American Popular Culture

AMERICAN STUDIES INFORMATION GUIDE SERIES

Series Editor: Donald Koster, Professor of English Emeritus, Adelphi University, Garden City, New York

Also in this series:

AFRO-AMERICAN LITERATURE AND CULTURE SINCE WORLD WAR II—*Edited by Charles D. Peavy*

AMERICAN ARCHITECTURE AND ART—*Edited by David M. Sokol*

AMERICAN LITERATURE AND LANGUAGE—*Edited by Donald N. Koster*

THE AMERICAN PRESIDENCY—*Edited by Kenneth E. Davison**

AMERICAN RELIGION AND PHILOSOPHY—*Edited by Ernest R. Sandeen and Frederick Hale*

AMERICAN STUDIES—*Edited by David W. Marcell*

HISTORY OF THE UNITED STATES OF AMERICA—*Edited by Ernest Cassara*

JEWISH WRITERS OF NORTH AMERICA—*Edited by Ira Bruce Nadel*

THE RELATIONSHIP OF PAINTING AND LITERATURE—*Edited by Eugene L. Huddleston and Douglas A. Noverr*

SOCIOLOGY OF AMERICA—*Edited by Charles Mark*

TECHNOLOGY AND VALUES IN AMERICAN CIVILIZATION—*Edited by Stephen H. Cutcliffe, Judith A Mistichelli, and Christine M. Roysdon*

WOMAN IN AMERICA—*Edited by Virginia R. Terris*

*in preparation

The above series is part of the

GALE INFORMATION GUIDE LIBRARY

The Library consists of a number of separate series of guides covering major areas in the social sciences, humanities, and current affairs.

General Editor: Paul Wasserman, Professor and former Dean, School of Library and Information Services, University of Maryland

Managing Editor: Denise Allard Adzigian, Gale Research Company

American Popular Culture

A GUIDE TO INFORMATION SOURCES

Volume 12 in the American Studies Information Guide Series

Larry N. Landrum

Associate Professor
Department of English
Michigan State University
East Lansing

Gale Research Company
Book Tower, Detroit, Michigan 48226

Library of Congress Cataloging in Publication Data

Landrum, Larry N.
American popular culture.

(Volume 12 in the American studies information
guide series) (Gale information guide library)
Bibliography: p.
Includes indexes.
1. United States—Popular culture—Bibliography.
I. Title. II. Series: American studies information
guide series ; v. 12.
Z1361.C6L28   1982   [E169.1]   016.7'00973   82-11902
ISBN 0-8103-1260-3

VITA

Larry N. Landrum is an associate professor of English at Michigan State University where he teaches literature and popular culture. He has served as bibliographer for the Popular Culture Association and THE JOURNAL OF POPULAR FILM AND TELEVISION and has conducted conferences and workshops on popular literature and popular culture. His publications include CHALLENGES IN AMERICAN CULTURE (Bowling Green, Ohio: Popular Press, 1970), a collection of papers from the Second National American Studies Association Conference; DIMENSIONS OF DETECTIVE FICTION (Bowling Green, Ohio: Popular Press, 1976); and THEORIES AND METHODOLOGIES IN POPULAR CULTURE (Bowling Green, Ohio: Popular Press, 1976).

CONTENTS

Contents

FOREWORD

To create a reliable and useful annotated bibliography on American popular culture would seem, at first blush, to be akin to the labor of Sisyphus. The present volume is proof, however, that, although Larry Landrum has worked perhaps as hard if not so long as the unfortunate Corinthian, he has achieved a happier result.

Professor Landrum's labors in the vineyards of popular culture have consumed much of his time for quite a few years past, during which he has accumulated a very large mass of bibliographical data. A large part of his task in doing this book has been to cull from this accumulation the more significant items and to organize them in such a way as to make them readily useful to students in this rapidly growing field. It seems to me that he has succeeded in doing so in face of the considerable problems involved in the process of selection. For it must be emphasized that this, despite, and probably because of, its enormous range, has had to be a highly selective bibliography.

AMERICAN POPULAR CULTURE is indeed a welcome and much needed addition to the Gale Information Guide Library series in American Studies.

Donald N. Koster
Series Editor

ACKNOWLEDGMENTS

No one who works through a task of this nature does so without help, much of which must be left unacknowledged. I would like to thank Ray B. Browne, Russel B. Nye, and Donald Koster for their encouragement and inspiration. I would also like to thank Marshall Fishwick who made useful suggestions during the early part of the project and Randall Scott for suggestions that improved the index. I have had advice from numerous librarians, particularly at the Michigan State University libraries, but also at the libraries of the University of Michigan, the Newberry Library, and the Library of Congress. Henry Koch, Jannette Fiore, and Kriss Ostrom were helpful with logistical problems. Erik Mattlin located and toted numerous books. Tamara Fish contributed to the accuracy of the entries in several sections. Betty Uphaus has earned my eternal gratitude for agreeing to type the manuscript from cards. Much of the film section appeared in another form in THE JOURNAL OF POPULAR FILM AND TELEVISION. I would also like to thank the authors cited in the bibliography, as well as many who are not, for leading me down diverse paths strewn with fresh information and ideas even though in doing so they helped delay the completion of this book. Finally, appreciation must be expressed to Denise Allard Adzigian and Donna Batten, my editors at Gale Research Company, for seeing the manuscript through to completion.

INTRODUCTION

The culture shared by Americans is probably the most complex the world has known. Not only does it encompass many ethnic cultures and elaborate political, economic, and social institutions, but also the diverse productions of the mass media and a rich mixture of life-styles, tastes, and leisure activities. Study of American popular culture has been largely carried out through interpretation of the meanings of imagery arising in the media, in leisure activities, and in the forms and uses of mass-produced consumer goods. It is generally recognized that such imagery carries with it meaning from a long cultural heritage, but that it also reflects the conditions and qualities of contemporary life. Since no single methodology or theoretical perspective has emerged to synthesize study of popular culture, the present bibliography is selective and unabashedly eclectic.

In traditional cultures imagery tends to be bound to geographical certainties, flora and fauna, weather, and seasonal changes. The creation of nation states and the growth of villages, towns, and cities as political and cultural centers led to the centralization of the image-making process and brought about the capacity for separating image making from everyday life. Until the early eighteenth century the preservation and dissemination of the culture of civilizations was controlled largely by powerful religious and political heirarchies. The culture of the majority of people survived, if at all, through custom, accident, or as borrowings by the elite culture. In Western civilizations political, religious, and social institutions created cultural ideals commensurate with the leisure and self-interest of those in power, a practice that effectively separated elite and folk cultures except, perhaps, for their common myths. The emergence of industrialism, and with it the transformation of the conditions of personal and cultural life, brought about a more complex and fluid system of imagery, one which retains something of tradition but which also transforms old or invents new imagery related to the experience of life in a technological society. With the growth of large urban areas and rapid transportation, the commercialization of leisure, and the emergence of a series of innovations in the technology of communication--printing, photography, motion pictures, radio, television, and their numerous offspring--a common fund of imagery, information, and consumer goods could be disseminated throughout society.

Introduction

Popular forms of expression exploit the tensions between tradition and change so that the inherited qualities of language and ritual are overlaid with current slang and jargon, inventive metaphors, and constantly changing ritualistic activities. This process of conservation, invention, and rediscovery is most clearly observed in leisure activities and entertainments, where imagery unbound from traditional ritual forms and imagery emerging from contemporary political, social, and material conditions coalesce spontaneously as fads, fashions, and happenings. Through the mutations of popular genres such expressions of impermanence themselves contribute to the substance of traditions. The ebb and flow of interest in and enthusiasm for sports, games, narratives of various kinds, clothing styles, music, and so on create difficulties for scholars, researchers, and critics who use interpretive models developed for the study of the products of more traditional cultures.

While there seems to be general agreement that the economic and technological forces which gave rise to modern popular culture are associated with a revolutionary transformation of the ways in which most people experience the world around them, there is little evidence of agreement about how this transformation is to be studied or interpreted. Part of the problem is that mass marketing and mass media not only make possible the diffusion of material culture and imagery, but also assume much of the responsibility for initiating and shaping them. But it must be stressed that marketing and media occur among, and often in competition with, numerous other areas of experience in everyday life. Mass media and mass marketing have their influence within a living culture where complex experiences evoke a wide range of emotional, intellectual, sensible, aesthetic, and kinesthetic responses; where values and beliefs interact with events in unpredictable ways; and where linguistic and nonverbal behavior precede their portrayal in media. For these reasons, the present bibliography includes selections from numerous disciplines and much information on numerous dimensions of American life.

A bibliography of popular culture can only hope to be representative because the enormous range of materials makes a definitive bibliography impractical. The study of popular culture having been conducted in many disciplines and often having an interdisciplinary focus, is not easily divided along disciplinary lines; nor, because it includes so much of the matter of everyday life and thought, can it be easily segmented into topical divisions or easily placed in any order of importance. The present bibliography includes items representative of numerous disciplines as well as lay contributions. Topic sections providing brief surveys of selected information on many areas of popular culture, and a large number of reference works, general studies, collections, and anthologies are indexed to specific topics.

Since the purpose of this bibliography is to provide a broad selection of publications, it contains few works on individual persons. The index does, however, provide references to numerous sources of biographical information. Because annotations for specific items identify contents, any book that is divided topically or thematically can be located through the index. I have attempted to indicate in the annotations something of the general or specific appeal of books and articles, and to suggest when possible the disciplinary or methodologi- cal perspective employed by the author.

The subject index has been made analytical by providing cross-indexing, cross- referencing, and alternative subject terms whenever possible. Any subject that is given coverage equivalent to a chapter or an article can be found in the index. The name index includes both authors and persons as subjects when they are given significant treatment.

Everday life refers to customs and manners common to styles of living. The notion of everyday life is important because it encourages those interested in studying popular culture to consider culture as both expression and experience, and as concerns of the community as well as the individual, as image and as act. While in its broadest sense everyday life includes both making a living and living on what is made, the bibliography is primarily concerned with the latter. Most of the works included emphasize experience apart from what most people consider to be work, although some information on the experience of work is included.

Ideology includes the association of culture with patterns of thought and value and with the ways in which such associations coalesce as enthusiasm, outrage, or other forms of collective expression. In practice it is difficult to separate ideology from the rest of cultural expression and experience, but it is useful to distinguish between relatively descriptive studies of the conditions and ar- rangements of everyday life and those oriented to the disclosure and examina- tion of popular values. Of particular interest in the diffusion of ideology are heroes and celebrities who, as Edgar Morin has observed, by virtue of their special charm spring out of their roles and into our imaginations.

Material culture is largely, in the modern world, the built environment, con- structed and manufactured on a vast scale. It includes objects that are per- manent or disposable, grand or miniscule, intentionally meaningful or seemingly insignificant. Aspects of the material culture which have been given consider- able attention are fashion and architecture. Although the emphasis of this bibliography is on clothing accessible to a broad range of people, it is also concerned with fashion change, which has long been studied in relation to social and economic factors, status orientation, individual and group psychol- ogy, and other matters. Domestic architecture, public and commercial archi- tecture, manufactured goods and crafts, and the shapes of cities and towns are included in material culture.

Leisure has often been considered the time spent away from work with hobbies, recreation, vacations, holidays, and similar matters. Though much of popular culture could be considered to be a part of leisure activity, leisure here is considered to be time available for leisure and places set aside for leisure pursuits, together with activities and pastimes most closely associated with specialized blocks of leisure time, such as holidays and vacations, and those recreations most likely to be enjoyed in leisure places.

Games include card and board games, party games, toys, interpersonal games, puzzles, pencil and paper diversions, playground and street games, and other activities involving one or more players and a system of rules. Games provide structure for fantasy and frameworks for social interaction.

Sports are often called games, but they are characterized by their greater emphasis on physical play and physical culture. Sports have traditionally been closely associated with education and it is not surprising that they are experienced directly or vicariously from childhood to old age, that sports are big business, and that a significant portion of media time is devoted to them. Since much scholarship and research has gone into the description and analysis of sports and their meaning to Americans, the section of this bibliography devoted to them is rather large.

Popular music is nearly omnipresent in contemporary America and it has always been an important part of the culture. It is distinct from classical music, to the extent that classical music is oriented to a relatively elite audience, and from folk music, which originates within isolated ethnic cultures, though it borrows from and influences both. Popular music is found in live performances, as underscoring for films and television programs, on most AM and FM radio frequencies, in the marketplace and the workplace, in automobiles, in homes, and on the streets. Considerable work has gone into the study of its performance, personalities, and business, as well as of the music itself both as a form of expression, as an influence on its audiences, and as it relates to classical and folk music.

Dance, like sport, is a patterned physical activity; it has been associated with cultural rituals, social occasions, and moments of intimacy. While the significance of dance as a popular form of expression has been widely noted, most of the study of dance has been devoted to professional dancers and to the dance as an art form. Studies of the meaning and fashion of social dancing are less plentiful.

Public art includes all forms of outdoor murals, statues and other fixed monuments, beautification projects involving art, street art of various kinds, and other forms of art and decoration that are publicly available. Advertising demonstrates the impact public art would have on the public if it were similarly endowed and motivated. Advertising permeates public life and much private experience; it draws from nature and art, and it has developed its own genres. As one of the oldest uses of media, advertising has spread from commerce to consumerism to the point that even personal items serve as billboards.

Theater is one of the oldest forms of art to have a significant influence on the emergence of popular culture, particularly before the development of technological media. It provided through melodrama an episodic structure borrowed by early popular novelists and adapted by current television programming. Drama, comedy, and musicals evolved from theater, which in turn led to more specialized forms. Many of the talents and techniques of the theater, as well as those developed in circuses and nightclubs, have led to a rich variety of entertainments not easily categorized. Entertainments included here derive from such forms as folk productions, shows and extravaganzas, carnivals, and amusement parks and arcades.

While popular literature might conceivably be seen as any printed matter that enjoys widespread popularity, here it includes both fiction and nonfiction books which are oriented to nonprofessional audiences or are cast into identifiable genres and those which contribute to or borrow from such genres. The periodical section provides corresponding information on magazines. Nonfiction includes publications on self-improvement, religion, schoolbooks, accounts of events and celebrities, almanacs, and other matters. Fictional genres include detective, crime, mystery, spy, gothic, juvenile, fantasy, Westerns, war, and science fiction among others. Both fiction and nonfiction best-sellers are covered.

Studies of media include those concerned with technical means of communication as well as descriptions of content and studies devoted to understanding the meaning and influence of media content. The emphasis of the bibliography is on the meaning and influence of the content of media. In addition to a general section on media, included are a brief section on book production and a section on periodicals. This part of the bibliography also includes information on ephemera, cartoons, comic strips, comic books, posters, illustrations, photography, radio, television, and film.

In short, the bibliography contains a broad selection of annotated items oriented to both academic libraries and those serving the general reader. In addition to a reference section, a collection of general works and one of anthologies and collections, the bibliography contains references to works on aspects of everyday life and ideology, and subject categories covering major areas of popular culture. A total of nearly twenty-two hundred items are annotated and keyed to an index of some sixty pages in length. The bibliography contains much information not previously collected and annotated, though another volume would be needed to include most of the significant work of the past twenty years, and a volume could be devoted to theory and methodology appropriate to the study of popular culture. In the meantime it is hoped that the present volume will, in its own small way, be useful to those who wish to know more about popular culture.

BIBLIOGRAPHIES, INDEXES, AND ABSTRACTS

1   ABSTRACTS OF POPULAR CULTURE. Bowling Green, Ohio: Popular
    Press, 1976-- . Biennial.

    Abstracts of articles on popular culture subjects from a wide
    range of periodicals, many of which do not appear in standard
    indexes. The only available source for abstracts particularly
    oriented to the study of popular culture.

2   ARTICLES IN AMERICAN STUDIES, 1954-1968: A CUMULATION OF
    THE ANNUAL BIBLIOGRAPHIES FROM AMERICAN QUARTERLY. 2 vols.
    Edited by Hennig Cohen. Ann Arbor: Pierian Press, 1972. Indexes.

    The volumes contain much useful information about articles in
    popular culture, primarily under the heading "Mass Culture."
    Since the items are reproduced as they appeared in AMERICAN
    QUARTERLY, it is necessary to consult the category index for
    the location of each year's entries. Indexes to authors and
    categories.

3   ARTS AND HUMANITIES CITATION INDEX. Philadelphia: Institute
    for Scientific Information, 1977-- . Annual.

    Contains a source index, citations index, and key-word index
    in several volumes. Identifies citations in journal articles and
    books, with a key-word index to article and chapter titles.

4   Ash, Lee. SUBJECT COLLECTIONS, A GUIDE IN SPECIAL BOOK
    COLLECTIONS AND SUBJECT EMPHASES AS REPORTED BY UNIVERSITY,
    COLLEGE, PUBLIC AND SPECIAL LIBRARIES AND MUSEUMS IN THE
    UNITED STATES AND CANADA. 4th ed. New York: R.R. Bowker,
    1978. 1,184 p.

    Invaluable guide to collections in various areas of popular
    culture. Probably the most complete book of its kind.

5   British Film Institute. Education Department. "Popular Culture and

Mass Media Studies." SCREEN 11, nos. 4-5 (1970): 148-71.

An annotated bibliography of books and monographs on mass media research, popular literature, the press, advertising, popular music, and general topics.

6   Browne, Ray B., and Geist, Christopher D., eds. POPULAR ABSTRACTS: JOURNAL OF POPULAR CULTURE, 1967-1977; JOURNAL OF POPULAR FILM, 1972-1977; POPULAR MUSIC AND SOCIETY, 1971-1975. Bowling Green, Ohio: Popular Press, 1978. 255 p. User's guide, index.

An annotated bibliography of books and monographs on mass media research, popular literature, the press, advertising, popular music, and general topics.

Contains abstracts of all articles and reviews appearing in the designated journals; arranged according to author.

7   Cawelti, John G. "Recent Trends in the Study of Popular Culture." AMERICAN STUDIES: AN INTERNATIONAL NEWSLETTER 10 (Winter 1971): 23-37.

A survey of recent publications in popular culture, with notes on the development of key areas.

8   Cluley, Leonard E., and Engelbrecht, Pamela N., eds. DICTIONARY CATALOG OF THE G. ROBERT VINCENT VOICE LIBRARY AT MICHIGAN STATE UNIVERSITY. Boston: G.K. Hall, 1975. 677 p.

Subject and speaker catalog for nearly seven thousand entries from Thomas Edison through contemporary figures. In an 1890 recording, the only surviving trumpeter from the Charge of the Light Brigade plays the "charge" on a trumpet borrowed for the occasion from the British Museum.

9   Council of Planning Librarians Exchange Bibliography. P.O. Box 229, Monticello, Ill. 61856.

An extremely useful collection of bibliographies on specialized subjects. Although the bibliographies are of uneven quality and do not ordinarily contain annotations, they do cover such areas as information and communication systems, landscape design, leisure research, parks, periodical markets, recreation planning, science fiction and fantasy, stadiums, tourism, and world fairs. An index published in 1979 indexes items 1-1565 (1958-1978). Some sixteen hundred bibliographies have appeared to date.

10   Dougherty, James J., comp. and ed. WRITINGS ON AMERICAN HISTORY, 1974-75: A SUBJECT BIBLIOGRAPHY OF ARTICLES. 4 vols. Washington, D.C.: American Historical Association, 1975.

Four-column coverage of popular culture, with items appearing also in other sections.

11   ESSAY AND GENERAL LITERATURE INDEX. New York: H.W. Wilson, 1900-- . Semiannual.

Indexes about forty-five hundred articles in three hundred volumes of collections and miscellaneous works.

12   GAZETTE: INTERNATIONAL JOURNAL FOR MASS COMMUNICATION STUDIES. The Hague: Martinus Nijhoff, 1955-- . Quarterly.

International bibliography of research appears in each issue. The bibliography is arranged by topic. See especially "Leisure and Popular Culture," though other sections contain useful material. Emphasis is on social science.

13   Harrison, Cynthia Ellen. WOMEN'S MOVEMENT MEDIA: A SOURCE GUIDE. New York: R.R. Bowker, 1975. 269 p. Indexes.

A classified listing of some 550 organizations arranged by publishers and news services, research centers and collections, organizations, governmental agencies, and special interests. Indexes to locations, media titles, groups, and subjects.

14   HUMANITIES INDEX. Bronx, N.Y.: H.W. Wilson, June 1974-- . Quarterly.

Formerly INTERNATIONAL INDEX, which began in 1916 and split in 1974 into HUMANITIES INDEX and SOCIAL SCIENCE INDEX, the HUMANITIES INDEX cites essays and book reviews in some one hundred general and specialized periodicals according to author, title, and subject. Although some items do appear under "Popular Culture," it is necessary to consult a wide range of headings to identify contributions in particular areas.

15   INDEX TO THE CONTEMPORARY SCENE: AN ANALYTICAL GUIDE TO THE CURRENT CONTENTS OF 299 RECENT MONOGRAPHS, COLLECTIONS, SYMPOSIA, ANTHOLOGIES, HANDBOOKS, GUIDES, SURVEYS, AND OTHER WORKS OF NONFICTION DEALING WITH TOPICS OF CURRENT INTEREST. Vol. 2. Edited by David W. Brunton. Detroit: Gale Research Co., 1975. 120 p. List of and key to books indexed.

This volume covers books reviewed during 1972. For books reviewed during 1971 see INDEX TO THE CONTEMPORARY SCENE: AN ANALYTICAL GUIDE TO THE CONTENTS OF 322 RECENT MONOGRAPHS, COLLECTIONS, SYMPOSIA, ANTHOLOGIES, HANDBOOKS, GUIDES, SURVEYS, AND OTHER WORKS OF NONFICTION DEALING WITH TOPICS OF CURRENT INTEREST (Vol. 1. Edited by David W. Brunton. Detroit: Gale Research Co., 1973. 122 p. List of and key to books indexed.)

15a   Inge, M. Thomas, ed. HANDBOOK OF AMERICAN POPULAR CULTURE.
       3 vols. Westport, Conn.: Greenwood Press, 1979-81. 1,200 p.
       Index, bibliog.

       A collection of bibliographical essays which discuss history and
       critical approaches to some forty-eight topics in popular culture.
       Included in volume 1 are: Thomas W. Hoffer on animation,
       Maurice Duke on the automobile, R. Gordon Kelly on chil-
       dren's literature, M. Thomas Inge on comic art, Larry Landrum
       on detective and mystery novels, Robert A. Armour on film,
       Kay J. Mussell on gothic novels, Mark W. Booth on popular
       music, Bill Blackbeard on the pulps, Nicholas A. Sharp on
       radio, Marshall B. Tymn on science fiction, Robert J. Higgs
       on sports, Don B. Wilmeth on stage entertainments, Robert S.
       Alley on television, and Richard W. Etulain on the Western.
       Volume 2 includes Elizabeth Williamson on advertising, Suzanne
       Ellery Greene on best-sellers, Don B. Wilmeth on circus and
       outdoor entertainments, Robert A. Armour and J. Carol Williams
       on death, Nancy Pogel and Paul Somers, Jr., on editorial
       cartoons, Charles Camp on foodways, Bernard Mergen on games
       and toys, R. Gordon Kelly on historical fiction, Robert Galbreath
       on occult and the supernatural, Richard N. Masteller on pho-
       tography, Richard Guy Wilson on architecture, Roy M. Anker
       on popular religion and theories of self-help, Kay J. Mussell
       on romantic fiction, Janice Radway on poetry, Katherine Fish-
       burn on women in popular culture. Volume 3 includes Robert
       K. Dodge on almanacs; Robert H. Janke on debate and public
       address; James J. Best on illustration; Bill Bennett on jazz;
       Bernard Mergen on leisure vehicles, pleasure boats, and air-
       craft; Dorothy Schmidt on magazines; Earle J. Coleman on magic
       and magicians; Anne Hudson Jones on medicine and the physician;
       Faye Nell Vowell on minorities; Richard A. Schwarzlose on news-
       papers; Claudius W. Griffin on physical fitness; Paul P. Somers,
       Jr., and Nancy Pogel on pornography; Richard Alan Nelson on
       propoganda; James Von Schilling on records and the recording
       industry; Anne Rowe on regionalism; Annette M. Woodlief on
       science; John Bryant on stamp and coin collecting; and Arthur
       H. Miller, Jr., on trains and railroading.

16   Kiell, Norman, comp. and ed. PSYCHOANALYSIS, PSYCHOLOGY
       AND LITERATURE: A BIBLIOGRAPHY. Madison: University of Wis-
       consin Press, 1963. 225 p. Subject index.

       Books and journal articles divided into fourteen sections in-
       cluding material on comics, drama, fairy tales and fables,
       film, journalism, myth, wit, and humor.

17   Landrum, Larry. "Recent Books in Popular Culture." INDIANA SOCIAL
       STUDIES QUARTERLY 26 (Winter 1973-74): 76-83.

       A survey of some areas in popular culture where publication
       has been most active, with emphasis on innovative approaches
       to the field.

18   McKee, Kathleen Burke. WOMEN'S STUDIES: A GUIDE TO REFER-
      ENCE SOURCES. Storrs Bibliography Series, no. 6. Storrs: University
      of Connecticut Library, 1977. Author, title, and subject indexes.

      Annotated bibliography of sources on women and women's studies,
      arranged according to guide and collections, handbooks,
      directories, statistical sources, indexes, abstracts, and bibliog-
      raphies. An appendix annotates feminist periodicals in the
      University of Connecticut Library's Alternate Press Collection.

19   Meckler, Alan M., and McMullin, Ruth, comps. and eds. ORAL
      HISTORY COLLECTIONS. New York and London: R.R. Bowker, 1975.
      344 p.

      Subject listing with a sixty-page listing of oral history centers
      in the United States; seven pages of foreign sources. Many
      omissions, but useful as preliminary source; subjects spotty.

20   ORAL HISTORY COLLECTION OF COLUMBIA UNIVERSITY. New York:
      Oral History Research Office, Columbia University, 1964. 181 p. Index.

      A description of the collection based on biographical sketches
      of represented figures, with sections on popular arts and other
      areas indicated.

21   "Popular Culture in the Round." CULTURAL INFORMATION SERVICE,
      February 1976, pp. 1-6. Bibliog.

      Introduction to popular culture through interviews with several
      scholars.

22   POPULAR PERIODICAL INDEX. Collingswood, N.J.: 1973-- . Semiannual.

      Currently indexes thirty-nine periodicals not included in many
      other indexes, often with brief notes.

23   READER'S GUIDE TO PERIODICAL LITERATURE. New York: H.W.
      Wilson, 1900-- . Monthly.

      Author, subject, and title index to popular middle-class
      periodicals.

24   SOCIAL SCIENCES AND HUMANITIES INDEX. New York: H.W.
      Wilson, 1965-74. Quarterly, annual cumulation.

      Split into HUMANITIES INDEX and SOCIAL SCIENCE INDEX
      with the April 1974 issue. Each cumulation indexes about
      three hundred journals and specialized magazines.

25   Stevenson, Gordon. "The Wayward Scholar: Resources and Research
      in Popular Culture." LIBRARY TRENDS 25 (April 1977): 779-818.

An excellent survey of materials, collections, and areas for
library acquisition in the field of popular culture.

26   Tingley, Donald F., ed. SOCIAL HISTORY OF THE UNITED STATES:
      A GUIDE TO INFORMATION SOURCES. American Government and
      History Information Guide Series, vol. 3. Detroit: Gale Research Co.,
      1979. 260 p.

      Chapter 22 contains twelve pages of annotated citations on
      popular culture.

27   Wasserman, Paul, and Herman, Esther, eds. LIBRARY BIBLIOGRAPHIES
      AND INDEXES: A SUBJECT GUIDE TO RESOURCE MATERIAL FROM
      LIBRARIES, INFORMATION CENTERS, LIBRARY SCHOOLS AND LI-
      BRARY ASSOCIATIONS IN THE UNITED STATES AND CANADA.
      Detroit: Gale Research Co., 1975. 301 p.

      Organized by subject, the volume contains five thousand
      indexes compiled by about 750 libraries on a broad range of
      subjects.

GENERAL WORKS

28   Albrecht, Milton C.; Barnett, James H.; and Griff, Mason, eds. THE
SOCIOLOGY OF ART AND LITERATURE: A READER. London: Gerald
Duckworth, 1970. 752 p. Bibliog., index.

        Essays in this volume center on the arts, particularly literature,
painting and sculpture, as institutions in the broadest sense.
Of particular interest are: Nelson Graburn's essay on the commercialization of Eskimo art; Harold Rosenberg, the art establishment; Rosenberg and Norris Fliegel, the artist and his pub-
lics; Alvin Toffler, the art of measuring the arts; Quentin Bell,
conformity and nonconformity in the fine arts; Hugh Duncan,
Burke's dramatistic conception; and Walter Abell, the conception of a unified field in critical studies.

29   Barfield, Owen. SAVING THE APPEARANCES: A STUDY IN IDOLATRY.
London: Faber and Faber, 1957. 190 p. Index.

        Philosophical essays on collective representations, figuration,
participation, appearances, medieval thought, metaphor, the
origins of language, and new slants on old problems.

30   Barthes, Roland. CRITICAL ESSAYS. Chicago: Northwestern University
Press, 1972. 279 p.

        Of particular interest are essays on costume, newspaper filler
items, imagination of the sign, structuralism, and reading from
a critical perspective.

31   Bateson, Gregory. STEPS TO AN ECOLOGY OF MIND. New York:
Ballantine, 1972. 517 p.

        A collection of Bateson's writing on a variety of cultural sub-
jects, focusing on conceptualizing cultural phenomena. Of
particular interest are essays on semantics, national character,
and play theory. Includes a checklist of Bateson's writings.

32   Bogart, Leo. SILENT POLITICS: POLLS AND THE AWARENESS OF
        PUBLIC OPINION. New York: Wiley-Interscience, 1972. 250 p.
        Notes, index.

        A discussion of the potential, limitations, and omissions in
        opinion surveys, with thoughts on opinion change, ambiguity,
        and the uses of opinion surveys.

33   Brown, Richard Harvey, and Lyman, Stanford M. STRUCTURE, CON-
        SCIOUSNESS, AND HISTORY. New York: Cambridge University Press,
        1978. 284 p.

        An important collection of essays on the development of sym-
        bolic realism and cognitive aesthetics as evolving perspectives
        which mediate between positivist reductionism and intuitive
        idealism.

34   Burns, Elizabeth. THEATRICALITY: A STUDY OF CONVENTION IN
        THE THEATRE AND IN SOCIAL LIFE. London: Longman, 1972. 246 p.
        Index.

        Drawing on literary analogies and the symbolic interactionism
        of such sociologists as Erving Goffman, Burns explores sociology
        and the theater, the theatrical paradigm, conventions of per-
        formance, and other matters that relate the practices and ex-
        pectations of theater with those of life.

35   Cawelti, John G. "Popular Culture: Coming of Age?" JOURNAL
        OF AESTHETIC EDUCATION 10 (July-October 1976): 165-82.

        A discussion of the transformation of critical thinking about
        popular culture that has taken place since the 1950s, and of
        the sophisticated artistic awareness that has emerged among
        artists in several media.

36   _____. WHY POP? A CONVERSATION ABOUT POPULAR CULTURE
        WITH JOHN CAWELTI CONDUCTED BY DON F. ROGERSON. Intro-
        duction by Russel B. Nye. National Humanities Faculty Why Series.
        San Francisco: Chandler and Sharp, 1973. 30 p.

        An interview with Cawelti on the importance of studying popu-
        lar culture in the high school and college classroom.

37   Combs, James E., and Mansfield, Michael W., eds. DRAMA IN LIFE:
        THE USES OF COMMUNICATION IN SOCIETY. New York: Hastings
        House, 1976. 444 p. Index.

        A collection of thirty-six articles on dramatic interpretations
        of behavior; organized into sections on life as theater, social
        interactions, culture, and history. Many of the contributions
        are key essays on the symbolic interactionist approach.

38   Diamond, Edwin. THE SCIENCE OF DREAMS. Garden City, N.Y.:
      Doubleday, 1962. 264 p. Index.

      A survey of dream research, with chapters on early beliefs,
      Freud's contributions, and contemporary perspectives.

39   Dichter, Ernest. HANDBOOK OF CONSUMER MOTIVATIONS: THE
      PSYCHOLOGY OF THE WORLD OF OBJECTS. New York: McGraw-
      Hill, 1964. 486 p. Bibliog., index.

      The classic handbook for symbol manipulators of the psychology
      of consumer goods. Now dated.

40   Eister, Allan W., ed. CHANGING PERSPECTIVES IN THE SCIENTIFIC
      STUDY OF RELIGION. New York: Wiley, 1974. 370 p. Notes,
      bibliog.

      Includes essays on the social context of religion. Victor
      Turner discusses metaphors of antistructure; Benjamin Nelson,
      the play of eros, logos, nomas, and polis; and David Ruth,
      body symbols.

41   Erikson, Erik H. TOYS AND REASONS: STAGES IN THE RITUALIZA-
      TION OF EXPERIENCE. New York: Norton, 1977. 182 p.

      Erikson examines the relationships of play and the use of toys
      in life-cycle stages from infancy through adult experiences in
      politics and everyday life. The book is useful for its review
      of Erikson's ego psychology in relation to his understanding of
      the turmoil of the sixties.

42   Firth, Raymond. SYMBOLS: PUBLIC AND PRIVATE. Ithaca, N.Y.:
      Cornell University Press, 1973. 469 p. Bibliog., index.

      Includes discussions of food, hair, flags, gifting, and bodily
      symbols, with emphasis on symbol theory in anthropology.

43   Furay, Conal. THE GRASS-ROOTS MIND IN AMERICA: THE AMERICAN
      SENSE OF ABSOLUTES. New York: New Viewpoints, A Division of
      Franklin Watts, 1977. 170 p. Notes, bibliog., index.

      This provocative little volume argues that the "grass-roots mind"
      of ordinary Americans is built around absolutes that provide
      stability in a world seen by intellectuals as constantly under-
      going change. Furay discusses the grass-roots mind as it is
      influenced by popular culture, geography, and the structure
      of such mental retreats as business, the military, religion,
      Americanism, and ethnic self-investment.

44   Goffman, Erving. FRAME ANALYSIS: AN ESSAY ON THE ORGANI-

ZATION OF EXPERIENCE. Cambridge, Mass.: Harvard University
Press, 1974. 586 p. Notes, index.

An analysis of the way people define situations among people
which results in interactions that are sequences of everyday
activities bound by rules capable of being exploited by deception. Goffman draws on news items, popular biographies, cartoons, comics, novels, films, and theater.

45   Gowans, Alan. ON PARALLELS IN UNIVERSAL HISTORY, DISCOVER-
ABLE IN ARTS AND ARTIFACTS: AN OUTLINE STATEMENT. Victoria,
B.C.: University of Victoria, 1972. 126 p.

An exploration of universal themes in art; the notion that
"arts and artifacts must be seen as records of successive
ideological convictions held through the ages."

46   Gregory, R.L., and Gombrich, E.H., eds. ILLUSION IN NATURE
AND ART. New York: Scribner's, 1973. 288 p. Illus., bibliog.,
index.

Six useful essays on the qualities, sources, and effects of
illusion in nature and art. Colin Blakemore discusses the
physiological bases of illusion; R.L. Gregory identifies the
optic process; H.E. Hinton surveys illusion in nature; Jan B.
Deregowski discusses culturally conditioned differences in
perception; E.H. Gombrich discusses the problems of the
analysis of illusion in art and life; and Roland Penrose cele-
brates the qualities of illusion that are basic to art and links
it to deeper emotional levels in those who experience it.

47   Hall, Edward T. BEYOND CULTURE. Garden City, N.Y.: Anchor
Press, Doubleday, 1976. 256 p. Bibliog., index.

Theoretical framework for the analysis of both traditional and
contemporary cultures. Discussion of kinesics, proxemics,
high and low context cultures, action chains and situational
contexts, and identity in culture.

48   Harper, Ralph. NOSTALGIA: AN EXISTENTIAL EXPLORATION OF
LONGING AND FULFILLMENT IN THE MODERN AGE. Cleveland:
Press of Western Reserve University, 1966. Published as THE SLEEPING
BEAUTY. New York: Harper, 1955. 146 p.

Meditations on the sleeping beauty tale as a timeless expression of hidden truth.

49   Henle, Mary, ed. VISION AND ARTIFACT. New York: Springer
Publishing Co., 1976. 186 p. Illus.

A collection of essays divided into three sections: "Visual

Perception," "Visual Thinking," and "Artifact." The third part is especially useful. See Wolfgang M. Zucker's essay on Christian hermeneutics, Walter Hess's formal analysis of a Vermeer painting, and Dore Ashton's essay on the considerations necessary for social interpretation of art.

50   Henry, Jules. CULTURE AGAINST MAN. New York: Random House, 1963. 495 p. Index.

A personal anthropological investigation into American culture. The volume contains chapters on the American character and contemporary American life, advertising as a philosophical system, the cold war, parents and children, teens, education, family case studies, and three institutions for the aged. Appendixes chart mother-son contacts and reprint an extract from V.A. Kral's manuscript, "Recent Research in Prevention of Mental Disorders at Later Age Levels."

51   Huizinga, Johan. HOMO LUDENS: A STUDY OF THE PLAY ELEMENT IN CULTURE. London: Routledge and Kegan Paul, 1950. Reprint. Boston: Beacon, 1955. Reprint. New York: J.J. Harper, 1970. 220 p. Notes, index.

Arguing that play is a basic form of human expression that cannot be further reduced, Huizinga traces the influence of play in the formation of such phenomena as language and civilization, and in institutions such as war, law, knowledge, poetry, philosophy, art, and selected aspects of contemporary civilizations.

52   Jones, Russell A. SELF-FULFILLING PROPHECIES: SOCIAL, PSYCHOLOGICAL, AND PHYSIOLOGICAL EFFECTS OF EXPECTANCIES. Hillsdale, N.J.: Lawrence Erlbaum Associates, 1977. 275 p. Bibliog., index.

An examination of the implications of stereotyping, labeling, expectancies and goals, variables and performance, and health-associated practices.

53   Larrabee, Eric. THE SELF-CONSCIOUS SOCIETY. Garden City, N.Y.: Doubleday, 1960. 188 p. Notes.

An important attempt to understand how intellectuals have become isolated from their native culture, and how Americans have continually attempted to reconceptualize themselves. Perceptive chapters on the status system, critics of popular culture, characteristics of mass audiences, jazz, pornography, attitudes toward children, Americans abroad, and the culture of abundance.

54   Lefebvre, Henri. EVERYDAY LIFE IN THE MODERN WORLD. Translated

by Sacha Rabinovitch. Paris: Gallimard, 1968. Reprint. New York: Harper Torchbook, 1971. 206 p.

Examines the perspectives gained through the exploration of thought about everyday life, including a critique of readings of Joyce's ULYSSES which stress its realism, an investigation of the emergence and pervasiveness of the bureaucratic mode, the consumption of signs, terrorism, and notes toward a permanent cultural revolution.

55 Lowenthal, Leo. LITERATURE, POPULAR CULTURE, AND SOCIETY. Englewood Cliffs, N.J.: Prentice-Hall, 1961. 169 p. Index.

An important sociological study composed of essays (previously published) on definition, the popular culture debate on aesthetics, pop heroes found in biographical essays in magazines, and the relationship of literature to society.

56 Loye, David. THE LEADERSHIP PASSION. San Francisco: Jossey-Bass Publishers, 1977. 249 p. Bibliog., tables, charts, index.

A psychosocial examination of political ideology and leadership, with a review of earlier work and tests of findings that suggest an emerging middle-range leadership belief system.

57 Lynes, Russell. THE TASTEMAKERS. New York: Harper, 1954. 362 p. Illus., bibliog., index.

Lynes documents what he sees as the most influential arbiters of taste from the 1920s, the Age of Public Taste, through the Age of Private Taste, to the Age of Corporate Taste ushered in by the growth of the mass media. Since taste is a matter of "personal delight . . . private dilemma and . . . public facade," those who attempted to dictate or influence American taste were themselves largely representative of the ebb and flow of larger fashions in ideas and opinions. A useful introduction to the history of tastes in architecture, art, fashion, interior decoration, and related matters.

58 McCormack, William C., and Wurm, Stephen A., eds. WORLD ANTHROPOLOGY: LANGUAGE AND THOUGHT. The Hague: Mouton Publishers, 1977. 525 p. Index.

A collection of twenty-eight essays on linguistic models, ethnoscience, ethnohermeneutics, oppositions, and functions, structures and values. The focus of the volume is on exploration of the Sapir-Whorf hypothesis, isomorphic oppositions as in the Levi-Strauss formulation, and the grounded interests of field research.

59   McLuhan, Marshall. UNDERSTANDING MEDIA: THE EXTENSIONS OF MAN. New York: McGraw-Hill, 1964. 318 p. Bibliog.

Part 1, the author's fullest statement on media as the extension of human faculties, provides a theoretical perspective which discusses media form as message, distinguishes between "hot" and "cool" media, narcissism and gadgetry, and other matters. Part 2 explores specific categories of expression, including oral and written language, maps, numbers, clothing, housing, money, clocks, comics, vehicles, photography, news, advertising, games, telegraphy, typewriters; and the telephone, phonograph, movies, radio, television, weaponry, and automation, with further consideration of ideas developed in part 1.

60   Nye, Russel B. THE CULTURAL LIFE OF THE NEW NATION, 1776-1830. New York: Harper, 1960. 324 p. Bibliog., index.

An extensive cultural history of the United States during the period. The volume considers the framework for belief and thought and the emergence of an American perspective through social life, education, religion, literature, and the arts.

61   _____. SOCIETY AND CULTURE IN AMERICA, 1830-1860. New York: Harper and Row, 1974. 432 p. Bibliog., index.

A companion volume to THE CULTURAL LIFE IN THE NEW NATION (above entry), the volume traces the change and continuity of established institutions, the emergence of new forces, ideas, and crafts, and examines the evolving framework of belief.

62   _____. THE UNEMBARRASSED MUSE: THE POPULAR ARTS IN AMERICA. New York: Dial Press, 1970. 497 p. Illus., notes, bibliog.

Essential reading for any student or teacher who wishes to understand America's popular arts. A historical approach includes sections on most popular forms, placing them in their social and cultural contexts.

63   Shayon, Robert Lewis. OPEN TO CRITICISM. Boston: Beacon Press, 1971. 324 p. Index.

A "record of one critic's intellectual development" that attempts a "critique of criticism" and encompasses "criticism, biography" and other matters, compiled from pieces written for the SATURDAY REVIEW and various newspapers.

64   Stannard, David E. SHRINKING HISTORY: ON FREUD AND THE FAILURE OF PSYCHOHISTORY. New York: Oxford, 1980. 187 p. Bibliog., notes, index.

A critique of psychohistorical investigation, focussing on
Freud's Leonardo essay, therapy, logic, theory, and psychohistorical methodology.

65   Swingewood, Alan. THE MYTH OF MASS CULTURE. Atlantic High-
lands, N.J.: Humanities Press, 1977. 146 p. Notes, bibliog., index.

A critique of theories of mass society developed in the Frankfurt school by conservative social critics and among post-World
War II Marxists, together with speculation about the differences
between democratization and the ideology of mass culture theorists.

66   Ulanov, Barry. THE TWO WORLDS OF AMERICAN ART: THE PRIVATE
AND THE POPULAR. New York: Macmillan, 1965. 528 p. Notes,
index.

Included are chapters on popular music and jazz, photography,
mysteries, science fiction and fantasy, dance, film, radio,
television, and criticism, as well as the traditional arts.

67   Warner, William Lloyd. THE LIVING AND THE DEAD: A STUDY OF
THE SYMBOLIC LIFE OF AMERICANS. Yankee City Series, Vol. 5.
New Haven, Conn.: Yale University Press, 1959. 528 p. Bibliog.,
index.

A theoretical discussion of symbolic life through analysis of a
political hero, the segmentation and structure of time, and
religious and secular values in Yankee City. Part 5 is particularly concerned with a formal discussion of signs and symbols.

68   Woods, Ralph L., and Greenhouse, Herbert B., eds. THE NEW WORLD
OF DREAMS. New York: Macmillan, 1974. 439 p. Index.

The volume collects articles on people who dream, dream
themes, and paranormal dreams, with extensive sections on
research and theory, both historical and contemporary.

69   Wright, John K. HUMAN NATURE IN GEOGRAPHY: FOURTEEN
PAPERS, 1925-1965. Cambridge, Mass.: Harvard University Press,
1966. 359 p. Notes, index.

A useful collection of essays that discuss history and geography,
the subjectivity of maps, human motives in scientific research,
imagination in geography, the Arctic land bridge, Coleridge's
Florida sources for KUBLA KHAN and ANCIENT MARINER,
among other subjects.

ANTHOLOGIES AND COLLECTIONS

70   AMERICA NOW: AN INQUIRY INTO CIVILIZATION IN THE UNITED
STATES BY THIRTY-SIX AMERICANS. Edited and introduction by Harold
E. Stearns. New York: Literary Guild of America, Charles Scribner's
Sons, 1938. 606 p.

> Of the wide range of essays included, especially worth noting
> are those by Louis R. Reid on radio and movies, Bruce Bliven
> on public opinion, and John Kieran on sports.

71   Arens, W., and Montague, Susan P., eds. THE AMERICAN DIMENSION:
CULTURAL MYTHS AND SOCIAL REALITIES. Port Washington, N.Y.:
Alfred Publishing Co., 1976. 221 p.

> A collection of papers originally presented at the 1974 Ameri-
> can Anthropological Association Conference, which includes
> studies of football, television, rock concerts, fictional detec-
> tive Nancy Drew, bagels, coffee, health-care seeking, poker,
> moonshining, astrology, and middle-class friendships.

72   Berger, Arthur Asa. POP CULTURE. Dayton, Ohio: Pflaum, Standard,
1973. 192 p. Bibliog., study aids.

> A collection of brief essays and quips on a variety of popular
> culture topics, with a useful section on definition and critical
> perspectives. Other topics include comics, sports, media, food,
> artifacts, styles, and symbols.

73   Berger, Bennett M. LOOKING FOR AMERICA: ESSAYS ON YOUTH,
SUBURBIA, AND OTHER AMERICAN OBSESSIONS. Englewood Cliffs,
N.J.: Prentice-Hall, 1971. 331 p. Index.

> A collection of Berger's articles on defining the youth culture,
> the identity myth, hippies, suburban life-styles, racism, black
> culture, and the sociology of leisure. One section on prob-
> lems of conceptualization in sociology.

74   Bigsby, C.W.E., ed.   APPROACHES TO POPULAR CULTURE.   Bowling
        Green, Ohio: Bowling Green University Popular Press, 1976.   280 p.
        Index.

        Presents approaches to popular culture from the perspectives
        of communications, sociology, history, structuralism, linguis-
        tics, Marxism, politics, and photography (as a photo-essay);
        with examinations of screen violence, media executives,
        television comedy, blues music, the thirties, and writing
        about Watergate.

75   _____.   SUPERCULTURE: AMERICAN POPULAR CULTURE AND EUROPE.
        Bowling Green, Ohio: Bowling Green University Popular Press, 1975.
        225 p.   Notes, illus.

        Essays include Bigsby on Europe, America and the cultural
        debate; Leslie Fiedler on defining popular culture, David
        Crystal on American English in Europe, Reyner Banham on
        mediated environments, Magnus Pike on the influence of
        American food practices on Europe, Peter Masson and Andrew
        Thorburn on American advertising's influence, Bryan Wilson
        on U.S. religious sects in Europe, Michael Watts on the
        influence of American popular music, Paul Oliver on the
        European experience of jazz, Jens Peter Becker on the in-
        fluence of the "hard-boiled school" on European detective
        fiction, Gerard Cordesse on the impact of American science
        fiction, Roger Lewis on the comic form in Britain and the
        United States, Martin Esslin on the television series as folk
        epic, and Thomas Elsasser on Hollywood and European film-
        making.

76   Boorstin, Daniel J.   DEMOCRACY AND ITS DISCONTENTS: REFLEC-
        TIONS ON EVERYDAY AMERICA.   New York: Random House, 1974.
        136 p.

        A collection of essays on the saturation of communication,
        the ways public opinion has been assessed, the lack of ma-
        turity in television, advertising the good life, the prevailing
        image of the present, an anticipation of the kind of thought
        that led to the Bakke case, the iconographic landscape, self-
        liquidating ideals, and technological innovations that have led
        to changes in the commercial ecology.

77   _____.   THE IMAGE: A GUIDE TO PSEUDO-EVENTS IN AMERICA.
        New York: Atheneum, 1971.   315 p.   Bibliog., index.

        A valuable collection of the author's thoughts on managed
        news, the celebrity process, modern tourism, disposable
        media, self-fulfilling prophecies, and the decay of the
        American dream into American illusions.   The essays form a
        critical interpretation of contemporary American tendencies
        toward modernization and media.

78   Brossard, Chandler, ed. THE SCENE BEFORE YOU: A NEW APPROACH TO AMERICAN CULTURE. New York: Rinehart, 1955. 307 p.

A collection of essays, drawn primarily from COMMENTARY and PARTISAN REVIEW, which provide critical perspectives on American culture. Of particular interest are the essays on film, black imagery, comics, television, best sellers, magazines, life-styles, Dashiell Hammett, popular music, and painting.

79   Browne, Ray B., and Madden, David. THE POPULAR CULTURE EXPLOSION. Dubuque, Iowa: W.C. Brown Co., 1972. 203 p. Bibliog.

An anthology in magazine format of newspaper and magazine articles on contemporary popular treatments of timeless subjects. An excellent seventy-five page INSTRUCTOR'S MANUAL (1972) keyed to the text provides an overview; ideas for discussions on about fifty topics; keys to elements of writing; background essays by Russel B. Nye, Marshall Fishwick, and John Cawelti; lists of plays, songs, films, magazines, and distributors.

80   Browne, Ray B., ed. POPULAR CULTURE AND THE EXPANDING CONSCIOUSNESS. New York: John Wiley and Sons, 1973. 200 p.

Sixteen essays on popular formulas (the Western, crime in science fiction, John G. Cawelti on formula), Kurt Vonnegut, Marvel comics, LOVE STORY, Burt Bacharach, JESUS CHRIST SUPERSTAR, black consciousness in film, BONNIE AND CLYDE. Other essays include Cawelti's essay on the aesthetics of popular culture and three essays on perspectives toward popular culture.

81   Browne, Ray B.; Crowder, Richard H.; Lokke, Virgil L.; and Stafford, William T., eds. FRONTIERS OF AMERICAN CULTURE. West Lafayette, Ind.: Purdue University Press, 1968. 201 p. Illus.

Twelve essays on American symbols, paperback publishing, the new Western, utopian fiction, jazz, folklore and American studies, electronic music, literary aesthetics, literature (William Styron, Melville's Israel Potter), modern comedy, and sculptor Herbert M. Schueller.

82   Browne, Ray B.; Grogg, Sam, Jr.; and Landrum, Larry, eds. THEORIES AND METHODOLOGIES IN POPULAR CULTURE. Bowling Green, Ohio: Bowling Green University Popular Press, 1976. 156 p. Bibliog.

Essays from JOURNAL OF POPULAR CULTURE on the critical perspective, mass art, formalism, popular culture's relationship to literary studies and folklore, the notion of a "mass mind," sociological perspectives, content analysis, museum and street imagery, entertainment conventions, geographical perspectives, foreign languages, history, philosophy, political science, religious studies, antimethod, and methodological constrictions.

83   Browne, Ray B.; Landrum, Larry N.; and Bottorff, William K., eds. CHALLENGES IN AMERICAN CULTURE. Bowling Green, Ohio: Bowling Green University Popular Press, 1970. 278 p.

Twenty-five essays on American studies and popular culture from the Second National American Studies Conference. Included are essays on early American genre painting, posters, Brooklyn Bridge symbolism, avant garde art, new directions for American studies, public programs for authors, television censorship, popular Catholic fiction, God and Darwin in fiction, early science fiction, Whitman, Twain, Dreiser, Tennessee Williams, Henry James, the little Lord Fauntleroy series, the little colonel series, gangster films, and Harry Stephen Keeler's detective fiction.

84   Cantor, Norman F., and Werthman, Michael S., eds. THE HISTORY OF POPULAR CULTURE: Volume 1: TO 1815; volume 2: SINCE 1815. New York: Macmillan, 1968. 792 p. Index to authors.

Volume 1 includes essays on Greek games, drama values, rites of passage, prostitution, homosexuality, markets, everyday life; Roman travel, lust and blood lust, baths, the good life, soldiers' lives and beliefs; medieval worldview, barbarian life, beliefs and ritual practices, the crusades, tournaments, legal practice, university life, Arthurian legend, and the impact of the plague; the early modern era, the survival of medieval attitudes, Reformation and counter Reformation, court life, aristocratic life, popular politics, the bourgeois, the poor, military life, and the emergence of print and the discovery of the New World. Part 4 covers violence and blood sports, drinking and gambling, financial speculation, clubs and salons, travel in the eighteenth century, the growth of literacy, opera, proletarian life, evangelism, military life, discontent and uprisings, and the Romantic sensibility. Volume 2 contains essays and excerpts on material improvements, industrial lifestyles, politics, entertainments and recreations, diversions, Victorian immorality, nationalism, wealth, women's emancipation, automobiles, soldiers, the democratization of education, recreation and spectator sports in the twentieth century, mass entertainments before television, movies, the great crash, political extremism, urban life. Articles on contemporary life cover the quality of suburban life, uses of increased leisure, television, football, mass protest, the sexual revolution, and the "turned-on generation."

85   Coffin, Tristram, III, ed. AMERICAN FOLKLORE. N.p.: Voice of America, 1968. 325 p.

A collection of essays prepared from the Voice of America Forum lectures. The essays cover definition, ballads, the lyric tradition, hymns, musical structures in folk songs, folk dance, magic folktales, legends and tall tales, the trickster figure, folk games, proverbs and proverbial expressions, riddles, superstition, folk speech, folklore in literature, labor lore, the hillbilly movement, urbanization of black musical traditions, and the commercialization of folk music. This is a handy introduction to American folklore through the words of eminent folklorists.

86   Cooper, Susan. BEHIND THE GOLDEN CURTAIN: A VIEW OF THE U.S.A. London: Hodder and Stoughton, 1965. 256 p.

This collection of essays by a British American is useful as a balancing view of religious institutions, schools, cultural change, wealth, the weapons credo, sports and recreation, and other matters.

87   Deer, Irving, and Deer, Harriet, eds. THE POPULAR ARTS: A CRITI-CAL READER. New York: Charles Scribner's Sons, 1967. 356 p. Study questions, bibliog.

A useful anthology of previously published essays on architecture, popular literature, television, photography, the Western, science fiction, gangster films, pornography, kitsch, musicals, comic strips, film epics, film comedy, best sellers, and aesthetics.

88   Dégh, Linda; Glassie, Henry; and Oinas, Felix J., eds. FOLKLORE TODAY: A FESTSCHRIFT FOR RICHARD M. DORSON. Bloomington: Indiana University, Research Center for Language and Semiotic Studies, 1976. 537 p.

Although the volume is primarily of use to folklorists, those interested in popular culture should note Rolf Wilhelm Brednich's "Comic Strips as a Subject of Folk Narrative Research."

89   DeMott, Benjamin. HELLS AND BENEFITS: A REPORT ON AMERICAN MINDS, MATTERS, AND POSSIBILITIES. New York: Basic Books, 1962. 264 p.

Lively, provocative essays on the emergence of such a maga-zine as MAD, contemporary fiction, "Instant Redefinition" of literature and other things, the National Book Award, tele-vision, Washington politics, the Peace Corps, Jewish writers, the math controversy, Robert D. Bowen's THE NEW PROFES-SORS (New York: Holt, Rinehart and Winston, 1960), the Adams-Jefferson letters, and other books; and the suburban spirit.

90   _____. SUPERGROW: ESSAYS AND REPORTS ON IMAGINATION
IN AMERICA. New York: Dutton, 1969. 188 p.

> Provocative essays on homosexual art, Marshall McLuhan as
> a prophet, rock music, teaching in a cultural enrichment
> program in Mississippi, failure of the American imagination,
> pressuring children to excel, technological sexology, poetry,
> teaching English, student rebels, Charles Horton Cooley's
> LIFE AND THE STUDENT (1927), contemporary uses of exis-
> tentialism, and working Hollywood.

91   _____. SURVIVING THE SEVENTIES. New York: E.P. Dutton, 1971.
153 p.

> Impressionistic essays on contemporary styles of coping: women's
> liberation, husbands, the ecology movement, the WHOLE EARTH
> CATALOGUE (1969-74), personal reactions to contemporary issues,
> and confrontations.

92   _____. YOU DON'T SAY: STUDIES OF MODERN AMERICAN IN-
HIBITIONS. New York: Harcourt, Brace and World, 1966. 240 p.

> Perceptive essays on PLAYBOY magazine, greeting cards,
> sport parachuting, "literary silence," Massachusetts politics,
> Richard Hofstadter's ANTI-INTELLECTUALISM IN AMERICAN
> LIFE (1963), Lee Oswald, the domestic Peace Corps, Third
> World fiction, Portugal, political writing, anti-Americanism in
> England, alumni magazines as resources, culture through
> writing, educational reform. The essays, which experiment
> with various methods and styles, first appeared in magazines
> such as HARPER'S, COMMENTARY, and NEW REPUBLIC.

93   Denney, Reuel. THE ASTONISHED MUSE, 1957. Reprint. Introduction
by John Cawelti. Chicago: University of Chicago Press, 1974. 273 p.

> A collection of critical pieces adapted to book form on the
> uses of leisure, audiences, popular literary forms, television
> programs, the decline of "lyric" sport, spectator sports, hot-
> rod culture, comics, science fiction, advertising, skyscrapers,
> and other subjects. The 1974 edition contains a foreword by
> David Reisman and an afterword by the author.

94   ESSAYS IN HONOR OF RUSSEL B. NYE. Edited by Joseph Waldmeir.
East Lansing: Michigan State University Press, 1978. 265 p.

> A collection of sixteen essays on literature and cultural
> history, including John Cawelti on John Buchan and the
> spy thriller, Marshall Fishwick on the thingness of things,
> William McCann on midwestern journalistic humor, and
> C. David Mead's profile of Nye.

95   Frye, Northrup. NORTHRUP FRYE ON CULTURE AND LITERATURE:
      A COLLECTION OF REVIEW ESSAYS. Edited by Robert D. Denham.
      Chicago: University of Chicago Press, 1978. 264 p. Notes, index.

      Organized into sections on "Grammars of the Imaginations"
      and "Orders of Poetic Experience," the brief essays are linked
      by Denham's extensive introduction.

96   Goldman, Albert Harry. FREAKSHOW: THE ROCKSOULBLUESJAZZ-
      SICKJEWBLACKHUMORSEXPOPPSYCH GIG AND OTHER SCENES FROM
      THE COUNTER-CULTURE. New York: Atheneum, 1971. 387 p.

      A collection of brief essays on rocktheater, soul, blues,
      nostalgia, rock music and jazz, current comedians, erotic
      fantasy, and numerous short subjects.

97   Goodman, Paul, and Gatell, Frank Otto. AMERICA IN THE TWENTIES:
      THE BEGINNINGS OF CONTEMPORARY AMERICA. New York: Holt,
      Rinehart and Winston, 1972. 247 p. Illus., bibliog., index.

      A textbook approach to the culture of the period that features
      chapters on mass consumption (especially the automobile), mass
      styles (the new morality), anxiety, and politics. Excerpts
      from the newspapers and biographies of the time are included.

98   Hall, James B., and Ulanov, Barry. MODERN CULTURE AND THE
      ARTS. New York: McGraw-Hill, 1967. 560 p. Author and title
      indexes.

      A varied collection of previously printed essays on the arts
      with several on popular culture, including Andre Malraux,
      Abraham Kaplan, and others on the popular arts; Constant
      Lambert, Aaron Copland and Roger Sessions on listening to
      music, E.H. Gombrich's seminal essay on artistic form;
      Clement Greenberg on kitsch, Richard Lippold's perceptive
      essay on crafting artifacts; a section of essays on television,
      film, and photography; and a final section on the design arts,
      including Leslie Fiedler's essay on comics from NO! IN
      THUNDER (1972).

99   Hall, Stuart, and Whannel, Paddy. THE POPULAR ARTS. New York:
      Pantheon, 1965. 480 p. Index, appendixes.

      This pioneering work is arranged into four parts covering
      definitions, with distinctions among minority, folk and popu-
      lar art, and considerations of media and society, and popular
      art within mass culture. Topics for study consider popular
      forms and popular artists, screen violence, crime fiction, love
      stories, romantic fantasies, television dramas, youth as audi-
      ence, and advertising. Part 3 considers institutions and the
      debate about the massification of society; part 4 considers

curriculum, teaching, and various topics for classroom development. Appendixes include a bibliography, discography, filmography, and other information.

100   Hammel, William M. THE POPULAR ARTS IN AMERICA: A READER.
       2d ed. Chicago: Harcourt Brace Jovanovich, 1977. 501 p.

       Forty-five previously published essays and excerpts collected
       in sections on the popular arts, movies, television and radio,
       music, and print; with a rhetorical table of contents. Dis-
       cussion questions.

101   Hougan, Jim. DECADENCE: RADICAL NOSTALGIA, NARCISSISM,
       AND DECLINE IN THE SEVENTIES. New York: Morrow, 1975.

       A potpourri of essays on contemporary culture. Organized
       around the conflict between technology and sensibility, the
       brief essays touch, often incisively, on media, Charles Manson,
       advertising, and other subjects.

102   Hoyt, Edwin P. THE GOLDEN ROT: A SOMEWHAT OPINIONATED
       VIEW OF AMERICA. Indianapolis: Bobbs-Merrill, 1964. 226 p.

       A series of essays on the state of institutions and values in
       contemporary America. Among Hoyt's targets are scientists,
       the legal system, race, Kennedy publicity, and medical bills.

103   INDIANA SOCIAL STUDIES QUARTERLY 26 (Winter 1973-74): entire
       issue.

       Special issue devoted to popular culture, edited by Joseph F.
       Trimmer. The issue contains "Literature, the Public, and the
       Critic" by Russel B. Nye and "Notes on the Typology of
       Literary Formulas" by John G. Cawelti, with essays on icons,
       THE GODFATHER, the West in rock music, and other topics.

104   Kaiser, Robert G., and Lowell, Jon. GREAT AMERICAN DREAMS:
       A PORTRAIT OF THE WAY WE ARE. New York: Harper and Row,
       1979. 255 p.

       A survey of the beliefs of "middle Americans" through inter-
       views conducted mainly at Las Vegas. Chapters are topical
       and intended to be metaphorical--the great American buffet
       is a champagne breakfast offered to attract hotel guests, but
       it also represents for the authors the way Americans experience
       reality within the context of "democratized conspicuous con-
       sumption."

105   Kando, Thomas M. LEISURE AND POPULAR CULTURE IN TRANSITION.
       St. Louis: C.V. Mosby Co., 1975. 308 p.

A textbook designed for sociology courses at the high school or college level. Includes sections on leisure, high culture, mass culture aspects of print and cinema, mass leisure aspects of sports, the outdoors and travel, and a section on youth, culture, and social change.

106   Kouwenhoven, John A. THE BEER CAN BY THE HIGHWAY: ESSAYS ON WHAT'S "AMERICAN" ABOUT AMERICA. Garden City, N.Y.: Doubleday, 1961. 255 p. Index.

Ten essays on various aspects of American material culture that provide useful insights into the qualities of Americanness. The essays range from a consideration of architecture and design (including auto tail fins) through advertising and the abundance of waste.

107   Krout, John Allen. AMERICAN THEMES: SELECTED ESSAYS AND ADDRESSES. Edited by Clifford Lord and Henry F. Graff. New York: Columbia University Press, 1963. 227 p. Illus.

Essays on American culture, including several of particular interest to students of popular culture: on colonial drinking habits, the development of turnpikes in the late eighteenth and early nineteenth centuries, the emergence of American sport, and amateur athletics. A checklist of the author's publications is included.

108   Krutch, Joseph Wood, et al. IS THE COMMON MAN TOO COMMON? AN INFORMAL SURVEY OF OUR CULTURAL RESOURCES AND WHAT WE ARE DOING ABOUT THEM. Norman: University of Oklahoma Press, 1954. 146 p.

A collection of informal essays that consider the common man as reader, viewer, listener, and in his relation to news, business, education, art, and taste.

109   Lahr, John. ASTONISH ME: ADVENTURES IN CONTEMPORARY THEATER. New York: Viking Press, 1973. 269 p. Notes, index.

Lahr's provocative thoughts on sports, contemporary theater, Jules Feiffer, Neil Simon and Woody Allen, open theatre, Ike and Tina Turner, Maurice Chevalier, Lenny Bruce, Little Richard, and Muhammed Ali.

110   Leighton, Isabel, ed. THE ASPIRIN AGE, 1919-1941. New York: Simon and Schuster, 1949. 491 p.

Twenty-two essays by contemporary writers on a variety of phenomena. Of interest are the essays on Aimee Semple McPherson, a Kokomo, Indiana Klan gathering, Jack Dempsey,

Lindbergh; radio religion; the death of Starr Faithfull; the Dionne quintuplets; the fire on the luxury liner, MORRO CASTLE; the Duke of Windsor's marriage to Mrs. Simpson; the Republic Steel strike; and THE WAR OF THE WORLDS (1938) broadcast.

111   Lewis, George H., comp. SIDE-SADDLE ON THE GOLDEN CALF: SOCIAL STRUCTURE AND POPULAR CULTURE IN AMERICA. Pacific Palisades, Calif.: Goodyear, 1972. 388 p. Bibliog.

The volume of essays is divided into three parts, the first including essays in the mainstream of popular culture on Marlboro cigarettes, demolition derbies, roller derbies, radio religion, patriotic country music, romance magazines, PLAY-BOY, middle-class values, adult bookstores, Vietnam war fiction, movie-making and audiences, Arthur Penn, television censorship, playing bridge, bicycles, fast food, frozen dinners, diffusion of popular culture among elites. The second part, "Antithesis," provides representative voices from the black community, youth culture (comics and comic artists, tatooing, movie radicalism), rock music culture, and street theater. The final section, "Synthesis?," is composed of an essay on a communal experiment. Essays are drawn from the JOURNAL OF POPULAR CULTURE and other sources, and a running commentary is provided by the editor.

112   Lieber, Joel, ed. AMERICA THE BEAUTIFUL: A MODERN GUIDE TO SEX, SECURITY AND THE SOFT BUCK. New York: David White, 1968. 207 p.

Essays on children's toys, beauty contests, computer mating, careers, husband hunting, honeymoons, cemeteries, life insurance, gambling, divorce, fat, self-improvement, anxiety, old age, and a vision of the future.

113   Locke, Raymond Friday, ed. THE HUMAN SIDE OF HISTORY: MAN'S MANNERS, MORALS AND GAMES. New York: Hawthorne Books, 1970. 256 p. Index.

A collection of light essays from MANKIND MAGAZINE. Of interest are the essays on valentines, the invention of the ice cream cone, the film hero-lover, early television, cosmetics, football, and the chautauqua.

114   Macdonald, Dwight. AGAINST THE AMERICAN GRAIN. New York: Random House, 1962. 427 p.

A collection of essays critiquing "the influence of mass culture on High culture." Of particular interest is the revised version of Macdonald's essay "A Theory of Popular Culture," which in 1944 favored integrating "mass" culture with "high" culture, but which in the present version, "Masscult and Midcult," favors separating culture into one for the masses and one for the intellectual elite. In addition to this lead essay, other essays attack the elite cultural viability of contemporary novelists, the great books enterprise, modern dictionaries, revisions of the BIBLE, how-to books, journalism, and matters of fact.

115   MOM, THE FLAG, AND APPLE PIE: GREAT AMERICAN WRITERS ON GREAT AMERICAN THINGS. By Max Apple et al. New York: Doubleday, 1976. 255 p.

Essays on popular culture from ESQUIRE.

116   Nelson, John Wiley. YOUR GOD IS ALIVE AND WELL AND APPEARING IN POPULAR CULTURE. Philadelphia: Westminster Press, 1976. Notes, bibliog.

A provocative collection of essays oriented to the thesis, "Popular culture is to what most Americans believe as worship services are to what the members of institutional religious believe." Chapters consider popular culture as a belief system, the classic Western film and the anti-Western, country, music, popular magazines, television, and detective fiction; a chapter on implications for the church concludes the volume.

117   Newfield, Jack. BREAD AND ROSES TOO. New York: E.P. Dutton, 1971. 429 p. Index.

A collection of articles written for the VILLAGE VOICE on aspects of American culture during the late 1960s through the turn of the decade on race relations, the hippies and radical organizations, Vietnam, New York politics, the news media, jails, and other subjects. A self-styled advocacy journalist, Newfield writes with the heat of the battle.

118   Nye, Russel, ed. NEW DIMENSIONS IN POPULAR CULTURE. Bowling Green, Ohio: Popular Press, 1972. 246 p. Notes.

Based on Nye's seminar at Michigan State University, the essays examine Sunday school books; nineteenth century gift books; little blue books; women's magazine fiction, 1900–1920; celebrity magazines; the demise of the SATURDAY EVENING POST; American Victorian sentimental novels; the dime novel Western hero; country-life novels; Rinehart's mysteries; religious poetry, 1820–1860; the counter culture and rock music; folk music and popular culture; and John D. MacDonald's Travis McGee stories.

119   Ohlgren, Thomas, and Berk, Lynn, eds. THE NEW LANGUAGES: A RHETORICAL APPROACH TO THE MASS MEDIA AND POPULAR CULTURE. Englewood Cliffs, N.J.: Prentice-Hall, 1977. 395 p.

A collection of essays on popular culture and the mass media,
commercial and public propaganda, print language, film, television, and radio. Selected for discussion in composition
classes, the essays are intended as well as models of argument,
exposition, description, and narration.

120   Paredes, Américo, and Stekert, Ellen J., eds. THE URBAN EXPERIENCE
        AND FOLK TRADITION. Publications of the American Folklore Society
        Bibliography and Special Series, no. 22. Austin: University of Texas
        Press, 1971. 207 p. Notes, bibliog., index.

        A useful collection of essays and comments on the question
        of urban folklore, Negro riot stereotypes, folk medical be-
        liefs in Detroit, country and Western music in urban areas,
        and rural migrants to cities. An extensive bibliography covers
        ethnic and folkloristic materials.

121   Popular Culture Association. PROCEEDINGS. Fifth National Con-
        vention, St. Louis, Missouri, March 20-22, 1975. Compiled by Michael
        Marsden. Bowling Green, Ohio: The Association, 1976. Microfilm.

122   Real, Michael R. MASS-MEDIATED CULTURE. Englewood Cliffs, N.J.:
        Prentice-Hall, 1977. 289 p. Bibliog., index.

        An excellent collection of essays on the influences of the
        media, Disneyland, the super bowl on television, Marcus
        Welby and the medical genre, media campaigning, Billy
        Graham, an Indian fiesta in the Andes, and a theoretical
        perspective.

123   Rissover, Fredric, and Birch, David C. MASS MEDIA AND THE POPU-
        LAR ARTS. 2d ed. New York: McGraw-Hill Book Co., 1977. 494 p.
        Bibliog., media sources, index.

        An anthology of essays arranged according to information on
        advertising, journalism, cartoons and comic strips, popular
        literature, radio and television, photography and film, music,
        education; with alternate thematic and multimedia categories.
        Discussion questions.

124   Rosenberg, Bernard, and White, David Manning, eds. MASS CULTURE
        REVISITED. New York: Van Nostrand-Reinhold, 1971. 473 p.

        An updated version of MASS CULTURE (see no. 145), the volume
        includes revised essays by Rosenberg and White, theoretical
        perspectives on the mass aspects of contemporary culture, es-
        says on television, film, journalism, spy fiction, advertising,
        and alternative life-styles.

125   Rosenberg, Samuel. THE CONFESSIONS OF A TRIVIALIST. Baltimore: Penguin, 1972. 219 p.

Essays on being a serious trivialist, Mary Shelley's creation of FRANKENSTEIN (1817), how William James Sidis passed from corporate genius to a collector of streetcar transfers, the origins of Santa Claus, Albert Schweitzer, Lot's wife, and Herman Melville's creative source.

126   Rourke, Constance. THE ROOTS OF AMERICAN CULTURE: AND OTHER ESSAYS. Edited by Van Wyck Brooks. New York: Harcourt, Brace, 1952. 305 p. Index.

An influential collection on the complexities of American culture, "theatricals" and popular literature, music, shakers, folklore, the popular artist Voltaire Combe, Negro literature, and the future of American art.

127   Salzman, Jack, ed. PROSPECTS: AN ANNUAL JOURNAL OF AMERICAN CULTURAL STUDIES. Vol. 1. New York: Burt Franklin, 1975. 445 p. Illus.

Essays on popular culture include Ray B. Browne on whale lore in popular print, David H. Cuthbert on humor in the World War II army film, Allen Guttmann on baseball fiction, Lawrence E. Mintz on Art Buchwald, Russel B. Nye on the Jean Goldkette Orchestra, Bruce A. Rosenberg on the martyrdom of General Custer, and Anne Tropp Trensky on the saintly child in nineteenth-century fiction.

128   _____. PROSPECTS: AN ANNUAL OF AMERICAN CULTURAL STUDIES. Vol. 3. New York: Burt Franklin, 1977. 602 p. Notes, illus.

Twenty-three essays, including those on artifacts, jazz, mobility and stability, frontier literature, Thomas Moran's illustrations of Yellowstone, girls' serial novels from 1900 to 1920, Harrison Cady's cartoons, and violence in autobiography.

129   _____. PROSPECTS: AN ANNUAL OF AMERICAN CULTURAL STUDIES. Vol. 4. Edited by Jack Salzman. New York: Burt Franklin, 1979. 634 p. Illus.

A collection of essays on various aspects of American culture, including Susan Kennedy on P.T. Barnum, Kenneth Roemer on illustrations in utopian fiction, Carl Smith on Thomas Eakin's boxing paintings, Karal Marling on New Deal art, William Alexander on documentary films of the 1930s, Fred Matthews on mental hygiene as ideology, Alan Gowans on comic strips, and John Cawelti on clandestinity and spy fiction.

130   Schrank, Jeffrey. SNAP, CRACKLE, AND POPULAR TASTE: THE
       ILLUSION OF FREE CHOICE IN AMERICA. A Delta Original. New
       York: Dell Publishing Co., 1977. Index.

       Contains essays on television, food technology, automobiles,
       advertising, "packaged" architecture and artifacts, institutions,
       mythologizing in contemporary culture, and sports.

131   Seldes, Gilbert. THE PUBLIC ARTS. New York: Simon and Schuster,
       1956. 303 p.

       More optimistic than THE GREAT AUDIENCE (1950) and more
       concerned with media content, this volume includes chapters on
       film, radio, and television, with special attention to comedy
       and comedians, and the problem of power in broadcasting. In
       many ways, this is a pioneering work.

132   _____. THE SEVEN LIVELY ARTS. 1924. Reprint. New York:
       Harper, 1962. 398 p. Appendixes, index.

       Informal essays on Chaplin, popular songs, jazz, popular
       writing, Florenz Ziegfeld's Follies, blacks on Broadway, one-
       man shows, a plan for a lyric theater, Al Jolson and Fanny
       Brice, comic strips and Krazy Kat, vaudeville, dance, humor-
       ous newspaper columnists, burlesque and circus, clowns, bogus
       high arts, movie magnates, Picasso and authentic art.

133   Shayon, Robert Lewis. OPEN TO CRITICISM. 3 vols. Boston: Beacon
       Press, 1971. 793 p. Illus., bibliog., index.

       A compendium of writings by American travelers about the
       manners and customs of their countrymen, written from about
       the late eighteenth century to the last quarter of the nine-
       teenth century. The volumes cover most of the nation and
       many interesting scenes, from jails and asylums to dancing,
       holidays, resorts, dandies, high and low life, and Indian
       games in the West.

134   Sontag, Susan. AGAINST INTERPRETATION AND OTHER ESSAYS.
       New York: Farrar, Straus and Giroux, 1966. 304 p.

       A provocative collection of Sontag's essays on a variety of
       subjects. Of particular interest are "Against Interpretation,"
       "The Imagination of Disaster" (science fiction films), "Notes
       on 'Camp,'" and "One Culture and the New Sensibility"
       which argues for a perspective on art that includes popular
       forms.

135   Spradley, James P., and Rynkiewich, Michael A. THE NACIREMA:
       READINGS ON AMERICAN CULTURE. Boston: Little, Brown and Co.,
       1975. 417 p. Bibliog., index.

An anthology of forty-one articles that apply anthropological perspectives to contemporary America, with sections on schooling, informal communication, the family, social structure, technology and economics, law and politics, religion and magic, values, and cultural change. Essays on sports, games, and informal activities are especially useful.

136   Susman, Warren, ed. CULTURE AND COMMITMENT, 1929-1945. New York: George Braziller, 1973. 372 p. Photos, notes, bibliog.

Contemporary middle-class reactions to various aspects of culture during the period. Included are reactions to landscape, success, work, leisure, love, sex (by Mae West), religion, consumerism, soap operas, films, family life, technology, housing, the world's fair, design, and ideas about the future.

137   Tanner, Louise. ALL THE THINGS WE WERE: A SCRAPBOOK OF THE PEOPLE, POLITICS, AND POPULAR CULTURE IN THE TRAGICOMIC YEARS BETWEEN THE CRASH AND PEARL HARBOR. Garden City, N.Y.: Doubleday, 1968. 362 p. Notes, index.

Nostalgic essays on comic strips, Sunday diversions, radio programs, popular fiction in magazines and books, music, advertising, automobiles, sports, news, clothing fashions, interior decoration, the socialites, movies and other matters, with a chapter on the contemporary heritage of thirties styles.

138   Thompson, Denys, ed. DISCRIMINATION AND POPULAR CULTURE. Middlesex, Engl.: Penguin Books, 1964. 198 p.

An anthology of essays written by various critics to advance critical education about advertising, radio and television, the press, film, magazines, recorded music, and design.

139   Toffler, Alvin. THE CULTURE CONSUMERS: ART AND AFFLUENCE IN AMERICA. Baltimore: Penguin, 1965. 288 p. Notes, bibliog., index.

A counterattack on elite critics who deplored the growing audiences for the arts and the emergence of new popular arts. Toffler includes chapters on quantitative increases in consumption, changes in attitudes of consumers and related social changes, increased costs of art, the debate over government support, aesthetic issues and tastes, and an epilogue defending the expansion of the audience for the arts.

140   Trachtenberg, Alan, ed. DEMOCRATIC VISTAS, 1860-1880. New York: George Braziller, 1970. 368 p.

A collection of period pieces demonstrating middle-class attitudes toward popular forms of entertainment.

141   Ulanov, Barry. THE TWO WORLDS OF AMERICAN ART: THE PRIVATE AND THE POPULAR. New York: Macmillan, 1965. 528 p. Index.

> This is a curious, contentious book that explores popular music, jazz, photography, mystery stories, science fiction and fantasy, movies, radio, television, and other matters of popular culture. Ulanov seems fated to say over and over that the popular arts are box office, facile, and only very occasionally skilled or moving. His grudging style begins in the preface and continues through the footnotes.

142   Warshow, Robert. THE IMMEDIATE EXPERIENCE: MOVIES, COMICS, THEATRE, AND OTHER ASPECTS OF POPULAR CULTURE. New York: Doubleday, 1962. 282 p.

> A classic series of essays on the popular arts, including pieces on the ideology of the 1930s, "Krazy Kat," Clifford Odets, the Rosenbergs, horror comics, E.B. White, the gangster as tragic hero, movie Westerns, THE BEST YEARS OF OUR LIVES, MY SON JOHN, the use of the camera in DEATH OF A SALESMAN, and THE CRUCIBLE as a vehicle for liberal conscience. Two pieces on Chaplin, several on the art film, and a memoir of the author's father fill out the collection.

143   White, David Manning, ed. POP CULTURE IN AMERICA. Chicago: Quadrangle, New York Times Book, 1970. 279 p. Bibliog., index.

> A collection of NEW YORK TIMES articles, together with an introduction by White. Includes essays on using leisure, being cultured, paying for art, television programming, contemporary radio, the importance of movies, of drama; Bob Dylan as a writer; DeMott on rock, rock lyrics, rock audience psychology; pop art, Charles Schulz, books in Muncie, Indiana.

144   White, David Manning, and Averson, Richard, eds. SIGHT, SOUND, AND SOCIETY: MOTION PICTURES AND TELEVISION IN AMERICA. Boston: Beacon Press, 1968. 466 p. Index.

> A useful general anthology of writing about film and television divided into parts focusing on audiences, media, communicators, issues, and speculations. Thirty-two contributors discuss aesthetics, audiences, the nature of film and television media, the psychology of the male movie star, news, film violence, politics on television, and related matters. An appendix containing a bibliographic essay by White and Averson covers art, education, career training, and recommendations for further research and scholarship.

145   White, David Manning, and Rosenberg, Bernard, eds. MASS CULTURE: THE POPULAR ARTS IN AMERICA. New York: Free Press of Glencoe, 1957. 561 p.

Collects the following essays: Bernard Rosenberg, "Mass Culture in America"; David M. White, "Mass Culture in America: Another Point of View"; Jose Ortega y Gasset, "The Coming of the Masses"; Leo Lowenthal, "Historical Perspectives of Popular Culture"; Dwight Macdonald, "A Theory of Mass Culture"; Gilbert Seldes, "The People and the Arts"; Clement Greenberg, "Avant-Garde and Kitsch"; Paul F. Lazarsfeld and Robert K. Merton, "Mass Communication, Popular Taste and Organized Social Action"; Marshall McLuhan, "Sight, Sound, and the Fury"; Irving Howe, "Notes on Mass Culture"; Ernest Van Den Haag, "Of Happiness and of Despair We Have No Measure"; Leslie A. Fiedler, "The Middle Against Both Ends"; and Melvin Tumin, "Popular Culture and the Open Society."

146 White, Edward M., ed. THE POP CULTURE TRADITION: READINGS WITH ANALYSIS FOR WRITING. New York: W.W. Norton, 1972. 196 p.

An anthology for writing students concerned with popular culture themes. The volume is divided into sections on "Art and Society," "Art and Behavior," and "Art and Popular Art," with essays and fiction by Wolfe, Updike, and others. An appendix on perceptive rewriting is included.

147 Wolfe, Tom. THE KANDY-KOLORED TANGERINE-FLAKE STREAMLINE BABY. New York: Farrar, 1965. 339 p.

An excellent collection of essays on American styles, places, and personalities written in Wolfe's personal prose. Includes essays on Las Vegas, demolition derbies, disc jockey Murray the K, the Peppermint Lounge, teenage tycoon Phil Spector, custom cars, Cassius Clay, stock car racer Junior Johnson, Cary Grant, exposé magazines, socialite Jane Holzer, sketches of New York types, Huntington Hartford, art gallery society, clothing styles, and various New York scenes.

148 _____. MAUVE GLOVES AND MADMEN, CLUTTER AND VINE, AND OTHER STORIES, SKETCHES, AND ESSAYS. New York: Farrar, 1976. 243 p.

Stories, sketches, and essays on Americana, including navy pilots over Vietnam, the intellectual climate of the sixties according to its most travelled representatives, the "me" generation, taking hostages (published shortly before the Hearst kidnapping), pornoviolence, Freud, funky chic, class and status language usage, and fighting for taxis in New York.

149 _____. THE PUMP HOUSE GANG [British Title: THE MID-ATLANTIC MAN]. New York: Farrar, Straus and Giroux, 1968. 309 p.

Sketches of American and British scenes: a quasi gang from
La Jolla, an Englishman who has gone American, Hugh Hefner,
Carol Doda, young hip London workers, a customized motor-
cycle, the Harvey's drive-in boys, Marshall McLuhan, art
collector Robert Scull, new etiquette, London Dollies, gambling in London, the New York Hilton, Natalie Wood meets
the master painters, Edward T. Hall.

150 _____. RADICAL CHIC AND MAU-MAUING THE FLAK CATCHERS.
New York: Farrar, Straus and Giroux, 1970. 184 p.

The title essays on fashionable radicalism and the ghetto-
bureaucrat confrontations in Chicago.

151 Wolfe, Tom, and Johnson, E.W., eds. THE NEW JOURNALISM, WITH
AN ANTHOLOGY. New York: Harper and Row, 1973. 394 p.

Part 1 is a perceptive introduction to journalistic writing in
the late sixties and early seventies that tended to blur the
distinctions between fiction and objective reporting. Part 2,
comprising the bulk of the volume, includes selections by
Rex Reed, Gay Talese, Richard Goldstein, Michael Herr,
Truman Capote, Joe Eszterhas, Terry Southern, Hunter Thomp-
son, Norman Mailer, Nicholas Tomalin, Barbara Goldsmith,
Joe McGinnis, George Plimpton, James Mills, John Gregory
Dunn, John Sack, Joan Didion, "Adam Smith," Robert Christgau,
Gary Wills, and Wolfe.

152 Zelomek, A.W. A CHANGING AMERICA: AT WORK AND PLAY.
New York: John Wiley and Sons, 1959. 181 p.

Useful, statistically infused essays on the modern woman,
automation, the uses of leisure time, elite and popular consumption of culture, suburbia, and the growth of the service
industry.

153 Zinsser, William. POP GOES AMERICA. New York: Harper and Row,
1966. 174 p.

Observations on fads, fashions, and interests of the sixties.

ASPECTS OF EVERYDAY LIFE

154 Abrahams, Roger D. DEEP DOWN IN THE JUNGLE . . ., NEGRO
NARRATIVE FOLKLORE FROM THE STREETS OF PHILADELPHIA. Rev. ed.
Chicago: Aldine Publishing Co., 1970. 278 p. Glossary, bibliog.,
type and motif list, index.

> A perceptive revision of the 1963 edition which provides
> analysis of the tellers and tales in everyday Negro life. Chap-
> ters treat verbal contests, heroes, style and performance,
> toasts, and jokes.

155 _____. POSITIVELY BLACK. Englewood Cliffs, N.J.: Prentice-Hall,
1970. 177 p.

> An attempt to bring about an understanding of the differences
> "between lower-class blacks and the rest of America," drawing
> on the expressive folklore of South Philadelphia and elsewhere.

156 _____. TALKING BLACK. Rowley, Mass.: Newbury House, 1976.
102 p. Bibliog., index.

> A discussion of the varieties of black discourse, including
> that corresponding to particular situations.

157 Abrahams, Roger D., and Szwed, John, eds. DISCOVERING AFRO-
AMERICA. Leiden: E.J. Brill, 1975. 94 p. Notes, index.

> A collection of six essays on ghetto research of the 1960s,
> African labor in early South Carolina, Afro-American emanci-
> pation celebrations, black art, black sensibility, and black
> music.

158 Adams, Ramon F. THE COWMAN SAYS IT SALTY. Tucson: University
of Arizona Press, 1971. 163 p.

> Anecdotes of the language found in various situations in the
> West, with emphasis on cowboy slang.

159 _____. SIX GUNS AND SADDLE LEATHER: A BIBLIOGRAPHY OF
BOOKS AND PAMPHLETS ON WESTERN OUTLAWS AND GUNMEN
Rev. ed. Norman: University of Oklahoma Press, 1969. 808 p. Index.

Contains 2,491 carefully annotated items on outlaws and gunmen.

160 Allen, Everett S. A WIND TO SHAKE THE WORLD: THE STORY OF
THE 1938 HURRICANE. Boston, Mass.: Little, Brown and Co., 1976.
340 p. Illus.

A reconstruction from oral reports and documentary sources of
the hurricane that swept northeastern United States.

161 Altschuler, Richard, and Regush, Nicholas. OPEN REALITY: THE WAY
OUT OF MIMICKING HAPPINESS. New York: G.P. Putnam's Sons,
1974. 224 p.

A critique of consumer society and an appeal for "open reality,"
the shared psychological condition of people in modern consumer societies who are subject to images of consumer ideals
that promise closure (cognitive integration), but deny it since
it is linked to endless buying. Open reality rejects patterned
responses in favor of continuous personal creation of possibilities. The essay critiques standard views of sex appeal, marriage and family, leisure, religion, politics, and provides
suggestions for making conscious the appeals. Discussions of
vogue psychology.

162 American Library Association. Reference and Adult Services Division.
THE BLACK EXPERIENCE: A BIBLIOGRAPHY OF BIBLIOGRAPHIES, 1970-
1975. Composed and edited by Ron Blazek. Chicago: 1978. 67 leaves.
Index.

This is a 209-item bibliography of bibliographies on the black
experience; 185 entries are annotated.

163 Amory, Cleveland. THE LAST RESORTS. Vol. 2. New York: Harper
and Brothers, 1952. 527 p. Index.

An anecdotal account of the resorts of the rich.

164 _____. WHO KILLED SOCIETY? New York: Harper and Brothers,
1960. 599 p. Brief bibliog., index.

Amory's anecdotes about the world of high society, its people
and opinions, with a list of (registered and proved) coats of
arms.

165 Asbury, Herbert. THE BARBARY COAST: AN INFORMAL HISTORY OF

THE SAN FRANCISCO UNDERWORLD. New York: Alfred A. Knopf, 1933. 330 p. Illus., bibliog., index.

A lively account of the San Francisco area from the gold rush in 1849 to the early twentieth century. Asbury covers the brothels, gambling houses, opium dens, hoodlums, and gang wars through the reforms of 1912, with accounts of the tactics employed to prey on the unwary.

166 Barker, Roger Garlock, and Schoggen, Phil. QUALITIES OF COM-MUNITY LIFE. San Francisco: Jossey-Bass, 1973. 562 p. Illus., bibliog.

Behavior of people in public settings in the traditions of community studies. Focus is on children in British and U.S. towns.

167 Baron, Stanley. BREWED IN AMERICA: THE HISTORY OF BEER AND ALE IN THE UNITED STATES. Boston: Little, Brown and Co., 1962. 424 p. Notes, bibliog., index.

An extensive examination of the universality, borrowed practices, and American contributions to brewing and consuming beer and ale, with emphasis on the historical development through Prohibition. The first part covers the introduction and colonial development of home brewing. Part 2 covers eighteenth-century practices, and part 3 includes a variety of events through Prohibition, with chapters on Washington, Jefferson, Vassar, and the development of commercial brewing and distribution. Part 4 concentrates on manufacturing innovations, brewing dynasties, labor disputes, and popular resistance to the beverages. Part 5 covers issues leading to Prohibition and its repeal, as well as a summary history of events following Prohibition. Appendixes incorporate an early recipe and the Act of 1789 that encouraged production.

168 Beck, Warren A., and Clowers, Myles L., eds. UNDERSTANDING AMERICAN HISTORY THROUGH FICTION. 2 vols. New York: McGraw-Hill, 1975. 410 p.

A collection of excerpts from fiction which illustrate aspects of the colonial experience, the path to independence, nation-building, the rise of the common man, social reform, manifest destiny, slavery, the Civil War, reunion, the last frontier, capitalism in America, World Wars I and II, the interval between wars, the counterculture, and the cold war, Korean War, and Vietnam War.

169 Berrey, Lester V., and Van den Bark, Melvin. THE AMERICAN THE-SAURUS OF SLANG, WITH SUPPLEMENT: A COMPLETE REFERENCE

BOOK OF COLLOQUIAL SPEECH. New York: Thomas Y. Crowell, 1953. 1,272 p. Indexes to words.

> Standard words with slang equivalents and variations; sections on special sources of slang: underworld, trades, commerce, art, entertainment, sports and games, transportation, electricity, food, education, military and western sources. Supplement contains teen slang and further military slang.

170 Birmingham, Stephen. THE RIGHT PEOPLE: A PORTRAIT OF THE AMERICAN SOCIAL ESTABLISHMENT. Boston: Little, Brown, 1968. 360 p. Index, illus.

> Revelations of high society and the people of the decade who qualify. Divided into three parts, the book treats the social establishment, how money lives, and playgrounds of the rich; with a chapter on how the class structure is maintained from one generation to the next.

171 Boas, Max, and Chain, Steve. BIG MAC: THE UNAUTHORIZED STORY OF McDONALD'S. New York: E.P. Dutton and Co., 1976. 212 p.

> A history of Ray Kroc and his hamburger chain.

172 Boatright, Mody Coggin. FOLKLORE OF THE OIL INDUSTRY. Dallas: Southern Methodist University Press, 1963. 220 p. Notes, index.

> The lore of finding oil, popular stereotypes of the geologist, oil promoter, shooter, driller, and landowner; stories and songs.

173 Boatright, Mody Coggin, and Owens, William. TALES FROM THE DERRICK FLOOR: A PEOPLE'S HISTORY OF THE OIL INDUSTRY. Garden City, N.Y.: Doubleday, 1970. 268 p. Chronology, bibliog., index.

> The lore of strikes, boom towns, women, characters, jargon, hazards, and working knowledge.

174 Bode, Carl. THE ANATOMY OF AMERICAN POPULAR CULTURE, 1840–1861. Berkeley and Los Angeles: University of California Press, 1959. 292 p. Notes, index.

> An examination of fine and popular arts, books and other print materials, and the revelation of the American character through cultural preferences. The book is oriented to four motifs: patriotism, including chauvinism and feelings of European superiority; aggressiveness and its dominant expression in the notions about success, materialism, restlessness and optimism; religion and its varieties of expression; and the various forms of love that characterized the sentimental

productions of the period. Bode provides examinations of drama, music, popular architecture and furnishings, decoration, painting and sculpture; manuals, religious publications and inspirational fiction, best sellers, poetry, adventure fiction, popular histories, the political press, and related matters.

175 Botkin, Benjamin Albert. SIDEWALKS OF AMERICA; FOLKLORE, LEGENDS, SAGAS, TRADITIONS, CUSTOMS, SONGS, STORIES, AND SAYINGS OF CITY FOLK. Indianapolis, Ind.: Bobbs-Merrill, 1954. 605 p.

An extensive collection of excerpts and brief pieces gathered to show "as many cities, types, and aspects of city life and folklore as possible," in order to "create the mood of the city" through biography, memoirs, historical and travel writing, reportage, manuscripts, interviews, and recordings.

176 Branch, E. Douglas. THE SENTIMENTAL YEARS, 1836-1860. New York: D. Appleton-Century, 1934. 432 p. Index.

Sentimentalism is defined as "the refusal to recognize the reality; or the inability to pass judgment upon it; and the clinging to the myth." The volume explores the myth of "the first generation of the American middle class" as it emerged in the free states. Branch surveys the development of paternalistic capitalism and the rise of labor unions; literature, both elite and popular; fashions; temperance; pseudosciences, children, religion, and the growing abolitionist movement.

177 Brandes, Paul D., and Brewer, Jentonne. DIALECT CLASH IN AMERICA: ISSUES AND ANSWERS. Metuchen, N.J.: Scarecrow Press, 1977. 586 p. Bibliog., index.

A general discussion of language development in the United States, with chapters on differences in English and American development, dialect, the clash of dialect in schools, and the historical description of various dialects.

178 Browne, Joy. THE USED-CAR GAME: A SOCIOLOGY OF THE BARGAIN. Lexington, Mass.: Lexington Books, 1973. 184 p.

An analysis of the perspectives and social context of selling used cars.

179 Burke, W.J. THE LITERATURE OF SLANG. Introduction by Eric Partridge. New York: New York Public Library, 1939. Reprint. Detroit: Gale Research Co., 1965. 180 p. Index.

This is an invaluable annotated guide to information concerning reference works, cant, occupational jargon, war slang, school slang, and the slang of sports, the theater, gambling, and other institutions and subcultures. References to regional dialects are included, but little on ethnic speech.

180 Carson, Gerald. CORNFLAKE CRUSADE. 1959. New York: Arno Press, 1976. 305 p. Chronology, illus.

The history of the breakfast cereal empire centered in Battle Creek, Michigan. Emphasis is on the relationship of Adventist activity, health fads, and other matters, to the building of the Kellogg and Post cereal empires.

181 _____. MEN, BEASTS, AND GODS: A HISTORY OF CRUELTY AND KINDNESS TO ANIMALS. New York: Charles Scribner's Sons, 1972. 268 p. Notes, bibliog., index.

A perceptive examination of the relationships of animals to culture with emphasis on the American experience. Chapters highlight key events, with a final series dealing with declining contact, unwanted animals, rodeos, furs, animal experiments, and the exploitation of animals.

182 _____. THE SOCIAL HISTORY OF BOURBON: AN UNHURRIED ACCOUNT OF OUR STAR-SPANGLED AMERICAN DRINK. New York: Dodd, Mead, 1963. 280 p. Index, chap. notes, glossary, chronology, illus.

A useful account of the development of bourbon whiskey from colonial to modern times.

183 Chudacoff, Howard. THE EVOLUTION OF AMERICAN URBAN SOCIETY. Englewood Cliffs, N.J.: Prentice-Hall, 1975. 280 p. Bibliog., index.

An urban history from colonial times to the present, emphasizing the assimilation of migrants, the standardization of social and economic activities, and the incorporation of technological innovations in transportation and communication.

184 Churchill, Allen. A PICTORIAL HISTORY OF AMERICAN CRIME, 1849-1929. New York: Holt, Rinehart and Winston, 1964. 180 p. Illus., bibliog., index.

Brief illustrated accounts of fifty celebrated murder cases.

185 _____. THE SPLENDOR SEEKERS: AN INFORMAL GLIMPSE OF AMERICA'S MULTIMILLIONAIRE SPENDERS--MEMBERS OF THE $50,000,000

CLUB. New York: Grosset and Dunlap, 1974. 278 p. Bibliog., index.

Chapters on the life-styles of nineteenth-century robber barons.

186   Cohn, David L. LOVE IN AMERICA: AN INFORMAL STUDY OF MANNERS AND MORALS IN AMERICAN MARRIAGE. New York: Simon and Schuster, 1943. 234 p.

Interesting and provocative comments on society pages and commentators, radio soap operas, lovelorn columns, cosmetics, women's magazines, and related matters. The focus is on the influence of advertising and peer group pressure on women of the time.

187   Cornell, James, comp. and ed. IT HAPPENED LAST YEAR!: EARTH EVENTS, 1973. New York: Macmillan Co., 1974. 254 p. Illus., bibliog.

Disasters, astrophysical, biological, ecological, and geophysical events in the world described by the Smithsonian Institution's Center for Short-Lived Phenomena.

188   Cox, Frank D., comp. AMERICAN MARRIAGE: A CHANGING SCENE? 2d ed. Dubuque, Iowa: W.C. Brown, 1972. 272 p. Notes, index.

A collection of twenty-seven essays oriented to the future, with emphasis on tomorrow's morality, the popular romantic ideal, ethnic ideals, and the family of the future.

189   Cummings, Richard O. THE AMERICAN AND HIS FOOD: A HISTORY OF FOOD HABITS IN THE UNITED STATES. Rev. ed. Chicago: University of Chicago Press, 1941. 291 p. Illus., tables, diagrams, bibliog., notes, index.

Though focusing on nutrition, the volume contains much information on food habits of early Americans (though it continues many erroneous assumptions) and the attitudes of nutritionists of the early forties. Includes material on transportation of food and food preservation. Appendixes chart food classification, consumption trends, life expectancy, seasonal foods, budgets, and wage percentages for food, calorie cost, and related matters.

190   Dietz, Lawrence. SODA POP: THE HISTORY, ADVERTISING, ART AND MEMORABILIA OF SOFT DRINKS IN AMERICA. New York: Simon and Schuster, 1973. 184 p. Illus.

Although written by an inspired fan of the memorabilia, this is an informative and highly readable account of soft drinks, especially Coca Cola and Pepsi Cola.

191   Dill, Stephen, and Bebeau, Donald, eds. "Current Slang." Vols. 1-4, 1966-70. Department of English, University of South Dakota. Mimeographed sheets.

Brief definitions for terms, with locations noted. Most collections were made on college campuses and in Watts.

192   Dillard, Joey Lee. ALL-AMERICAN ENGLISH. New York: Random House, 1975. 369 p. Notes, bibliog., index.

A history of American-English diffusion, with chapters on maritime English, American koine, migrants and immigrants, frontier speechways, Puerto Rican bilingualism, and world English.

193   _____. AMERICAN TALK: WHERE OUR WORDS COME FROM. New York: Random House, 1976. 187 p. Notes, bibliog., index.

A survey of pidgin English, Dutch influences, New Orleans and Louisiana influences; gambling, drinking, smoking, and chewing words; cowboy and mountain men usages; black English; and the influences of Madison Avenue and politics.

194   _____. BLACK NAMES. The Hague: Mouton, 1976. 114 p. Notes, bibliog.

Discussions of personal names, names in music, church names, vehicle names, and shops, vendors, and things for sale.

195   _____. LEXICON OF BLACK ENGLISH. New York: Continuum, Seabury, 1977. 199 p. Notes, bibliog., index.

A perceptive discussion of aspects of black English, including chapters on the language of sex, religion, music (especially blues), street hustlers, and conjure and root work. Other chapters discuss the social significance of a lexicon, distinctions between black usage and slang, discourse patterns, and problems with the reliance on literary sources for the understanding of black English.

196   _____, ed. PERSPECTIVES ON BLACK ENGLISH. Paris and The Hague: Mouton, 1975. 391 p. Notes, bibliog., index.

A collection of twenty-three essays on black English, focusing on dialectology, history of black usages, acculturation, and psycholinguistics.

197   Dohan, Mary Helen. OUR OWN WORDS. New York: Alfred A. Knopf, 1974. 315 p.

A popular history of American words and usages with a brief bibliographical essay and an index to words and phrases.

198 Donaldson, Scott. THE SUBURBAN MYTH. New York: Columbia University Press, 1969. 272 p. Notes, annot. bibliog., index.

An attempt to correct the mistaken image of suburban life fostered by numerous critics. Donaldson draws on a range of statistics, impressions, observations by other writers, and fiction to argue that the reality of the suburbs is a practical realization of the pastoral dream.

199 Dubois, Betty Lou, and Crouch, Isabel, eds. PAPERS IN SOUTHWEST ENGLISH IV: PROCEEDINGS OF THE CONFERENCE ON THE SOCIOLOGY OF THE LANGUAGES OF AMERICAN WOMEN. San Antonio: Trinity University, 1976. 196 p. Illus., bibliog.

Essays on features of women's speech, interaction cues, and other matters related to examination of sexual differences in language usage.

200 Duhamel, Georges. AMERICA THE MENACE: SCENES FROM THE LIFE OF THE FUTURE. Translated by Charles Miner Thompson. Boston: Houghton Mifflin, 1931. 217 p.

An early denouncement of the Baconian technological thrust that has overtaken America and threatens, in another twenty years, to take over the consciousness of Europe, destroying the last vestiges of civilization there. The critique is novelized as an encounter with a future civilization in which the Frenchman is abused in his encounters with the scientific perspective, goes to a movie, argues about Prohibition, evades automobiles, complains about the state of art, observes Chicago and the stockyards, notes the prevalence of advertising, comments on racial segregation, is horrified by a football game, is confounded by insurance, and thinks about what is to come of it all.

201 Dundes, Alan, and Pagter, Carl R., comps. URBAN FOLKLORE FROM THE PAPERWORK EMPIRE. Austin: American Folklore Society, 1975. 223 p.

A collection of form letters, informal dictionaries, memos, tests, drawings, and double entendres circulated through institutions, with a refreshing redefinition of folklore that avoids the oral bias.

202 Emrich, Duncan. FOLKLORE ON THE AMERICAN LAND. Boston: Little, Brown, 1972. 707 p. Bibliog., notes, index.

Contains useful sections on the urban belief tale; names; children's lore; street cries and epitaphs; legends, songs and ballads; and beliefs and superstitions.

203 Evans, Walker. AMERICAN PHOTOGRAPHS. New York: Museum of
Modern Art, 1938. 198 p.

Evans's striking photographs with an essay by Lincoln Kerstein.

204 _____. PHOTOGRAPHS FOR THE FARM SECURITY ADMINISTRATION,
1935-38: A CATALOG OF PHOTOGRAPHIC PRINTS AVAILABLE FROM
THE FARM SECURITY ADMINISTRATION COLLECTION IN THE LIBRARY
OF CONGRESS. Introduction by Jerald C. Maddox. New York: Da Capo,
1975. 244 p. Index.

A collection of 488 photographs taken from 1935 through 1938
along the eastern seaboard, Appalachia, and the South. Many
scenes, storefronts, poster walls, and people are shown.

205 Fairfield, Richard, ed. UTOPIA, U.S.A.: WRITINGS ON CONTEM-
PORARY ALTERNATIVE LIFESTYLES. San Francisco, Calif.: Alternatives
Foundation, 1972. 231 p. Illus.

Descriptive and inspirational articles on communes and alternative
settlements in the style of THE MODERN UTOPIAN (1966?-72?).

206 Feldman, Sandor. MANNERISMS OF SPEECH AND GESTURE IN EVERY-
DAY LIFE. New York: International Universities Press, 1959. 309 p.

Psychological interpretations based on psychiatric patients'
habitual use of such a common phrase as "I think, as usual,"
but, more importantly, of gestures and expressions.

207 Feldstein, Stanley. THE LAND THAT I SHOW YOU: THREE CENTURIES
OF JEWISH LIFE IN AMERICA. Garden City, N.Y.: Anchor, 1978.
512 p. Bibliog., index.

Traces Jewish presence on the continent from 1654 to the
1970s.

208 _____. ONCE A SLAVE: THE SLAVE'S VIEW OF SLAVERY. New
York: William Morrow, 1971. 329 p. Notes, bibliog., index.

A survey of everyday life, the business of slavery, beliefs
and customs, and the slave's perspective on slavery.

209 Feldstein, Stanley, and Costello, Lawrence, eds. THE ORDEAL OF
ASSIMILATION: A DOCUMENTARY HISTORY OF THE WHITE WORKING
CLASS. Garden City, N.Y.: Anchor, Doubleday, 1974. 500 p. Index.

Excerpts from books, articles, and other sources, with chapter
introductions to sections on initial experiences, nativism,
ghettos, industrialization, unionism, assimilation, and pluralism.

210 Ferrara, Grace M., ed. THE DISASTER FILE: THE 1970S. New York: Facts on File, 1979. 173 p. Illus., index.

Encyclopedic entries on aviation, highway, sea, railroad, earthquake, volcano, storm, flood, fire, explosion, drought, famine, oil spills, mine, and other disasters. No secondary sources cited.

211 Filene, Peter Gabriel. HIM/HER/SELF: SEX ROLES IN MODERN AMERICA. New York: Harcourt, 1975. 351 p. Bibliog., essay, notes, index.

An exploration of the social aspects of masculinity and femininity as they have been sanctioned and expressed from 1890 to 1974. In two parts, the volume focuses on the formation of role expectations formed in the home, in wartime, and at work through World War I and later. Appendix on the female labor force.

212 Flanagan, Cathleen C., and Flanagan, John T. AMERICAN FOLKLORE: A BIBLIOGRAPHY, 1950-1974. Metuchen, N.J.: Scarecrow Press, 1977. 406 p. Obituaries, author index.

A bibliography, with many items annotated, of over thirty-six hundred items, collected into categories covering reference material, teaching, and various genres.

213 Flexner, Stuart Berg. I HEAR AMERICA TALKING: AN ILLUSTRATED TREASURY OF AMERICAN WORDS AND PHRASES. New York: Van Nostrand Reinhold Co., 1976. 505 p. Index.

This large format volume contains brief chapters on about 175 words, names, and phrases; each discussion lists synonyms.

214 Fogarty, Robert S. DICTIONARY OF AMERICAN COMMUNAL AND UTOPIAN HISTORY. Westport, Conn.: Greenwood Press, 1980. 271 p. Appendixes, bibliog., index.

Descriptive biographical and community entries, with an annotated list of communal and utopian societies, 1787-1919, by Otohiko Okugawa, and a bibliographical history of communalism in America.

215 Forma, Warren. THEY WERE RAGTIME. New York: Grosset and Dunlap, 1976. 245 p. Index, bibliog.

A history, from about 1892 to 1920, of urbanizing and industrializing America through a text based largely on Thorstein Veblen and Freud and a magnificent collection of photographs. Forma focuses on the class conflict implicit in the laissez faire development of predatory capitalism.

216   Fulton, Robert, comp. DEATH, GRIEF AND BEREAVEMENT: A BIBLIOG-
       RAPHY, 1845-1972. Minneapolis: University of Minnesota, Center for
       Death Education and Research, 1973. 173 p. Index.

       A total of 2,639 items, arranged alphabetically. Only those
       having empirical value are included and those dealing with
       suicide have been excluded.

217   Gans, Herbert J. THE LEVITTOWNERS: WAYS OF LIFE AND POLITICS
       IN A NEW SUBURBAN COMMUNITY. New York: Random House, 1967.
       474 p. Methodological appendix, bibliog., index.

       An influential study of Levittown, New York, one of the
       first postwar suburban developments, and its lower middle-
       and working-class people during the period between 1958
       and 1962. Sections cover origins, quality of life, and com-
       munity politics.

218   _____. THE URBAN VILLAGERS: GROUP AND CLASS IN THE LIFE
       OF ITALIAN-AMERICANS. New York: Free Press, 1962. 367 p.
       Methodological appendix, bibliog., index.

       A community study of the old Boston West End before the
       federal renewal project. Chapters describe everyday life
       and ethnicity, with a description and critique of the dislo-
       cation caused by urban renewal.

219   Gardner, Hugh. THE CHILDREN OF PROSPERITY: THIRTEEN MODERN
       AMERICAN COMMUNES. New York: St. Martin's Press, 1978. 281 p.
       Notes on fieldwork and ethnographic protocols, bibliog., index.

       Beginning with a chapter on the development of the modern
       commune movement, Gardner then discusses Drop City, Libre,
       Guild of Colorado, Lama Foundation, LILA, Morning Star
       East and the Reality Construction Company, Maharaj Ashram,
       Wheeler Ranch, Ananda Cooperative Village, Talsalsan, Crook's
       Creek, Saddle Ridge Farm. Two final chapters interpret the
       viability of the communes and discuss the legacy of the com-
       mune movement.

220   Garfinkle, Harold. "Studies in the Routine Grounds of Everyday Activi-
       ties." SOCIAL PROBLEMS 11 (Winter 1964): 225-50.

       Examination of the assumptions behind linguistic exchanges
       among people in domestic and other intimate situations.

221   Garman, E. Thomas, and Monroe, Sarah D. AVOIDING CONSUMER
       FRAUDS AND MISREPRESENTATIONS: A LEARNING MODULE. Blacks-
       burg: Virginia Cooperative Extension, Virginia Polytechnic Institute and
       State University, 1977. 79 leaves.

A handbook text for consumer education groups, including masters for making transparencies.

222   Garson, Barbara. ALL THE LIVELONG DAY. New York: Doubleday, 1975. 221 p.

A series of interviews with workers in a ping pong factory, tuna fish plant, a cosmetics factory, an automobile plant, a mink-fleshing factory, a pharmaceutical plant, keypunching, clerical work and typing; with chapters on unions and division of labor in assembly lines. The volume concludes with a plea for worker-controlled conditions and notes on the dehumanization of workers through management practices.

223   Gelman, Woody, and Jackson, Barbara. DISASTER ILLUSTRATED: TWO HUNDRED YEARS OF AMERICAN MISFORTUNE. New York: Harmony Books, 1976. 191 p. Illus.

A survey of the disasters caused by earthquakes, floods, fires, blizzards, the sea, explosions, railroads, hurricanes, tornadoes, airplanes, mines, epidemics, together with disappearances. Includes charts, photographs, newspaper clippings, and drawings.

224   Giedion, Sigfried. MECHANIZATION TAKES COMMAND: A CONTRIBUTION TO ANONYMOUS HISTORY. 1948. Reprint. New York: W.W. Norton, 1969. 743 p. Indexes to illustrations and subjects, chapter notes.

The classic study of the impact of technology on everyday life, Giedion's volume covers the notion of movement, progress, and the means of mechanization from classical times through the mid-twentieth century. The development of the tool is traced from simple forms of extension of the hand to the assembly line and scientific management; then the impact of mechanization is considered in agriculture, comfort, the tastes of the ruling classes, furniture, household appliances, food preservation, streamlining, and the bathroom throughout history. A conclusion discusses the illusion of progress.

225   Glick, Paul C. AMERICAN FAMILIES. New York: Wiley, 1957. Revised edition. New York: Russell and Russell, 1976. 230 p. Charts, graphs, tables, bibliog., index.

An updated interpretation of statistics related to family life that first appeared in 1957.

226   Gold, Robert S. JAZZ TALK: A DICTIONARY OF THE COLORFUL LANGUAGE THAT HAS EMERGED FROM AMERICA'S OWN MUSIC. New York: Bobbs-Merrill, 1975. 322 p.

A lexicon with sources, for a wide range of slang and colloquial words and phrases.

227 Goldin, Hyman E.; O'Leary, Frank; and Lipsius, Morris. DICTIONARY OF AMERICAN UNDERWORLD LINGO. New York: Twayne, 1950. 327 p.

Brief definitions of terms in use among prison inmates, collected and defined by the editors, who were themselves convicts.

228 Goldstine, Daniel, et al. THE DANCE-AWAY LOVER; AND OTHER ROLES WE PLAY IN LOVE, SEX, AND MARRIAGE New York: Morrow, 1977. 251 p.

A therapeutic book about couples and individual styles of coping that attempts, in the tradition of role theory, to provide the social context for understanding common scenarios and problems.

229 Graff, Harvey J. THE LITERACY MYTH: LITERACY AND SOCIAL STRUCTURE IN THE NINETEENTH-CENTURY CITY. New York: Academic Press, 1979. 352 p. Illus., notes, index.

An extensive study that finds literacy overrated as an important aspect of the developing industrial societies of western Europe and North America.

230 Greenwood, Val D. THE RESEARCHER'S GUIDE TO AMERICAN GENE-ALOGY. Baltimore, Md.: Genealogical Publications, also distr. by Scribner. 1973. 535 p. Illus., bibliog., index.

A thorough guide to genealogical research, including chapters on recording practices, research materials, analyzing information, using various kinds of evidence, with notes on Canadian research.

231 Gurko, Leo. HEROES, HIGHBROWS AND THE POPULAR MIND. Indianapolis, Ind.: Bobbs-Merrill, 1953. 319 p. Index.

This is a wary venture into the complexities of examining the popular mind through various media and entertainments. The study begins with cautions about reading American imagery directly from media, traces several popular myths and examines such intellectuals as teachers, artists and policy advisors in the public milieu. The second part examines print media, radio, film and television, and provides an examination of the popular heroic figure. The last part explores the notion of the whole man and his prospects in contemporary society.

232   Hall, Susan. GENTLEMAN OF LEISURE: A YEAR IN THE LIFE OF A
       PIMP. New York: Prairie House Book, New American Library, 1972.
       192 p. Glossary.

> An essay with photographs of a pimp and his whores in New
> York; largely based on tape-recorded interviews.

233   Harder, Kelsie B., ed. ILLUSTRATED DICTIONARY OF PLACE NAMES:
       UNITED STATES AND CANADA. A Hudson Group Book. New York: Van
       Nostrand Reinhold, 1976. 631 p. Illus., bibliog.

> Lists probable sources for place names, often with a brief
> explanation, along with later derivations.

234   Hareven, Tamara K., ed. ANONYMOUS AMERICANS: EXPLORATIONS
       IN NINETEENTH-CENTURY SOCIAL HISTORY. Englewood Cliffs, N.J.:
       Prentice-Hall, 1971. 314 p. Notes, index.

> Essays on everyday life in rural New England, mobility, images
> of the plains frontier, melodrama, slave songs, immigrant reli-
> gious life, mental hospitals, and violence in Chicago.

235   Harris, Louis. THE ANGUISH OF CHANGE. New York: Norton, 1973.
       306 p. Notes, index.

> National trends in opinions, interests, concerns, and beliefs
> based on 436 polls, from 1960 to 1973. Prose summaries of the
> statistics cover the Vietnam war and its aftermath, the status
> of women, blacks, the poor, youth, the quality of life, joy,
> and despair.

236   Harrison, Deborah Sears, and Trabasso, Tom, eds. BLACK ENGLISH:
       A SEMINAR. Hillsdale, N.J.: Lawrence Erlbaum, 1976. 301 p. Index.

> Essays on the definition of black English, its historical origins,
> use, and the implications of its ethnic connections.

237   Hauser, Arnold. THE SOCIAL HISTORY OF ART. 4 vols. 1951. Re-
       print. New York: Knopf, 1968. 1,007 p. Illus., notes, index.

> A broad history that includes in volumes 3 and 4 discussions
> of the English social novel, film, the new reading public,
> domestic drama, and other movements and themes.

238   Hemphill, Paul. THE GOOD OLD BOYS. New York: Simon and
       Schuster, 1974. 255 p.

> A series of magazine and newspaper pieces on southern Ameri-
> cana and the individuals who liven the scenes. Subjects in-
> clude sports, entertainers, evangelists, and moods.

239   Hess, John L., and Hess, Karen. THE TASTE OF AMERICA. New
      York: Grossman Publishers, 1977. 384 p. Bibliog., index.

      An excellent corrective to the many glosses on the develop-
      ment of modern food and food processing. In this delight-
      fully written book are chapters on plagiarism in cookbooks,
      the nonsensical anecdotes regarding food heritage, "gourmet
      food," food hustlers who write for newspapers and magazines,
      and many other matters regarding food and chemical concoc-
      tions that are packaged as food.

240   Homer, Joel. JARGON: HOW TO TALK TO ANYONE ABOUT ANY-
      THING. New York: Times Books, 1979. 223 p. Illus.

      Informal definitions for words and phrases circulating among
      power brokers, the media, technocrats, and others.

241   Hook, J.N. THE GRAND PANJANDRUM, & 1,999 OTHER RARE, USE-
      FUL, AND DELIGHTFUL WORDS AND EXPRESSIONS. New York:
      Macmillan, 1980. 392 p. Index, quizzes.

      Definitions of rarely used but useful words for which there
      are no common counterparts. The volume is divided into sec-
      tions of topical interest.

242   Horan, James D. DESPERATE WOMEN. New York: G.P. Putnam's
      Sons, 1952. 356 p. Bibliog., index.

      Biographical sketches and adventures of women spies, despera-
      does, and others more noted for their activities than their sex.
      Included are confederate spies Rose O'Neale Greenhow and
      Belle Boyd, union spy and frontierswoman Pauline Cushman,
      union spy Elizabeth Van Lew, calamity Jane, outlaw Belle
      Starr, Ella "Cattle Kate" Watson, outlaw Rose "of Cimarron"
      Dunn, outlaws Genie Carter and Mollie Merrill, road agent
      Pearl Hart, Little Jo Monoghan, "China Polly," and "Poker
      Alice" Ivers.

243   Hotten, J.C. THE SLANG DICTIONARY: ETYMOLOGICAL, HISTORI-
      CAL AND ANECDOTAL. London: Chatto and Windus, 1874. 382 p.
      Bibliog.

      Includes brief histories of cant slang and notes the hieroglyphics
      used by vagabonds. A glossary of rhyming slang and back
      slang, a "secret" language in which words are pronounced back-
      ward, is provided. The main dictionary is cross-referenced and
      provides some notes on early appearances in print.

244   Hunter, Carman St. John, and Harman, David. ADULT ILLITERACY IN
      THE UNITED STATES: A REPORT TO THE FORD FOUNDATION. New
      York: McGraw-Hill, 1979. 206 p. Illus., bibliog., index.

A survey of data on definitions, the isolation of illiteracy, approaches to the problems of illiteracy, and proposed remedies. The tables, figures, and annotated bibliography are particularly useful.

245 Inglis, Brian. THE FORBIDDEN GAME: A SOCIAL HISTORY OF DRUGS. New York: Scribner's, 1975. 256 p. Sources, bibliog., index.

A heady survey of the social effects of drugs, with chapters on their uses in various cultures, and chapters on spirits, opium, hemp, heroin, and cannibis. Other chapters treat efforts at control as well as uses of drugs to achieve altered states of consciousness.

246 Ireland, Norma Olin, comp. INDEX TO AMERICA: LIFE AND CUSTOMS-- SEVENTEENTH CENTURY. Westwood, Mass.: F.W. Faxon, 1978. 254 p.

Indexes aspects of everyday life and customs from approximately 120 books.

247 Irwin, Godfrey. AMERICAN TRAMP AND UNDERWORLD SLANG: WORDS AND PHRASES USED BY HOBOES, TRAMPS, MIGRATORY WORKERS AND THOSE ON THE FRINGES OF SOCIETY, WITH THEIR USES AND ORIGINS. London: Eric Partridge, 1931. 264 p.

Includes brief definitions and a number of tramp songs.

248 Jenkins, Alan. THE THIRTIES. New York: Stein and Day, 1976. 240 p. Index.

A potpourri of themes is covered in this richly illustrated volume, including chapters on glamor, transportation, the popular arts, scandal, violence, and media.

249 Jerome, Judson. FAMILIES OF EDEN: COMMUNES AND THE NEW ANARCHISM. New York: Continuum: Seabury, 1974. 271 p.

A useful discussion of the definition and styles of communes and communal life written by an academic dropout who appears to continue a thoughtful life.

250 Kalish, Richard A., and Reynolds, David K. DEATH AND ETHNICITY: A PSYCHOCULTURAL STUDY. Los Angeles: University of Southern California, Ethel Percy Andrus Gerontology Center, 1976. 224 p. Bibliog., appendix, index.

Based on community surveys and other sources, the volume discusses dying in relation to age, sex, education, and religiosity for black, Japanese, and Mexican Americans.

251 Kane, Joseph Nathan, and Alexander, Gerard L. NICKNAMES AND SOBRIQUETS OF U.S. CITIES, STATES, AND COUNTIES. 3d ed. Metuchen, N.J.: Scarecrow Press, 1979. 429 p.

This book is cross-indexed.

252 Kanter, Rosabeth Moss. COMMUNES: CREATING AND MANAGING THE COLLECTIVE LIFE. New York: Harper, 1973. 544 p.

Sociological study of various contemporary communities.

253 Kett, Joseph F. RITES OF PASSAGE: ADOLESCENCE IN AMERICA, 1790 TO THE PRESENT. New York: Basic Books, 1977. 327 p. Notes, index.

A historical account of the distortions introduced by society in its effort to provide children with guidance. The volume treats three major periods: to 1840, 1840-1900, and the emergence of the idea of adolescence in modern times.

254 Key, Mary Ritchie. MALE/FEMALE LANGUAGE: WITH A COMPRE-HENSIVE BIBLIOGRAPHY. Metuchen, N.J.: Scarecrow Press, 1975. 200 p. Notes, illus., bibliog., index.

An extensive discussion of language differences between males and females as they relate to social structure; labels and descriptors; titles, names, and greetings; discrimination; education; nonverbal behavior; authors' usages; language change; and androgynous language.

255 King, Larry L. OF OUTLAWS, CON MEN, WHORES, POLITICIANS, AND OTHER ARTISTS. New York: Viking, 1980. 274 p.

Essays on the American redneck, Herbert Hoover, high school yearbook prophecies, going home, bad musicians, the Chicken Ranch whorehouse, big stakes poker, horse trading, the Willie Nelson concert, John Connally, Mo Udall, politicians and sex, LBJ and politics.

256 Kornblum, William. BLUE COLLAR COMMUNITY. Studies of Urban Society. Chicago: University of Chicago Press, 1974. 260 p. Notes, bibliog., index.

A study that elucidates the role of local political institutions in South Chicago in channeling and shaping ethnic values and cultural change.

257 Kronenberger, Louis. THE CART AND THE HORSE. New York: Alfred A. Knopf, 1964. 211 p.

A collection of essays on the condition of contemporary

American culture, on the new Babbitts, personal ethnics, pretentious vulgarity, New York vulgarity, pills, on late middle age, and on writing and the writer's situation in society.

258 Lacour-Gayet, Robert. EVERYDAY LIFE IN THE UNITED STATES BE-FORE THE CIVIL WAR, 1830-1860. Translated by Mary Ilford. New York: Frederick Ungar, 1969. 300 p. Bibliog., index.

A survey of cities, houses and furnishings, dress and fashions, food and beverages, communications and transportation; women-love-marriage, manners and etiquette, hygiene and sports, recreation and entertainment; and matters of professional, intellectual, moral, and civic life.

259 Lamb, Ruth deForest. AMERICAN CHAMBER OF HORRORS: THE TRUTH ABOUT FOOD AND DRUGS. New York: Farrar and Rinehart, 1936. Reprint. New York: Arno Press, 1976. 418 p.

A critical examination of food, beauty aids, health gimmicks as advertised and packaged for consumption.

260 Landy, Eugene E. THE UNDERGROUND DICTIONARY. New York: Simon and Schuster, 1971. 206 p.

Current slang expressions with pronunciations; appended is a very brief list of signs and gestures.

261 Langdon, William Chauncy. EVERYDAY THINGS IN AMERICAN LIFE, 1776-1876. 2 vols. New York: Scribner's Sons, 1941. 456 p. Illus., bibliog., index.

A useful set that covers, in volume 1, shelters, the fire-place, regional ethnics, furniture, wrought iron, pewter, silver, money, glass, ships, trails and roads, mail, agri-culture, and small towns from 1607 to 1776. Volume 2 covers travel by various means, early retail trade, news-papers, domestic life and furnishings, clothing, fairs and exhibitions, and other matters through 1876.

262 Lathrop, Elise. EARLY AMERICAN INNS AND TAVERNS. New York: Tudor, 1976. 365 p. Illus., bibliog.

Accounts and descriptions of inns and taverns still extant from nineteenth century or earlier origins.

263 Lawless, Edward W. TECHNOLOGY AND SOCIAL SHOCK. New Brunswick, N.J.: Rutgers University Press, 1977. 606 p. Notes, index.

A study of episodes resulting in public alarm and recurrent

news stories since World War II. Several dozen case studies
with synopses of many more provided; analyses of the process
of publicity and reaction are included. Appendixes review
methodology, technological assessment, and the technological
causes of public concern.

264   LeMasters, E.E.   BLUE-COLLAR ARISTOCRATS: LIFE-STYLES AT A
      WORKING-CLASS TAVERN. Madison: University of Wisconsin Press,
      1975. 218 p. Notes, index.

      The author examined the life-styles in a working-class bar as
      a participant-observer from 1967 through 1972. Most of the
      tavern goers are in the construction trade and are relatively
      affluent. LeMasters divides his observations into sections on
      work, marriage, sex, children, social life, drinking patterns,
      such issues as politics, race and religion, and the new young
      workers, with observations on the tavern's function in the lives
      of its patrons.

265   _____. PARENTS IN MODERN AMERICA. 3d ed. Homewood, III.:
      Dorsey Press, 1977. 210 p. Bibliog.

      A textbook that attempts to understand parents in complex
      "sick society." Chapters on parenting lore, roles parents
      play, media, social change, and counseling.

266   Lerner, Max. AMERICA AS A CIVILIZATION: LIFE AND THOUGHT
      IN THE UNITED STATES TODAY. 2 vols. New York: Simon and
      Schuster, 1957. 1,010 p. Notes, index.

      A midcentury discussion of the institutions and culture shaping
      the American experience. Volume 1 treats the idea of Ameri-
      can civilization, a survey of the people, technological culture,
      capitalism, and politics; volume 2 emphasizes cultural aspects,
      especially class and status, everyday life, the American char-
      acter, beliefs, popular culture, and international influence.

267   Liebow, Elliot. TALLY'S CORNER. Boston: Little, Brown, 1967. 260 p.
      Bibliog.

      Observations on low-income black social life by a white
      sociologist.

268   Lockridge, Kenneth A. LITERACY IN COLONIAL NEW ENGLAND:
      AN ENQUIRY INTO THE SOCIAL CONTEXT OF LITERACY IN THE
      EARLY MODERN WEST. New York: Norton, 1974. 164 p. Illus.,
      notes, bibliog., index.

      Based on the frequency of signatures as opposed to marks on
      wills and correlated with social and economic data, the study

raises questions and provides tentative answers about the meaning of literacy during this period of history.

269 Mathews, Mitford M. AMERICANISMS: A DICTIONARY OF SELECTED
AMERICANISMS ON HISTORICAL PRINCIPLES. Abridged ed. Chicago:
University of Chicago Press, 1951. 304 p.

Definitions and sources of early appearance of words and
phrases.

270 Medved, Michael, and Wallechinsky, David. WHAT REALLY HAPPENED
TO THE CLASS OF '65. New York: Random House, 1976. 285 p.
Photos.

A reconstruction of the lives and present status of some members of the 1965 class of Palisades High School that was
featured in a TIME article in January 1965, based on interviews with the authors' classmates and other material. About
thirty people are represented in some depth, with impressions
divided into life-styles and rites of passage.

271 Mehrabian, Albert. PUBLIC PLACES AND PRIVATE SPACES: THE
PSYCHOLOGY OF WORK, PLAY, AND LIVING ENVIRONMENTS.
New York: Basic Books, 1976. 354 p. Illus., bibliog., index.

An interesting and provocative discussion of environments--
intimate, residential, work, therapeutic, play, and communal--
with attention to the general adaptation syndrome.

272 Miller, Albert Jay, and Acri, Michael James. DEATH: A BIBLIO-
GRAPHICAL GUIDE. Metuchen, N.J.: Scarecrow Press, 1977. 420 p.
Index.

About 3,850 partially annotated items are included under the
categories of general works, education, humanities, medical
and nursing experiences, science, social sciences, and media.

273 Miller, Casey, and Swift, Kate. WORDS AND WOMEN: NEW LAN-
GUAGES IN NEW TIMES. Garden City, N.Y.: Anchor, Doubleday,
1976. Bibliog., notes, index.

A lively discussion of naming practices, standard English
biases, religious uses of language, the self-serving male
view, unisex, and liberation from sexist forms.

274 Miller, Wayne Charles. A COMPREHENSIVE BIBLIOGRAPHY FOR THE
STUDY OF AMERICAN MINORITIES. 2 vols. New York: New York
University, 1976. 1,380 p. Index.

An extensive, briefly annotated bibliography of materials on

ethnic groups arranged according to place of origin, and including references to fiction, the arts, everyday life, music,
folklore, and culture.

275 Mindel, Charles H., and Haberstein, Robert W. ETHNIC FAMILIES IN
AMERICA: PATTERNS AND VARIATIONS. New York: Elsevier, 1976.
429 p. Bibliog.

Essays on the history and life-styles of sixteen ethnic minorities, focusing on family life.

276 Minnigerode, Meade. THE FABULOUS FORTIES, 1840-1850: A PRESEN-
TATION OF PRIVATE LIFE. New York: G.P. Putnam's Sons, 1924.
345 p.

An "effort to apprehend a little of the mentality, of the intellectual point of view, of the daily manners" of the decade,
focusing on popular music, drama, fiction, fashion and entertainments. Included are chapters on Fanny Elssler the dancer,
the William Henry Harrison campaign, woman's life, sentimental fiction, popular drama (and the first live nude statues),
a riot at the opera; dioramas and panoramas, minstrel shows
and P.T. Barnum; dandies about town; parades and celebrations; the gold rush.

277 Montagu, Ashley. THE ANATOMY OF SWEARING. New York: Macmillan,
1967. 370 p. Chap. notes, index.

This unique study is concerned with all aspects of swearing,
from its etiology and history to its psychology and situational
ethnics. Montagu includes information on cursing and oaths,
the words and variants used to swear, Shakespearean swearing,
English-language swearing by centuries; with chapters devoted
to bloody, damn, the four-letter words, and a miscellany of
anecdotes.

278 Noling, A.W., comp. BEVERAGE LITERATURE: A BIBLIOGRAPHY.
Metuchen, N.J.: Scarecrow Press, 1971. 865 p. Subject index.

List of works on beverages of all kinds, with a general subject index and a list of collections of works on beverages.

279 Nye, Russel B., and Morpurgo, J.E. A HISTORY OF THE UNITED
STATES. 2 vols. 1955. Reprint. Baltimore, Md.: Penguin, 1967.

A cultural history, written as a collaboration between an
American and an English historian, that traces the develop-
ment of the idea of America through its fruition prior to
World War II.

280 Packard, Vance. A NATION OF STRANGERS. New York: David McKay, 1972. 368 p. Notes, index.

> An incisive impression of the patterns of fragmentation caused by migrating corporations, urban and ethnic changes, colleges and other sources, with emphasis on emerging styles of personal and social adaptation. Appendixes chart worldwide mobility, indicate high mobility states, and designate states with high rates of in- and out-flow of population.

281 _____. THE STATUS SEEKERS: AN EXPLORATION OF CLASS BE-HAVIOR IN AMERICA AND THE HIDDEN BARRIERS THAT AFFECT YOU, YOUR COMMUNITY, YOUR FUTURE. New York: David McKay, 1959. 376 p. Notes, index.

> The popular sociology of status seeking among Americans. Packard's section on status indicators is particularly interesting in its treatment of housing, job prestige, consumer items, sex and friendship, clubs, religious organizations, voting, and education. Also included are chapters on changes, strains, trends, and implications.

282 _____. THE WASTE MAKERS. New York: David McKay, 1960. 340 p. Notes, index.

> Attempts to answer questions about where the wastefulness of American business will lead, with chapters on increasing consumption, planned obsolescence and hard-sell promotion, the implications of such practices, and suggestions for achieving a more rational and satisfying style of living.

283 Partridge, Eric. A DICTIONARY OF CATCH PHRASES, BRITISH AND AMERICAN, FROM THE SIXTEENTH CENTURY TO THE PRESENT DAY. London: Routledge and Kegan Paul, 1977. 278 p.

> Brief definitions of phrases with literary sources when available and dates of frequent usage.

284 _____. A DICTIONARY OF CLICHES. 5th ed. London: Routledge and Kegan Paul, 1978. 261 p.

> Brief definitions of phrases used often enough to be considered ubiquitous at various times, with a useful introduction by the author.

285 _____. A DICTIONARY OF THE UNDERWORLD--BRITISH AND AMERI-CAN: BEING THE VOCABULARIES OF CROOKS, CRIMINALS, RACKE-TEERS, BEGGARS AND TRAMPS, CONVICTS, THE COMMERCIAL UNDER-WORLD, THE DRUG TRAFFIC, THE WHITE SLAVE TRAFFIC, SPIVS. London: Routledge and Kegan Paul, 1968. 886 p.

Extensive lexicon with origins, usages, and source references.

286 Pawley, Martin. THE PRIVATE FUTURE. New York: Random House, 1974. 217 p. Index.

A polemical argument on the decline of community and the malignant growth of self-indulgent private consumerism; uses popular sources.

287 Pei, Mario. DOUBLE-SPEAK IN AMERICA. New York: Hawthorne, 1973. 216 p. Indexes to subjects and words.

A popular exploration of the use and misuse of language in many contexts, including weasel words in advertising, student usage, erotic situations, feminism, newspapers, the Pentagon, taxation, violence, and other sources and contexts; with discussions of "beautiful" and "ugly" words, and euphemisms.

288 PLAYBOY'S BOOK OF FORBIDDEN WORDS: A LIBERATED DICTIONARY OF IMPROPER ENGLISH, CONTAINING OVER 700 UNINHIBITED DEFINITIONS OF EROTIC AND SCATOLOGICAL TERMS. Edited by Robert A. Wilson. Chicago: Playboy Press, 1972. 302 p.

A compilation of earthy words with commentaries.

289 Plowden, David. COMMONPLACE. New York: Sunrise Books, 1974. 117 p. Photos.

Everyday life in nonurbanized America through photographs of the milieu.

290 Psathas, George, ed. EVERYDAY LANGUAGE: STUDIES IN ETHNO-METHODOLOGY. New York: Irvington Publishers, 1979. 299 p. Subject index.

A collection of eleven essays on hot-rodder language, conversational shifts, telephone conversation openings, inviting laughter, beliefs, directional maps, traffic court, and court proceedings. Appendixes identify transcript symbols and a transcription system.

291 Rapport, Samuel, and Schartle, Patricia, eds. AMERICA REMEMBERS: OUR BEST-LOVED CUSTOMS AND TRADITIONS. Garden City, N.Y.: Hanover House, 1956. 669 p.

An extensive five-part compendium of nostalgic essays of many writers on home and family, country days, home town, city sidewalks, and across the nation. The home and family section includes pieces on holidays, rites of passage, family relationships; county days section covers visitors, everyday life,

entertainments, and catalogs and almanacs; home town contains
descriptions of games, events, holidays, the model T, character
types, and town life. City sidewalks cover sports, city sketches,
high life, and holiday events. The last section touches on
matters associated with particular places across the nation:
clambakes, possum hunts, the Kentucky Derby, Mardi Gras,
play parties, barbecues, rodeos, the Rose Bowl, and the Wild
West.

292   Reiss, Ira L., ed. THE SEXUAL RENAISSANCE IN AMERICA. Vol. 22.
Ann Arbor, Mich.: Society for the Psychological Study of Social Issues,
April 1966. 140 p.

A special issue of JOURNAL OF SOCIAL ISSUES which includes essays on adolescent sexual behavior, interpersonal relations, parent-child conflict, class aspects, and speculations
about the contemporary mood.

293   Robertson, Jerry. OIL SLANGUAGE. Evansville, Ind.: Petroleum Publishers, 1954. 181 p.

Brief definitions of terms and phrases found around oil producing areas, with cartoon illustrations and sketches of types
of people in the chain of command and types of women associated with oil workers. Contains production tips.

294   Rose, Howard N., comp. A THESAURUS OF SLANG. New York:
Macmillan, 1934. Reprint. Detroit: Gale Research Co., 1972. 120 p.

Categories include aviation, college, detective, hobo, lumber-
jack, New England, newspaper, oil field, railroad, sea-fishing,
sports, theater, western slang, war.

295   Ross, Ishbel. TASTE IN AMERICA: AN ILLUSTRATED HISTORY OF THE
EVOLUTION OF ARCHITECTURE, FURNISHINGS, FASHIONS, AND
CUSTOMS OF THE AMERICAN PEOPLE. New York: Thomas Y. Crowell,
1967. 343 p.   Notes, bibliog., index.

Illustrated with a lavish hodgepodge of illustrations, this useful survey of customs and manners covers sports and games,
domestic decoration, architecture, women's fashions, men's
fashions, the great parties and feasts, travel, and changes in
social customs.

296   Rossi, Alice S.; Kagan, Jerome; and Hareven, Tamara K., eds. THE
FAMILY. New York: Norton, 1978. 267 p. Notes, index.

Among the twelve essays are useful perspectives on family
time and historical time, child care, the history of the
family, and the city and the family.

297 Sagarin, Edward. THE ANATOMY OF DIRTY WORDS   New York: Lyle Stuart, 1968. 220 p. Notes, bibliog., indexes.

Discussions of the contexts of the words and usages in brief topical chapters.

298 Sann, Paul. THE ANGRY DECADE: THE SIXTIES. New York: Crown Publishers, 1979. 324 p. Index, photos.

A year-by-year summary of the decade through coverage of newsworthy events and news photographs.

299 _____. FADS, FOLLIES AND DELUSIONS OF THE AMERICAN PEOPLE. New York: Crown Publishers, 1967. 370 p. Illus., subject index.

Brief commentary on Batman, Superman, Zorro, Hopalong Cassidy, Davy Crockett, James Bond, flag pole sitting, the promoter C.C. Pyle, dance marathons, contests, technocracy, Townsend's pension plan, Upton Sinclair, chain letters, Emile Coué, Wilhelm Reich's orgone box, dianetics, diet fads, Hadacol, chlorophyll, ouija boards, hula hoops, skate boards, Mah-Jongg, miniature golf, bubble gum, Silly Putty, rebel flags, Scrabble, yo-yos, theosophy, Jiddu Krishnamurti, Father Divine, Frank Buchman's moral rearmament, Billy Sunday, Aimee Semple McPherson, Billy Graham, Timothy Leary, hippies, styles in grooming, new dance forms, rock music, campus fads, Valentino's funeral, quiz shows, and popular singers.

300 _____. THE LAWLESS DECADE: A PICTORIAL HISTORY OF A GREAT AMERICAN TRANSITION: FROM THE WORLD WAR I ARMISTICE AND PROHIBITION TO REPEAL AND THE NEW DEAL. New York: Crown Publishers, 1957. 240 p. Index, photos.

A year-by-year summary of the decade through featured events and news photographs.

301 Schaefer, Jack. AN AMERICAN BESTIARY. New York: Houghton Mifflin, 1975. 287 p.

Based on Schafer's experiences as an enlightened amateur, the volume offers an informal history of intellectual perspectives on animals, followed by discussions of a dozen species.

302 Seldes, Gilbert. THE STAMMERING CENTURY. New York: John Day, 1928. Reprint. Gloucester, Mass.: P. Smith, 1972. 414 p. Index.

This volume surveys the sects, cults, fads, religious excitements and related matters, in part as an answer to H.L. Mencken's claim that it is the masses rather than the intellectual aristocracy that succumb to various deceptions. Seldes demonstrates that it is more likely the educated and social elites that first become interested, but his focus is on the relationship of the sects to their environments and it is here that the interest of the volume lies. Included are chapters on Jonathan Edwards, the Great Awakening camp meetings, George Rapp's New Eden and Robert Owen's New Harmony, evangelists, Robert Matthews's Mormonism, John Humphrey Noyes's communism, Brook Farm and Fruitlands, Hopedale, William Lloyd Garrison; Frances E. Willard, Carry Nation and other prohibitionists, Mesmerism, phrenology, trance mediums such as Andrew Jackson David and Phineas Parkhurst Quimby; New Thought, Christian Science, Dowieites, and other forms of radical sectarian thought.

303   Seligson, Marcia. THE ETERNAL BLISS MACHINE: AMERICA'S WAY OF WEDDINGS. New York: William Morrow, 1973. 304 p. Bibliog., index.

Accounts of weddings and wedding lore, especially flamboyant affairs.

304   Severn, William. PEOPLE WORDS. New York: Ives Washburn, 1966. 184 p. Indexes to names and words.

A popular account of words associated with going places, food and drink, clothes and fashions, science and invention, and other categories of experience.

305   Sheehy, Gail. HUSTLING: PROSTITUTION IN OUR WIDE-OPEN SOCIETY. New York: Delacorte Press, 1974. 273 p.

A series of vignettes recounting, while writing for NEW YORK magazine, the experiences of pimps and prostitutes in New York.

306   Shukair, Ali A. THE AMERICAN WAY OF LIFE. New York: Philosophical Library, 1972. 134 p. Bibliog.

Observations of a Jordanian who lived in the United States for nineteen years. Beginning with a chapter on the outsider's dream versus the reality, the volume covers the country's potential, socialization, religion, ethnic discrimination, advertising, mass communications, American ignorance of other peoples, freedom and alienation, the sexual revolution and the family, and the uses of leisure.

307   Simpson, Jeffrey. THE AMERICAN FAMILY: A HISTORY IN PHOTO-GRAPHS. New York: Viking Press, 1976. 239 p. Brief bibliog.

Photographic essay, with captions and chapter introductions, on aspects of family life. Chapters cover pre-1876 photographs, the public image, reunions, courting, babies, home life, work, mobility, displays of wealth, play, grandparents, stress, holidays, rites of passage, and couples.

308   Simpson, Michael A. DYING, DEATH, AND GRIEF: A CRITICALLY ANNOTATED BIBLIOGRAPHY AND SOURCE BOOK OF THANATOLOGY AND TERMINAL CARE. New York: Plenum, 1979. 288 p. Filmographies, indexes.

A bibliography of over seven hundred items.

309   Slater, Philip. THE PURSUIT OF LONELINESS: AMERICAN CULTURE AT THE BREAKING POINT. Rev. ed. Boston: Beacon Press, 1976. 206 p. Notes.

An interpretation of the deceptions of middle-class life-style, and the problems the individual faces in trying to relate to others in the culture around him. The first chapter sets the terms of interpretation, followed by a chapter on the Vietnam War, one on child rearing and sex roles, another on the uses and misuses of sexual energy; mainstream culture and the counter-culture; ideologies for change; recommendations for using cultural advantages for change.

310   Smitherman, Geneva. TALKIN AND TESTIFYIN: THE LANGUAGE OF BLACK AMERICA. Boston: Houghton Mifflin, 1977. 291 p. Study exercises, notes, bibliog., index.

A textbook on black English.

311   Sobel, Robert. THEY SATISFY: THE CIGARETTE IN AMERICAN LIFE. New York: Anchor, 1978. 255 p. Bibliog., index.

A social history of tobacco and smoking from the nineteenth century through modern marketing, health issues, politics, and "the habit."

312   Stannard, David E., ed. DEATH IN AMERICA. Philadelphia: University of Pennsylvania Press, 1975. 158 p.

A collection of eight essays on death in the American experience, including a bibliographic essay on death and the interpretation of culture, death in the pre-Civil War popular mind, consolation literature (1830-80), the rural cemetery movement, and changing attitudes.

313   Stewart, George R. AMERICAN GIVEN NAMES: THEIR ORIGIN AND HISTORY IN THE CONTEXT OF THE ENGLISH LANGUAGE. New York: Oxford University Press, 1979. 264 p. Brief notes, bibliog.

Historical sketch and alphabetical list of common names.

314 _____. AMERICAN PLACE-NAMES: A CONCISE AND SELECTIVE DICTIONARY FOR THE CONTINENTAL UNITED STATES OF AMERICA. New York: Oxford University Press, 1970. 550 p.

> Brief definitions of the names, with known or probable derivations and dates of settlement when available.

315 _____. AMERICAN WAYS OF LIFE. Garden City, N.Y.: Doubleday, 1954. 310 p. Index.

> This useful general volume on the activities of the American people includes chapters on language, religion, food and drink, clothing and shelter, sex, personal names, play, holidays, and the arts. The chapters are based on Stewart's Fulbright lectures and are marked by an elementary quality.

316 Stryker, Roy Emerson, and Wood, Nancy. IN THIS PROUD LAND: AMERICA 1935-1943 AS SEEN IN FSA PHOTOGRAPHS. Greenwich, Conn.: New York Graphic, 1973. 191 p. Bibliog.

> Collection from the Farm Service Administration of Stryker's photographs with a biographical essay by Wood. The volume includes a brief shooting schedule and notes on location.

317 Taggart, Jean E. PET NAMES. Metuchen, N.J.: Scarecrow Press, 1962. 387 p.

> Lists of names drawn from numerous sources for a wide variety of pets.

318 Tak, Montie. TRUCK TALK: THE LANGUAGE OF THE OPEN ROAD. Philadelphia: Chilton, 1971. 191 p.

> Brief definitions of terms, slang and other usages, with synonyms and comparable terms.

319 Taylor, A. Marjorie, comp. THE LANGUAGE OF WORLD WAR II: ABBREVIATIONS, CAPTIONS, QUOTATIONS, SLOGANS, TITLES AND OTHER TERMS AND PHRASES. Rev. ed. New York: H.W. Wilson, 1948. 265 p. Booklist, index.

> Definitions and sources for words and phrases; includes a list of song titles on war themes.

320 Tebbel, John. FROM RAGS TO RICHES: HORATIO ALGER, JR. AND THE AMERICAN DREAM. New York: Macmillan, 1963. 245 p. Descr. bibliog., index.

> After a brief chapter on the rise and fall of the American dream, Tebbel examines both Alger the man and his work in a perceptive psychological and literary study.

321 _____. THE INHERITORS: A STUDY OF AMERICA'S GREAT FOR-
TUNES AND WHAT HAPPENED TO THEM. New York: Putnam, 1962.
312 p. Index.

A survey of wealthy families with an eye to acquisition of
riches and the possession of vast wealth. Focus is on those
whose initial accumulation came in the nineteenth century.

322 Thomas, Sarah M., and Weddington, Bernadine. A GUIDE TO SOURCES
OF CONSUMER INFORMATION. Foreword by Virginia H. Knauer.
Washington, D.C.: Information Resources Press, Herner, 1973. Illus.,
bibliog., index.

Annotated bibliography of guides, textbooks, general information books and periodicals; with national, state and local
government, and national nongovernmental consumer organizations described.

323 Vasquez, Librado Keno, and Vasquez, Maria Enriqueta. REGIONAL
DICTIONARY OF CHICANO SLANG. Austin: Jenkins Publishing Co.,
Pemberton Press, 1975. 111 p. Bibliog., index.

Brief definitions of current words and phrases, with a list of
Chicano-Hispano-Americano phrases, a brief list of riddles,
some folk remedies, and several folk songs.

324 Wall, C. Edward, and Przebienda, Edward, comps. WORDS AND
PHRASES INDEX: A GUIDE TO ANTEDATINGS, NEW WORDS, NEW
COMPOUNDS, NEW MEANINGS, AND OTHER PUBLISHED SCHOLAR-
SHIP SUPPLEMENTING THE OXFORD ENGLISH DICTIONARY, DICTIO-
NARY OF AMERICANISMS, DICTIONARY OF AMERICAN ENGLISH AND
OTHER MAJOR DICTIONARIES OF THE ENGLISH LANGUAGE. 4 vols.
Ann Arbor: Pierian, 1969-70. 1,236 p.

Over 186,000 words and phrases appearing in AMERICAN
NOTES AND QUERIES, AMERICAN SPEECH, BRITANNIA
BOOK OF THE YEAR, NOTES AND QUERIES, COLLEGE
ENGLISH, DIALECT NOTES, PUBLICATIONS OF THE AMERI-
CAN DIALECT SOCIETY, CALIFORNIA FOLKLORE QUARTER-
LY and WESTERN FOLKLORE are listed, with references.

325 Wecter, Dixon. THE SAGA OF AMERICAN SOCIETY: A RECORD OF
SOCIAL ASPIRATION, 1607-1937. New York: Charles Scribner's Sons,
1937. 504 p. Illus., notes, index.

Though an oddly skewed book in many respects, it neverthe-
less contains useful chapters on the social register, etiquette
books and magazines, the blue book, gentlemen's clubs, society
news, the lust for pedigrees and social counters, sports, and self-
justifications.

326 Weingarten, Joseph Abraham. AN AMERICAN DICTIONARY OF SLANG
AND COLLOQUIAL SPEECH. New York: Author, 1954. 390 p.

A compilation of slang definitions with original contributions
by the author. Information includes early appearance dates
and citations of secondary sources.

327 Whitehouse, Roger. NEW YORK: SUNSHINE AND SHADOW: A
PHOTOGRAPHIC RECORD OF THE CITY AND ITS PEOPLE FROM 1850
TO 1915. New York: Harper, 1974. 357 p. Illus., index.

A topical photographic essay, with a brief historical text.

328 Whyte, William Foote. STREET CORNER SOCIETY: THE SOCIAL STRUC-
TURE OF AN ITALIAN SLUM. Rev. ed. Chicago: University of Chicago
Press, 1955. 364 p. Appendix, index.

An engaging study, based on personal interviews, of local
clubs and gangs, and of politics and the rackets.

329 Wolff, Edwin Daniel. WHY WE DO IT. New York: Macaulay Co.,
1929. Reprint. Freeport, N.Y.: Books for Libraries, 1968. 304 p.
Index.

Accounts of forty-four folkways and beliefs, such as why rice
is thrown at brides, why ladies wear rouge, men's hatbands.
Most explanations are historical.

330 Wood, Ann Douglas. "The Fashionable Diseases: Women's Complaints
and Their Treatment in Nineteenth-Century America." JOURNAL OF
INTERDISCIPLINARY HISTORY 4 (Summer 1973): 25-52.

The author argues that the nervous diseases attributed to women
in the nineteenth century were mainly the product of an un-
scientific science largely in the control of men, and that once
women became vocal and skilled in the medical sciences, they
were able to begin corrective propaganda.

331 Woolfolk, William, and Woolfolk, Joanna. THE GREAT AMERICAN
BIRTH RITE. New York: Dial, 1975. 294 p. Index.

Exposé of the consumer aspects of childbirth in American
society.

332 Wright, Richardson. HAWKERS AND WALKERS IN EARLY AMERICA:
STROLLING PEDDLERS, PREACHERS, LAWYERS, DOCTORS, PLAYERS,
AND OTHERS, FROM THE BEGINNING TO THE CIVIL WAR. Philadelphia: J.B. Lippincott, 1927. Reprint. New York: Arno Press, 1976.
317 p. Bibliog., illus., subject index.

A delightful account of all the itinerant types listed in the title, plus sections on artists, street cries, tramps, and a chapter on traveling shows that begins with the landing of the first elephant in New York in April 1796.

IDEOLOGY

333 Ackermann, Alfred Seabold Eli. POPULAR FALLACIES: A BOOK OF COMMON ERRORS EXPLAINED AND CORRECTED, WITH COPIOUS REFERENCES TO AUTHORITIES. 4th ed. London: Old Westminster Press, 1950. 843 p.

>An attempt to correct a wide range of fallacies culled from newspapers and other sources on a variety of subjects.

334 Adams, Ramon. THE ADAMS ONE-FIFTY: A CHECK-LIST OF THE 150 MOST IMPORTANT BOOKS ON WESTERN OUTLAWS AND LAWMEN. Austin: Jenkins, Pemberton, 1976. 91 p. Index.

>Annotated bibliography for collectors.

335 Akin, William E. TECHNOCRACY AND THE AMERICAN DREAM--THE TECHNOCRAT MOVEMENT, 1900-41. Berkeley and Los Angeles: University of California Press, 1977. 227 p. Notes, bibliog., index.

>A revealing examination of the men and ideas of technocracy, especially as it peaked in 1932 and 1933, and as it formed a basis for dialog about technology and social values.

336 Armbruster, Frank E., with Yokelson, Doris. THE FORGOTTEN AMERICANS: THE VALUES, BELIEFS, AND CONCERNS OF THE MAJORITY. New Rochelle, N.Y.: Arlington House, 1972. 454 p. Illus., bibliog., footnotes, tables, figures.

>An attempt to establish basic middle-of-the-road values held by Americans through comparative analysis of opinion data collected through polling services since the 1930s. The volume covers such issues as private morality, sex practices, gun laws, open housing, busing, election data; contemporary youth; Negro and white ethnic attitudes; changing attitudes of college graduates and other matters. The volume contains forty-five figures and 209 tables of data. The author finds "greater homogeneity in America than believed."

337   Barker, Charles A. AMERICAN CONVICTIONS: CYCLES OF PUBLIC
       THOUGHT 1600-1850. Philadelphia: J.B. Lippincott, 1970. 632 p.
       Bibliog., notes, index, illus.

       An examination of what the author calls public thought, the
       "main ideas and impulses, loyalties and traditions, which have
       concerned public-community life in America," as they are ex-
       pressed by public figures. Barker sees a tension between free-
       dom and organization as found in such enduring concerns as
       the colonists' heritage of English social, political, and legal
       practices; reformist religious thought; economic thought; and
       educational thought. Since his primary concern is with public
       rhetoric, little attention is given to the arts, science, or
       technology.

338   Barker-Benfield, G.J. THE HORRORS OF THE HALF-KNOWN LIFE:
       MALE ATTITUDES TOWARD WOMEN AND SEXUALITY IN NINETEENTH
       CENTURY AMERICA. New York: Harper and Row, 1976. 352 p.
       Notes, index.

       An extensive examination of the role of WASP men in de-
       fining sexuality in the nineteenth century, beginning with
       Tocqueville; discusses the decline of midwifery, the growth
       of popular books for young men, and handbooks for couples.

339   Beals, Carleton. THE GREAT REVOLT AND ITS LEADERS: THE HISTORY
       OF POPULAR AMERICAN UPRISINGS IN THE 1890'S. New York:
       Abelard-Schumann, 1968. 347 p. Bibliog., index.

       Focusing on leaders of various popular movements, Beals pro-
       vides chapters on Henry George, Oliver Kelley and his Grange,
       C.W. Macune and the Southern Farmer's Alliance, Ignatious
       Donnelly, Hamlin Garland, Jerry Simpson, James Baird Weaver,
       Davis Waite, J.S. Coxey, and William Jennings Bryan.

340   Blumenthal, Monica D.; Kahn, Robert L.; Andrews, Frank M.; and Head,
       Kendra B. JUSTIFYING VIOLENCE: ATTITUDES OF AMERICAN MEN.
       Ann Arbor: University of Michigan, Institute for Social Research, 1972.
       367 p. Appendixes, tables, bibliog., index.

       An attempt "to provide a baseline description of attitudes
       towards violence," together with the rationalizations for
       beliefs in violence, through attitude surveys.

341   Borneman, Ernest, ed. THE PSYCHOANALYSIS OF MONEY. New
       York: Urizen Books, 1976. 364 p. Bibliog.

       A collection of fifteen psychoanalytic essays on money, deriv-
       ing for the most part from Freud's relationship between money
       and anal eroticism. Divided into three parts, the essays ex-
       plore anal theory, cultural tendencies, and theoretical per-
       spectives other than anal theory.

342 Boslooper, Thomas David, and Hayes, Marcia. THE FEMININITY GAME. New York: Stein and Day, 1973. 224 p. Notes, bibliog., index.

Recounts the biases against women's success in the corporate society, and analyzes the "games" that perpetuate exclusion from a male-oriented world.

343 Brenton, Myron. THE RUNAWAYS: CHILDREN, HUSBANDS, WIVES AND PARENTS. Boston: Little, Brown, 1978. 237 p.

Part 1 of this informal account discusses the problem and gives a brief historical sketch of runaways; part 2 discusses children, especially adolescents, and their causes for running away; part 3 treats the situations leading to runaway husbands, wives, unsettled people, and oldsters. Part 4 considers what to do when someone runs and why the problem is so widespread. Includes sources for help and brief notes.

344 Brewer, E. Cobham. A DICTIONARY OF MIRACLES: IMITATIVE RE-ALISTIC, AND DOGMATIC. Philadelphia: Lippincott, 1884. Reprint. Detroit: Gale Research Co., 1966. 582 p. Index.

A range of miracles is presented, with Biblical text cited where appropriate.

345 Bruce, Dickson D., Jr. AND THEY ALL SANG HALLELUJAH: PLAIN-FOLK CAMPMEETING RELIGION, 1800-1845. Knoxville: University of Tennessee Press, 1974. 155 p. Bibliog., index to hymns and choruses, general index.

Emphasis on camp-meeting songs as a source of the symbol system that plain folk used to understand not only their faith, but also who they were and how they were to consider others. Bruce examines the context of the camp meeting, the place of religion in everyday life, the camp meeting itself, spirituals, and the meaning of the symbol system for the people.

346 Burnam, Tom. THE DICTIONARY OF MISINFORMATION. New York: Crowell, 1976. 324 p.

A correction of erroneous beliefs and tales about a wide variety of subjects.

347 Burns, Rex. SUCCESS IN AMERICA: THE YEOMAN DREAM AND THE INDUSTRIAL REVOLUTION. Amherst, Mass.: University of Massachusetts Press, 1976. 212 p. Notes, bibliog., index.

A useful study of the yeoman's dream of success as competence, independence, and morality as it emerged in the early nineteenth century and endured for a brief time in selected literature and some popular magazines.

348 Carson, Gerald. ONE FOR A MAN, TWO FOR A HORSE: A PICTORIAL HISTORY, GRAVE AND COMIC, OF PATENT MEDICINES. Garden City, N.Y.: Doubleday, 1961. 127 p. Illus., bibliog., index.

A light, heavily illustrated discussion of patent medicine advertising.

349 _____. THE POLITE AMERICANS: 300 YEARS OF MORE OR LESS GOOD BEHAVIOUR. New York: Morrow, 1966. 325 p. Bibliog., index.

An excellent introduction to the history of manners in America, particularly of the white middle class. Carson covers such matters as the manners inherited and modified from England, including the place of women and southern quasiaristocracy; duels, fashions in beards, parlor etiquette, etiquette books and practical manners; newspaper columns, women's freedom, business folkways, and contemporary fads.

350 Catoe, Lynn E. UFOS AND RELATED SUBJECTS: AN ANNOTATED BIBLIOGRAPHY PREPARED BY THE LIBRARY OF CONGRESS, SCIENCE AND TECHNOLOGY DIVISION, FOR THE AIR FORCE, OFFICE OF AEROSPACE RESEARCH, USAF. Washington, D.C.: Government Printing Office, 1969. 401 p. Illus., bibliog.

An extensive bibliography organized into sections on a wide range of UFO related subjects. Includes material on explanations and such beliefs as the Hollow Earth Theory, mirages, Atlantis and Lemuria, the Fatima miracle, Tuuguska Meteorite, prophecies, with a brief section of cartoons.

351 Cauthen, Wilfred Kenneth. THE ETHICS OF ENJOYMENT: THE CHRISTIAN'S PURSUIT OF HAPPINESS. Atlanta, Ga.: John Knox Press, 1975. 124 p. Notes.

An assessment of contemporary U.S. potential and a call for new values and actions to achieve an authentic interdependence among Americans and others.

352 Cavendish, Richard, ed. ENCYCLOPEDIA OF THE UNEXPLAINED: MAGIC, OCCULTISM AND PARAPSYCHOLOGY. New York: McGraw-Hill, 1974. 304 p. Bibliog., index, illus.

An extensive encyclopedia of beliefs, superstititions, and the occult, with entries on personalities and related phenomena. J.B. Rhine was consulted for entries on parapsychology.

353 Cawelti, John G. APOSTLES OF THE SELF-MADE MAN. Chicago: University of Chicago Press, 1965. 279 p. Notes, bibliog., index.

An examination of the success theme in biographies of famous men, in success manuals, and in fiction to discover connections between changing social patterns and ideals of self-improvement.

354 _____. "Myths of Violence in American Popular Culture." CRITICAL INQUIRY 1 (March 1975): 521-41.

Discusses four ways in which Americans have tended to justify violence.

355 Chenoweth, Lawrence. THE AMERICAN DREAM OF SUCCESS: THE SEARCH FOR SELF IN THE TWENTIETH CENTURY. North Scituate, Mass.: Duxbury Press, 1974. 237 p. Notes, bibliog., charts, index.

A perceptive analysis based on self-help guides, inspirational books, cartoons, comic strips, and popular magazines. Argues that strong, contending value systems have led to a loss of self.

356 Chesteron, Gilbert Keith. FANCIES VERSUS FADS. New York: Dodd, Mead, 1923. 274 p.

A potpourri of critiques of fashionable interpretations of human behavior and the fads of the day, ranging from psychoanalysis, drama theory, and feminists to fear of film and toys.

357 Clarie, Thomas C. OCCULT BIBLIOGRAPHY: AN ANNOTATED LIST OF BOOKS PUBLISHED IN ENGLISH, 1971 THROUGH 1975. Metuchen, N.J.: Scarecrow Press, 1978. 454 p. Indexes.

Covers a wide range of occult phenomena, including topical interests such as Uri Geller, the Bermuda Triangle, exorcism, extraterrestrials, psychic surgery, biorhythms, acupuncture, pyramid power, astral projection, the "other side" of death, voice phenomenon, altered consciousness, Bigfoot, Kirlian photography, dream research, and plant consciousness.

358 Clark, Joseph D. BEASTLY FOLKLORE. Metuchen, N.J.: Scarecrow Press, 1968. 326 p. Bibliog.

Background sketches and lists of sayings related to animals, particularly those found in North Carolina.

359 Clarke, Anne. BEASTS AND BAWDY. New York: Taplinger Publishing Co., 1975. 159 p. Illus., bibliog., index.

A study of sources of animistic lore, with chapters on the fabulous tales in the "Physiologus" of Byzantine times, fabulous beasts, men as beasts and beasts as men, sex and bawdy, beastly behavior, animal medicines, charms, and aphrodisiacs.

360   Coffin, Tristram Potter. THE PROPER BOOK OF SEXUAL FOLKLORE.
       New York: Seabury Press, 1978. 145 p.

       Informal discussions of love, obscenity, courtship, play-parties,
       the garden of Eden, and the lover-hero, all told with respect
       to taste and without respect to sources.

361   _____. THE SEX KICK: EROTICISM IN MODERN AMERICA. New
       York: Macmillan, 1966. 256 p. Bibliog.

       A survey of various topics related to sex, from "the erotic
       revolution," to marriage manuals, male magazines, gay life,
       movies, and related subjects.

362   Cohen, Daniel. MYTHS OF THE SPACE AGE. New York: Dodd,
       Mead, 1967. 278 p. Illus., bibliog.

       A "sceptic's" examination of such popular beliefs as those
       involving astrology, ESP, popular prophets, flying saucers,
       early discoverers of America, and modern monsters such as
       the Loch Ness monster and the yeti. Includes a chapter on
       Immanuel Velikovsky.

363   Coulson, William R. GROUPS, GIMMICKS AND INSTANT GURUS:
       AN EXAMINATION OF ENCOUNTER GROUPS AND THEIR DISTOR-
       TIONS. New York: Harper, 1972. 181 p.

       The author, a practitioner, finds both good and bad in en-
       counter groups and provides an assessment of his own successes
       and failures.

364   Davies, John D. PHRENOLOGY: FAD AND SCIENCE: A NINETEENTH-
       CENTURY AMERICAN CRUSADE. N.p.: Archon Books, 1971. 203 p.
       Bibliog., index.

       Considers the science and popular influence of phrenology
       in the early nineteenth century. The study provides a cul-
       tural history of the belief and insight into its diffusion as an
       idea into established and emerging categories of thought.

365   Davis, David Brion, ed. THE FEAR OF CONSPIRACY: IMAGES OF
       UN-AMERICAN SUBVERSION FROM THE REVOLUTION TO THE PRESENT.
       Ithaca, N.Y.: Cornell University Press, 1971. 369 p. Index.

       A collection of excerpts from various sources which express
       fear of events and belief in conspiratorial powers regarding
       the French Revolution, the American Revolution, internal
       security (1825-60), the slavery issue, labor, business, and
       international affairs (1865-1948). A final section traces the
       lack of consensus from 1936 to 1968.

366 Dickinson, Eleanor. REVIVAL! Text by Barbara Benziger. New York: Harper, 1974. 180 p. Illus.

A celebration of revival meetings, with excellent illustrations.

367 Ditzion, Sidney. MARRIAGE, MORALS AND SEX IN AMERICA: A HISTORY OF IDEAS. New York: W.W. Norton, 1969. 460 p. Notes, bibliog., index.

A history of the dialog on marriage and other relations between the sexes from the eighteenth century to the present, containing, according to the author, "a complete story of the woman's rights movement."

368 Dorough, C. Dwight. THE BIBLE BELT MYSTIQUE Philadelphia: Westminster, 1974. 217 p. Notes.

An examination of popular southwestern religion from the late eighteenth century through the mid-nineteenth century, with comments on contemporary revivals. Written for the layman, the study covers many of the features associated with revivalism, such as sensationalism, emotionalism, conservatism, and types of ministers.

369 Douglas, Ann. THE FEMINIZATION OF AMERICAN CULTURE. New York: Alfred A. Knopf, 1977. 403 p. Notes, index.

Finds an "intimate connection between critical aspects of Victorian culture and modern mass culture," in an extensive analysis of the way the "sentimental heresy" of the nineteenth century provided a rationalization for the expansion of capitalist influence in the minds of women and ministers of the northeastern United States. Sentimentalization precluded a more humanistic Romanticism that might have replaced declining Calvinism had the United States been a more mature culture. Appendixes identifying women and ministers.

370 Drago, Harry Sinclair. THE LEGEND MAKERS: TALES OF THE OLD-TIME PEACE OFFICERS AND DESPERADOES OF THE FRONTIER. New York: Dodd, Mead, 1975. 239 p. Illus., notes, bibliog., index.

Essays on Wild Bill Hickok, Ben Thompson, Mike Meagher, Bat Masterson, Wyatt Earp, Jim Courtright, Bill Mitchell, Butch Cassidy, Tom Horn, and Lee Hall, with further essays on border towns and feuds.

371 Durant, John. PREDICTIONS: PICTORIAL PREDICTIONS FROM THE PAST. New York: A.S. Barnes, 1956. 151 p.

Comic illustrations from LIFE, JUDGE, PUCK and other sources on the consequences of technology and on mores for the future.

372 Evans, Christopher. CULTS OF UNREASON. New York: Farrar, Straus and Giroux, 1974. 264 p. Index.

An exposé of scientology, "saviors from the skies," miraculous black boxes such as Wilhelm Reich's orgone box, and Eastern religions.

373 Feldstein, Stanley. THE POISONED TONGUE: A DOCUMENTARY HISTORY OF AMERICAN RACISM AND PREJUDICE. New York: Morris, 1971. 330 p.

Documents and notes on racism and anti-Semitism from Thomas Jefferson to contemporary individuals and associations.

374 Fisher, William H. THE INVISIBLE EMPIRE: A BIBLIOGRAPHY OF THE KU KLUX KLAN. Metuchen, N.J.: Scarecrow Press, 1980. 202 p. Indexes.

Divided into reference materials of the nineteenth and twentieth centuries, the volume contains annotated citations of dissertations, archival materials, government documents, monographs, and articles.

375 Fleming, Donald. "Roots of the New Conservation Movement." PERSPECTIVES IN AMERICAN HISTORY 6 (1972): 7-91.

Traces the origins of the ecology movement into early American history.

376 Fromm, Erich. THE REVOLUTION OF HOPE: TOWARDS A HUMANIZED TECHNOLOGY. New York: Harper and Row, 1968. 162 p.

A survey of kinds of hope, a projection of present technological tendencies, a discussion of the human condition, and suggestions for reorienting technology to serve authentic human ends.

377 Furay, Conal. THE GRASS-ROOTS MIND IN AMERICA: THE AMERICAN SENSE OF ABSOLUTES. New York: New Viewpoints, Division of Franklin Watts, 1977. 170 p. Notes, bibliog., index.

An attempt to understand the stability in popular thought as reflected in the thinking of farmers, small-townspeople, business, religion, the military, and Americanisms. An epilogue discusses the American sense of absolutes.

378 Gallup, George Horace. THE GALLUP POLL: PUBLIC OPINION 1935-1971. 3 vols. New York: Greenwood Press, 1972.

Contains the results of all polls conducted by the Gallup organization from the beginning in October 1935 through December 1971.

379 THE GALLUP POLLS OF ATTITUDES TOWARD EDUCATION, 1969-1973. Edited by Stanley Elam. Bloomington, Ind.: Phi Delta Kappa, 1973. 202 p. Index.

> The collected results of attitudes toward education and educational institutions, with chapters on trends and future possibilities.

380 Glanz, Rudolf. THE JEW IN EARLY AMERICAN WIT AND GRAPHIC HUMOR. New York: KTAV Publishing House, 1973. 269 p. Illus., notes, index.

> A survey of topics in which Jews were the subject of caricature and humor through the nineteenth century.

381 Gordon, Rosemary. STEREOTYPY OF IMAGERY AND BELIEF AS AN EGO DEFENCE. Cambridge, Engl.: University Press, 1962. 96 p. Bibliog.

> An investigation of stereotypical mental constructs based on tests for stereotyped responses.

382 Goshen, Charles E. DRINKS, DRUGS, AND DO-GOODERS. New York: Free Press, 1973. 268 p. Bibliog.

> The growth of the Prohibition movement, influx of organized crime, drinking patterns, drug use, myths of drugs, managing drinking and drug problems in industry and society, and prevention programs.

383 Habenstein, Robert W., and Lamers, William M. THE HISTORY OF AMERICAN FUNERAL DIRECTING. Milwaukee, Wis.: Bulfin Printers, 1955. 636 p. Appendixes, index.

> Traces mortuary practices from ancient times to modern America, focusing on undertaking, coffins, embalming, transportation, and behavior.

384 Hancock, Ralph. THE COMPLEAT SWINDLER. New York: Macmillan, 1968. 294 p.

> An informal discussion of the swindle in its many variations, together with a brief glossary of argot.

385 Handy, Robert T., ed. THE SOCIAL GOSPEL IN AMERICA, 1870-1920. New York: Oxford University Press, 1966. 399 p. Bibliog., index.

> Collected essays of Washington Gladden, Richard T. Ely, and Walter Rauschenbusch, with a historical introduction and author notes.

386   Harper, Ralph. NOSTALGIA: AN EXISTENTIAL EXPLORATION OF
      LONGING AND FULFILLMENT IN THE MODERN AGE. Cleveland:
      Press of Western Reserve University, 1966. 146 p. Notes.

      A meditation on the sleeping beauty tale as an expression of
      the transforming consciousness of the modern world with its
      longing for lost paradises.

387   Harrah, Barbara K., and Harrah, David F. FUNERAL SERVICE: A
      BIBLIOGRAPHY OF LITERATURE ON ITS PAST, PRESENT, AND FUTURE:
      THE VARIOUS MEANS OF DISPOSITION AND MEMORIALIZATION.
      Metuchen, N.J.: Scarecrow Press, 1976. 383 p. Appendixes, index.

      Contains 1,982 partially annotated items on funeral services,
      internment, and memorialization; audiovisual material, lists,
      and reference information.

388   Harrell, David Edwin. ALL THINGS ARE POSSIBLE: THE HEALINGS
      AND CHARISMATIC REVIVALS IN MODERN AMERICA. Bloomington:
      Indiana University Press, 1975. 304 p. Notes, bibliog., essay, index.

      An examination of popular evangelistic religions and the men
      who led them. Divided into three parts, the author discusses
      the origins, central figures who led healing cults and the
      problems of their movement, and major figures and problems
      after 1958. A final chapter discusses the amorphous quality
      of the movement in the 1970s.

389   Hechtlinger, Adelaide. THE GREAT PATENT MEDICINE ERA: OR WITH-
      OUT BENEFIT OF DOCTOR. New York: Madison Square, Grosset and
      Dunlap, 1970. 248 p. Illus.

      Reprints of advertisements and advice on a wide range of topics.

390   Heise, Juergen Arthur. MINIMUM DISCLOSURE: HOW THE PENTAGON
      MANIPULATES THE NEWS. New York: W.W. Norton, 1979. 221 p.
      Notes, index.

      Beginning with the suppression of news of the My Lai massacre,
      the book discusses Pentagon practices and ideological tenden-
      cies toward the disclosure of news.

391   Hills, Penney Chapin, and Hills, L. Rust, eds. HOW WE LIVE: CON-
      TEMPORARY LIFE IN CONTEMPORARY FICTION. New York: Macmillan
      Co., 1968. 1,008 p. Bibliog., notes.

      Divided into three parts, "The Way We Live Now," "Differ-
      entiations and Confusions," and "The Eye of Fiction." The
      first part is divided into sections titled "Alone," "In Families,"
      "In Communities," "At Work"; part 2 "In Religion--Jewish
      Conflicts in Cultural Assimilation," "In Race--The Visible

Negro," and "In Class--Minute Distinctions in the Middle"; part 3, "In Some Overviews," "In Some Stratagems." Contains on appendix defending contemporary fiction, with a final note apologizing for the lack of further inclusions. Writers included constitute the literary establishment.

392   Holbrook, Stewart. DREAMERS OF THE AMERICAN DREAM. Garden City, N.Y.: Doubleday and Co., 1957. 369 p. Bibliog., index.

Accounts of utopians, visionaries, prohibitionists; on land issues, women's rights, social services, and rebellions.

393   Huber, Richard M. THE AMERICAN IDEA OF SUCCESS. New York: McGraw-Hill, 1971. 563 p. Bibliog., notes, index.

An exploration of the idea of success in many of its forms from colonial times to the 1960s through examination of a wide range of materials and writing, but with an eye to its positive qualities.

394   Jackson, Herbert G., Jr. THE SPIRIT RAPPERS. Garden City: Doubleday and Co., 1972. 226 p. Bibliog.

A survey of the incidents that led to the widespread belief in spiritualism in the early nineteenth century, told in anecdotal form.

395   Jacobs, David Michael. THE UFO CONTROVERSY IN AMERICA. Bloomington: Indiana University Press, 1975. 362 p. Statistics, notes, bibliog., photos., index.

An explanation of the UFO controversy from 1897 to the mid-1970s that recounts the history of the controversy without drawing startling conclusions.

396   Jewett, Robert. THE CAPTAIN AMERICA COMPLEX: THE DILEMMA OF ZEALOUS NATIONALISM. Philadelphia: Westminster Press, 1973. 286 p. Notes.

An examination of the sense of mission Americans seem to share and the dilemmas it has produced by framing political thought and contemporary popular culture in religious antecedents.

397   Jewett, Robert, and Lawrence, John Shelton. THE AMERICAN MONO-MYTH. New York: Anchor Press, Doubleday, 1977. 263 p. Notes, illus., glossary, index.

A search through popular culture for the myth of redemption and a discussion of its relationships to folk and high culture.

Chapters examine "Star Trek" and Trekkies, DEATH WISH, PLAYBOY, WALKING TALL, "Little House on the Prairie," Disneyland, and JAWS, with a critique of American values.

398 Kennett, Lee, and Anderson, James La Verne. THE GUN IN AMERICA: THE ORIGINS OF A NATIONAL DILEMMA. Contributions in American History, no. 37. Westport, Conn.: Greenwood Press, 1975. 339 p. Notes, bibliog., index.

A history of the background and development of the idea of a weapons-bearing society, the gun industry, legal controversies, and the crisis of the 1960s.

399 Klapp, Orrin E. COLLECTIVE SEARCH FOR IDENTITY. New York: Holt, Rinehart and Winston, 1969. 383 p. Notes, index.

A general study of the failure of modern American society to provide meaning for individuals, so that substitute meanings are derived through popular forms. Chapters identify the seekers, discuss fashion, ritual language, cults, heroes and celebrities, crusades, and symbolic poverty.

400 Klinkowitz, Jerome. THE AMERICAN 1960S: IMAGINATIVE ACTS IN A DECADE OF CHANGE. Ames: Iowa State University Press, 1980. 111 p. Index.

Essays on Kennedy, Nixon, Larry McMurphy, Kurt Vonnegut, Donald Barthelme, CATCH-22, protest literature, Vietnam, Bob Dylan, Neil Young, and the sixties aesthetic.

401 Kraybill, Donald B. OUR STAR-SPANGLED FAITH. Scottsdale, Pa.: Herald Press, 1976. 215 p. Notes.

A text, with chapter questions, which explores the relations between political institutions and religious interests from the perspective of a Christian dissenter.

402 Krichmar, Albert. THE WOMEN'S RIGHTS MOVEMENT IN THE UNITED STATES 1848-1970: A BIBLIOGRAPHY AND SOURCEBOOK. Metuchen, N.J.: Scarecrow Press, 1972. 436 p. Author and subject indexes.

A partially annotated bibliography of 5,170 items on legal and political status, business and the professions, education, religion, biography, wages, and equal rights. A section of 402 entries identifying sources for papers, manuscripts, and collections is indexed separately. Sections on women's liberation, serial publications, and selected references used in the compilation completes the volume.

403 Krickus, Richard J. PURSUING THE AMERICAN DREAM. Bloomington: Indiana University Press, 1976. 424 p. Notes, index.

A history and analysis of the political life of working classes in the United States, with chapters on immigrant and working-class legacies, white ethnic politics, the McGovern failure, racial conflict, limits of the old politics, and the new populism.

404 Lane, Robert E. POLITICAL IDEOLOGY: WHY THE AMERICAN COMMON MAN BELIEVES WHAT HE DOES. New York: Free Press, 1962. 509 p. Appendixes, index.

A discussion of the roots of American working-class ideology based on in-depth interviews with fifteen workers on the eastern seaboard.

405 Leff, Arthur Allen. SWINDLING AND SELLING. New York: Free Press, 1976. 194 p. Bibliog., index.

An analysis of the selling situation common to both legitimate bargaining and swindling, with extensive examples of the many variants on basic swindling techniques.

406 Lemon, Richard. THE TROUBLED AMERICAN. New York: Simon and Schuster, 1970. 256 p. Tables, appendixes on research design, index.

An expanded use of data collected by the Gallup organization and others for the 6 October 1969 issue of NEWSWEEK on "middle America."

407 Leventhal, Herbert. IN THE SHADOW OF THE ENLIGHTENMENT: OCCULTISM AND RENNAISSANCE SCIENCE IN EIGHTEENTH-CENTURY AMERICA. New York: New York University Press, 1976. 330 p. Notes, bibliog., index.

A study of the influence of Elizabethan ideas on the Enlightenment, with emphasis on astrology, witchcraft, alchemy and the lore of rattlesnakes, as well as received images of the natural world, and the decline of the Elizabethan world view.

408 Levy, Lillian, ed. SPACE: ITS IMPACT ON MAN AND SOCIETY. New York: Norton, 1965. 228 p.

A collection of essays by key figures in and around the space program on various aspects of the space age.

409 McWilliams, Wilson Carey. THE IDEA OF FRATERNITY IN AMERICA. Berkeley and Los Angeles: University of California Press, 1973. 695 p. Bibliog., notes, index.

A historical exploration of the expression of "intense interpersonal affection" within small groups with specified values
and goals which are in some tension with the larger society.
McWilliams draws on literature, the history of ideas, and
social movements to develop his perspective.

410 Manheim, Jarol B., and Wallace, Melanie. POLITICAL VIOLENCE IN
THE UNITED STATES 1875-1974: A BIBLIOGRAPHY. New York: Garland Publishing, 1975. 116 p. Index.

Contains 1,521 items arranged in categories designated as
strikes and labor strife, race riots and urban violence, anarchism and terrorism, assassination, vigilantism and police
violence, gun control, and general studies.

411 Manwaring, David R. RENDER UNTO CAESAR: THE FLAG-SALUTE
CONTROVERSY. Chicago: University of Chicago Press, 1962. 321 p.
Notes, index.

An analysis of the legal controversy surrounding the compulsory
flag salute through examination of citizenship training, the
Jehovah's Witness case, and Supreme Court decisions.

412 Mencken, H.L., and Nathan, George Jean. THE AMERICAN CREDO:
A CONTRIBUTION TOWARD THE INTERPRETATION OF THE NATIONAL
MIND. New York: A.A. Knopf, 1920. Reprint. New York: Octagon
Books, 1977. 266 p.

A long harangue about the American booboisie, together with
869 alleged beliefs.

413 Meyer, Donald B. THE POSITIVE THINKERS: A STUDY OF THE AMERI-
CAN QUEST FOR HEALTH, WEALTH AND PERSONAL POWER FROM
MARY BAKER EDDY TO NORMAN VINCENT PEALE. New York:
Doubleday, 1965. 358 p. Notes, index.

A history and interpretation of popular enthusiasms for health,
wealth, and peace of mind. Chapters cover the religious
and secular ideas promoted by those professing mind cures,
business and industry success schemes, and the rise of therapeutic psychology. Included are postscripts on William James,
and mind cures among Catholics and Jews.

414 Miller, Albert Jay, and Acri, Michael James. DEATH: A BIBLIOGRAPHI-
CAL GUIDE. Metuchen, N.J.: Scarecrow Press, 1977. 420 p. Author
and subject indexes.

A checklist of 3,848 books, articles, and films arranged by
discipline.

415 Mizruchi, Ephraim. SUCCESS AND OPPORTUNITY: A STUDY OF ANOMIE. Glencoe, Ill.: Free Press, 1964. 204 p. Appendixes, bibliog., index.

A discussion, based on interview information, of the tensions between aspiration and reality among Americans, with comments on anomie, alienation, deviant behavior, and work satisfaction in relation to social structure.

416 Moscovici, Serge, ed. THE PSYCHOSOCIOLOGY OF LANGUAGE. Chicago: Markham, 1972. 462 p. Notes, charts, diagrams.

Pages 143–57: David McNeill, "Speaking of Space," an essay on the slang and technical terminology of NASA personnel.

417 Murray, Robert K. RED SCARE: A STUDY IN NATIONAL HYSTERIA, 1919–1920. Minneapolis: University of Minnesota Press, 1955. 337 p. Bibliog., notes, index.

A discussion of the historical context and rise of fear leading to the infamous red scare.

418 Nash, Jay Robert. HUSTLERS AND CON MEN: AN ANECDOTAL HISTORY OF THE CONFIDENCE MAN AND HIS GAMES. New York: M. Evans, 1976. 372 p. Glossary of argot, bibliog., index.

Accounts of big-name swindlers, together with a "Chronology of Con" from 1800–1975.

419 Nash, Roderick. WILDERNESS AND THE AMERICAN MIND. Rev. ed. New Haven, Conn.: Yale University Press, 1973. 300 p. Notes, index.

An examination of the concept of wilderness from Old World roots through the counterculture of the 1960s, with attention to Romanticization, Americanization, conservation, cults, and key figures in the formulation and diffusion of the ideas.

420 Newall, Venetia. AN EGG AT EASTER: A FOLKLORE STUDY. Bloomington: Indiana University, 1971. 423 p. Illus., notes, bibliog., index.

A world study of the egg in creation myths, sacrifice, witchcraft and magic, bird lore, fertility, purity, Resurrection, celebrations, games and pastimes; with techniques of decoration.

421 Noyes, John Humphrey. HISTORY OF AMERICAN SOCIALISMS. Philadelphia: J.B. Lippincott, 1870. Reprint. New York: Hillary House, 1961. 678 p. Index.

A sympathetic examination of the experimental and utopian

communities that flourished in the nineteenth century, with much documentary evidence on the aims and practices of numerous settlements.

422   Packard, Vance. THE NAKED SOCIETY. New York: McKay, 1964. 369 p. Notes, Bill of Rights, index.

Identifies five forces that undermine privacy: the increase in organized living, the garrison state mentality, pressures generated by abundance, growth of investigation as a private industry, and the miniaturization of electronics. The volume is divided into chapters on likely opportunities for intrusion, assaults on traditional rights, and suggestions for actions to maintain personal liberty.

423   _____. THE PEOPLE SHAPERS. Boston: Little, Brown, 1977. 398 p. Notes, index.

An examination of the techniques for controlling behavior and reshaping the human species, with a section on concerns and countermeasures. The study concludes with a chapter summarizing views of man from the perspectives of the leading schools of psychology and philosophy.

424   _____. THE PYRAMID CLIMBERS. New York: McGraw-Hill, 1962. 339 p. Notes, bibliog., index.

A popular account of how executives rise in the business world, what businesses look for, and in what ways the system fails.

425   Parker, William. HOMOSEXUALITY: A SELECTIVE BIBLIOGRAPHY OF OVER 3,000 ITEMS. Metuchen, N.J.: Scarecrow Press, 1971. 323 p. Index.

In addition to articles, books, documents, and other non-fiction publications, references to literature and media are included.

426   _____. HOMOSEXUALITY BIBLIOGRAPHY: SUPPLEMENT 1970-1975. Metuchen, N.J.: Scarecrow Press, 1977. 337 p.

Extended coverage of categories in the earlier volume (cited above).

427   Patai, Raphael. MYTH AND MODERN MAN. Englewood Cliffs, N.J.: Prentice-Hall, 1972. 359 p. Notes, index.

After introductory chapters on the interpretation of myth, Patai discovers myth in science fiction, contemporary radical-

ism, general strikes, Marxism, Nazism, Che Gueverra, Marion
Delgado, religion, "demythologizing," the God is Dead
theology, Negro beliefs, comic and cartoon figures, advertising, self-destructive behavior, sex, and beliefs in planetary
escape. The volume ends with a call for a new democratic
myth.

428   Paul, Rodman W., and Etulain, Richard W. THE FRONTIER AND
AMERICAN WEST. Goldentree Bibliographies in American History.
Arlington Heights, Ill.: AHM Publishing Corp., 1977. 168 p. Index.

A checklist of 2,973 items arranged by topics including brief
sections on the visual and performing arts, journalism, and
literature.

429   Petersen, William J. THOSE CURIOUS NEW CULTS. New Canaan,
Conn.: Keats Publishing, 1973. 214 p.

A Christian's survey of a wide variety of cults and ethnic
faiths in vogue in the late 1960s and early 1970s.

430   Phillips, David R., ed. THE WEST: AN AMERICAN EXPERIENCE.
New York: A and W Visual Library, 1975. 232 p. Illus., bibliog.

An extensive photographic history of the post-Civil War West.

431   Rosa, Joseph G. THE GUNFIGHTER: MAN OR MYTH? Norman:
University of Oklahoma Press, 1969. 229 p. Illus., notes, bibliog.,
index.

An account of the historical evidence available about a wide
range of Western figures, well-known feuds and gunfights,
dangerous towns, and other matters that have entered into
legend through the media.

432   Roszak, Theodore. WHERE THE WASTELAND ENDS: POLITICS AND
TRANSCENDENCE IN POSTINDUSTRIAL SOCIETY. Garden City, N.Y.:
Doubleday and Co., 1972. 492 p. Notes.

A sprawling critique of the decline of values in the technological age and a call for a new unified vision.

433   Rowland, Beryl. ANIMALS WITH HUMAN FACES: A GUIDE TO ANI-
MAL SYMBOLISM. Knoxville: University of Tennessee Press, 1973.
192 p. Illus., bibliog., notes, index.

An encyclopedia of the mythological and folklore heritages
of both real and imaginary animals.

434 Sable, Martin H. UFO GUIDE: 1947-1967; CONTAINING INTERNA-
TIONAL LISTS OF BOOKS AND MAGAZINE ARTICLES ON UFO'S,
FLYING SAUCERS, AND ABOUT LIFE ON OTHER PLANETS: WORLD-
WIDE DIRECTORIES OF FLYING SAUCER ORGANIZATIONS, PROFES-
SIONAL GROUPS AND RESEARCH CENTERS CONCERNED WITH SPACE
RESEARCH AND ASTRONAUTICS, A PARTIAL LIST OF SIGHTINGS, AND
AN INTERNATIONAL DIRECTORY OF FLYING SAUCER MAGAZINES.
Beverly Hills, Calif.: Rainbow Press, 1967. 100 p.

435 Sanford, Charles L. THE QUEST FOR PARADISE: EUROPE AND THE
AMERICAN MORAL IMAGINATION. Urbana: University of Illinois
Press, 1961. 282 p. Bibliog., notes.

Edenic theme in American thought and action.

436 Sann, Paul. FADS, FOLLIES AND DELUSIONS OF THE AMERICAN
PEOPLE. New York: Crown Publishers, 1967. 370 p. Illus., subject index.

For annotation, see no. 299.

437 Sansweet, Stephen J. THE PUNISHMENT CURE: HOW AVERSION
THERAPY IS BEING USED TO ELIMINATE SMOKING, DRINKING,
OBESITY, HOMOSEXUALITY . . . AND PRACTICALLY ANYTHING
ELSE. New York: Mason-Charter Publishers, 1976. 211 p. Bibliog.,
index.

A critique of behavior modification.

438 Savage, William W., Jr., ed. COWBOY LIFE: RECONSTRUCTING AN
AMERICAN MYTH. Norman: University of Oklahoma Press, 1975. 208 p.

A collection of essays from various sources on aspects of cowboy life, written from 1874 to 1943, covering everyday life.

439 Schlesinger, Arthur M. LEARNING HOW TO BEHAVE: A HISTORICAL
STUDY OF AMERICAN ETIQUETTE BOOKS. New York: Macmillan,
1947. Bibliog., notes, index.

An important contribution to the study of American manners
through etiquette books and other sources from colonial times
through the first quarter of the twentieth century.

440 Schneider, Louis, and Dornbusch, Sanford M. POPULAR RELIGION:
INSPIRATIONAL BOOKS IN AMERICA. Chicago: University of Chicago
Press, 1973. 174 p. Appendixes, index.

A sociological examination of popular inspirational literature,
based on a content analysis of forty-six best-sellers published
between 1875 and 1955. Appendixes identify the books, coding categories, and methodology.

441 Schwartz, David C., and Schwartz, Sandra Kenyon, eds. NEW DIREC-
TIONS IN POLITICAL SOCIALIZATION. New York: Free Press, 1975.
340 p. Index, bibliog., charts.

> Especially useful are chapters on health and body images,
> sources of children's political concepts, and popular music
> as an agency of political socialization.

442 Scott, Gini Graham. CULT AND COUNTERCULT: A STUDY OF A
SPIRITUAL GROWTH GROUP AND A WITCHCRAFT ORDER Contributions in Sociology, no. 38. Westport, Conn.: Greenwood, Press, 1980.
213 p. Notes, bibliog., index.

> A comparison of the Inner Peace movement, a slickly promoted
> organization for developing inner growth, and the Aquarian
> Age Order, countercultural association of witches.

443 Simpson, Jeffrey, comp. THE WAY LIFE WAS: A PHOTOGRAPHIC
TREASURY FROM THE AMERICAN PAST. New York: Praeger, 1974.
Unpaged.

> A collection of carefully reproduced photographs by various
> hands taken between 1880 and 1915, arranged according to
> themes.

444 Sladek, John Thomas. THE NEW APOCRYPHA: A GUIDE TO STRANGE
SCIENCE AND OCCULT BELIEFS. New York: Stein and Day, 1974.
375 p. Notes, bibliog., index.

> Debunks many enthusiasms based on pseudoscience, such as
> UFOs, food claims, astrology, spirits, cult figures, miracu-
> lous inventions, and doomsday predictions.

445 Slater, Peter Gregg. CHILDREN IN THE NEW ENGLAND MIND: IN
DEATH AND IN LIFE Hamden, Conn.: Shoe String Press, 1978. 248 p.
Notes, bibliog., index.

> Adult perceptions of children between the seventeenth and
> mid-nineteenth centuries in New England changed from
> "twisted toward evil, as totally plastic and as inclined toward
> good"; the study of the perceptions of children can be seen
> as a subject for intellectual history.

446 Sloane, Eric. FOLKLORE OF AMERICAN WEATHER. New York: Duell,
Sloan and Pearce, 1963. 63 p.

> A collection of weather sayings, with discussion of almanacs,
> weather instruments, and the context for the rise of American
> weather lore. Sayings are designated with true, false, and
> probable evaluations.

447 Slotkin, Richard. REGENERATION THROUGH VIOLENCE: THE MYTHOL-
     OGY OF THE AMERICAN FRONTIER, 1600–1860. Middleton, Conn.:
     Wesleyan University Press, 1973. 670 p. Notes, bibliog., index.

> An extensive consideration of the myth of regeneration in
> American literature from 1625 through 1841, with chapters on
> captivity narratives, literary genres, heroes, and romance.

448 Smith, Henry Nash. VIRGIN LAND: THE AMERICAN WEST AS SYM-
     BOL AND MYTH. Cambridge, Mass.: Harvard University Press, 1950.
     298 p. Notes, index.

> A consideration of the American West as "an intellectual con-
> struction that fuses concept and emotion into an image." Smith's
> seminal volume deals with Westward expansion; the Western hero
> as Daniel Boone, Cooper's Leatherstocking, Charles W. Webber,
> Kit Carson, and the dime novel hero and heroine; and the West
> as a garden in an extensive treatment of themes.

449 Spence, Lewis. AN ENCYCLOPEDIA OF OCCULTISM: A COMPENDIUM
     OF INFORMATION ON THE OCCULT SCIENCES, OCCULT PERSONALI-
     TIES, PSYCHIC SCIENCE, MAGIC, DEMONOLOGY, SPIRITISM, MYSTI-
     CISM AND METAPHYSICS. New Hyde Park, N.Y.: University Books,
     1968. 440 p. Illus., bibliog., index.

> Brief entries on a wide range of occult terms, personalities
> both in this life and others, and related matters.

450 Starkes, M. Thomas. CONFRONTING POPULAR CULTS. Nashville,
     Tenn.: Broadman Press, 1972. 122 p. Notes.

> A Christian assessment of the weaknesses and strengths of
> Mormonism, Jehovah's Witnesses, Anglo-Israelism, Christian
> Science, Black Muslims, Eastern religions, and Unitarianism.

451 Steckmesser, Kent Ladd. THE WESTERN HERO IN HISTORY AND LEGEND.
     Norman: University of Oklahoma Press, 1965. 281 p. Illus., notes,
     bibliog., index.

> Detailed examinations of the facts and subsequent legends of
> Kit Carson, Billy the Kid, Wild Bill Hickok, and George
> Armstrong Custer as representatives of occupations around which
> Western folklore has often centered.

452 Strunk, Mildred. PUBLIC OPINION, 1935–1946. Princeton, N.J.:
     Princeton University Press, 1951. 1,191 p.

> Compilation of the polls conducted by twenty-three organiza-
> tions in sixteen countries on such subjects as politics, taxa-
> tion, industry, agriculture, religion, unemployment, the atom
> bomb, crime, entertainment, and World War II.

453 Summers, Anthony. CONSPIRACY. New York: McGraw-Hill, 1980.
640 p. Illus., notes, bibliog., index.

Argues that the Kennedy assassination resulted from a successful conspiracy.

454 Swingewood, Alan. THE MYTH OF MASS CULTURE. London: Macmillan, 1977. 146 p. Notes, bibliog., index.

A critique of the Frankfurt school's assertion that Western
society's working classes have declined into atomistic masses,
of cultural critics who see the general decline of society,
and of the cultural pluralists.

455 Szwed, John F.; Abrahams, Roger D.; et al. AFRO-AMERICAN FOLK
CULTURE: AN ANNOTATED BIBLIOGRAPHY OF MATERIALS FROM
NORTH, CENTRAL, AND SOUTH AMERICA, AND THE WEST INDIES.
2 vols. Philadelphia: Institute for the Study of Human Issues, 1978.
1,628 p. Index.

A partially annotated compilation of folklore articles, books,
documents, and other materials on Afro-American folklore.

456 Thorwald, Jürgen. THE CENTURY OF THE DETECTIVE. Translated by
Richard Winston and Clara Winston. New York: Harcourt, Brace, 1965.
500 p. Bibliog., index.

A history of criminal detection from the early nineteenth century through the late 1920s, with emphasis on technical innovations in identification, forensic medicine, toxicology, and
ballistics.

457 Veysey, Laurence. THE COMMUNAL EXPERIENCE: ANARCHIST AND
MYSTICAL COUNTERCULTURES IN AMERICA. New York: Harper and
Row, 1973. 495 p. Notes, index.

Attempts to explain the roots of the communal experiences of
the 1960s through examination of lesser known experimental
communities, including the Ferrer colony, the Modern School
of Stelton, New Jersey, the Vedanta monasteries, and contemporary communities.

458 Walsh, William S. CURIOSITIES OF POPULAR CUSTOMS AND OF
RITES, CEREMONIES, OBSERVANCES, AND MISCELLANEOUS ANTIQ-
UITIES. 1897. Reprint. Philadelphia: J.B. Lippincott, 1925. 1,018 p.

An illustrated encyclopedia of traditions and customs associated
with personages, places, events, and religious beliefs.

459 Webb, James. THE OCCULT UNDERGROUND. LaSalle, Ill.: Library
Press; Open Court, 1974. 387 p. Notes, index.

Emphasis is on the occult revival in the nineteenth century,
but is useful for interpretations of contemporary phenomena.
Webb's analysis finds occult roots in social change and the
influential effects of Darwin's ORIGIN OF THE SPECIES,
and traces the emergence of the necromancers, Orientalism,
Theosophy, Protestant sects, the "occult revival" in late
nineteenth-century Paris, secret traditions, and other occult
beliefs and practitioners.

460   Weinberg, Arthur, and Weinberg, Lila, eds. PASSPORT TO UTOPIA:
      GREAT PANACEAS IN AMERICAN HISTORY. Chicago: Quadrangle,
      1968. 329 p. Bibliog.

      An anthology of twenty-eight essays and excerpts by writers
      from 1825 to 1935 on proposals for improving the human condi-
      tion. The topics covered range from those in the antebellum
      period which advocated abolition, utopian communities, and
      economic changes; during the postbellum nineteenth century,
      George's single tax, Steward's eight-hour day, Anthony's suf-
      frange for women, and Bellamy's internationalism; before the
      First World War, Coxey's army, Harvey's proposal for a bi-
      metalic standard, Bryan's for free silver, Nation's for Pro-
      hibition, and Straus's for thrift; after World War I, Sanger's
      for birth control, Sunday's for repentance and faith, Garvey's
      for Negro improvement, Lindsey's for companionate marriage,
      Scott's for technocracy, Teagle's for work sharing, Sinclair's
      for industrial democracy in California, Long's concept to share
      the wealth, Father Coughlin's for the eradication of poverty,
      Father Devine's for peace, and Townsend's for the old-age
      pension. The bibliography covers general matters and the
      individual writers.

461   Weiss, Richard. THE AMERICAN MYTH OF SUCCESS: FROM HORATIO
      ALGER TO NORMAN VINCENT PEALE. New York: Basic Books, 1969.
      276 p. Notes, bibliog., index.

      Chapters develop the idea of success, the Horatio Alger phe-
      nomenon, the Christian novel, success manuals, the transcen-
      dental revival, and the mystique of mind over matter.

462   White, Ronald C., and Hopkins, C. Howard. THE SOCIAL GOSPEL:
      RELIGION AND REFORM IN CHANGING AMERICA. Philadelphia:
      Temple University Press, 1976. 306 p. Notes, index.

      A reexamination of the later nineteenth- and early twentieth-
      century impact of the Social Gospel movement which focuses
      on the strategies, movement, and popular literary expression
      of the gospelists.

463 Wyllie, Irvin. THE SELF-MADE MAN IN AMERICA: THE MYTH OF RAGS TO RICHES. New Brunswick, N.J.: Rutgers University Press, 1954. 210 p. Notes, bibliog., index.

Traces the idea of material success and its businessman hero from colonial times to the Depression.

464 Young, James Harvey. THE MEDICAL MESSIAHS: A SOCIAL HISTORY OF HEALTH QUACKERY IN TWENTIETH-CENTURY AMERICA. Princeton University Press, 1967. 460 p. Bibliog., illus., index.

A sequel to THE TOADSTOOL MILLIONAIRES (entry below), the volume traces medical quackery from 1906 to 1966.

465 _____. THE TOADSTOOL MILLIONAIRES: A SOCIAL HISTORY OF PATENT MEDICINES IN AMERICA BEFORE FEDERAL REGULATION. Princeton: Princeton University Press, 1961. 282 p. Illus., notes, index.

A history of patent medicines from the appearance of English imports during colonial times through the nineteenth century, with an afterword on current practices. Contains chapters on the press, outdoor advertising, almanacs, medicine shows, the psychology of patent medicine advertising, and the Pure Food and Drugs Act of 1906.

466 Zenderland, Leila, ed. RECYCLING THE PAST: POPULAR USES OF AMERICAN HISTORY. Philadelphia: University of Pennsylvania Press, 1978. 131 p.

Essays dealing with various uses made of historical material: commercial uses, emotional props, the "lessons of history," and intellectual and artistic uses. Essays cover the treatment of Merrymount in fiction, the commercial and propagandistic use of Archibald M. Willard's "Yankee Doodle" (The Spirit of '76), Noah Webster's dictionary as an attempt to define how an American should behave, the reasons for the popularity of Thomas Dixon's fiction, Constance Rourke's use of legend in her attempt to create a democratic criticism, the attempt to promote internationalism in Darryl F. Zanuck's WILSON (1945), and an examination of how Wilson's warning about checking international aggressions became one of the lessons of history that presidents are fond of evoking. Most of the essays first appeared in AMERICAN QUARTERLY.

HEROES AND CELEBRITIES

467 Basso, Hamilton. MAINSTREAM. New York: Reynal and Hitchcock, 1943. 246 p. Index.

> Informal essays on influential figures in U.S. history and their particular kind of influence. Included are Cotton Mather and John Smith (in the beginning), Thomas Jefferson (Democrat), John Calhoun (aristocrat), Abe Lincoln (patron saint), Andrew Carnegie (success), P.T. Barnum (educator), Henry Adams and William Jennings Bryan (turn of the century), Theodore Rossevelt (Progressive), Huey Long (demagogue), Franklin Delano Roosevelt (revolutionary).

468 Blair, Walter, and Meine, Franklin J., eds. HALF HORSE HALF ALLI-GATOR: THE GROWTH OF THE MIKE FINK LEGEND. Chicago: University of Chicago Press, 1956. 288 p.

> Collection of printed accounts of contributions to Fink's (1770-1823) legend.

469 Borges, Jorge Luis. A UNIVERSAL HISTORY OF INFAMY. New York: E.P. Dutton, 1972. 146 p. Bibliog. note.

> Sixteen brief essays on infamous persons, including several Americans.

470 Brown, William R. IMAGEMAKER: WILL ROGERS AND THE AMERI-CAN DREAM. Columbia: University of Missouri Press, 1970. 304 p. Illus., bibliog.

> Will Rogers is a representative man whose image as American Adam, American Democrat, self-made man, and American Prometheus provides a richer understanding of American dreams.

471 Browne, Ray B., ed. LINCOLN-LORE: LINCOLN IN THE POPULAR MIND. Bowling Green, Ohio: Bowling Green State University Popular Press, 1974. 510 p. Bib.

A collection of popular writing arranged into sections on
wit and humor, songs, satires, and other writings.

472 Browne, Ray B.; Fishwick, Marshall; and Marsden, Michael, eds.
HEROES OF POPULAR CULTURE. Bowling Green, Ohio: Popular
Press, 1972. 190 p. Illus.

Includes Marshall Fishwick, "Heroic Style in America"; Fred
MacFadden, "The Pop Pantheon"; Bruce E. Coad, "The
Alger Hero"; H.D. Piper, "Dick Whittington and the Middle
Class Dream of Success"; Michael Mehlmann, "Hero of the
Thirties--The Tenant Farmer"; Leverett T. Smith, "Ty Cobb,
Babe Ruth and the Changing Image of the Athletic Hero";
Gerald O'Connor, "Where Have You Gone, Joe Di Maggio?";
Ronald Cummings, "The Superbowl Society"; Anthony Hopkins,
"Contemporary Heroism--Vitality in Defeat"; Patricia Kaye,
"Perry Mason: Modern Culture Hero"; Marshall McLuhan,
"The Popular Hero and Anti-Hero"; Jerome Rodnitzky, "A
Pacifist St. Joan--The Odyssey of Joan Baez"; Bruce Lohof,
"The Bacharach Phenomenon"; David Stupple, "A Hero for
the Times"; John Stevens, "The Dog as Hero"; Epilogue, by
Ray Browne.

473 Calder, Jenni. HEROES: FROM BYRON TO GUEVARA. London:
Hamish Hamilton, 1977. 211 p. Illus., bibliog., index.

Twelve chapters on heroic styles, including the Romantic,
revolutionary, historical, enterprising, imperialist, frontier,
exiled, leisure, disenchanted, professional, and anarchist,
and dispossessed heroes.

474 Coffin, Tristram Potter. THE FEMALE HERO IN FOLKLORE AND
LEGEND. New York: Seabury Press, 1975. 223 p.

A survey of the legends and lore surrounding mythical and
historical women, and modern women whose images emerge
in the media.

475 Coffin, Tristram Potter, and Cohen, Hennig, eds. THE PARADE OF
HEROES: LEGENDARY FIGURES IN AMERICAN LORE. Garden City,
N.Y.: Anchor, 1978. 630 p. Notes, index.

Transcriptions and reproductions of mostly original sources
for hero legends and stories in the American experience,
with source notes and some interpretation.

476 Deford, Frank. THERE SHE IS: THE LIFE AND TIMES OF MISS AMERICA.
New York: Viking Press, 1972. 351 p. Name index.

A tongue-in-cheek history of the Miss America pageants,

complete with an appendix of statistics on everything from measurements to television ratings.

477 Dorson, Richard Mercer. DAVY CROCKETT: AMERICAN COMIC LEGEND. New York: Printed at the Spiral Press for Rockland editions, 1939. Reprint. Westport, Conn.: Greenwood Press, 1977. 171 p. Illus., bibliog.

Collection of Crockett legends from the Crockett almanacs, selected according to themes.

478 Fishwick, Marshall. AMERICAN HEROES: MYTH AND REALITY. Washington, D.C.: Public Affairs Press, 1954. Reprint. Westport, Conn.: Greenwood Press, 1975. 242 p. Notes, index, chronology.

Contains chapters on seven historical figures and a series of types, including the self-made man, the cowboy, Paul Bunyan and Joe Magarac, Douglas Fairbanks and Mickey Mouse, villains, and changing conceptions of the hero.

479 Greene, Theodore. AMERICA'S HEROES: THE CHANGING MODELS OF SUCCESS IN AMERICAN MAGAZINES. New York: Oxford University Press, 1970. 387 p. Notes, index.

An examination of magazines that results in collective portraits of the hero characterized by: order (1787-1820), power (1894-1903), justice (1904-13), and organization (1914-18); with an epilogue.

480 Hamilton, Charles. THE SIGNATURE OF AMERICA: A FRESH LOOK AT FAMOUS HANDWRITING. New York: Harper and Row, 1979. 278 p. Index.

An extensive collection of autographs, ranging from the pictographs of early Indians and frontiersmen to authors, presidents, murderers, composers, inventors, and entertainers.

481 Klapp, Orrin E. HEROES, VILLAINS AND FOOLS: THE CHANGING AMERICAN CHARACTER. Englewood Cliffs, N.J.: Prentice-Hall, 1962. 176 p.

An exploration of major role-models that are found imbedded in the popular language of newspaper accounts, biographies, and other sources.

482 Krause, Herbert, and Olson, Gary D. PRELUDE TO GLORY: NEWSPAPER ACCOUNTING OF CUSTER'S 1874 EXPEDITION TO THE BLACK HILLS. Sioux Falls, S.D.: Brevet Press, 1974. 279 p. Illus., bibliog., index.

Collected newspaper accounts, military reports, and reminiscences.

483 Lewis, David L. THE PUBLIC IMAGE OF HENRY FORD: AN AMERI-CAN FOLK HERO AND HIS COMPANY. Detroit: Wayne State University Press, 1976. 598 p. Notes, index.

> This is perhaps the definitive biography of Ford and the history of his public image.

484 Nimmo, Dan, and Savage, Robert L. CANDIDATES AND THEIR IMAGES: CONCEPTS, METHODS AND FINDINGS. Pacific Palisades, Calif.: Goodyear Publishing Co., 1976. 250 p. Notes, charts, index.

> Definition of image, with the relationship of candidates' images to voting behavior. Chapters discuss image content, complexities of images, campaign styles and images, presidential images of 1952-72, and the effect of victory and defeat on images.

485 Ward, John W. "The Meaning of Lindbergh's Flight." In STUDIES IN AMERICAN CULTURE, edited by Joseph J. Kwiat and Mary C. Turpie, pp. 27-40. Minneapolis: University of Minnesota Press, 1960.

> A useful examination of the double meaning of Lindbergh's Atlantic crossing, which made the pilot a popular hero and his machine a metaphor for the potentialities of technology. Ward sees the heroic image as a form of nostalgia for the simpler past, and the machine as foreshadowing the reality of increasingly collectivized behavior necessary to complex technology.

486 Wecter, Dixon. THE HERO IN AMERICA: A CHRONICLE OF HERO WORSHIP. Ann Arbor: University of Michigan Press, 1941. 524 p. Notes, index.

> An examination of the legends of standard American heroes such as John Smith, Ben Franklin, George Washington, Thomas Jefferson, Daniel Boone and David Crockett, Andrew Jackson, Robert E. Lee, Ulysses Grant, Buffalo Bill, Teddy Rossevelt, the unknown soldier, Thomas Edison, Henry Ford, and Charles Lindbergh. A final chapter discloses how Americans choose their heroes.

MATERIAL CULTURE

487   Allen, Jon L. AVIATION AND SPACE MUSEUMS OF AMERICA. New
York: Arco, 1975. 287 p. Illus.

Guide to the historical development and contents of fifty-
seven aviation and aerospace museums.

488   Battersby, Martin. THE DECORATIVE THIRTIES. New York: Walker,
1971. 208 p. Illus., bibliog., index.

A useful discussion of the interiors and furnishings in vogue
during the decade.

489   Blake, Peter. GOD'S OWN JUNKYARD: THE PLANNED DETERIORA-
TION OF AMERICA'S LANDSCAPE. New York: Holt, Rinehart and
Winston, 1964. 144 p. Photos.

Rich in photographs, the volume attempts to capture the dese-
cration of the natural landscape by illustrating the impact of
towns, roads, cars, planes, advertising, and mindless cluttering.

490   Bracegirdle, Brian, et al. THE ARCHAEOLOGY OF THE INDUSTRIAL
REVOLUTION. Madison, N.J.: Fairleigh Dickinson University Press,
1973. 207 p. Illus., index.

Introduction to the study of industrial archaeology, together
with essays, written around more than 250 photographs illustrating contemporary work in industrial archaeology.

491   Brooks, John. TELEPHONE: THE FIRST HUNDRED YEARS. New York:
Harper, 1976. 369 p. Illus., notes, index.

A general history of the telephone, particularly the Bell
system, based primarily on AT&T files.

492   Bush, Donald J. THE STREAMLINED DECADE. New York: Braziller,
1975. 214 p. Illus., bibliog., index.

On design in the thirties.

492a Butterworth, Benjamin, comp. THE GROWTH OF INDUSTRIAL ART. Washington, D.C.: Government Printing Office, 1892. Reprint. New York: Knopf Publishing, 1902. 200 p. Illus.

> A monster-sized (16" X 20") facsimile of a two thousand picture celebration of American industrial development (everything from farm equipment and hydraulic motors to music boxes, boots, bottle stoppers, and beehives).

493 Christensen, Erwin O. THE INDEX OF AMERICAN DESIGN. New York: Macmillan and the National Gallery of Art, Washington, D.C., 1950. 229 p. Illus., subject list, bibliog., index.

> Topical sections on domestic, commercial, frontier, and entertainment design of artifacts.

494 Clark, Robert Judson, ed. THE ARTS AND CRAFTS MOVEMENT IN AMERICA, 1876-1916. Princeton, N.J.: Princeton University and Art Institute of Chicago, 1972. 170 p. Illus.

> A generously illustrated survey of the movement that sprang up in reaction to the Industrial Revolution and became something of a craftsman's crusade to imbue functional, everyday design--inkwells and manicure cases, furniture, fabrics, opalescent glassware--with grace, style, and beauty.

495 Clark, Ronald William. THE SCIENTIFIC BREAKTHROUGH: THE IMPACT OF MODERN INVENTION. New York: Putnam, 1974. 208 p. Illus., index.

> Brief chapters on photography, flying, electronics, man-made materials, nuclear energy, and speculation about the future.

496 Cowan, Ruth Schwartz. "The 'Industrial Revolution' in the Home: Household Technology and Social Change in the Twentieth Century." TECHNOLOGY AND CULTURE 17 (January 1976): 1-23.

> Basing her findings on a survey of such middle-class magazines as the LADIES' HOME JOURNAL, AMERICAN HOME, PARENTS' MAGAZINE, GOOD HOUSEKEEPING and McCALL'S as well as on available statistics, Cowan attempts to show how domestic technology affected family life and the self-image of the housewife.

497 Flink, James J. AMERICA ADOPTS THE AUTOMOBILE, 1895-1910. Cambridge: MIT Press, 1970. 343 p. Illus., bibliog., notes, index.

> An introduction to the development of the automobile's use, with consideration of beginnings, the mass market, motives for adoption, governmental and press response, auto clubs,

regulations, road systems, technology, and corporate development.

498 _____. THE CAR CULTURE. Cambridge: MIT Press, 1975. 260 p. Notes, index.

A history of the impact of the automobile on American culture, primarily through the institutions and personalities associated with it. The final chapter traces the changes effected by concerns for ecological attitudes and the scarcity of fuel.

499 Gies, Joseph, and Gies, Frances. THE INGENIOUS YANKEES. New York: Crowell, 1976. 376 p. Illus., bibliog., index.

Focusing on inventors and innovations important to the development of technology in the United States.

500 Gowans, Alan. IMAGES OF AMERICAN LIVING: FOUR CENTURIES OF ARCHITECTURE AND FURNITURE AS CULTURAL EXPRESSION. Philadelphia: J.B. Lippincott, 1964. 498 p. Illus., notes, index.

A history and interpretation of American architecture and furniture from the colonial period to the early sixties, with emphasis on the meaning and expression of psychological predispositions through form.

501 Gunn, Angus Macleod. HABITAT: HUMAN SETTLEMENTS IN AN URBAN AGE. Oxford, Engl.: Pergamon Press, 1978. 272 p. Illus., bibliog., index.

An issue-oriented discussion of human settlements based on information gathered for the Vancouver U.N. Habitat Conference of 1976, with chapters on the rural-urban system, population, wealth, life support, hazards, energy, and shelter.

502 Harling, Robert, ed. STUDIO DICTIONARY OF DESIGN AND DECORATION. New York: Viking, 1973. 538 p.

Includes some two thousand articles culled from HOUSE AND GARDEN on design and decoration. Included are materials on art, architecture, furniture, and various household artifacts.

503 Herkimer County Historical Society. THE STORY OF THE TYPEWRITER, 1873-1923. Herkimer, N.Y.: Press of A.H. Kellogg Co., 1923. 142 p. Illus.

A useful early account of the development of the typewriter which attributes women's emancipation to its invention.

504   Hillier, Bevis. THE DECORATIVE ARTS OF THE FORTIES AND FIFTIES:
AUSTERITY/BINGE. New York: Clarkson N. Potter, 1975. 200 p.
Illus., index, notes.

A topical history of the period's decorative arts, with a concluding chapter on contemporary nostalgic revivals.

505   Holstein, Jonathan. ABSTRACT DESIGN IN AMERICAN QUILTS. New
York: Whitney Museum of American Art, 1971. 15 p.

Catalog of the exhibition that ran from 1 July to 12 September
1971.

506   Hope, Adrian. WHY DIDN'T I THINK OF IT FIRST? New York: Drake,
1974. Illus., index.

An entertaining account of some of the patents granted to
Englishmen and Americans for gadgets.

507   Hornung, Clarence P. TREASURY OF AMERICAN DESIGN. 2 vols.
New York: Abrams, 1973. 846 p. Index, illus.

Pictorial survey of popular craft-making from colonial times
to the early seventies, arranged in sections on land and sea,
home, house and garden, women's world, children's world,
and regional styles.

508   Hume, Ivor Noël. A GUIDE TO ARTIFACTS OF COLONIAL AMERICA.
New York: Alfred A. Knopf, 1970. 323 p. Index, illus.

An excellent discussion of artifacts of the period, with an
introductory chapter that is essential reading for anyone interested in the study of artifacts. Each category of artifacts is treated in a section that varies in length according
to what is known about the subject, with bibliographical
items appended. A total of forty-four categories is included,
with one hundred illustrations, ranging from armor to wig
curlers.

509   Isaacson, Philip M. THE AMERICAN EAGLE. Boston: New York Graphic
Society; Little, Brown, 1975. 210 p. Illus., notes, bibliog., index.

A history and analysis of the eagle as an American symbol
from its inception in 1782 through various folk, commercial,
and political manifestations.

510   Kaye, Myrna. YANKEE WEATHERVANES. New York: Dutton, 1975.
236 p. Index, bibliog., notes, illus., list of makers and vendors.

History, European heritage, thematic iconography, and significance of weathervanes in New England through the present time.

511 Knight, Arthur. THE HOLLYWOOD STYLE. London: Collier-Macmillan, 1969. 219 p. Illus.

>A brief introduction is followed by lavish photographs by Eliot Elisofon of the homes of two dozen stars.

512 Larsen, Egon. A HISTORY OF INVENTION. New York: Roy Publishers, 1969. 382 p. Index.

>Divided into sections on energy, transport, and communications, the volume provides summaries of major innovations and inventions.

513 Ludwig, Allan I. GRAVEN IMAGES: NEW ENGLAND STONECARVING AND ITS SYMBOLS, 1650-1815. Middletown, Conn.: Wesleyan University Press, 1966. 482 p. Notes, illus., bibliog., maps, index.

>Burial rituals and the iconography of New England religious symbolism.

514 Luebbers, David J. THE 1950-1972 BICYCLE BIBLIOGRAPHY. Part 1. Denver: Silers Printing Co., 1977. 96 p.

>One in a series of books by the author compiling a wide range of source materials on bicycles and other pedal-powered vehicles and machines.

515 Lynch, Kevin. THE IMAGE OF THE CITY. Cambridge: MIT Press; Harvard University Press, 1960. 194 p. Illus., bibliog., index.

>An exploration and analysis of the "look" of cities, with focus on the elements of the image. Notes on method and matters of perception and orientation.

516 Mastai, Boleslaw, and Mastai, Marie-Louise D'Otrange. THE STARS AND STRIPES: THE AMERICAN FLAG AS ART AND HISTORY FROM THE BIRTH OF THE REPUBLIC TO THE PRESENT. New York: Knopf, 1973. 248 p. Index, charts.

>Pictorial history of the flag in peace, war, and art. Only tasteful examples of the flag's use in art are included.

517 Mehrabian, Albert. PUBLIC PLACES AND PRIVATE SPACES: THE PSYCHOLOGY OF WORK, PLAY, AND LIVING ENVIRONMENTS. New York: Basic Books, 1976. 354 p. Illus., bibliog., index.

>A discussion of the psychology of intimate environments, residences, work places, therapeutic environments, play environments, and communal environments.

518 Morris, Lloyd. NOT SO LONG AGO. New York: Random House, 1949. 504 p. Index.

An informal history of the motion picture, the automobile, and the radio from 1896 to the late forties. The sections are divided into readable accounts of episodes in the development of each of the topics, with illustrations keying on the more photogenic aspects.

519 Norman, Bruce. THE INVENTING OF AMERICA. London: British Broadcasting Corp., 1976. 240 p. Bibliog., index, illus.

A cursory history of technical innovations in transportation, weaponry, communications, and many other areas.

520 THE OXFORD COMPANION TO THE DECORATIVE ARTS. Edited by Harold Osborne. London: Oxford University Press, Clarendon, 1975. 865 p. Illus., bibliog.

Encyclopedic entries on personalities, movements, and styles in a broad range of artifacts, but with few examples from folk or popular culture.

521 Papanek, Victor. DESIGN FOR THE REAL WORLD: HUMAN ECOLOGY AND SOCIAL CHANGE. Introduction by Buckminster Fuller. New York: Pantheon, 1972. 378 p. Extensive bibliog., random notes, diagrams.

This perceptive volume begins with a chapter on definitions of design, then provides a brief general history, identifies the aesthetic isolation of contemporary designers, social and moral responsibilities, designed obsolescence, design myths, ideas toward utilizing the structures found in nature, ecology and design, education of designers, and designing in the real world.

522 Paulus, Virginia, ed. HOUSING: A BIBLIOGRAPHY, 1960-1972. New York: AMS Press, 1974. 339 p. Index.

Includes a section on political and social information.

523 Pons, Valdo. IMAGERY AND SYMBOLISM IN URBAN SOCIETY. Hull, Engl.: University of Hull, 1975. 25 p.

A review of research on urban imagery by Kevin Lynch, Anselm Strauss, Daniel Boorstin, and others, with suggestions for further research.

524 Price, Edward T. "The Central Courthouse Square in the American County Seat." GEOGRAPHICAL REVIEW 58 (January 1968): 29-60.

Diffusion of forms of the courthouse square throughout the East and Midwest.

525 Quimby, Ian M.G., ed. MATERIAL CULTURE AND THE STUDY OF AMERICAN LIFE. New York: Norton; published for the Henry Francis DuPont Winterthur Museum, 1978. 250 p. Illus., index.

Essays cover a wide range of material culture. Of particular interest are essays on the visual and psychological dimensions of objects, vernacular architecture, development of department stores and world's fairs as sources of popular taste, and several essays on the effective use of artifacts in teaching and in presenting museum materials to the public.

526 Rae, John B. THE AMERICAN AUTOMOBILE: A BRIEF HISTORY. Chicago: University of Chicago Press, 1965. 265 p. Chronology, illus., bibliog., index.

A useful study of the corporate growth of the automobile industry, and related societal changes.

527 _____. THE ROAD AND THE CAR IN AMERICAN LIFE. Cambridge: MIT Press, 1971. 390 p. Illus., bibliog., index.

A study of automobiles and highways based largely on information made available from the Automobile Manufacturers Association. Chapters cover preautomobile roads, contemporary highways and policies, urban systems, and prospects.

528 Rapoport, Amos. HUMAN ASPECTS OF URBAN FORM: TOWARDS A MAN-ENVIRONMENT APPROACH TO URBAN FORM AND DESIGN. New York: Pergamon Press, 1977. 438 p. Illus., bibliog., index.

An examination of urban imagery in relation to human use, with chapters on perception of quality, environmental cognition; social, cultural, and territorial variables; distinctions between associational and perceptual worlds; and related matters.

529 Reyburn, Wallace. FLUSHED WITH PRIDE: THE STORY OF THOMAS CRAPPER. Englewood Cliffs, N.J.: Prentice-Hall, 1971. 95 p.

A tongue-in-cheek biography of the inventor of the indoor toilet.

530 Seale, William. THE TASTEFUL INTERLUDE: AMERICAN INTERIORS THROUGH THE CAMERA'S EYE, 1860-1917. American Decorative Arts. New York: Praeger, 1975. 256 p.

Examples from the rich, middle class, and poor.

531 Sealock, Richard B., and Seely, Pauline A. BIBLIOGRAPHY OF PLACE-NAME LITERATURE: UNITED STATES AND CANADA. 2d ed. Chicago: American Library Association, 1967. 352 p. Index.

Supplemented annually in NAMES: JOURNAL OF THE AMER-
ICAN NAME SOCIETY (1953--), this partially annotated volume
of 3,599 articles and books about place naming is a key source.

532 Smeets, René. SIGNS, SYMBOLS & ORNAMENTS. New York: Van
Nostrand Reinhold, 1975. 176 p. Illus., index.

Illustrated discussion of signs, pictorial symbols, and orna-
mentation in folk, industrial products, and architecture,
among other topics.

533 Stafford, Maureen, and Ware, Dora. AN ILLUSTRATED DICTIONARY
OF ORNAMENT. New York: St. Martin's Press, 1975. 246 p. Illus.,
bibliog., index.

Brief illustrated entries on a wide variety of ornaments and
designs associated with architecture and artifacts.

534 Stern, Jane, and Stern, Michael. AMAZING AMERICA. New York:
David Obst Books; Random House, 1978. 463 p. Photos, indexes.

This delightful collection of "sights"--described in brief essays,
sometimes with photographs--are covered in the following chapter headings: shrines to animals, architecture, birthplaces,
celebrations, contests, crime, folk and fine art environments,
halls of fame, monuments, museums, music, natural phenomena,
places to stay, religion, science, sports, superlatives, tours,
and travel and transportation, throughout the United States.
It is organized according to state and contains both a general
index and a subject index.

535 Tashjian, Dickran, and Tashjian, Ann. MEMORIALS FOR CHILDREN
OF CHANGE: THE ART OF EARLY NEW ENGLAND STONECARVING.
Middletown, Conn.: Wesleyan University Press, 1974. 309 p. Notes,
bibliog., index, illus.

A useful attempt to relate the art and verse of gravestones
to their cultural heritage through consideration of their iconology and verbal expression.

536 Thompson, Hunter. FEAR AND LOATHING IN LAS VEGAS. New York:
Random House, 1971. 288 p. Illus.

A drug odyssey through Las Vegas and the frontal lobes of
the American nightmare, by the innovator of "Gonzo" journalism.

537 Townroe, P.M., ed. SOCIAL AND POLITICAL CONSEQUENCES OF
THE MOTOR CAR. London: David and Charles, 1974. 189 p. Illus.,
bibliog., index.

A collection of essays on problems, contexts, the environmental impact, congestion, public transport, new technology, and future planning, in relation to the automobile, primarily in Britain.

538 Trachtenberg, Alan. BROOKLYN BRIDGE: FACT AND SYMBOL. New York: Oxford University Press, 1965. 182 p.

Symbolic analysis of the Brooklyn Bridge through discussion of its origin and heritage, construction, and appearance in literature and thought.

539 Trachtenberg, Marvin. THE STATUE OF LIBERTY. New York: Viking Press, 1976. 224 p. Notes, illus.

An essay that discusses the circumstances, site, construction, artist Auguste Bartholdi, and reactions relating to the conception and construction of the statue.

540 Train, Arthur, Jr. THE STORY OF EVERYDAY THINGS. New York: Harper and Brothers, 1941. 428 p. Bibliog., index, photos, drawings.

A useful informal account of houses, furniture, food, clothing, transportation and communication, but "also . . . agriculture, handicraft, industry, community life, the life of the intellect, and amusements." This is a history according to periods of artifacts and other aspects of material culture.

541 Tunnard, Christopher, and Reed, Henry Hope. AMERICAN SKYLINE: THE GROWTH AND FORM OF OUR CITIES AND TOWNS. Boston: Houghton Mifflin, 1956. 302 p. Illus., bibliog., index.

A standard informal history of urban development from 1607 through 1950, with emphasis on architectural styles in public and commercial buildings.

542 Vries, Leonard de, with Ilonka Van Amstel, comps. VICTORIAN INVENTIONS. New York: American Heritage; McGraw-Hill, 1972. 192 p.

An absolutely charming--and eye-opening--compendium of engravings and articles reproduced from popular scientific magazines of 1865-1900.

543 Wagner, Walter. MONEY TALKS: HOW AMERICANS GET IT, SPEND IT, USE IT AND ABUSE IT. Indianapolis, Ind.: Bobbs-Merrill, 1978. 295 p.

Interviews with psychologists, entertainers, socialites, ghetto dwellers, speculators, senior citizens, immigrants, doctors, the unemployed and employed.

544 Winner, Langdon. AUTONOMOUS TECHNOLOGY: TECHNICS-OUT-OF-CONTROL AS A THEME IN POLITICAL THOUGHT. Cambridge: MIT Press, 1977. 386 p. Notes, index.

>An attempt to provide a middle ground for discussions of technology among disciplines, with consideration of technological autonomy, change, flaws, technocracy, artifice and order, politics, complexity, and creation and control.

545 Winslow, David C. "Trade Cards, Catalogs, and Invoice Heads." PENNSYLVANIA FOLKLORE 19 (Spring 1970): 16-23.

>The importance of old catalogs, stationery, and business cards in identification of artifacts.

546 Wright, Lawrence. WARM AND SNUG: THE HISTORY OF THE BED. London: Routledge and Kegan Paul, 1962. 360 p. Bibliog., index, illus.

>Brief anecdotal chapters on more than fifty aspects of the bed, illustrated with sketches and reproductions.

FASHION AND DRESS

547 Adburgham, Alison, ed. VIEW OF FASHION. London: George Allen and Unwin, 1966. 285 p. Illus., index.

>A collection of comment and criticism culled from PUNCH, THE GUARDIAN, HARPER'S BAZAAR, the OBSERVER, and THE QUEEN. Topics cover the general fashion scene, Victorian and Edwardian sportswomen, the social scene, the cult of beauty, fashion abroad (New York, Paris, Rome, etc.), lingerie, personalities, London fashions, exhibitions, and men's fashions.

548 Angeloglou, Maggie. HISTORY OF MAKE-UP. London: Studio Vista, 1970. 143 p. Bibliog., index.

>A world history of cosmetics written in a lucid style, with information on American practices in the twentieth century.

549 Anspach, Karlyne. THE WHY OF FASHION. Ames: Iowa State University Press, 1967. 378 p. Notes, index.

>A useful contribution to the economic aspects of fashion, with sections on social need, economics, and marketing, and contemporary fashion through discussions of symbolism, conservatism, the youth, and casual looks.

550 Beaton, Cecil Walter Hardy. THE GLASS OF FASHION. Garden City, N.Y.: Nelson Doubleday, 1954. 397 p. Sketches.

> An informed account of twentieth-century fashion leaders and designers.

551 Chalmers, Helena. CLOTHES, ON AND OFF THE STAGE: A HISTORY OF DRESS FROM THE EARLIEST TIMES TO THE PRESENT DAY. New York: D. Appleton, 1928. Reprint. Detroit: Gale Research Co., 1979. 292 p. Illus.

> A handbook for the stage which provides notes on dress throughout history, with practical hints on dressing and preparing costumes.

552 Colle, Doriece. COLLARS-STOCKS-CRAVATS: A HISTORY AND COSTUME DATING GUIDE TO CIVILIAN MEN'S NECKPIECES 1655-1900. Emmaus, Pa.: Rodale Press, 1972. 255 p. Illus., appendixes, bibliog.

> Summaries of styles, with sketches and plates.

553 Copeland, Peter F. WORKING DRESS IN COLONIAL AND REVOLUTIONARY AMERICA. Contributions in American History, no. 58. Westport, Conn: Greenwood Press, 1977. 223 p. Glossary, bibliog., index, notes.

> Sketches of occupational groups including sailors and fishermen, farmers, craftsmen, tradesmen, frontiersmen, transportation workers, servants and slaves, soldiers, professionals, and criminals, with brief documented notes on features.

554 Corson, Richard. FASHIONS IN HAIR: THE FIRST FIVE THOUSAND YEARS. London: Peter Owen, 1965. 701 p. Bibliog., index, illus.

> Corson tries to cover the entire history of men's and women's fashions, devoting a small chapter to categories and the ideas of change, then providing three chapters on the ancients, four chapters on the era from the Middle Ages through the seventeenth century, and chapters on men and women from the eighteenth through the twentieth centuries. Sources include museums, libraries, periodicals, and books.

555 Crawford, M.D.C., and Guernsey, Elizabeth A. THE HISTORY OF CORSETS IN PICTURES. New York: Fairchild Publications, 1951. 41 p. Illus.

> History of the development of corsets from ancient times through the 1940s.

556 Daves, Jessica. READY-MADE MIRACLE: THE AMERICAN STORY OF

FASHION FOR THE MILLIONS. New York: G.P. Putnam's Sons, 1967. 256 p. Index.

A perceptive account of the emergence of the industry from shirtwaists to modern styles, with emphasis on the promotion and manufacture of ready-made clothing for women.

557 Dorner, Jane. FASHION: THE CHANGING SHAPE OF FASHION THROUGH THE YEARS. London: Octopus Books, 1974. 128 p. Illus., bibliog., index.

An outline history of fashion, with compact chapters on conscious display, trousers and sport clothes, dandies, and American influences.

558 _____. FASHION IN THE FORTIES AND FIFTIES. New Rochelle, N.Y.: Arlington House, 1975. 160 p. Bibliog., illus.

Collage of fashion designs and accessories that range from high- to middle-brow tastes. Illustrations are culled primarily from manufacturer's plates.

559 Earle, Alice Morse. COSTUME OF COLONIAL TIMES. New York: C. Scribner's Sons, 1894. Reprint. Detroit: Gale Research Co., 1974. 263 p.

A studious social history and glossary of colonial dress and hair fashions, primarily of the northern colonies, drawn from newspapers, wills, letters, inventories of estates, and court records.

560 Evans, Mary. COSTUME THROUGHOUT THE AGES. Philadelphia: Lippincott, 1950. 360 p. Illus., bibliog., indexes.

A textbook on the history of costume throughout the world.

561 Ewing, Elizabeth. FASHION IN UNDERWEAR. London: B.T. Batsford, 1971. 160 p. Bibliog., illus., index.

A useful history of undergarments for women from ancient times to 1970. Illustrated with ink sketches and some reproductions, the volume has a detailed text and includes a chapter on manufacturing innovations.

562 _____. HISTORY OF TWENTIETH CENTURY FASHION. New York: Scribner's, 1974. 244 p. Bibliog., index.

Ewing sees the emancipation of fashion from the control of the upper classes as occurring with the emancipation of women around the turn of the century. Though primarily concerned with British fashion, the volume has many insights applicable to the emergence of styles in the United States to the middle 1970s. The emphasis is on high fashion.

563 Fehr, Barbara. YANKEE DENIM DANDIES. Blue Earth, Minn.: Piper
Publications, 1974. 96 p. Illus., bibliog.

History of jeans, with much interspersed miscellanea.

564 Flugel, J.C. THE PSYCHOLOGY OF CLOTHES. International Psycho-
Analytical Library, no. 18. London: Hogarth Press, 1930. 257 p.
Bibliog., index.

An early exploration of the ideas of decoration, modesty,
protection, and motives in wearing apparel, together with
consideration of sex differences, clothing types, forces and
vicissitudes of fashion, the ethics of dress, and speculation
on the future of fashion.

565 Garland, Madge. THE CHANGING FORM OF FASHION. New York:
Praeger, 1970. 130 p. Illus., index.

An interesting approach to fashion that emphasizes physical
features rather than history. Chapters treat shape, modesty,
hair styling and hats, footwear, fabrics, fashion creators,
English fashions, and ready-made clothes.

566 Gold, Annalee. SEVENTY-FIVE YEARS OF FASHIONS. New York:
Fairchild Publications, 1975. 112 p. Illus.

An introductory text illustrated with sketches and brief descriptions of women's fashions from the turn of the century.

567 Gottwald, Laura, and Gottwald, Jarusz. FREDERICK'S OF HOLLY-
WOOD, 1947-1973: TWENTY-SIX YEARS OF MAIL ORDER SEDUCTION.
New York: Strawberry Hill, 1973. 255 p. Illus.

Reproductions of advertisements.

568 Hall, Carrie A. FROM HOOPSKIRTS TO NUDITY: A REVIEW OF THE
FOLLIES AND FOIBLES OF FASHION, 1866-1936. Caldwell, Idaho:
Caxton Printers, 1938. 240 p. Bibliog., illus., index.

A decade-by-decade account of changes in fashions, with
chapters on accessories and the eternal fashion machine by
a woman who made twenty thousand dresses over a fifty-year
period.

569 Horn, Marilyn J. THE SECOND SKIN: AN INTERDISCIPLINARY
STUDY OF CLOTHING. 2d ed. Boston: Houghton Mifflin, 1975.
468 p. Source notes, illus., index.

One of the most useful sources, this illustrated textbook discusses the interrelationship of clothing to cultural values,
clothing symbolism, aesthetics, comfort and appearance,

economic aspects of marketing and the clothing industry, and consumer decisions. Horn draws on a wide variety of secondary sources.

570   Jarnow, Jeannette A., and Judelle, Beatrice. INSIDE THE FASHION BUSINESS. 2d ed. New York: Wiley, 1974. 432 p. Bibliog., glossary, index.

A textbook that stresses the business side of fashion through chapter introductions and essays by various contributors. Sections focus on socioeconomics, fabrics, U.S. women's apparel and accessories, foreign producers, retailing, auxiliary industries, men's fashions, and changing directions.

571   Kern, Stephen. ANATOMY AND DESTINY: A CULTURAL HISTORY OF THE HUMAN BODY. New York: Bobbs-Merrill, 1975. 307 p. Notes, index.

A descriptive interpretation of body imagery, with chapters on clothing, the Victorian morality and its decline, art, public hygiene, opinions of intellectuals, theories of bodily determinants of gender roles and family relations, scientific studies of sexuality, sex education, Freud's contributions, the impact of World War I on attitudes toward the body, and major developments in England, America, Germany, and France. Also considered are D.H. Lawrence, Henry Miller, physical culture in Nazi Germany, and Sartre's philosophy of the body.

572   Keyes, Jean. A HISTORY OF WOMEN'S HAIRSTYLES, 1500-1965. London: Methuen, 1967. 86 p. Bibliog., index, drawings.

A compact history of hairstyles, with a brief section on accessories and jewelery.

573   Kidwell, Claudia B., and Christman, Margaret C. SUITING EVERYONE: THE DEMOCRATIZATION OF CLOTHING IN AMERICA. Washington, D.C.: Published for the National Museum of History and Technology by the Smithsonian Institution Press, 1974. 208 p. Bibliog., illus.

Extensively illustrated history of the development of ready-to-wear clothing from early fabrics to contemporary manufactured products.

574   Kohler, Karl. A HISTORY OF COSTUME. New York: Dover, 1928. 464 p. Bibliog., illus., index.

A detailed study, with patterns, of costume from antiquity to 1870.

575   Lambert, Eleanor. WORLD OF FASHION: PEOPLE, PLACES, RESOURCES. New York: Bowker, 1976. 361 p. Bibliog, index.

Essays arranged geographically on social and economic development, with biographical notes on important figures.

576   Laver, James. CLOTHES. London: Burke, 1952. 272 p. Bibliog., index.

Another of Laver's attempts to come to grips with clothing fashions, though more heavily laden with quotation than TASTE AND FASHION (see below). Highlights of the volume include dress in poetry, satire, and fiction; admonitions; hoops, bloomers, hair and hats, fans and gloves, undergarments, make-up; some speculations about why people wear clothes; and notes on the cost of famous wardrobes in the past.

577   _____. THE CONCISE HISTORY OF COSTUME AND FASHION. New York: Abrams, 1969. 288 p. Bibliog., illus., index.

A brief international survey of high fashion from ancient times to date of publication, featuring excellent black and white and color illustrations.

578   _____. TASTE AND FASHION: FROM THE FRENCH REVOLUTION UNTIL TODAY. New York: Dodd, Mead, 1938. 267 p. Illus., index.

Based on fashion plates, dated portraits and caricatures, the volume discusses decolletage, corsets and lingerie, colors, furs, bathing costumes and sports clothing, hair and hats, and men's fashions, in addition to a general history of dress. Laver draws a connection between fashion and the styles of architecture and interior decoration.

579   Levin, Phyllis Lee. THE WHEELS OF FASHION. Garden City, N.Y.: Doubleday and Co., 1965. 244 p. Illus.

Anecdotal survey of the fashion industry.

580   Ley, Sandra. FASHION FOR EVERYONE: THE STORY OF READY-TO-WEAR, 1870S TO 1970S. New York: Scribner's, 1974. 153 p. Bibliog., illus., index.

An informal history of women's ready-made clothing, with illustrations. Although the economics is naive and the general level of discussion light, this is a useful introduction to general trends in available fashions.

581 Lister, Margot. COSTUMES OF EVERYDAY LIFE: AN ILLUSTRATED HISTORY OF WORKING CLOTHES. Boston: Plays, 1972. 178 p. Illus., glossary, index.

Includes 250 sketches of figures with descriptions for typical occupations from 1900 to 1910.

582 Lynam, Ruth, ed. PARIS FASHION: THE GREAT DESIGNERS AND THEIR CREATIONS. London: Michael Joseph, 1972. 256 p. Illus., index.

Eleven contributors discuss the classic tradition, couture, the 1920s and 1930s, "Coco," Dior, Fath, models, and contemporary designers.

583 McLaughlin, Terence. THE GILDED LILY. London: Cassell, 1972. 188 p. Illus., index.

A useful overview of the uses of cosmetics in modern Western societies. The author's thesis is that cosmetics are used to create masks or personas in order that the wearer may become "more of a type, an undifferentiated female." Though the emphasis is on England, there is much useful information on the United States as well, together with a chapter on the grooming of household pets and one on warpaint and tattoos.

584 Monro, Isabel Stevenson, and Cook, Dorothy, eds. COSTUME INDEX: A SUBJECT INDEX TO PLATES AND TO ILLUSTRATED TEXT. New York: H.W. Wilson, 1937. 338 p.

An index to plates in 942 volumes, arranged according to subject matter.

585 Monro, Isabel Stevenson, and Monro, Kate M., eds. COSTUME INDEX: A SUBJECT INDEX TO PLATES AND TO ILLUSTRATED TEXT. SUPPLEMENT. New York: H.W. Wilson, 1957. 210 p.

An additional 347 books are included, primarily from the period 1937 to 1953.

586 Newton, Stella Mary. HEALTH, ART AND REASON: DRESS REFORMERS OF THE NINETEENTH CENTURY London and New York: John Murray, 1974. 191 p. Notes, illus., bibliog., index.

A useful social history, not only of dress reformers, but also of the cultural contents and influences on fashion during the century.

587 Nystrom, Paul H. ECONOMICS OF FASHION. New York: Ronald Press Co., 1928. 521 p. Illus., bibliog., index.

Discusses the fashion cycle, fashion psychology, factors that influence the character of fashion and its directions of change, Haut Couture, modesty, modern innovations, men's fashions, furniture styles in the nineteenth century, American originals, production trends, and standardization of sizes and types of apparel.

588 Reyburn, Wallace. BUST-UP: THE UPLIFTING TALE OF OTTO TITZLING AND THE DEVELOPMENT OF THE BRA. Englewood Cliffs, N.J.: Prentice-Hall, 1972. 106 p. Illus.

An imaginative reconstruction of incidents leading to the invention and development of the brassiere in the twentieth century.

589 Roach, Mary Ellen, and Eicher, Joan B. THE VISIBLE SELF: PERSPECTIVES ON DRESS. Englewood Cliffs, N.J.: Prentice-Hall, 1973. 246 p. Notes, illus., index.

A textbook which surveys types of studies, body and dress, art and meaning, societal influences, and economics; with a summary.

590 Robinson, Julian. FASHION IN THE FORTIES. New York: St. Martin's Press, 1976. 103 p. Illus.

A useful introduction to the high fashion trends of the decade, with emphasis on several centers of fashion and the leading designers of Europe and America.

591 Rudofsky, Bernard. THE UNFASHIONABLE HUMAN BODY. Garden City, N.Y.: Doubleday, 1974. 288 p. Notes, illus., index.

A thoughtful and provocative contribution to the dialog on the meaning and origins of clothes, with an exceptional choice of illustrations. Rudofsky's examination of the symbolism and myth considers the Edenic myth, modesty, imaginative monsters, customs of body distortion, tattooing, clothing, dress reform and reformers' fashions, Sartoriasis, garments for two, and artistic uses of clothing.

592 Severn, William [Bill]. HERES YOUR HAT. New York: David McKay, 1963. 209 p. Glossary, bibliog., index.

Informal account of the history, customs and styles associated with hats, with a section on hat tricks.

593 _____. THE LONG AND SHORT OF IT: FIVE THOUSAND YEARS OF FUN AND FURY OVER HAIR. New York: David McKay, 1971. 136 p. Illus., index.

A lighthearted survey of the styles and controversies regarding hair on heads and faces of men and women.

594 Stabile, Toni. COSMETICS: TRICK OR TREAT? Introduction by Congressman James J. Delaney. New York: Hawthorn Books, 1966. 223 p. Notes, index.

An impassioned investigation into the cosmetics industry and the results of its marketing of harmful products, and products that are misrepresented in advertising copy.

595 Stuart, Jessie. THE AMERICAN FASHION INDUSTRY. Boston: Simmons College, 1951. 78 p. Award list, bibliog.

A presentation for store use, this little volume contains brief chapters on the development of the industry, with sections on style piracy, promotion, and American designers.

596 Verrill, Alpheus Hyatt. PERFUMES AND SPICES, INCLUDING AN ACCOUNT OF SOAPS AND COSMETICS: THE STORY OF THE HISTORY, SOURCE, PREPARATION, AND USE OF THE SPICES, PERFUMES, SOAPS, AND COSMETICS WHICH ARE IN EVERYDAY USE. 1940. Reprint. Boston: L.C. Page and Co., 1945. 304 p. Index.

Brief international history of uses and preparations.

597 Warwick, Edward; Pitz, Henry C.; and Wyckoff, Alexander. EARLY AMERICAN DRESS: THE COLONIAL AND REVOLUTIONARY PERIODS. New York: B. Blom, 1965. 428 p. Bibliog., illus., index.

Undoubtedly the most thorough treatment of middle- and upper-class clothing during this period. Sketches and reproduced illustrations supplement the detailed text. The volume covers European influences, with chapters on Virginia, New England, Dutch New York to 1675; the colonies through 1775, with chapters on Pennsylvania and the Quakers; the Revolutionary period; a special chapter on children's clothing, and one on frontier life. The volume concludes with ninety-six pages of plates with notes on artists.

598 Wilcox, Ruth Turner. FIVE CENTURIES OF AMERICAN COSTUME. New York: Scribner's, 1963. 207 p. Bibliog., illus.

A concise history, through text and sketches, of "ordinary" dress from the Vikings and Indians to contemporary times. Chapters on military, civilian, and children's clothing.

599 _____. THE MODE IN COSTUME. New York: Scribner's, 1958. 463 p. Bibliog., illus., sketches.

Covers both male and female fashion from the ancient Egyptians to the Western world in 1958. Treats inner and outer garments, and accessories.

600 Wykes-Joyce, Max. COSMETICS AND ADORNMENT. New York: Philosophical Library, 1961. 190 p. Bibliog., index.

An extensive historical survey with contemporary quotations of beauty practices. The volume focuses primarily on England and the United States.

601 Yarwood, Doreen. THE ENCYCLOPEDIA OF WORLD COSTUME. New York: Charles Scribner's Sons, 1978. 471 p. Illus., bibliog., index.

Informal encyclopedic entries on costume, dress, and fashion.

602 Young, Agatha (Agnes) Brooks. RECURRING CYCLES OF FASHION, 1760-1937. New York: Cooper Square, 1966. 216 p. Illus., charts, index.

Originally begun to test the fashion-business cycle hypothesis, the study expanded to cover a much broader range of information. Young concludes that fashions occur in three cycles per century and that the cycles follow a prescribed pattern based on principles of change.

ARCHITECTURE

603 Andrews, Wayne. ARCHITECTURE IN AMERICA: A PHOTOGRAPHIC HISTORY FROM THE COLONIAL PERIOD TO THE PRESENT. Rev. ed. New York: Atheneum, 1977. 185 p. Illus., bibliog., index.

A brief text supplements the photographs. The volume is concerned with a survey of the styles of the modern period, with major artists representing modern design in commercial and domestic building.

604 Barnard, Julian. THE DECORATIVE TRADITION. New York and London: Pyne, distributed by Scribner's; Architectural Press, 1974. 144 p.

An important discussion of the contribution of decorative architecture to human values from its roots in antiquity and direct influence in the nineteenth century, to the informal decoration of modern functionalist buildings.

605 Becker, Franklin D. HOUSING MESSAGES. Stroudsburg, Pa.: Dowden, Hutchinson and Ross, 1977. 142 p. Notes, index.

A useful introduction to architectural signs and the environ-

mental context provided by them. The volume begins with a
chapter on environmental messages, then deals with images of
"home," public housing, personalization of architectural space,
users' participation in planning, crime and vandalism, play
areas, and social change.

606 Blake, Peter. FORM FOLLOWS FIASCO: WHY MODERN ARCHITEC-
TURE HASN'T WORKED. Boston: Little, Brown, 1977. 169 p. Illus.

A critique of modern architectural dogma, with chapters on
the fantasy of function, the open plan, purity, technology,
the skyscraper, the ideal city, mobility, zoning, housing,
form, and architecture itself.

607 Brunskill, R.W. ILLUSTRATED HANDBOOK OF VERNACULAR ARCHI-
TECTURE. Boston: Faber and Faber, 1978. 249 p. Illus., appendixes,
notes, index.

An excellent handbook of styles, construction methods, and
diffusion of styles in England. This is a model for studies in
American vernacular architecture and the diffusion of commercial styles.

608 Fishwick, Marshall, and Neil, J. Merideth, eds. POPULAR ARCHITEC-
TURE. Bowling Green, Ohio: Bowling Green University Popular Press,
1974. 120 p. Illus., notes.

A collection of essays on vernacular architecture, the Wool-
worth Tower, cars and houses, squatter settlements, buildings
as signs, new art history, and the nineteenth-century aesthetic
of bigness.

609 Gowans, Alan. IMAGES OF AMERICAN LIVING: FOUR CENTURIES
OF ARCHITECTURE AND FURNITURE AS CULTURAL EXPRESSION. Philadelphia: J.B. Lippincott, 1964. 498 p. Illus., notes, index.

An exploration of the patterns of material expression from the
medieval, classical, literary, modern, international, and contemporary phases; with attention to the conquest of native
social change, concepts of art, and evolving democracy.

610 Heimsath, Clovis. BEHAVIORAL ARCHITECTURE: TOWARD AN AC-
COUNTABLE DESIGN PROCESS. New York: McGraw-Hill, 1977.
203 p. Illus., bibliog., index.

An introduction to behavioral logic in design processes, with
discussions of the current lack of behavioral considerations,
issues in behavioral architecture, current behavioral practices,
and the future of design based on behavioral principles.

611 Hirshorn, Paul, and Izenour, Steven. WHITE TOWERS. Cambridge: MIT Press, 1979. 216 p. Illus., geographical index.

A brief historical and architectural sketch of the hamburger chain, together with a photographic essay of selected White Towers from 1926 to 1972.

612 Kaufmann, Edgar, Jr.; Hitchcock, Henry-Russell; Fein, Albert; Weisman, Vincent; and Scully, Vincent, eds. THE RISE OF AN AMERICAN ARCHITECTURE. New York: Praeger Publishers, in association with the Metropolitan Museum of Art, 1970. 241 p. Notes, index.

Four excellent essays on American influence abroad (Hitchcock), the ideal and real American city (Fein), history of the sky-scraper (Weisman), and house design (Scully). Of particular interest is Fein's discussion of the nineteenth-century develop-ment of such urban features as parks, cemeteries, and other public spaces. Weisman notes seven stages based on tech-nological innovations and zoning codes.

613 Lohoff, Bruce A. "The Service Station in America: The Evolution of a Vernacular Form." INDUSTRIAL ARCHEOLOGY 11 (May 1974): 1-13.

A consideration of the form, social impact, and influence of the gasoline service station.

614 Marc, Olivier. PSYCHOLOGY OF THE HOUSE. London: Thames and Hudson, 1977. 144 p. Bibliog., index, illus.

A psychoanalytic examination of the house as a universal symbol of the body and self, through comparisons of house styles from many cultures with representation in children's art and religious symbolism.

615 Poole, Gray Johnson. ARCHITECTS AND MAN'S SKYLINE. New York: Dodd, Mead, 1972. 176 p. Illus., index.

A series of career sketches of twelve major architects from the fifth century B.C. to Constantinos Doxiadis, all of whom were in some way individualists.

616 Quantrill, Malcolm. RITUAL AND RESPONSE IN ARCHITECTURE. London: Lund Humphries, 1974. 151 p. Illus., notes, index.

An exploration of the "lack of correlation between ritual and building form" in contemporary architecture, and critique of current theories and practices.

617 Rapoport, Amos. HOUSE FORM AND CULTURE. Foundations of Cul-tural Geography. Englewood Cliffs, N.J.: Prentice-Hall, 1969. 150 p.

Provides a conceptual framework through the discussion of
form as it is related to sociocultural factors, climate, materials, and other influences.

618   Rickert, John E. "House Facades of the Northeastern United States: A
       Tool of Geographic Analysis." ANNALS OF THE ASSOCIATION OF
       AMERICAN GEOGRAPHERS 57 (June 1967): 211-38. Illus.

       An extensive discussion of sources for the study of house fa-
       cades together with changes associated with building periods
       from 1830 to 1960.

619   Scully, Vincent. AMERICAN ARCHITECTURE AND URBANISM. New
       York: Frederick A. Praeger, 1969. 275 p. Index, Illus.

       A history and interpretation of architectural styles in the
       United States from the earliest times through the late sixties.
       The author draws parallels between architecture and life-
       styles, and treats vernacular as well as public and commer-
       cial architecture. Extensively illustrated with an afterword
       on method and bibliography.

620   "Signs of Life--Venturi/Rauch." ARCHITECTURAL DESIGN 46 (August
       1976): 496-98.

       Photographs and discussion of the Venturi/Rauch exhibit show-
       ing derivative architectural motifs in domestic housing.

621   Stern, Robert A.M. NEW DIRECTIONS IN AMERICAN ARCHITECTURE.
       New Directions in Architecture Series. New York: George Braziller,
       1977. 152 p. Illus., notes, bibliog., index.

       Essays on Kahn, Roche, Rudolph, Johnson, Venturi, Giurgola
       and Charles Moore, with commentary on urban renewal and
       the formal preoccupations of architects.

622   Tobey, G.B. A HISTORY OF LANDSCAPE ARCHITECTURE: THE RELA-
       TIONSHIP OF PEOPLE TO ENVIRONMENT. New York: Elsevier, 1973.
       305 p. Illus., chronologies, bibliog., index.

       A history from ancient times through 1970 of changes made to
       the environment by man, with emphasis on American values
       from discovery to contemporary times. Chapters cover ideas
       of beauty, the Arcadian myth, the city beautiful movement,
       garden cities, the form-function issue, structures and land,
       and perception.

623   Zevi, Bruno. THE MODERN LANGUAGE OF ARCHITECTURE. Seattle:
       University of Washington Press, 1978. 241 p. Illus., index.

A dissent against the classical language of architecture and an attempt to evolve a language of architecture based on semiotic and other analytic perspectives, so that classical form is deconstructed in order to allow for the emergence of an innovative form.

LEISURE

624 Belasco, Warren James. AMERICANS ON THE ROAD: FROM AUTO-CAMP TO MOTEL, 1910-1945. Cambridge: MIT Press, 1979. 288 p. Illus., notes, bibliog., index.

> An excellent study of the origins and development of auto-camping, or "gypsying," and the emergence from about 1925 of motels.

625 Braithwaite, David. FAIRGROUND ARCHITECTURE: THE WORLD OF AMUSEMENT PARKS, CARNIVALS & FAIRS. Excursions into Architecture Series. New York: Praeger, 1968. 195 p. Illus., bibliog., glossary, index.

> Illustrated with photographs, maps, and construction diagrams, the volume considers joy rides, booths and joints, transportation, innovations, and construction and decoration.

626 Brightbill, Charles Kestner. THE CHALLENGE OF LEISURE. Englewood Cliffs, N.J.: Prentice-Hall, 1963. 118 p.

> An interpretation and philosophy of the values of leisure. A chatty, but level-headed account of the uses of leisure in contemporary society which is strong on recreational matters, offering an assessment of programs for the present and the future.

627 Burby, Raymond J. III. RECREATION AND LEISURE IN NEW COM-MUNITIES. Cambridge, Mass.: Ballinger, 1976. 366 p. Appendixes, bibliog., index.

> A questionnaire-based study of recreational service systems in fifteen new communities representing several regions, with chapters on services, administrative practices, resources, recreational preferences, target groups, community planning, and quality of life.

628   Cheek, Neil H., and Burch, William R., Jr. THE SOCIAL ORGANI-
       ZATION OF LEISURE IN HUMAN SOCIETY. New York: Harper and
       Row, 1976. 283 p. Notes, bibliog., index.

       A sociological overview of leisure and its relation to every-
       day life, time segmentation, work, identification, taste,
       locales, myth, sport, and recreation.

629   Cheek, Neil H., Jr.; Field, Donald R.; and Burdge, Rabel J. LEISURE
       AND RECREATION PLACES. Ann Arbor, Mich.: Ann Arbor Science,
       1976. 172 p. Bibliog., index.

       An attempt to discover some of the "underlying dimensions of
       human behavior" in leisure and recreational activities, and
       in particular to identify behavior in such places as parks,
       bowling alleys, and concert halls.

630   Domhoff, G. William. THE BOHEMIAN GROVE AND OTHER RETREATS:
       A STUDY IN RULING-CLASS COHESIVENESS. New York: Harper,
       1974. 250 p.

       An account of retreats of the rich, with an appendix listing
       corporate executives, politicians, and military elite and their
       club affiliations.

631   Dulles, Foster Rhea. A HISTORY OF RECREATION: AMERICA LEARNS
       TO PLAY. New York: D. Appleton-Century, 1965. 441 p. Bibliog.
       essay, notes, index, illus.

       An important contribution toward understanding the development
       of play and recreation in the United States, this volume
       covers Puritan resistance to play, colonial recreations, popu-
       lar drama, P.T. Barnum, spectator sports, fashion, movies,
       autos, and many games, entertainments, and diversions in
       the context of the historical milieu.

632   Durant, Henry. THE PROBLEM OF LEISURE. London: George Rout-
       ledge, 1938. 276 p. Bibliog., index.

       An interesting perspective, on the Anglo-American state of
       leisure in the late 1930s, which explores the British class
       structure, sports, gambling, film, and recreational organiza-
       tions.

633   Faris, John T. ROAMING AMERICAN PLAYGROUNDS. New York:
       Farrar and Rinehart, 1934. 331 p. Index.

       A survey of the attractions throughout the United States in
       the early 1930s. The author notes beaches, taverns, fishing
       spots, geological sites, scenic highways, and hunting areas;
       he describes national forests, steamboat trips, winter sport

locales, and many other places for those living in the time of the Depression to explore.

634 Gregory, Ruth W. ANNIVERSARIES AND HOLIDAYS. Rev. ed. Chicago: American Library Association, 1975. 246 p.

A bibliography of 1,002 annotated items, together with descriptions of particular fixed and moveable anniversary and holiday dates.

635 Grimes, Ronald L. SYMBOL AND CONQUEST: PUBLIC RITUAL AND DRAMA IN SANTE FE, NEW MEXICO. Ithaca, N.Y.: Cornell University Press, 1976. 336 p. Bibliog., index.

A study of the icons, symbols, emblems, insignia, and commercial imagery associated with the Indian and Hispanic traditions in the city, together with Anglo elaborations and contributions. The focus is on fiesta and processional symbolism, especially symbols of power, and other performances such as pageants and melodramas. Our Lady of the Conquest and the fiesta are emphasized.

636 Jury, Mark. PLAYTIME! AMERICANS AT LEISURE. New York: Harcourt Brace Jovanovich, 1977. 192 p. Illus.

This striking photographic essay and text illustrate the relationships of leisure activities to identity and life-style, as well as to needs and interests.

637 Kaplan, Max. LEISURE: THEORY AND POLICY. New York: Wiley, 1975. 444 p. Notes, charts, index.

An extensive discussion of leisure theory and the practice of leisure research within a set of models that relate leisure to other aspects of society.

638 Keown, Ean M. LOVERS' GUIDE TO AMERICA. New York: Collier; Macmillan, 1974. 325 p. Illus.

Annotated list of about 135 inns and hotels--offering relative seclusion from everyday hassles and having a pleasing environment--mostly for the well-to-do.

639 Kerr, Walter. THE DECLINE OF PLEASURE. New York: Simon and Schuster, 1962. 319 p.

A personal essay on the failure of the dream of leisure.

640 Lavery, Patrick, ed. RECREATIONAL GEOGRAPHY. New York: John Wiley and Sons, 1974. 335 p. Illus., bibliog.

A collection of essays on demand, perception of values in recreation, routing patterns, urban parks, national parks, forest lands, resorts, water recreation management, economic considerations, ecology, and planning.

641 Linn, Edward A. BIG JULIE OF VEGAS. New York: Walker, 1974. 217 p.

Biography of Julie Weintraub, a tour guide for the Dunes Hotel in Las Vegas.

642 Logan, Harry Britton. A TRAVELER'S GUIDE TO NORTH AMERICAN GARDENS. New York: Scribner's, 1974. 253 p. Illus., index.

Accounts of the major gardens which are available to the public in the fifty states, Puerto Rico, the Virgin Islands, and Canada, with notes on garden societies.

643 Lundberg, George A.; Komaravsky, Mirra; and McInerny, Mary Alice. LEISURE: A SUBURBAN-STUDY. New York: Columbia University Press, 1934. 396 p. Notes, tables, bibliog., index.

Based on field work carried out between January 1932 and April 1933, this is a useful contribution to understanding leisure in relation to quantified socioeconomic factors in suburban Westchester County, New York. Although Lundberg is convinced that the choices for improving "adjustment to the environment" are confined to manipulating the environment or conditioning the individual, his ideal of leisure remains humanistic and his general comments in the introduction relate to contemporary society. Chapters consider the suburban social setting, a range of organizations devoted to leisure activities, quantitative measures of leisure time, family, church, schools, the arts, adult education, and the community's responsibility for the extent and quality of leisure.

644 Myers, Robert J., with the editors of Hallmark Cards. CELEBRATIONS: THE COMPLETE BOOK OF AMERICAN HOLIDAYS. Garden City, N.Y.: Doubleday, 1972. 386 p. Bibliog., illus., index.

Origins, traditions, and gifting practices associated with forty-five American holidays are covered in essays of several pages each, with brief entries for fifteen others, and a list of dates for fifty-eight more.

645 Owen, John D. THE PRICE OF LEISURE. Montreal: McGill-Queen's University Press, 1970. 169 p. Bibliog.

A study of leisure time and the role played in the determination of leisure time by the commercial recreation industry, education, commuting, working conditions, fatigue, productive consumption, and unemployment.

646 Patten, Marjorie. THE ARTS WORKSHOP OF RURAL AMERICA: A STUDY OF THE RURAL ARTS PROGRAM OF THE AGRICULTURAL EXTENSION SERVICE. New York: Columbia University Press, 1937. 202 p.

A supportive study of the use of extension programs for the development of drama, music, hobbies, arts and crafts, and art exhibitions. The study concludes with the belief that such programs will continue to thrive and attract more sophisticated guidance.

647 Peck, Esther Alice. A CONSERVATIVE GENERATION'S AMUSEMENTS: A PHASE OF CONNECTICUT'S SOCIAL HISTORY. Bangor, Maine: Jordan-Frost Printing Co., 1938. 119 p. Notes, bibliog., index.

An account of exhibitions, holiday observances, music and dancing, lectures and readings, and informal activities from 1818 to about 1850.

648 THE SPORTING SET. Leisure Class in America Collection. New York: Arno Press, 1975. Irregular pagination.

Reprints of early essays: Ruth Painter's "Tavern Amusements in Eighteenth Century America" (1916); Frederic Paxon's "The Rise of Sport" (1919); John Krout's "Some Reflections on the Rise of American Sport" (1928); George Wright's "Sketch of National Game of Baseball" (1920); Andrew Davis's "College Athletics" (1883); Aleck Quest's "The Fast Set at Harvard University" (1888); Ira Hollis's "Inter-Collegiate Athletics" (1902); Robert Dunn's "The Country Club" (1905); and Alfred Lewis's "The Racing Game" (1907).

649 Steiner, Jesse Frederick. AMERICANS AT PLAY: RECENT TRENDS IN RECREATION AND LEISURE TIME ACTIVITIES. New York: McGraw-Hill, 1933. 201 p. Tables, notes, index.

A statistical history of playgrounds and parks, outdoor sports, spectacle sports, commercial amusements, rural recreation, administration of facilities, and expenditures.

650 Taraporevala, Dinoo Jal. LEISURE TIME EXPENDITURES: THE DEMAND FOR PARTICIPANT SPORTS IN THE UNITED STATES. Bombay: D.B. Taraporevala Sons, 1968. 206 p. Bibliog., appendixes.

Statistical analysis of leisure participation.

651 Thomas, Bill. TRIPPING IN AMERICA: OFF THE BEATEN TRACK. Radnor, Pa.: Chilton, 1974. 223 p. Illus.

Out-of-the-way places and attractions in America.

652 Torbert, William R., and Rogers, Malcolm P. BEING FOR THE MOST PART PUPPETS; INTERACTIONS AMONG MEN'S LABOR, LEISURE AND POLITICS. Cambridge, Mass.: Schenkman Publishing Co.; distributed by General Learning Press, Morristown, N.J., 1973. 193 p. Charts, bibliog.

A questionnaire-based study of the relationship between work and leisure, particularly among blue-collar workers.

653 Tunnard, Christopher. A WORLD WITH A VIEW: AN INQUIRY INTO THE NATURE OF SCENIC VALUES. New Haven, Conn.: Yale University Press, 1978. 196 p. Notes, illus., index.

An exploration of the paradigms of aesthetic values through consideration of landscapes in relation to science, art, scenic preservation, gardens, and townscapes as these appear in paintings.

654 Van der Zee, John. THE GREATEST MEN'S PARTY ON EARTH: INSIDE BOHEMIAN GROVE. New York: Harcourt, 1974. 182 p. Bibliog.

Account of the club that changed from an artist's colony to a retreat for rich executives.

655 Wrenn, Charles Gilbert, and Harley, D.L. TIME ON THEIR HANDS: A REPORT ON LEISURE, RECREATION AND YOUNG PEOPLE. Washington, D.C.: American Council on Education, 1941. 266 p. Illus., index.

Discussion, with recommendations, of the state of constructive recreation as administered by various public and private organizations.

GAMES

656 Abrahams, Roger D., ed. JUMP-ROPE RHYMES: A DICTIONARY.
Austin: University of Texas Press, for the American Folklore Society,
1969. 228 p. Bibliog.

    A collection of 619 rhymes with notes on sources and cross-
references. Appendixes list names and terms of games, and
proper names appearing in the rhymes.

657 Arpad, Joseph J. "The Fight Story: Quotation and Originality in Native
American Humor." JOURNAL OF THE FOLKLORE INSTITUTE 10, no. 3
(1973): 141-72.

    An examination of the oral roots and popular literary tradi-
tions associated with the often-quoted fight story in the early
nineteenth century.

658 Asbury, Herbert. SUCKER'S PROGRESS: AN INFORMAL HISTORY OF
GAMBLING IN AMERICA FROM THE COLONIES TO CANFIELD. New
York: Dodd, Mead, 1938. 493 p. Bibliog., index.

    Includes the history through the nineteenth century of casino
games, lotteries, a survey of the spread of gambling into the
western territories with the pioneers, and chapters on John
Morrissey and Richard Canfield.

659 Avedon, Elliott M., and Sutton-Smith, Brian. THE STUDY OF GAMES.
New York: J. Wiley, 1971. 530 p. Bibliog.

    Both an anthology of interpretations and bibliography of games,
this volume is also an anthropological introduction to the
study of games and gaming.

660 Bellew, Frank. THE ART OF AMUSING. Popular Culture in America
1800-1925. New York: Carleton, 1866. Reprint. New York: Arno
Press, 1974. 302 p. Illus.

    An illustrated guide to tricks, games, puzzles, and other
entertainments.

661 Brady, Maxine. THE MONOPOLY BOOK. New York: McKay, 1975. 144 p.

On playing the game; some statistics, information.

662 CONTEMPORARY GAMES: DIRECTORY. Vol. 1. Detroit: Gale Research Co., 1973. 560 p. Index, bibliog.

Covers about nine hundred games, mostly simulations.

663 DICTIONNAIRE DES JEUX. Edited by René Alleau. Paris: Firmin-Didot, 1964. 555 p. Illus., index.

An encyclopedia of world games and sports.

664 Cors, Paul B. RAILROADS. Spare Time Guides: Information Sources for Hobbies and Recreation. Littleton, Colo.: Libraries Unlimited, 1975. 152 p. Index.

Selected, annotated bibliography of railroadiana.

665 Frey, Richard, and Truscott, Alan F. OFFICIAL ENCYCLOPEDIA OF BRIDGE. Rev. ed. New York: Crown, 1976. 858 p. Illus., stat., lists, bibliog.

Contains definitions, historical and strategic information, biographies, tournament results.

666 Fritzsch, Karl Ewald, and Bachmann, Manfred. AN ILLUSTRATED HISTORY OF TOYS. London: Abbey Library, 1965. 194 p. Bibliog., illus.

Primarily a history of German toys, but with many counterparts in America and elsewhere.

667 Fry, William F., Jr. SWEET MADNESS: A STUDY OF HUMOR. Palo Alto, Calif.: Pacific Books, 1963. 178 p. Bibliog.

A study of the context for humor and its similarities to and differences from play.

668 Gordon, Lesley. PEEPSHOW INTO PARADISE: A HISTORY OF CHILDREN'S TOYS. London: George G. Harrap, 1953. 264 p. Illus., bibliog., museum list, index.

A survey of toys and games from primitive and classical cultures through types of toys and notes on international styles.

669 Hall, Carrie A., and Kretsinger, Rose G. THE ROMANCE OF THE

PATCHWORK QUILT IN AMERICA IN THREE PARTS. Part 1: HISTORY AND QUILT PATCHES; Part 2: QUILTS--ANTIQUE AND MODERN; Part 3: QUILTING AND QUILTING DESIGNS. Caldwell, Idaho: Caxton Printers, 1935. 299 p. Illus., index.

A brief history of the craft.

670 Hannas, Linda. THE ENGLISH JIGSAW PUZZLE, 1760-1890, WITH A DESCRIPTIVE CHECK-LIST OF PUZZLES IN THE MUSEUMS OF GREAT BRITAIN AND THE AUTHOR'S COLLECTION. London: Wayland Publishers, 1972. 164 p. Illus., puzzle checklist, index, bibliog.

Historical background, the inventor, eighteenth- and nineteenth-century dissections, publishers, the trade, puzzles in education, and literature.

671 Hargrave, Catherine Perry. A HISTORY OF PLAYING CARDS AND A BIBLIOGRAPHY OF CARDS AND GAMING. New York: Houghton Mifflin, 1930. Reprint. New York: Dover, 1966. 462 p. Illus., bibliog., index.

An international history with the U.S. chapter indicating early sales, styles, and common card games.

672 Hartt, Rollin Lynde. THE PEOPLE AT PLAY: EXCURSIONS IN THE HUMOR AND PHILOSOPHY OF POPULAR AMUSEMENTS. Boston: Houghton Mifflin, 1909. 316 p. Illus.

A sympathetic investigation of burlesque, amusement parks, dime museums, moving pictures, melodrama, dating habits, the East Gissing Street popular arts, and baseball.

673 Jackson, Mrs. F. Nevill [Emily]. TOYS OF OTHER DAYS. New York: Scribner's, 1908. Reprint. New York: Benjamin Blom, 1968. 309 p. Index, illus.

A history of the influence of toys on the imagination, with chapters on various dolls and accessories, silver and pewter toys, war toys, animal toys, percussion toys, rattles, ball games, sacred and education toys, board games, kites and fireworks, and mechanical toys.

674 Kagan, Diane, and Joseph, Meryl. WHO WON SECOND PLACE AT OMAHA? A JOURNEY. New York: Random House, 1975. 86 p. Illus.

Survey of the doll collection of Mrs. Lenon Holder Hoyte, an unusual collector.

675 Ludovici, Laurence J. THE ITCH FOR PLAY: GAMBLERS AND GAM-

BLING IN HIGH LIFE AND LOW LIFE. London: Jarrolds, 1962. 255 p. Illus.

> A history of gambling and various gaming styles with emphasis on England.

676 McClintock, Inez, and McClintock, Marshall. TOYS IN AMERICA. Washington, D.C.: Public Affairs Press, 1961. 480 p. Illus., bibliog., directory of pre-1900 toy manufacturers, index.

> Presented as a topical history, the volume surveys colonial play, games after the Revolution, toy craftsmen and factories, early nineteenth-century Christmas toys, mechanical toys, toys oriented to sports, vehicles, and other interests of the latter nineteenth century; metal toys, board games, sound effects, teddy bears, the promotion of toys, competition among manufacturers, mass market toys, and prospects for the future.

677 McNamara, Brooks. STEP RIGHT UP. New York: Doubleday, 1975. 233 p. Bibliog.

> On medicine shows to 1951.

678 Mebane, John. COLLECTING NOSTALGIA: THE FIRST GUIDE TO THE ANTIQUES OF THE 30'S AND 40'S. New Rochelle, N.Y.: Arlington House, 1972. 367 p. Directory of clubs, bibliog., index.

> Good informal topical study of the popular artifacts of the fifties written for dealers. Included are sections on art and photography, autographs, business antiques, ceramics, collectibles of Coca-Cola, entertainment, furniture, general background, glass, politics, smoking accessories, toys, transportation, Walt Disney collectibles, and World War II.

679 Messick, Hank, and Goldblatt, Burt. THE ONLY GAME IN TOWN: AN ILLUSTRATED HISTORY OF GAMBLING. New York: Thomas Y. Crowell, 1976. 214 p. Index.

> Generously illustrated history of some of the sensational aspects of gambling. The authors suggest that gambling may have begun in the garden of Eden, and cite mythical and religious sources to indicate its universality. The volume covers George Washington's wagers, the American frontier, organized gambling in the twentieth century, and the development of gaming devices.

680 Murray, H.J.R. A HISTORY OF BOARD-GAMES OTHER THAN CHESS. Oxford, Engl.: Clarendon Press, 1952. 267 p. Illus.

> A survey of board games throughout the world, with information on playing and history, and an attempt to "investigate

the ultimate origin of board-games in general and the circumstances which made possible their invention." The author
does not consider contemporary commercially derived games.

681 Nueckel, Susan, ed. SELECTED GUIDE TO SPORTS AND RECREATION
BOOKS. New York: Fleet Press Corp., 1974. 168 p. Directory of
publishers, index.

Contains 1,233 references to how-to books on sports and
games.

682 Packard, Vance. THE SEXUAL WILDERNESS: THE CONTEMPORARY
UNHEAVAL IN MALE-FEMALE RELATIONSHIPS. New York: David
McKay, 1968. 553 p. Notes, index.

Beginning with a discussion of six forces that affect the context of sexual relations in contemporary America (contracep-
tives, social changes brought about by technology, changes
in the age distribution of the population, the expansion of
higher education, changes in ideals, beliefs and national
mood, and the effects of wars and international tensions on
individuals), Packard surveys some of the changes that are
taking place in current society and speculates on possible
futures. Appendixes list tables regarding sexual practices.

683 Phelan, Rev. John J. POOL, BILLIARDS AND BOWLING ALLEYS AS
A PHASE OF COMMERCIALIZED AMUSEMENTS IN TOLEDO, OHIO.
Social Survey Series 1. Toledo: Little Book Press, 1919. 195 p. Illus.

A valuable handbook of the commercial vices available to
minors in Toledo, Ohio, in 1919, together with results of a
questionnaire and a digest of the ordinances of sixty-two
cities regulating pool, billiards, and bowling alleys.

684 Scarne, John. SCARNE'S ENCYCLOPEDIA OF GAMES. New York:
Harper and Row, 1973. 628 p. Illus., glossary, index.

Rules and strategies for over one thousand parlor, board,
and table games, with chapters on cheating, guessing games,
and lotteries.

685 Sherrill, Robert. THE SATURDAY NIGHT SPECIAL. New York: Charterhouse, 1973. 338 p. Illus.

Contains chapters on gun collectors, gun fighter myths, and
the relationship between the National Rifle Association and
military.

686 Shields, Joyce F. MAKE IT: AN INDEX TO PROJECTS AND MA-
TERIALS. Metuchen, N.J.: Scarecrow Press, 1975. 477 p.

Index to projects found in about 475 crafts books published from 1968 through 1973.

687   Wagenvoord, James. HANGIN'OUT: CITY KIDS, CITY GAMES. New York: Lippincott, 1974. 120 p. Illus.

Photographic essay on kids playing games in the city.

688   Wilgus, D.K., and Rosenberg, Bruce A. "A Modern Medieval Story: 'The Soldier's Deck of Cards.'" In MEDIEVAL LITERATURE AND FOLKLORE STUDIES: ESSAYS IN HONOR OF FRANCIS LEE UTLEY, edited by Jerome Mandel and Bruce A. Rosenberg, pp. 291-303. New Brunswick, N.J.: Rutgers University Press, 1970. 408 p. Illus.

SPORTS

689 Alderman, Richard B. PSYCHOLOGICAL BEHAVIOR IN SPORT. Philadelphia: Saunders, 1974. 280 p. Bibliog., index.

Develops the psychology of play, the social-psychological
aspects of games, sport and physical activity, the psychology
of competition; personality and sports involvement; and aggression, achievement, and application in sport.

690 Allen, Lee. THE WORLD SERIES: THE STORY OF BASEBALL'S ANNUAL
CHAMPIONSHIP. New York: Putnam, 1969. 253 p.

An account based on secondary sources and interviews.

691 ALMANAC 1979: SPORTS AND GAMES. New York: Facts on File,
1979. 442 p.

Statistics and summaries for 1978 or 1977-78 seasons for about
160 individual and team sports and games. Profiles major
professional and amateur events through statistics and other
data, and provides a five-page section of obituary notes for
1978.

692 Anderson, Bob, ed. SPORTSOURCE. Mountain View, Calif.: World
Publications, 1975. 430 p. Illus.

Accounts, often with further references, of over two hundred
sports, games, and related matters such as magic; folk, jazz
and belly dancing; circus skills; cheerleading; beachcombing;
and hitchhiking.

693 Angell, Roger. THE SUMMER GAME. New York: Viking Press, 1972.
303 p.

A decade of baseball from March 1962 to 1971, based on
Angell's NEW YORKER pieces.

694 THE ANTHROPOLOGICAL STUDY OF PLAY: PROBLEMS AND PROS-
PECTS. Proceedings of the First Annual Meeting of the Association
for the Anthropological Study of Play. Edited by David F. Lancy and
B. Allan Tindall. Cornwall, N.Y.: Leisure Press, 1976. 245 p.

> Twenty-seven essays on play, including Susan Boyd on poker,
> Frank Manning on Pentecostal play, and Lawrence La Fave
> and Roger Mannell on ethnic humor and humor judgments.
> An appendix contains the organization's constitution.

695 Appel, Martin, and Goldblatt, Burt. BASEBALL'S BEST: THE HALL OF
FAME GALLERY. New York: McGraw-Hill, 1977. 420 p. Illus.

> Profiles and photographs of inductees.

696 Associated Press. THE SPORTS IMMORTALS. Englewood Cliffs, N.J.:
Prentice-Hall, 1972. 320 p. Illus.

> Brief biographical pieces by various hands on fifty-one sports
> heroes.

697 Athletic Institute, Chicago. SPORTS FILM GUIDE: A LISTING OF
OVER 2,000 16MM FILMS. 3d ed. Chicago: n.d. 76 p.

> A guide to films on training and appreciation.

698 Baillie-Grohman, William Adolph. SPORT IN ART: AN ICONOGRAPHY
OF SPORT DURING FOUR HUNDRED YEARS FROM THE BEGINNING OF
THE FIFTEENTH TO THE END OF THE EIGHTEENTH CENTURIES. New
York: Benjamin Blom, 1969. 422 p. Index, notes on artists, illus.

> History of sport art that focuses on major artists and topical
> themes.

699 Ball, Donald W., and Loy, John W., eds. SPORT AND THE SOCIAL
ORDER: CONTRIBUTIONS TO THE SOCIOLOGY OF SPORT. Reading,
Mass.: Addison-Wesley, 1975. 574 p. Bibliog.

> Chapters on geographical aspects, social differentiation, poli-
> tics, consumerism, violence, subcultures, college coaches,
> professional baseball and hockey players' careers, and wres-
> tlers' "identity work-up." With overviews of sociological study
> and of methodology.

700 Balter, Sam, and Rice, Cy. ONE FOR THE BOOK OF SPORTS. New
York: Citadel Press, 1955. 148 p.

> A youth's book of brief accounts of sports events and per-
> formers.

701 Barkow, Al. GOLF'S GOLDEN GRIND: THE HISTORY OF THE TOUR. New York: Harcourt, Brace, 1974. 310 p. Photos, index.

History of the golf tour.

702 Bartlett, Arthur. BASEBALL AND MR. SPALDING: THE HISTORY AND ROMANCE OF BASEBALL. New York: Farrar, Straus and Young, 1951. 295 p.

A history of the sport based on newspaper accounts.

703 BASEBALL YEAR AND NOTE BOOK. MAJOR LEAGUE. St. Petersburg, Fla.: Baseball Blue Book, 1912-- . Annual.

704 Beisser, Arnold R. THE MADNESS IN SPORTS. 2d ed. Bowie, Md.: Charles Press, 1977. 207 p.

A psychosocial approach to sports that examines ritual, sea-sonal masculinity rites, fans, winning, tribal fandom, stars, and related matters.

705 Beddoes, Richard; Fischler, Stan; and Gitler, Ira. HOCKEY! THE STORY OF THE WORLD'S FASTEST SPORT. New York: Macmillan, 1969. 384 p. Records, photos, index.

Accounts of the teams, players, game highlights, and con-troversies.

706 Benagh, Jim. MAKING IT TO #1: HOW COLLEGE FOOTBALL AND BASKETBALL TEAMS GET THERE. New York: Dodd, Mead, 1976. 302 p. Bibliog., chronology of NCAA sanctions, index.

A critique of the practices regarding sports in universities and colleges, with chapters on recruiting, coaching, sports dynasties, and related matters.

707 THE BEST OF SPORTS ILLUSTRATED. Boston: Little, Brown, 1973. 213 p. Illus.

A collection of eleven articles from the magazine.

708 BEST SPORTS STORIES, 1980: A PANORAMA OF THE 1978 SPORTS WORLD INCLUDING THE 1978 CHAMPIONS OF ALL SPORTS, WITH THE YEAR'S TOP PHOTOGRAPHS. Edited by Irving T. Marsh and Edward Ehre. New York: E.P. Dutton, 1981. 258 p. Photos., lists.

Contains best news coverage, news features, magazine stories, and other articles representing all major sports. The 1979 edition is representative of this annual, which began in 1944.

709 Betts, John Rickards. AMERICA'S SPORTING HERITAGE, 1850–1950.
Addison-Wesley Series in the Social Significance of Sport. Reading,
Mass.: Addison-Wesley, 1974. 428 p. Index, bibliog., notes.

A social and cultural history, which focuses on the rise of
class sports, the development of organized sports related to
social stratification, technology, and urbanization; with the
effects of the Depression and World War II on participation,
and the interrelationship of sport with art, business, religion,
and education.

710 Boyle, Robert H. SPORT--MIRROR OF AMERICAN LIFE. Boston: Little,
Brown, 1963. 293 p. Bibliog., index.

Exploration of the impact of sports on American culture through
examination of class-oriented sports. Included are chapters on
the rise of sport, the psychology of sport, Negro baseball
players, the hot-rod cult, country clubs, the Harvard-Yale
weekend, and the Merriwell stories. Appendixes provide 1962
statistics for attendance, sports consumer goods, together with
a graph of consumer expenditures for sporting goods since 1929.

711 Brasch, R. HOW DID SPORTS BEGIN? A LOOK INTO THE ORIGINS
OF MAN AT PLAY. London: Longmans, 1972. 279 p. Illus., index.

Useful short discussions of forty-four sports and their possible
origins.

712 Brohm, Jean-Marie. SPORT: A PRISON OF MEASURED TIME. Translated by Ian Fraser. London: Ink Links, 1978. 185 p.

A collection of critical essays first published in France on
the political uses of sport, primarily by repressive societies.
The essays are keyed to contemporary regimes in Europe and
Argentina, with several dealing with the Olympics.

713 Burkholder, Ed. BASEBALL IMMORTALS. Boston: Christopher, 1955.
136 p.

A book for youth of biographical sketches of twenty-five baseball personalities.

714 Butt, Dorcas Susan. PSYCHOLOGY OF SPORT: THE BEHAVIOR,
MOTIVATION, PERSONALITY, AND PERFORMANCE OF ATHLETES.
New York: Van Nostrand Reinhold, 1976. 196 p. Sketches, bibliog.,
index.

A useful introduction to the broad psychological perspective
on sport, with chapters on psychological and social motivation, personality, sex roles, culture, improving performance,
and social change.

715 Carrick, Peter. ALL HELL AND AUTOCROSS--MORE HELL AND RALLYCROSS. London: Pelham, 1971. 160 p. Illus., records, index.

A history and description of the sport, primarily as practiced in England.

716 Carrick, Robert W. THE PICTORIAL HISTORY OF THE AMERICA'S CUP RACES. New York: Viking, 1964. 194 p. Illus., bibliog., records.

History of the development of the sport, featuring the great races.

717 Carrick, Robert W., and Rosenfeld, Stanley Z. DEFENDING THE AMERICA'S CUP. New York: Knopf, 1969. 189 p. Illus.

The story of the INTREPID and its 1967 crew.

718 Cascio, Chuck. SOCCER U.S.A. Washington, D.C.: R.B. Luce, distributed by McKay, 1975. 220 p. Illus.

A survey history of soccer, with highlights on heroes, American soccer to 1968, the renaissance after 1968, and discussion of the sport's appeal.

719 Chalk, Ocania. BLACK COLLEGE SPORT. New York: Dodd-Mead, 1976. 376 p. Index.

A determined examination of the emergence of black stars on white college teams, and the stars of black college teams in baseball, basketball, football, and track and field.

720 Chew, Peter. THE KENTUCKY DERBY: THE FIRST 100 YEARS. Boston: Houghton, 1974. 303 p. Illus., index, notes, statistics.

A heavily illustrated history of the race.

721 Coakley, Jay J. SPORT IN SOCIETY: ISSUES AND CONTROVERSIES. St. Louis: Mosby, 1978. 349 p. Illus., bibliog., index.

The eleven issues considered include sport as inspiration or opiate, competition, youth sports, problems of sports in educational institutions, exploitation or entertainment in professional sports, coaches, women, blacks, and the future.

722 Coffin, Tristram P. THE OLD BALL GAME: BASEBALL IN FOLKLORE AND FICTION. New York: Herder and Herder, 1971. p. 206. Index.

An informal introduction to the appeal of baseball, with chapters on its emergence, the framework for its folklore, words and phrases, hero making, folk types in the game, and baseball in juvenile, pulp, and mainstream fiction.

723 Cohane, Tim. BYPATHS OF GLORY: A SPORTSWRITER LOOKS BACK.
New York: Harper and Row, 1963. 239 p.

Reminiscences on such sports personalities as Vince Lombardi,
Rocky Marciano, Duffy Daugherty and others from many sports,
as well as the events that made these figures famous.

724 Cohen, Marvin. BASEBALL THE BEAUTIFUL: DECODING THE DIAMOND.
Introduction by Jim Bouton. Illustrated by Paul Spina. New York:
Links Books, 1974. 120 p. Illus.

An appreciation and interpretation.

725 Corum, Bill. OFF AND RUNNING. Edited by Arthur Mann. New
York: Holt, 1959. 303 p.

Reminiscences of a sportswriter.

726 Cozens, Frederick W., and Stumpf, Florence Scovil. SPORTS IN
AMERICAN LIFE. Chicago: University of Chicago Press, 1953. 366 p.
Notes, index.

An ambitious attempt to provide a social history of sports in
modern America through their relationships to the family,
commerce, labor, industry, schools, churches, media coverage, vehicles, government interests, wartime, democratization, ideology and jargon, race relations, international aspects, and the problems of spectator sports in a democracy.

727 Cummings, Parke, ed. THE DICTIONARY OF SPORTS. New York:
A.S. Barnes, 1949. 472 p.

Definitions for about fifty sports, more extensive than those
provided by Salak (no. 866), with appendixes that isolate
terms by individual sports, provide sample box scores, code
signals for officials in basketball and football, tournament
pairings, and the weight-for-age scale for horse racing.

728 Cutter, Robert, and Fendell, Bob. THE ENCYCLOPEDIA OF AUTO
RACING GREATS. Englewood Cliffs, N.J.: Prentice-Hall, 1973.
675 p. Illus.

Total of 550 biographical articles.

729 Daley, Arthur. SPORTS OF THE TIMES. New York: Dutton, 1959.
270 p.

A collection of brief pieces from Daley's NEW YORK TIMES
columns, mostly on personalities from baseball, but many on
boxing, football, track, golf, racing, and other sports.

730   Danzig, Allison, and Brandwein, Peter, eds. SPORT'S GOLDEN AGE: A CLOSE-UP OF THE FABULOUS TWENTIES. New York: Harper, 1948. 296 p.

> Journalists write brief surveys of the major contributions to many sports, with regional coverage for football, and national coverage for other major sports for the decade.

731   Davis, Mac. THE GIANT BOOK OF SPORTS. New York: Grosset and Dunlap, 1967. 191 p.

> A child's book of biographical sketches.

732   DeKoven, Bernard. THE WELL-PLAYED GAME: A PLAYER'S PHILOSO-PHY. Garden City, N.Y.: Anchor, 1978. 183 p.

> An informal guide to sports and sportsmanship, with advice for players.

733   Demmert, Henry G. THE ECONOMICS OF PROFESSIONAL TEAM SPORTS. Lexington, Mass.: Lexington Books, 1973. 106 p. Notes, bibliog., index, statistics.

> An economic analysis of baseball, football, basketball, and hockey, taking into consideration their special legal status and offering suggestions for public policy.

734   Denlinger, Ken, and Shapiro, Len. ATHLETES FOR SALE. New York: Crowell, 1975. 262 p.

> The emphasis of the book, by reporters of the WASHINGTON POST, is on recruiting of college and professional athletes. Includes a chapter on early recruiting practices, but the focus is on contemporary athletics.

735   Deutsch, Jordan A., et al., comps. THE SCRAPBOOK HISTORY OF BASEBALL. New York: Bobbs-Merrill, 1975. 320 p. Illus.

> Ephemera from 1876 to 1974.

736   Devaney, John, and Goldblatt, Burt. THE WORLD SERIES: A COM-PLETE PICTORIAL HISTORY. Chicago: Rand McNally, 1976. 384 p. Illus., statistics.

> A year-by-year account of the series from 1903 to date of publication.

737   Dickey, Glenn. THE JOCK EMPIRE: ITS RISE AND DESERVED FALL. Radnor, Pa.: Chilton Book Co., 1974. 235 p. Index.

> An informal critique of the sporting life that considers sex,

chauvinism, myth making, finances, contemporary sports
personalities, sportswriters, sports management, and racism.

738 Dickinson, John. A BEHAVIORAL ANALYSIS OF SPORT. Princeton,
N.J.: Princeton Book Company, 1977. 134 p. Bibliog., index.

Emphasis on sports determinants, deterrents to participation,
skill acquisition, social phenomena, and the implications of
behavioral technology goals.

739 Dugdale, John. GREAT MOTOR SPORT OF THE THIRTIES: A PERSONAL
ACCOUNT. New York: Two Continents, 1977. 256 p. Illus., index.

An account of the men, machines, and racing organizations
of the 1930s, with emphasis on British competitors and cars.

740 Dunning, Eric, comp. SPORT: READINGS FROM A SOCIOLOGICAL
PERSPECTIVE. Toronto: University of Toronto Press, 1972. 382 p.
Notes, index.

Essays are divided into concepts and theories, historical development, and a general section with subsections on socialization, class and race, occupation, and social control.

741 Durant, John. THE HEAVYWEIGHT CHAMPIONS. 6th ed. New York:
Hastings, 1976. 244 p. Illus., glossary, index, records.

Accounts of boxing greats through the ages, from bare-knuckle
champions to contemporary fighters.

742 _____. HIGHLIGHTS OF THE OLYMPICS FROM ANCIENT TIMES TO
THE PRESENT. 5th ed. New York: Hastings House, 1977. 240 p.
Records, illus., index.

Features recent games, together with stars of the past.

743 _____. HIGHLIGHTS OF THE WORLD SERIES. New York: Hastings
House, 1963. 187 p. Glossary, illus., index.

A series of pieces that seize on the dramatic moments, from
the first World Series to its "new look" after 1959.

744 _____. THE STORY OF BASEBALL IN WORDS AND PICTURES. 3d ed.
New York: Hastings House, 1973. 312 p. Index, statistics, illus.

An informal history of the game.

745 _____. YESTERDAY IN SPORTS: MEMORABLE GLIMPSES OF THE
PAST AS SELECTED FROM THE PAGES OF SPORTS ILLUSTRATED. New
York: A.S. Barnes, 1956. 136 p. Illus.

A collection of brief pieces on historical events and curiosities relating to many sports.

746   Durant, John, and Bettmann, Otto. PICTORIAL HISTORY OF AMERICAN SPORTS, FROM COLONIAL TIMES TO THE PRESENT. New York: A.S. Barnes, 1952. 280 p. Illus., index.

A decade-by-decade account of the rise of sport in America from 1607 to 1952, with sketches, cartoons, photographs, and a brief text.

747   Durso, Joseph. THE ALL-AMERICAN DOLLAR: THE BIG BUSINESS OF SPORTS. Boston: Houghton Mifflin, 1971. 294 p. Index.

Discusses through anecdotes, personalities, and statistics how professional sports were revolutionized by money in the late sixties. Durso reports on television's influence, the escalation of purses in football, racing, baseball, golf, and other sports.

748   _____. CASEY: THE LIFE AND LEGEND OF CHARLES DILLON STENGEL. Englewood Cliffs, N.J.: Prentice-Hall, 1967. 211 p. Index, statistics, photos.

A biography.

749   _____. THE DAYS OF MR. McGRAW. Englewood Cliffs, N.J.: Prentice-Hall, 1969. 243 p. Records, photos., index.

A biography of John J. McGraw and his career as a player and manager from 1891 to 1932.

750   _____. MADISON SQUARE GARDEN: ONE HUNDRED YEARS OF HISTORY. New York: Simon and Schuster, 1979. 255 p. Illus.

A pictorial survey of the history of the three arenas called Madison Square Garden and their attractions.

751   _____. YANKEE STADIUM: FIFTY YEARS OF DRAMA. Boston: Houghton Mifflin, 1972. 155 p. Illus.

A pictorial history of the stadium, major events, and the fans.

752   Durso, Joseph, and the New York Times Sports Department. THE SPORTS FACTORY: AN INVESTIGATION INTO COLLEGE SPORTS. New York: Quadrangle, distributed by Harper, 1975. 207 p. Illus., index.

Draws on the reports in the NEW YORK TIMES and from the Carnegie Foundation Report of 1929 and the 1974 Carnegie-Ford Foundation report to discuss the social and economic costs of college athletics.

753 Edwards, Harry. SOCIOLOGY OF SPORT. Homewood, Ill.: Dorsey Press, 1973. 395 p. Notes, bibliog., methodological appendix, index.

> Discusses definition; the creed with respect to the coach, athlete, fan, economics, related beliefs, and social change. Focus is on the relation of sports to American ideology.

754 Eitzen, D. Stanley, and Sage, George H. SOCIOLOGY OF AMERICAN SPORT. Dubuque, Iowa: W.C. Brown Co., 1978. 337 p. Chapter notes, index.

> A textbook that considers the influences on sport, with chapters on sport and values, education, religion, politics, economics, social stratification and mobility, racism, women, and trends in sports.

755 Emrich, Linn. THE COMPLETE BOOK OF SKY SPORTS. New York: Macmillan, 1970. 208 p. Illus., bibliog., glossary, index.

> Primer of sky sports, including parachuting, soaring, balloon draft, gyrocraft, and power plane fundamentals.

756 Enhagen, Carl Olof. SPORTS STAMPS. New York: Arco, 1961. 275 p. Illus., charts.

> Handbook of international issues for philatelists.

757 Fetros, John G. THIS DAY IN SPORTS: A DIARY OF MAJOR SPORTS EVENTS. Novato, Calif.: Newton K. Gregg, 1974. 264 p.

> Daily record of sporting events.

758 Fischler, Stan, and Baliotti, Dan. THIS IS HOCKEY. Englewood Cliffs, N.J.: Prentice-Hall, 1975. 224 p. Illus.

> Lavishly illustrated discussion of the professional game.

759 Fischler, Stan, and Fischler, Shirley. FISCHLER'S HOCKEY ENCYCLO-PEDIA. New York: Crowell, 1975. 628 p. Photos.

> Biographical sketches of one thousand hockey personalities.

760 Flath, Arnold, ed. ATHLETICS IN AMERICA. Corvallis Publications for Convocations and Lecture Committee. Eugene: Oregon State University Press, 1972. 90 p. Notes, bibliog.

> Essays on sport and society, women's participation, excellence, amateurism, and the Greek ideal.

761 Friedman, Arthur. THE WORLD OF SPORTS STATISTICS: HOW THE

FANS AND PROFESSIONALS RECORD, COMPILE AND USE INFORMA-
TION. New York: Atheneum, 1977. 302 p.

The statistical book for intense fans, with sections on hockey,
football, basketball, betting, broadcasting, and trivia.

762 Fuller, Peter. THE CHAMPIONS: THE SECRET MOTIVES IN GAMES
AND SPORTS. New York: Urizen Books, 1977. 310 p.

A psychological interpretation of sports through analyses of
chess master Bobby Fischer, bullfighter El Cordobes, boxer
Muhammad Ali, and racing drivers Jackie Stewart, Alberto
Ascari, and the Campbells.

763 Gardner, Paul. NICE GUYS FINISH LAST: SPORT AND AMERICAN
LIFE. New York: Universe Books, 1975. 264 p. Bibliog., index.

Sport as a key to the American character through discussions
of the emergence of sport, media sports, sport as frontier,
football, violence, blacks, college athletics, the Black Sox
scandal, soccer, and sports myth.

764 Gee, Ernest Richard. EARLY AMERICAN SPORTING BOOKS, 1734-
1844: A FEW BRIEF NOTES. New York: Derrydale Press, 1928. 61 p.

Chapters on THE AMERICAN TURF REGISTER, NEW YORK
SPORTS MAGAZINE, and U.S. SPORTING MAGAZINE.
A final chapter describes other books and magazines in the
author's library.

765 Gerber, Ellen W.; Felshin, Jan; Berlin, Pearl; and Wyrick, Waneen.
THE AMERICAN WOMAN IN SPORT. Reading, Mass.: Addison-Wesley
Publishing Co., 1974. 562 p. Charts, bibliog., index.

Covers the history of participation, social aspects, the woman
athlete, and biophysical perspectives.

766 Gibson, Nevin H. THE ENCYCLOPEDIA OF GOLF, WITH THE OFFI-
CIAL ALL-TIME RECORDS. Rev. ed. New York: A.S. Barnes, 1964.
310 p. Illus., statistics.

A brief history, with chapters on the USGA, PGA, championships, important players.

767 _____. A PICTORIAL HISTORY OF GOLF. Rev. ed. New York:
A.S. Barnes, 1974. 282 p. Illus.

Extends coverage through 1972.

768 Gilmore, Al-Tony. BAD NIGGER! THE NATIONAL IMPACT OF JACK

JOHNSON. Introduction by John Blassingame. New York: Kennikat Press, 1975. 162 p. Illus., bibliog., index.

The account of Johnson's boxing career and life, with emphasis on the reaction of white society to this flamboyant champion.

769 Gipe, George. THE GREAT AMERICAN SPORTS BOOK: A CASUAL BUT VOLUMINOUS LOOK AT AMERICAN SPECTATOR SPORTS FROM THE CIVIL WAR TO THE PRESENT TIME. Garden City, N.Y.: Doubleday, 1978. 570 p. Index.

A compendium of history, anecdotes, illustrations from popular magazines, and other information arranged by decades from the end of the Civil War through 1977, with a year featured in each decade and interspersed chapters on fixes, flaps, presidential sport interest, language, films, technology, rules, leagues, stadia, feats performed while handicapped, endurance contests, failed sports, failed promotions, intersport competitions, ethnic and women athletes, sport tragedies, spectators, superstitions, losing records, upsets, strikes, dissenters, exported sports and athletes, and oddities.

770 Gregory, Paul Michael. THE BASEBALL PLAYER: AN ECONOMIC STUDY. Washington, D.C.: Public Affairs Press, 1956. 213 p. Index.

A general study that identifies value, reward, legal aspects, and representation.

771 Grimsley, Will. A CENTURY OF SPORTS. New York: Associated Press, 1971. 434 p. Index, illus.

A sport-by-sport account of major events, illustrated with action photographs.

772 Grobani, Anton, ed. GUIDE TO BASEBALL LITERATURE. Detroit: Gale Research Co., 1975. 363 p. Index.

A checklist to books on clubs, record books, annuals, histories, biographies, how-to books, anthologies, periodicals, fiction, humor, drama, verse, ballads, pictorials, event books, dictionaries, recollections, technical booklets, officiating, annuals, and other items.

773 _____. GUIDE TO FOOTBALL LITERATURE. Detroit: Gale Research Co., 1975. 363 p. Bibliog., illus.

Includes sections on periodicals, fiction, humor, drama, verse, ballads, and pictorials as well as technical and statistical aspects of the game.

774 Gutkind, Lee. BIKE FEVER. Chicago: Follett, 1973. 233 p.

Informal essay on biking in America, with excursions into the history, land, people, machines and experience of riding motorcycles.

775 Guttmann, Allen. FROM RITUAL TO RECORD: THE NATURE OF MODERN SPORTS. New York: Columbia University Press, 1978. 198 p. Notes, index.

After discussing relationships between play and sports, Guttmann offers seven characteristics which distinguish modern sports from those of earlier times, then considers various theoretical perspectives and examines baseball, football, and individualism in some depth.

776 Hart, Mabel Marie, comp. SPORT IN THE SOCIOCULTURAL PROCESS. 2d ed. Dubuque, Iowa: W.C. Brown, 1976. 509 p. Notes, bibliog.

Essays devoted to theories and definitions, cultural perspectives, cultural contexts, and the social systems and socialization within sport.

777 Harvey, Charles, ed. SPORT INTERNATIONAL. New York: A.S. Barnes, 1961. 416 p. Illus., records.

Records, with many photographs, of competitions in numerous sports.

778 Henderson, Robert W. EARLY AMERICAN SPORT: A CHECKLIST OF BOOKS BY AMERICAN AND FOREIGN AUTHORS PUBLISHED IN AMERICA PRIOR TO 1860; INCLUDING SPORTING SONGS. 3d ed., rev. and enl. Rutherford, N.J.: Fairleigh Dickinson University Press, 1977. 309 p. Index.

The volume contains a brief bibliography of bibliographies and a subject index. Annotations identify illustrations and content features.

779 Heward, Bill, with Gnat, Dimitri V. SOME ARE CALLED CLOWNS: A SEASON WITH THE LAST OF THE BARNSTORMING BASEBALL TEAMS. New York: Crowell, 1974. 354 p. Photos.

Story of a season with the Indianapolis Clowns.

780 Heyn, Ernest V., ed. TWELVE SPORT IMMORTALS. New York: Bartholomew House, 1951. 304 p.

Baseball players and boxers are captured in anecdotes.

781 Higgs, Robert J., and Isaacs, Neil D., eds. THE SPORTING SPIRIT: ATHLETES IN LITERATURE AND LIFE. Foreword by Heywood Hale Broun. New York: Harcourt Brace Jovanovich, 1977. 304 p. Bibliog., index.

An anthology of stories and essays.

782 Hoch, Paul. RIP OFF THE BIG GAME: THE EXPLOITATION OF SPORTS BY THE POWER ELITE. Garden City, N.Y.: Anchor, 1972. 222 p. Bibliog.

A critique of the prevailing sport ideology.

783 Hollander, Zander. BASEBALL LINGO. New York: W.W. Norton, 1967. 135 p. Illus.

An informal glossary of words common to baseball.

785 _____, ed. BASKETBALL'S GREATEST GAMES. Englewood Cliffs, N.J.: Prentice-Hall, 1971. 242 p. Illus.

Accounts of the twenty-one favorite games determined by a poll of coaches, players, and fans.

786 _____. THE PRO BASKETBALL ENCYCLOPEDIA. Los Angeles: Corwin Books, Associated Features, 1977. 404 p. Illus., statistics, index.

A brief history, followed by accounts of player awards, drafts, season and team accounts, biographical sketches of players and coaches, accounts of the Globetrotters, officials, and the Hall of Fame. Official rules and an all-time player roster is included.

787 Hollander, Zander, and Bock, Hal, eds. THE COMPLETE ENCYCLO-PEDIA OF ICE HOCKEY: THE HEROES, TEAMS, GREAT MOMENTS AND RECORDS OF THE NATIONAL HOCKEY LEAGUE, PLUS THE WORLD HOCKEY ASSOCIATION. Rev. ed. Englewood Cliffs, N.J.: Associated Features and Prentice-Hall, 1974. 702 p. Index, statistics, illus.

Historical introduction, with chapters on players, the Stanley Cup, great moments, important games, the Hall of Fame, records, rules, a player register, and miscellaneous information.

788 Holliman, Jennie. AMERICAN SPORTS (1785-1835). Perspectives in American History, no. 34. Durham, N.C.: Seeman Press, 1931. Reprint. Philadelphia: Porcupine Press, 1975. 222 p. Bibliog., index.

A social history of sports and amusements during the time that
covers shooting, hunts, ball-playing, physical contests, quoits,
nine pins, skittles, bowls, dollar pitching, long bullets, archery, swimming, skating, sleighing, horse racing, cockfighting
and animal baiting, gouging and boxing, women's and children's sports, and opinions of the period on sports.

789 Holtzman, Jerome, ed. NO CHEERING IN THE PRESS BOX. New
York: Holt, 1974. 287 p.

Taped interviews with eighteen sports writers from 1971 to
1973.

790 Honig, Donald. BASEBALL WHEN THE GRASS WAS REAL: BASEBALL
FROM THE TWENTIES TO THE FORTIES TOLD BY THE MEN WHO
PLAYED IT. New York: Coward, McCann and Geoghegan, 1975.
320 p. Illus., statistics, index.

Biographical sketches of eighteen players.

791 Hunt, Sarah Ethridge. GAMES AND SPORTS THE WORLD AROUND.
3d ed. New York: Ronald Press, 1964. 271 p. Index.

A sweeping discussion of games played throughout the world
at various times, oriented to teachers and recreation leaders
as a means to human understanding.

792 Isaacs, Neil D. ALL THE MOVES: A HISTORY OF COLLEGE BASKET-
BALL. Philadelphia: Lippincott, 1975. 319 p. Illus., index.

An informal history of the game, focusing on major college
games and players.

793 Izenberg, Jerry. HOW MANY MILES TO CAMELOT? THE ALL-AMERICAN
SPORT MYTH. New York: Holt, Rinehart and Winston, 1972. 227 p.

Accounts of the underside of the American sports myth, where
the myth reflects the values of the people who run it and
watch it. Chapters focus on the human themes related to
the 1968 Olympics, the NCAA, promoters, Muhammad Ali,
betting, fans, baseball, the new patriotism, and Little League
baseball.

794 Jones, Chris. CLIMBING IN NORTH AMERICA. Berkeley and Los Angeles: University of California Press, 1976. 392 p. Illus., bibliog., index.

A history of mountaineering in North America, with discussions of major climbers and the most interesting peaks.

795   Jones, Wally, and Washington, Jim. BLACK CHAMPIONS CHALLENGE AMERICAN SPORTS. New York: David McKay, 1972. 180 p. Index.

A history of the contribution of black athletes to American sports since 1870, with emphasis on the inequality and exploitation they have experienced.

796   Kaye, Ivan N. GOOD CLEAN VIOLENCE: A HISTORY OF COLLEGE FOOTBALL. New York: Lippincott, 1973. 288 p. Illus., bibliog., index.

History and development of college football, highlighting great players and successful innovations.

797   Keith, Harold. SPORTS AND GAMES. Rev. ed. New York: Crowell, 1976. 313 p.

Descriptions of sixteen sports, with tips on playing.

798   Kelley, Robert Fulton, ed. THE SPORTSMAN'S ANTHOLOGY. New York: Howell, Soskin, 1944. 396 p.

An eclectic selection of twenty-five stories and other writing on sport.

799   Kennedy, Charles William. SPORT AND SPORTSMANSHIP. Princeton, N.J.: Princeton University Press, 1931. 59 p.

An essay on the discipline, joy, and values of amateur sport.

800   Kieran, John. THE AMERICAN SPORTING SCENE. 1941. Reprint. New York: Macmillan, 1946. 211 p. Illus.

Informal accounts of boxing, baseball, tennis, racing, golf, and football.

801   Kieran, John; Daley, Arthur; and Jordan, Pat. THE STORY OF THE OLYMPIC GAMES, 776 BC TO 1976. Philadelphia: Lippincott, 1977. 575 p. Records, index.

An informal history of the Olympics through anecdotes.

802   Koppett, Leonard. THE NEW YORK TIMES GUIDE TO SPECTATOR SPORTS. New York: Quadrangle, 1971. 259 p.

Guide to twenty sports.

803   Kowet, Don. THE RICH WHO OWN SPORTS. New York: Random House, 1977. 271 p.

Sketches of Art Rooney, Phil Wrigley, Horace Stoneham,

Wellington Mara, Walter O'Malley, Lamar Hunt, Clint
Murchison, Roy Hofheinz, Charles Finley, Ewing Kauffman,
Ray Kroc, Joe Robbie, Al Davis, Arthur Wirtz, Jack Kent
Cooke, Gary Davidson, Gene Autry, and others.

804   Krawczyk, Chess. MOUNTAINEERING: A BIBLIOGRAPHY OF BOOKS
IN ENGLISH TO 1974. Metuchen, N.J.: Scarecrow Press, 1977.
180 p. Index.

A partially annotated bibliography of 1,141 items on all aspects of mountaineering and climbing.

805   Krout, John Allen. ANNALS OF AMERICAN SPORT. Pageant of
America, vol. 15. New Haven, Conn.: Yale University Press, 1929.
360 p. Illus., indexes, bibliog.

Brief entries on a wide range of popular activities, including
sections on angling, athletic clubs, gymnasiums, country clubs,
camping, and organized sports.

806   Landers, Daniel M., ed. SOCIAL PROBLEMS IN ATHLETICS: ESSAYS
IN THE SOCIOLOGY OF SPORT. Urbana: University of Illinois Press,
1976. 251 p. Notes, index.

A useful collection of essays on competitions, informal versus
organized children's sports, cheating, hustling, hockey violence, black athletes and racism, and New Left criticism of
sport.

807   Leifer, Neil. SPORTS! Introduction by George Plimpton. New York:
H.N. Abrams, 1978. 192 p. Illus.

Excellent color photographs of contemporary sports.

808   Leonard, George Burr. THE ULTIMATE ATHLETE: RE-VISIONING
SPORTS, PHYSICAL EDUCATION, AND THE BODY. New York: Viking
Press, 1975. 273 p.

An Eastern-oriented perspective on discovering the self through
sport.

809   Lewis, Guy, and Redmond, Gerald. SPORTING HERITAGE: A GUIDE
TO HALLS OF FAME, SPECIAL COLLECTIONS AND MUSEUMS IN THE
UNITED STATES AND CANADA. South Brunswick and New York:
A.S. Barnes and Co., 1974. 181 p. Illus.

Illustrated and annotated listing of places and things.

810   Lipsyte, Robert. SPORTSWORLD: AN AMERICAN DREAMLAND. New
York: Quadrangle, distribution by Harper, 1975. 292 p. Index.

LIBRARY JOURNAL calls this "one of the best analyses of sport's last fifteen turbulent years." SPORTS WORLD is "an expression of a community of interest" controlled ultimately by banks, television networks, the press, and municipal and federal governments.

811 Lowe, Benjamin. THE BEAUTY OF SPORT: A CROSS-DISCIPLINARY INQUIRY. Englewood Cliffs, N.J.: Prentice-Hall, 1977. 327 p. Bibliog., illus., index.

An interesting approach to sport that considers the natural beauty of the athlete, sport and the arts, athletic performance, symbolic communication, superlative effects, and the prospects for quantification of the aesthetics of sport.

812 Lowe, Benjamin; Kanin, David B.; and Strenk, Andrew, eds. SPORT AND INTERNATIONAL RELATIONS. Champaign, Ill.: Stipes, 1978. 627 p. Bibliog., index.

A collection of previously published essays brought together for the purpose of exploring the political bridge between culture and sport. The essays are collected in five sections dealing with antecedents to political sport, olympism, ideological interpretations, national policies and their effects on international sport, and a section on the educative aspects of sport study.

813 Loy, John W.; McPherson, Barry D.; and Kenyon, Gerald. SPORT AND SOCIAL SYSTEMS: A GUIDE TO THE ANALYSIS, PROBLEMS, AND LITERATURE. Reading, Mass.: Addison-Wesley, 1978. 447 p. Bibliog., index.

A formal sociological discussion of sports as a microsocial system, macrosocial system, and social institution.

814 Loy, John W., and Kenyon, Gerald, eds. SPORT, CULTURE, AND SOCIETY: A READER ON THE SOCIOLOGY OF SPORT. New York: Macmillan, 1969. 464 p. Bibliog., notes.

Important essays on the sociological problems related to the study of sport within a broad cultural framework. Of interest are sections on sport and social processes, institutions, ethnic cultures, and subcultures.

815 Lucas, John Apostal, and Smith, Ronald A. SAGA OF AMERICAN SPORT. Philadelphia: Lea and Febiger, 1978. 439 p. Notes, index, illus.

A general history of sport and leisure, the volume covers the social and cultural aspects to the present.

816   Ludwig, Jack Barry. THE GREAT AMERICAN SPECTACULARS: MARDI GRAS, THE KENTUCKY DERBY, AND OTHER DAYS OF CELEBRATION. Garden City, N.Y.: Doubleday, 1976. 247 p.

Chapters on the rich at play, the Derby, the Indianapolis "500," the Miami Beach Republican Convention, the Rose Bowl, and the Mardi Gras as focuses for pageantry, informal recreation, and circus.

817   Lüschen, Günther, ed. THE CROSS-CULTURAL ANALYSIS OF SPORT AND GAMES. Champaign, Ill.: Stipes, 1970. 192 p. Bibliog., index.

Essays on theory, primitive culture, cross-cultural analysis, and sport in modern society. The latter section contains a comparison of baseball and the bullfight, an essay on children's play, and a study of attitudes toward sport and physical activity among adolescents.

818   McWhirter, Norris Dewar, comp. GUINNESS SPORTS RECORD BOOK: TAKEN FROM THE GUINNESS BOOK OF WORLD RECORDS. New York: Sterling Publishing Co., 1972. 160 p. Index.

Includes many arcane items of information about sports and pseudo sporting events.

819   Magill, Richard A.; Ash, Michael J.; and Smoll, Frank L., eds. CHILDREN IN SPORT: A CONTEMPORARY ANTHOLOGY. Champaign, Ill.: Human Kinetics, 1978. 259 p.

Sections on physiological, psychological, moral and social development in child athletics, with a brief history of highly organized sports for children.

820   Manchester, Herbert. FOUR CENTURIES OF SPORT IN AMERICA, 1490–1890. New York: Derrydale Press, c. 1931. New York: Benjamin Blom, 1968. 245 p.

All kinds of sports, from Indian jaguar hunting to lady's croquet--in short, social manners in America as reflected in fun and games.

821   Mann, Arthur William. BASEBALL CONFIDENTIAL: SECRET HISTORY OF THE WAR AMONG CHANDLER, DUROCHER, MAC PHAIL, AND RICKEY. New York: David McKay, 1951. 184 p.

An account by the assistant to Branch Rickey, of the fiery career of Leo Durocher and the New York Giants.

822   Marsh, Irving T., and Ehre, Edward, eds. BEST OF THE BEST SPORTS

STORIES, WITH ALL THE PRIZE-WINNING PHOTOGRAPHS. New York: Dutton, 1964. 480 p. Photos.

Collected stories from 1944 to 1963 by various reporters on sports news and personalities.

823 Martens, Rainer. JOY AND SADNESS IN CHILDREN'S SPORTS. Champaign, Ill.: Human Kinetics, 1978. 360 p.

Contains thirty-six articles, with comments, on the controversy, competition, issues, bellwethers (coaches and parents), and alternatives to contemporary children's sports.

824 Meany, Tom, ed. COLLIER'S GREATEST SPORTS STORIES. New York: R.S. Barnes, 1955. 299 p.

Essays and fiction on a wide range of sports and heroes from 1899 to 1955.

825 Menke, Frank G. THE ENCYCLOPEDIA OF SPORTS. 6th rev. ed. New York: A.S. Barnes, 1978. 1,132 p. Lists, stats., illus., index.

Accounts of and statistics for about seventy sports and sports topics.

826 Michener, James Albert. SPORTS IN AMERICA. New York: Random House, 1976. 466 p. Index.

A useful discussion of principles, ways of participating, sports in relation to health, children and women in sport, status, education, media, financing, government control, competition and violence, with chapters on athletes and their problems. An epilogue returns to the delight to be found in sports.

827 Miller, Donna Mae, and Russell, Kathryn R.E. SPORT: A CONTEMPORARY VIEW. Philadelphia: Lea and Febiger, 1971. 202 p. Notes, index.

Covers the personal, social, cultural, and educational aspects of sport, with chapters on participation, spectation, sport and art, women, entertainment, physical education and athletics.

828 Moore, Robert A. SPORTS AND MENTAL HEALTH. Springfield, Ill.: Charles C Thomas, 1966. 115 p. Bibliog., index.

A psychoanalytic interpretation of the role of sports and play in human experience, with attention to their role in education. Considered briefly are theories, sports as social control, and sport as a therapeutic technique.

829   Moss, Peter. SPORTS AND PASTIMES THROUGH THE AGES. New York: Arco, 1963. 222 p. Illus., bibliog., index.

A light history of diversions, recreations, and entertainment, primarily in England, with a chapter on American sports.

830   National Football League Properties. THE FIRST FIFTY YEARS: A CELEBRATION OF THE NATIONAL FOOTBALL LEAGUE IN ITS FIFTIETH SEASON. New York: NFL Properties, distribution by Simon and Schuster, 1969. 256 p. Illus., statistics.

Pictorial and statistical coverage.

831   Neft, David S.; Johnson, Roland T.; and Cohen, Richard M. THE SPORTS ENCYCLOPEDIA: PRO FOOTBALL. Text by Jordan A. Deutsch. New York: Grossett and Dunlap, 1974. 496 p.

Statistical summaries and profiles of teams and players with variants for most phases of the game.

832   Nicholson, Timothy R. SPORTS CARS: 1928-39. Cars of the World in Color. New York: Macmillan, 1969. 183 p. Illus.

Brief, technical essays and appreciations.

833   Nixon, Howard L. SPORT AND SOCIAL ORGANIZATION. Indianapolis: Bobbs-Merrill, 1976. 75 p. Bibliog.

Considers social strains and the emphasis on conformity, group behavior, social stratification, big business, and social change.

834   Noakes, Aubrey. SPORTSMEN IN A LANDSCAPE. Philadelphia: J.B. Lippincott, 1954. 224 p. Index.

A history of English sporting art which antedates similar art in the United States.

835   Noll, Roger G., ed. GOVERNMENT AND THE SPORTS BUSINESS: PAPERS PREPARED FOR A CONFERENCE OF EXPERTS, WITH AN IN-TRODUCTION AND SUMMARY. Studies in the Regulation of Economic Activity. Washington, D.C.: Brookings Institution, 1974. 445 p. Bibliog., index, tables.

Analysis of the operation of professional team sports in the United States, with emphasis on the effects of government policy on profits. Chapters treat ticket prices, social bene-fits of restrictions on team quality, taxation, labor relations, discrimination, broadcasting, stadium subsidies, self-regulation, leagues and antitrust law; with a conclusion on alternatives.

836 NORTH AMERICAN SOCIETY OF SPORT HISTORIANS: PROCEEDINGS AND NEWSLETTER. University Park, Pa.: 1973–– . Annual.

Abstracts of conference papers and business reports.

837 Novak, Michael. THE JOY OF SPORTS: END ZONES, BASES, BASKETS, BALLS AND THE CONSECRATION OF THE AMERICAN SPIRIT. New York: Basic Books, 1976. 357 p. Bibliog., index, notes.

Informal essays on Homeric deeds, religion, metaphysics, rural myth in baseball, immigrant and corporate myths in football, the jazz myth of basketball, seven seals of sports, women, and others in the sports monomyth.

838 Nueckel, Susan, ed. SELECTED GUIDE TO SPORTS AND RECREATION BOOKS. New York: Fleet Press, 1974. 168 p. Index.

Annotated bibliography of how-to books.

839 Nunn, Marshall E. SPORTS. Spare Time Guides: Information Sources for Hobbies and Recreation, no. 10. Littleton, Colo.: Libraries Unlimited, 1976. 217 p. Directory, list of assoc., index.

Annotated bibliography of 743 items covering general sport books, baseball, basketball, boxing, equestrian sports, aerial sports, football, golf, hockey, motorcycling, olympics, self-defense, winter sports, racing, tennis, track and field, water sports, and a periodical list.

840 OFFICIAL WORLD SERIES RECORDS. St. Louis: Charles C. Spink and Sons, 1966. 384 p.

Complete box scores and synopses from 1903 to 1966.

841 Oglesby, Carole A., ed. WOMEN AND SPORT: FROM MYTH TO REALITY. Philadelphia: Lea and Febiger, 1978. 256 p. Notes.

Fifteen essays on female exclusion, stereotyping, sexual attitudes, sport and values, and governing practices.

842 Osterhoudt, Robert G. AN INTRODUCTION TO THE PHILOSOPHY OF PHYSICAL EDUCATION AND SPORT. Champaign, Ill.: Stipes, 1978. 260 p. Bibliog.

An outline of philosophical contributions to the study of sport, with abstracts of major works, summaries of philosophical perspectives, and a course outline.

843 THE OXFORD COMPANION TO WORLD SPORTS AND GAMES. Edited by John Arlott. New York: Oxford University Press, 1975. 1,143 p. Illus.

Accounts by various contributors of games and sports played around the world, exclusive of children's games and board and table games.

844 Paretchan, Harold. THE WORLD SERIES: THE STATISTICAL RECORD. South Brunswick, N.J.: A.S. Barnes, 1968. 136 p.

Statistics of the series broken down into thirty-six categories.

845 Patterson, Jerry E. ANTIQUES OF SPORT. New York: Crown, 1975. 150 p. Photos., bibliog., index.

Guide to collecting sports artifacts.

846 Phillips-Birt, Douglas. FAMOUS SPEEDBOATS OF THE WORLD. New York: St. Martin's Press, 1950. 141 p. Illus.

Accounts of innovative speedboats from about 1895 to 1950.

847 PLAY: ANTHROPOLOGICAL PERSPECTIVES. Edited by Michael A. Salter. Proceedings of the Association for the Anthropological Study of Play. West Point, N.Y.: Leisure Press, 1978. 262 p. Appendixes.

Twenty essays on the anthropology of play, most prepared for the third annual meeting of the Association for the Anthropological Study of Play. Of particular interest are John Grayzel on the play motif at a state penitentiary; Patrick Doyle on children's preschool play activities; Bernard Mergen on leisure activities among shipyard workers, 1917-1977; Susan Boyd on native American powwow play; Helen Schwartzman on dancing in a mental health center; Nancy Theberge on women's professional golf; and John Bowman on the organization of spontaneous adult social play. Appendixes review the organization, identify its executive council, and reprint its constitution.

848 Pratt, John Lowell. THE OFFICIAL ENCYCLOPEDIA OF SPORTS. New York: F. Watts, 1964. 344 p. Bibliog., index, records, illus.

Brief histories and descriptions for thirty-four sports.

849 _____, ed. BASEBALL'S ALL-STARS. Garden City, N.Y.: Doubleday, 1967. 151 p. Illus., records, index.

One man's ideal team.

850 Ralbovsky, Martin. DESTINY'S DARLINGS: A WORLD CHAMPIONSHIP LITTLE LEAGUE TEAM TWENTY YEARS LATER. New York: Hawthorn, 1974. 255 p.

A follow-up on the 1954 Schenectady, New York, players
through interviews and commentary.

851 _____. LORDS OF THE LOCKER ROOM: THE AMERICAN WAY OF
COACHING AND ITS EFFECT ON YOUTH. New York: P.H. Wyden,
1974. 236 p.

Essentially a critique of coaching and parenting practices
which covers little league baseball, coaching, ploys, symbolism
and patriotism, media, recruiting, public relations; with a
guide for parents.

852 Reichler, Joe, and Olan, Ben. BASEBALL'S UNFORGETTABLE GAMES.
New York: Ronald Press Co., 1960. 362 p. Photos., box scores, index.

Over a hundred essays on favorite games.

853 Reiger, John F. AMERICAN SPORTSMEN AND THE ORIGINS OF CON-
SERVATION. New York: Winchester Press, 1975. 316 p. Notes, illus.,
bibliog., index.

An apology of sportsmen's development of conservation policy,
with chapters on the sportsmen's code, the concept of national
parks, and related matters.

854 Reisman, Marty. THE MONEY PLAYER: CONFESSIONS OF THE
WORLD'S GREATEST TABLE TENNIS CHAMPION AND HUSTLER. Morrow, 1974. 241 p. Illus.

Autobiography of table tennis player, with seventeen major
championships to his credit. First autobiography in table
tennis.

855 Remington, Frederic. FREDERIC REMINGTON'S OWN OUTDOORS.
Introduction by Harold McCracken. Edited by Douglas Allen. New
York: Dial, 1964. 190 p.

Collection of articles and plates of Remington's sporting experiences.

856 Rice, Grantland. SPORTLIGHTS OF 1923. New York: G.P. Putnam's
Sons, 1924. 212 p. Illus.

A collection of essays on the year's stars and events.

857 _____, ed. THE OMNIBUS OF SPORT. New York: Harper, 1932. 809 p.

Collection of fiction, commentary, articles, and verse on
football, baseball, golf, tennis, ancient pageant passes,
combat, racing, hunting, and fishing.

858 Roberts, John M. SPORTS FACILITIES. McLean, Va.: American Society of Landscape Architects Foundation, 1973. 79 p. Bibliog., diagrams, tables.

Handbook for the planning of outdoor sports facilities, with emphasis on net sports and golf courses.

859 Roberts, Michael. FANS! HOW WE GO CRAZY OVER SPORTS. Washington, D.C.: New Republic Book Co., 1976. 209 p. Index.

Informal essays on the Washington Redskins and the capitol, Jewish jocks, college athletics, Yankee Stadium, salaries, endorsements, Wilt Chamberlain's meeting with Richard Nixon, football superstars, personal lives of celebrities, politics and sports, hockey brutality, Nazi propaganda, and the Olympics.

860 Roe, Frederic Gordon. SPORTING PRINTS OF THE EIGHTEENTH AND EARLY NINETEENTH CENTURIES. London: Connoisseur, 1927. 50 p. Illus., index.

Collection of color plates with explanatory material.

861 Ronberg, Gary. THE HOCKEY ENCYCLOPEDIA. New York: Rutledge, Macmillan, 1974. 392 p. Illus., statistics.

History and guide to professional hockey.

862 Rooney, John F., Jr. A GEOGRAPHY OF AMERICAN SPORT, FROM CABIN CREEK TO ANAHEIM. Addison-Wesley Series in the Social Significance of Sport. Menlo Park, Calif.; Reading, Mass.: Addison-Wesley Publishing Co., 1974. 306 p. Charts, maps, bibliog., index.

Geographical interpretation of the diffusion of sports, focusing on the origins of players and spectators for major and minor sports on college and professional levels. Emphasis is on the origins of players and recruiting for baseball, basketball, and football, but the study includes chapters on women's sport, minor sports, and spatial organization of conferences.

863 Russell, Fred. BURY ME IN AN OLD PRESS BOX: GOOD TIMES AND LIFE OF A SPORTSWRITER. New York: Barnes, 1957. 235 p. Name index.

864 Rust, Art. "GET THAT NIGGER OFF THE FIELD!" A SPARKLING, INFORMAL HISTORY OF THE BLACK MAN IN BASEBALL. New York: Delacorte Press, 1976. 228 p. Charts, illus., index.

History of black baseball, with profiles of the great players.

865 Sage, George Harvey, comp. SPORT AND AMERICAN SOCIETY:

SELECTED READINGS. 3d ed. Reading, Mass.: Addison-Wesley, 1980. 395 p. Bibliog.

Essays discuss heritage, socialization, stratification, women, blacks, school, and change with respect to sport.

866 Salak, John S. DICTIONARY OF AMERICAN SPORTS. New York: Philosophical Library, 1961. 491 p.

Brief definitions of some six thousand terms for some eighty familiar sports.

867 Sandys, Edwyn. SPORTING SKETCHES. New York: Macmillan, 1905. 389 p.

Sketches, many from OUTING magazine, on wildlife and woodcraft.

868 Schiffer, Don, ed. WORLD SERIES ENCYCLOPEDIA. New York: T. Nelson, 1961. 256 p. Illus., statistics.

Synopses of periods, with individual records of players and managers, all-time records, and major league rosters for the year.

869 Scott, Jack. THE ATHLETIC REVOLUTION. New York: Free Press, 1971. 242 p. Bibliog.

A counter-cultural view of sports which argues that professionalism is counter to the needs of students and athletes.

870 Senzel, Howard. BASEBALL AND THE COLD WAR: BEING A SOLILO-QUY ON THE NECESSITY OF BASEBALL. New York: Harcourt Brace Jovanovich. 1977. 298 p.

Reminiscences of a writer who discovers baseball to be the source of metaphors for explaining events of the cold war era and for discovering his own identity.

871 Seymour, Harold. BASEBALL: THE EARLY YEARS. Vol. 1. New York: Oxford University Press, 1960. 373 p. Illus., notes, index.

A history from early forms to 1903 which focuses on "economic and social aspects," and its development as Americana. See also next entry.

872 _____ . BASEBALL: THE GOLDEN AGE. Vol. 2. New York: Oxford University Press, 1971. 492 p. Bibliog., index.

A history from 1903 to 1930, with emphasis on the professional structure. See also above entry.

873　Shapiro, Harvey. FASTER THAN SOUND. New York: A.S. Barnes, 1975. 176 p. Illus.

On land speed records and the people who drive the vehicles.

874　Shecter, Leonard. THE JOCKS. Indianapolis: Bobbs-Merrill, 1969. 278 p. Index.

Reminiscences and observations on television sports, organizations, stars, losers, Casey Stengel, scandals, baseball origins, yacht racing, boxing, basketball and football betting, and getting caught in the games surrounding sports.

875　Slaughter, Frances Elizabeth. THE SPORTSWOMAN'S LIBRARY. 2 vols. Westminster: A. Constable, 1898. 415 p. Index.

Volume 1 discusses fox hunting, hare hunting, shooting, fishing for tarpon, archery, skating, golf, and croquet for the English-woman. Volume 2 covers small craft racing, deer hunting, fishing, driving, cycling, tennis, and miscellanea.

876　Slusher, Howard S. MAN, SPORT, AND EXISTENCE: A CRITICAL ANALYSIS. Philadelphia: Lea and Febiger, 1967. 243 p. Bibliog., index.

The first extensive exploration of the athlete's existential predicament.

877　Smith, Ken. BASEBALL'S HALL OF FAME. New York: Grosset and Dunlap, 1962. 263 p. Illus.

878　Smith, Leverett T., Jr. THE AMERICAN DREAM AND THE NATIONAL GAME. Bowling Green, Ohio: Popular Press, 1975. 285 p. Notes, index.

Organized around both high culture and popular culture, the author grounds his study in Huizenga's (see no. 51) perspective, considers the uses of leisure advocated by mainstream authors, then examines the professional sports world depicted in Ring Lardner's fiction, the implications of the Black Sox scandal, and Vince Lombardi's sports ethic.

879　Smith, Robert. SPORTS: THE AMERICAN SCENE: MEMORABLE MOMENTS FROM THE PAGES OF SPORTS ILLUSTRATED. New York: McGraw-Hill, 1963. 283 p.

Twenty-five essays on sports, hustling, and commuter poker.

880　_____. WORLD SERIES: THE GAME AND THE PLAYERS. Garden City, N.Y.: Doubleday, 1967. 310 p.

A history of the series from 1903 to 1966, with synopses of each year's results.

881 Smits, Ted, ed. THE YEAR IN SPORTS: THE ASSOCIATED PRESS RE-VIEW OF THE MEMORABLE SPORTS EVENTS. Englewood Cliffs, N.J.: Prentice-Hall, 1958. 256 p. Illus., records.

A typical volume, which includes profiles, highlights, the World Series games, and accounts of events in the major sports. Action photographs.

882 Snyder, Eldon E., and Spreitzer, Elmer. SOCIAL ASPECTS OF SPORT. Englewood Cliffs, N.J.: Prentice-Hall, 1978. 214 p. Bibliog., index.

A textbook on sports that covers social and institutional values, issues, media, sport as leisure activity, and related matters.

883 Somers, Dale A. THE RISE OF SPORTS IN NEW ORLEANS, 1850-1900. Baton Rouge: Louisiana State University Press, 1972. 320 p. Notes, bibliog., index.

An extensive history of sport and physical recreation in the city, with implications for a broader perspective on southern popular culture.

884 Spears, Betty Mary, and Swanson, Richard A. HISTORY OF SPORT AND PHYSICAL ACTIVITY IN THE UNITED STATES. Edited by Elaine T. Smith. Dubuque, Iowa: W.C. Brown, 1978. 402 p. Notes, bibliog., index.

A textbook, with study questions, of recreation. Chapters focus on history; influential people; pastimes; the change from informal to organized sports from 1840 to 1855; organizational practices, 1885-1917; sport and social change, 1917-45; democratization of sports after 1945; and the history of Olympic games.

885 SPORT AMERICANA BASEBALL CARD PRICE GUIDE, NO. 1. Laurel, Md.: Den's Collector's Den, 1979-- . 221 p. Glossary.

Contains a brief history of card collecting with prices.

886 THE SPORTING SET. Leisure Class in America. New York: Arno, 1975. 78 p. Illus.

Collection of essays on tavern amusements, the rise of sport, baseball, college athletics, social life at Harvard, the country club, and racing.

887 SPORTS, GAMES, AND PLAY: SOCIAL AND PSYCHOLOGICAL VIEW-
POINTS. Hillsdale, N.J.: L. Erlbaum Associates, 1979. 456 p.
Notes, index.

> Essays on make-believe play, the psychology of chess, pool,
> personality and change, sex roles, women, champions, ath-
> letes' attitudes, fans, aggression, spectation, home-field ad-
> vantage, and chance and skill.

888 Steiner, Jesse Frederick. AMERICANS AT PLAY: RECENT TRENDS IN
RECREATION AND LEISURE TIME ACTIVITIES. New York: McGraw-
Hill, 1933. 201 p. Index.

> Includes chapters on the development of urban playgrounds,
> the park system, commercial amusements, leisure organiza-
> tions and control, changes in rural recreation, and expenditures.

889 Stone, Gregory P., ed. GAMES, SPORT AND POWER. New Brunswick,
N.J.: Transaction Books, 1972. 228 p. Bibliog.

> Essays from TRANSACTION magazine on pool and poolrooms,
> poker playing and other card games, athletes, baseball, soc-
> cer; the relationships between social status and tastes for clas-
> sical music and jazz; dance studios, museums and comics.

890 STUDIES IN THE ANTHROPOLOGY OF PLAY: PAPERS IN MEMORY
OF B. ALLAN TINDALL. Proceedings, Association for the Anthropo-
logical Study of Play. No. 2. Edited by Phillips Stevens, Jr. West
Point, N.Y.: Leisure Press, 1976. 276 p. Bibliog. by Helen B.
Schwartzman.

> Essays on many aspects of play in a variety of cultures. Of
> interest are Susan Boyd on poker, Annette Rosenstiel on urban
> black children's games, Kendall Blanchard on the cultural
> component in physical recreation, Bernard Mergen on the
> acceptance of leisure in the U.S. (1880-1930), Helen Schwartz-
> man's review of research, Gilbert J. Botvin on children's
> fantasy narratives, and Ernestine Thompson and Tanya John-
> son on imaginary childhood figures.

891 Sullivan, George. SPORTS SUPERSTITIONS. New York: Coward,
McCann and Geoghegan, 1978. 71 p. Name index.

> Compilation of the superstitions of various players in major
> sports.

892 Telander, Rick. HEAVEN IS A PLAYGROUND. New York: St. Martin's
Press, 1976. 282 p.

> The experiences of the author during a summer of playground
> basketball in Brooklyn.

893 THRILL SPORTS CATALOGUE. By the editors of Consumer Guide. New York: Dutton, 1977. 192 p. Illus., catalogs, bibliog.

Accounts of rafting, hang gliding, skydiving, scuba diving, soaring, surfing, shark fishing, ballooning, speedboating, ice yachting, car racing, canoeing, bicycle racing, sailing, big game hunting, motorcycling, water skiing, mountain climbing, wilderness hiking, horseback riding, skiing, snowmobiling, judo and Karate, with notes on equipment and sources for further information.

894 Tunis, John R. THE AMERICAN WAY IN SPORT. New York: Duell, Sloan and Pearce, 1958. 180 p. Index.

Observations on the influence of the frontier on American sport, the effects of industrialization, competition, Hoosier basketball, sports heroism in the twenties, the first World Series, golf, Theodore Roosevelt as sportsman, and nationalism in sports.

895 Turkin, Hy, and Thompson, S.C. THE OFFICIAL ENCYCLOPEDIA OF BASEBALL. 9th rev. ed. New York: Doubleday, 1977. Statistics, illus.

Features an all-time register of players and other statistical matters.

896 Turkin, Hy, ed. THE OFFICIAL ENCYCLOPEDIA OF LITTLE LEAGUE BASEBALL. New York: Barnes, 1954. 238 p. Illus., bibliog., index.

Covers all aspects of the organization, including history, evaluation, establishing a franchise, rules, policies, press, tournaments, champions, anecdotes, play, and training.

897 Tutko, Thomas A., and Bruns, William. WINNING IS EVERYTHING AND OTHER AMERICAN MYTHS. New York: Macmillan, 1976. 240 p. Index.

Includes a players' Bill of Rights, with critical chapters on winning as everything, character building, early competition, participation, emotions, child abuse, superstars, injuries, coaches, and a chapter on alternative approaches to sport.

898 Twin, Stephanie L., ed. OUT OF THE BLEACHERS: WRITINGS ON WOMEN AND SPORT. Old Westbury, N.Y.: Feminist Press, 1979. 229 p. Photos, index.

Sections on physiology, confessions of sportswomen, and the structure of sports, with essays written by contemporaries.

899 Twombly, Wells. TWO HUNDRED YEARS OF SPORT IN AMERICA: A PAGEANT OF A NATION AT PLAY. New York: McGraw-Hill, 1976. 287 p. Illus.

Features many unusual paintings and photos.

900 Umminger, Walter. SUPERMEN, HEROES, AND GODS: THE STORY OF SPORT THROUGH THE AGES. Translation by James Clark. New York: McGraw Hill, 1963. 342 p.

An informal exploration of ancient and modern sports through the myths and legends of many lands, with anecdotes about individual athletes included throughout. The volume is divided into sections on worshippers and fans, hunters and fighters, gladiators, and those who strive for records.

901 Umphlett, Wiley Lee. THE SPORTING MYTH AND THE AMERICAN EX-PERIENCE. Studies in Contemporary Fiction. Lewisburg, Pa.: Bucknell University Press, 1975. 205 p. Notes, bibliog., index.

A study of selected American novels, centering on sports, which focus on the literary background, themes of encounter with nature and society, the neo-Romantic encounter. An epilogue discusses recent trends and variations.

902 U.S. Congress. House. Select Committee on Crime. ORGANIZED CRIME IN SPORTS (RACING), HEARINGS. 4 vols. 92d Cong., 2d sess. Washington, D.C.: Government Printing Office, 1973. 1,853 p.

Transcripts of the hearings held between May 9 and July 27, 1972.

903 VanderZwaag, Harold J. TOWARD A PHILOSOPHY OF SPORT. Reading, Mass.: Addison-Wesley, 1972. 261 p. Bibliog., index.

A general study of the interest, participation, and existential meaning of sport, with a scenario on sport in the educational system.

904 VanderZwaag, Harold J., and Sheehan, Thomas J. INTRODUCTIONS TO SPORT STUDIES: FROM THE CLASSROOM TO THE BALL PARK. Dubuque, Iowa: W.C. Brown, 1978. 286 p. Bibliog., illus., index.

A textbook, with discussion questions, that covers social processes, women in sport, issues, the experience, philosophy, history, sociology, psychology, physiology, careers, teaching, and coaching.

905 Vecsey, George. JOY IN MUDVILLE: BEING A COMPLETE ACCOUNT OF THE UNPARALLELED HISTORY OF THE NEW YORK METS FROM THEIR MOST PERTURBED BEGINNINGS TO THEIR AMAZING RISE TO

GLORY AND RENOWN. New York: McCall, 1970. 249 p.

A history from 1962 through their World Series win.

906   Voigt, David. AMERICAN BASEBALL: FROM GENTLEMAN'S SPORT TO THE COMMISSIONER SYSTEM. Vol. 1. Norman: University of Oklahoma Press, 1966. 336 p. Illus., bibliog., index.

Covers baseball from its antecedents to 1919, focusing on the professional system.

907   . AMERICA'S LEISURE REVOLUTION: ESSAYS IN THE SOCIOLOGY OF LEISURE AND SPORTS. Reading, Pa.: Albright College, Department of Sociology, 1971. 155 p. Notes, bibliog.

Exploratory essays into the social implications of leisure and sports.

908   . AMERICA THROUGH BASEBALL. Chicago: Nelson-Hall, 1976. 221 p. Notes, index.

The volume brings together baseball and nationalism, national purpose, unions, heroes, villains and national issues, with chapters on key events and change.

909   . A LITTLE LEAGUE JOURNAL. Bowling Green, Ohio: Bowling Green University Popular Press, 1974. 90 p.

The experiences of a sociologist and sometime coach of youth baseball.

910   Wallop, Douglass. BASEBALL: AN INFORMAL HISTORY. New York: Norton, 1969. 263 p. Bibliog., index, illus.

A useful discussion of the beginnings and development of the sport, with a section devoted to the rise and fall of the New York Yankees.

911   Ward, Arch, ed. GREATEST SPORT STORIES FROM THE CHICAGO TRIBUNE. New York: A.S. Barnes, 1953. 448 p.

Brief sports pieces from 1847 to 1952 on a variety of sporting events and personalities.

912   Watman, Melvyn, comp. THE ENCYCLOPAEDIA OF ATHLETICS. New York: St. Martin's, 1977. 240 p. Index, illus., tables.

Entries feature information on British and other countries' sports and sport personalities.

913 Weaver, Robert Bartow. AMUSEMENTS AND SPORTS IN AMERICAN LIFE. Chicago: University of Chicago Press, 1939. 195 p. Illus., bibliog.

> A brief general history of amusements, recreation and sports, with individual chapters on a dozen sports including billiards. Of particular interest are accounts of a wide range of informal pastimes before the twentieth century.

914 WEBSTER'S SPORTS DICTIONARY. Springfield, Mass.: G. and C. Merriam, 1976. 503 p. Illus.

> A useful dictionary of terms and catch phrases common to most sports, with a brief section on referee hand signals.

915 Weiss, Paul. SPORT: A PHILOSOPHIC INQUIRY. Carbondale: Southern Illinois University Press, 1969. 274 p. Bibliog., index.

> An examination of philosophy through sports, focusing on performance and the appeal of excellence for spectators.

916 Whiting, H.T.A., and Masterson, D.W., eds. READINGS IN THE AESTHETICS OF SPORT. London: Lepus Books; Kimpton, 1974. 160 p. Notes, bibliog., illus.

> A useful collection of essays on aesthetics and education, art, motion, and reporting of sports.

917 Wind, Herbert. GAME, SET, AND MATCH: THE TENNIS BOOM OF THE 1960'S AND 70'S. New York: Dutton, 1979. 229 p.

> Essays from the NEW YORKER during the years 1962-78 on both contemporary and past tennis seasons.

918 _____. THE STORY OF AMERICAN GOLF: ITS CHAMPIONS AND ITS CHAMPIONSHIPS. New York: Knopf, 1975. 563 p. Illus., records, bibliog., index.

> A standard history from 1888 to the mid-1970s.

919 _____, ed. THE REALM OF SPORT: A CLASSIC COLLECTION OF THE WORLD'S GREAT SPORTING EVENTS AND PERSONALITIES AS RECORDED BY THE MOST DISTINGUISHED WRITERS. New York: Simon and Schuster, 1966. 705 p.

> Essays on Zen archery, baseball, basketball, boating and sailing, boxing, fishing, football, golf, horses and horse racing, hunting and shooting, ice hockey, motoring, mountaineering, skiing and skating, swimming, tennis, track and field, and walking. A strong collection containing some excellent impressions.

920 Wood, Norton, ed. THE SPECTACLE OF SPORT, FROM SPORTS ILLUS-
TRATED. Englewood Cliffs, N.J.: Prentice-Hall, 1957. 319 p. Illus.

Lavish color photography of sports and spectators, with brief
essays.

921 Woodward, Stanley. SPORTS PAGE. New York: Simon and Schuster,
1949. Reprint. New York: Greenwood Press, 1968. 229 p.

An account of newspaper practices regarding sportswriting.

922 _____. SPORTSWRITER. Garden City, N.Y.: Doubleday, 1967.
177 p. List of journalism schools, index.

A handbook for aspiring sportswriters, with anecdotes of the
author's experiences.

923 THE WORLD SERIES. Compiled by Richard M. Cohen et al. Text by
Jordan Deutsch. New York: Dial, 1976. 416 p. Illus.

Contains thorough descriptions, box scores and player statistics
for each game through 1975, together with lists of leading
performances.

924 THE WORLD SERIES: A SEVENTY-FIFTH ANNIVERSARY. Edited by
Joseph L. Reichler. New York: Simon and Schuster, 1978. 290 p.
Illus., statistics, index, trivia quiz.

A collection of twenty-five essays on various World Series
topics, mostly by the editor, but also by Joe Durso, James T.
Farrell, Lillian G. Carter et al. Topics include humor, scandal, and series greats.

925 Yiannakis, Andrew; McIntyre, Thomas D.; Melnick, Merrill J.; and
Hart, Dale P., eds. SPORT SOCIOLOGY: CONTEMPORARY THEMES.
Dubuque, Iowa: Kendall; Hunt, 1976. 239 p. Notes, charts.

Chapters consider heroes, competition, juvenile sports organizations, interscholastic competitions, sport subcultures, sex
roles, violence, sport and society, and the future of sport.

926 Zeigler, Earle F., ed. HISTORY OF PHYSICAL EDUCATION AND
SPORT IN THE UNITED STATES AND CANADA. Champaign, Ill.:
Stipes, 1975. 537 p. Bibliog., index.

Essays on origins of sports, mind and body ideals, nationalism,
physical education, NCAA-AAU relations, the 1905 football
controversy, and related matters.

927 _____. HISTORY OF PHYSICAL EDUCATION AND SPORTS. Englewood

Cliffs, N.J.: Prentice-Hall, 1979. 292 p. Bibliog., index, illus.

A textbook on sport in early societies, the Middle Ages, modern times, and North America, with a chapter on sport and the historical perspective.

MUSIC

928 Adorno, Theodor W. INTRODUCTION TO THE SOCIOLOGY OF
MUSIC. New York: Seabury: Continuum, 1976. 233 p. Notes.

Included in this volume, based on the author's German lectures of 1961-62, are chapters on musical conduct, popular
music function, classes and strata, national music, and genres
of the musical arts.

929 Anderson, Robert, and North, Gail. GOSPEL MUSIC ENCYCLOPEDIA.
New York: Sterling Publishing Co., 1979. 320 p. Illus., index.

Encyclopedic accounts of performers, an award list, a list
of Hall of Fame members, radio and television station lists
by state, fifteen gospel arrangements, and a discography of
major recordings.

930 Armitage, Andrew D., and Tudor, Dean. ANNUAL INDEX TO POPU-
LAR MUSIC RECORD REVIEWS, 1973. Metuchen: Scarecrow, 1974.
Index.

Covers fifty-eight magazines in thirteen categories, with ratings for individual recordings.

931 Artis, Bob. BLUEGRASS: FROM THE LONESOME WAIL OF A MOUN-
TAIN LOVE SONG TO THE HAMMERING DRIVE OF THE SCRUGGS-
STYLE BANJO--THE STORY OF AN AMERICAN MUSICAL TRADITION.
New York: Hawthorn Books, 1975. 182 p. Illus., appendix, index.

A useful account of bluegrass, with chapters on Bill Monroe,
the Stanley Brothers, Flatt and Scruggs, Don Reno and Red
Smiley, Jimmy Martin, and Jim and Jesse, as well as information on contemporary variations. An appendix identifies recordings, radio stations, publications, and organizations.

932 Ashton, John. REAL SAILOR-SONGS. New York: C. Scribner's Sons,
1891. Reprint. New York: Benjamin Blom, 1971. Unpaged.

Two-hundred illustrations. Authentic sailor songs about sea fights, press gangs, disasters at sea and ashore, and love, with notes on origins and history.

933 Balliett, Whitney. AMERICAN SINGERS. New York: Oxford University Press, 1979. 178 p.

Interview-based, musically informed biographical sketches of popular singers Teddi King, Mary Mayo, Barbara Lea, Alberta Hunter, Joe Turner, Helen Humes, Ray Charles, Tony Bennett, Sylvia Syms, Hugh Shannon, Blossom Dearie, Bobby Short, Mabel Mercer, and Anita Ellis. These singers "join" popular songs with jazz singing, are excellent singers of "classic" American popular songs, and can "improvise or enlarge on them."

934 Baraka, Imamu Amiri [LeRoi Jones]. BLACK MUSIC. New York: William Morrow, 1967. 221 p. Index.

Essays on contemporary jazz and blues with emphasis on the changing black music scene and its artists.

935 _____. BLUES PEOPLE: NEGRO MUSIC IN WHITE AMERICA. New York: William Morrow, 1963. 244 p. Index.

A history of blues and early jazz from African roots through the early 1960s. Emphasis is on the social status and exclusion of blacks in America.

936 Bennett, Gertrude Ryder. BALLADS OF COLONIAL DAYS: WITH HISTORICAL BACKGROUND. Francestown, N.H.: Golden Quill Press, 1972. 160 p.

Reprints of about fifty-eight ballads, with sources and historical notes.

937 Bergman, Jo, comp. BOOK OF THE ROAD. Burbank, Calif.: Warner Brothers Records, 1975. 397 p. Illus.

Information on music facilities suitable for rock performers, together with other useful material on thirty-three cities.

938 Berlin, Edward A. RAGTIME: A MUSICAL AND CULTURAL HISTORY. Berkeley and Los Angeles: University of California Press, 1980. 248 p. Illus., notes, music checklist, bibliog., index.

A critical and musicological study of piano ragtime and its associated forms, with attempts to correct interpretations based on nostalgia and faulty memories. Consideration of origins, style, early impressions, and the development and erosion of a cohesive style.

939 Berton, Ralph. REMEMBERING BIX: A MEMOIR OF THE JAZZ AGE. New York: Harper and Row, 1974. 428 p. Bibliog., discography, index.

A biography or memoir, of the legendary Bix Beiderbecke.

940 Bierley, Paul E. JOHN PHILIP SOUSA: A DESCRIPTIVE CATALOG OF HIS WORKS. Urbana: University of Illinois Press, 1973. 177 p. Bibliog., chronology.

Includes an exhaustive listing of Sousa's music and prose, arranged according to genre.

941 _____. JOHN PHILIP SOUSA: AMERICAN PHENOMENON. New York: Appleton-Century-Crofts, 1973. 261 p. Illus., bibliog., index.

A standard biography and career assessment, with chapters on Sousa's music philosophy and his band.

942 BILLBOARD ENCYCLOPEDIA OF MUSIC. New York: Billboard Publications, 1939-- . Annual. Title varies. Index.

Articles on all aspects of music.

943 Blackstone, Orin. INDEX TO JAZZ: JAZZ RECORDINGS, 1917-1944. 4 vols. in 1. Fairfax, Va.: Record Changer, 1948. Reprint. Westport, Conn.: Greenwood Press, 1978. Unpaged.

Compiled from fourteen magazines devoted to jazz.

944 Blesh, Rudi. SHINING TRUMPETS: A HISTORY OF JAZZ. New York: Knopf, 1946. Reprint. New York: Da Capo Press, 1975. 452 p. Discography, illus., musical examples, index.

A history of jazz and related genres from the late nineteenth century until about 1940.

945 Blesh, Rudi, and Janis, Harriet. THEY ALL PLAYED RAGTIME. New York: Knopf, 1950. Reprint. New York: Oak Publications, 1971. 347 p. Chronology, lists of compositions and player piano rolls, discography, index.

A history of "a song that came from the people and then got lost," based on interviews and research conducted from 1949.

946 Botkin, B.A. THE AMERICAN PLAY-PARTY SONG. New York: Frederick Ungar Publishing Co., 1963. 400 p. Bibliog., indexes.

Emphasis on the Oklahoma experience from about 1889 through the middle thirties. Includes dance calls and rhymes.

947   Bowers, Q.D. THE ENCYCLOPEDIA OF AUTOMATIC MUSICAL IN-
      STRUMENTS. Vestal, N.Y.: Vestal Press, 1972. 1,008 p. Illus.

      Emphasis on commercial aspects, 1850–1930.

948   Brand, Oscar. SONGS OF '76: A FOLKSINGER'S HISTORY OF THE
      REVOLUTION. New York: M. Evans and Co., distribution by Lippin-
      cott, 1972. 178 p. Index, music, lyrics.

      Accounts of the historical contexts of songs of the period.

949   Burt, Olive Woolley. AMERICAN MURDER BALLADS AND THEIR STORIES.
      New York: Citadel Press, 1958. 272 p. Illus. Paperback, 1964.

      Contains chapters "Friends and Relations"; "Jealousy, Un-
      requited Love, and Madness"; "The Profit Motive"; "For the
      Love of God"; "A Matter of Pigment" (Indians); "Law at Any
      Price"; "A Way of Life"; and "Any Excuse Will Serve."

950   Burton, Jack. THE BLUE BOOK OF BROADWAY MUSICALS: WITH
      ADDITIONS BY LARRY FREEMAN. Watkins Glen, N.Y.: Century
      House, 1969. 327 p.

      Songs from the sound tracks and the stars who sang them since
      the birth of the talkies a quarter-century ago.

951   _____ . THE BLUE BOOK OF TIN PAN ALLEY: A HUMAN INTEREST
      ENCYCLOPEDIA OF AMERICAN POPULAR MUSIC. 2 vols. Watkins
      Glen, N.Y.: Century House, 1962-65. Illus.

      A history with career sketches of composers and lyricists, in-
      cluding song chronologies for most.

952   _____ . THE INDEX OF AMERICAN POPULAR MUSIC: THOUSANDS
      OF TITLES CROSS-REFERENCED TO OUR BASIC ANTHOLOGIES OF
      POPULAR SONGS. Watkins Glen, N.Y.: Century House, 1957. Var.
      pag.

      Indexes songs included in the BLUE BOOK OF TIN PAN
      ALLEY (1951), BLUE BOOK OF BROADWAY MUSICALS
      (1952), BLUE BOOK OF HOLLYWOOD MUSICALS (1953),
      and THE MELODIES LINGER ON (1951).

953   Charters, Samuel Barclay. JAZZ: NEW ORLEANS, 1885-1963: AN
      INDEX TO THE NEGRO MUSICIANS OF NEW ORLEANS. Rev. ed.
      New York: Oak Publications, 1963. 173 p. Illus., index.

      Biographical entries on musicians, with indexes to bands,
      nightclubs, and tunes.

954   _____ . THE POETRY OF THE BLUES. New York: Oak Publications,
      1963. 111 p.

An account of the blues that explores not only the poetry but also the racism and exploitation of the society in which this form of music has survived.

955 Charters, Samuel Barclay, and Kunstadt, Leonard. JAZZ: A HISTORY OF THE NEW YORK SCENE. Garden City, N.Y.: Doubleday, 1962. 382 p. Illus., notes, bibliog., discography, index.

A history of the New York scene, based on interviews, clippings, and other material from the 1890s.

956 Chilton, John. BILLIE'S BLUES: A SURVEY OF BILLIE HOLIDAY'S CAREER 1933-1959. New York: Stein and Day, 1975. 264 p. Illus.

Balanced interpretation based on interviews of acquaintances, secondary sources, and observations.

957 Cooper, David E. INTERNATIONAL BIBLIOGRAPHY OF DISCOGRAPHIES. Littleton, Colo.: Libraries Unlimited, 1975. 272 p. Bibliog.

In addition to classical music entries, the discography treats blues and jazz. Listings are chronological and according to labels, and include sections on general guides, subjects, and genres. A performer list is added, as well as an index.

957a Craig, Warren. SWEET LOWDOWN: AMERICA'S POPULAR SONG WRITERS. Metuchen, N.J.: Scarecrow Press, 1978. 645 p. Rankings, bibliog., indexes.

Arranged into sections treating writers before, during, and after Tin Pan Alley, the volume excludes such categories as rock, country and western music, and writers whose works did not sell well enough in sheets or discs. An interesting critique of other publications precedes the main entries, which consist of brief career sketches and chronological lists of song titles.

958 Cushing, Helen Grant. CHILDREN'S SONG INDEX. New York: H.W. Wilson, 1936. 798 p.

Title, author, and subject listings for some twenty-two thousand children's songs found in 189 anthologies selected by teachers and librarians.

959 Dance, Stanley. JAZZ ERA: THE 'FORTIES. London: Macgibbon and Kee, 1962. 252 p.

Career biographies for performers, with a brief overview of the period and the jazz scene.

960 _____. THE WORLD OF SWING. New York: Scribner's, 1974. 436 p. Illus., discography, index.

Background and career sketches for forty musicians.

961 Davies, Hunter, and Fast, Julius. THE BEATLES: THE AUTHORIZED BIOGRAPHY. New York: McGraw, 1968. 357 p. Illus.

An account of the origins of the Beatles from John Lennon's early efforts, through the German period, and into popular success.

962 Davies, J.H. MUSICALIA: SOURCES OF INFORMATION IN MUSIC. New York: Pergamon Press, 1966. 218 p. Index, appendixes.

A guide to information sources and archives in music, with chapters of interest on the ordinary listener, collector and dealer, folk singer and jazzman, broadcaster, record collector, and printing and copyrighting.

963 Davis, Clive, and Willwerth, James. CLIVE: INSIDE THE RECORD BUSINESS. New York: William Morrow, 1975. 300 p. Index, illus.

A Columbia Records executive reminisces about the move of the business from Broadway material to rock and roll.

964 Dearling, Robert; Dearling, Celia; and Rust, Brian. THE GUINNESS BOOK OF MUSIC FACTS AND FEATS. Enfield, Engl.: Guinness Superlatives, 1976. 278 p. Illus., bibliog., index.

An encyclopedia of information about instruments, composers, repertoire; opera, choral and vocal music, orchestras and concerts; music literature; the twentieth century scene; and mechanical music-taking, including a chronology.

965 Denisoff, R. Serge. GREAT DAY COMING: FOLK MUSIC AND THE AMERICAN LEFT. Urbana: University of Illinois Press, 1971. 219 p. Illus., discography, bibliog., index.

Chapter focus on folk consciousness and utopianism, urban folk, Almanac Singers, organizations, isolation, the radical Right, and new forms of protest.

966 _____. SONGS OF PROTEST, WAR AND PEACE: A BIBLIOGRAPHY AND DISCOGRAPHY. Santa Barbara, Calif.: ABC-Clio, 1973. 70 p. Index.

Includes books, periodicals, songbooks, Communist Party of America publications (1932-1949), SING OUT (1950-64), BROADSIDE (1962-72), discography of patriotic songs, and a bibliography of right wing attacks upon popular protest songs.

967 Denisoff, R. Serge, and Peterson, Richard A., eds. THE SOUNDS OF SOCIAL CHANGE: STUDIES IN POPULAR CULTURE. Sociology Series. Chicago: Rand McNally, 1972. 332 p. Notes, index.

A collection of twenty-five essays on protest music, music of social movements, rock tastes, the industry of music, and musicians.

968 Dexter, Dave, Jr. JAZZ STORY FROM THE '90S TO THE '60S. Englewood Cliffs, N.J.: Prentice Hall, 1964. 176 p. Bibliog., illus., discography, index.

An informal history of jazz, which features chapters on regional styles and major performers.

969 Dichter, Harry. HANDBOOK OF AMERICAN SHEET MUSIC: A CATALOG OF SHEET MUSIC. Philadelphia: H. Dichter, 1953. 297 p. Illus.

A catalog listing of 1,451 items.

970 Dichter, Harry, and Shapiro, Elliott. EARLY AMERICAN SHEET MUSIC: ITS LURE AND ITS LORE, 1768-1889. New York: R.R. Bowker, 1941. 287 p. Illus., publishers and artist list, bibliog., index.

Descriptive bibliography of sheet music, with a section of illustrations and publishing information, organized thematically.

971 Diehl, Katharine Smith. HYMMS AND TUNES--AN INDEX. New York: Scarecrow Press, 1966. 1,185 p. Glossary, bibliog.

Brief description of hymnals, with indexes to some eighty of them according to first lines and variants, authors, tune names and variants, composers, and melodies.

972 Dixon, Robert M.W., and Godrich, John. RECORDING THE BLUES. New York: Stein and Day, 1970. 85 p. Illus., charts, index, bibliog.

A discussion of blues recording artists and their releases from 1920-1945, with chapters on various changes.

973 Donakowski, Conrad L. A MUSE FOR THE MASSES: RITUAL AND MUSIC IN AN AGE OF DEMOCRATIC REVOLUTION, 1770-1870. Chicago: University of Chicago Press, 1977. 435 p. Notes, bibliog., index.

A history of the transformation of values that occurred in the transition from the Enlightenment to Romanticism through public, civic, ecclesiastical, utopian, and artistic agencies.

974 Drone, Jeanette Marie. INDEX TO OPERA, OPERETTA AND MUSICAL COMEDY SYNOPSES IN COLLECTIONS AND PERIODICALS. Metuchen, N.J.: Scarecrow Press, 1978. 171 p. Indexes, bibliog.

Indexes seventy-four collections and four periodical titles

and includes 1,705 titles by 627 composers. Contains title and composer indexes, and a bibliography of additional sources.

975   Edwards, Joseph. TOP 10'S AND TRIVIA OF ROCK & ROLL AND RHYTHM AND BLUES, 1950-1973. St. Louis: Blueberry Hill Publishing Co., 1974. 632 p. Index.

Statistical compilation from BILLBOARD magazine, with hundreds of trivia questions. Annual supplements.

976   Ewen, David. ALL THE YEARS OF AMERICAN POPULAR MUSIC. Englewood Cliffs, N.J.: Prentice-Hall, 1979. 850 p. Index.

A history of popular songs, composers, the musical theater and its variations and the roles of the media. Many areas such as festivals, social dancing, singing telegrams, and advertising jingles are discussed.

977   _____. AMERICAN POPULAR SONGS FROM THE REVOLUTIONARY WAR TO THE PRESENT. New York: Random House, 1966. 507 p.

Brief encyclopedia entries on performers, composers, songs, and presentations in media, with a chronological list of popular songs from 1765-1966 that is sketchy. Other sections include a list of the most popular songs according to performers, and a list of some popular performers together with some of their songs.

978   _____. COMPOSERS FOR THE AMERICAN MUSICAL THEATRE. New York: Dodd, Mead, 1968. 270 p. Illus., index.

Career biographies for fourteen composers active since the early 1900s, including Victor Herbert, Rudolf Friml, Sigmund Romberg, George M. Cohan, Jerome Kern, Irving Berlin, George Gershwin, Cole Porter, Richard Rodgers, Kurt Weil, Frederick Loewe, Frank Loesser, Jerry Bock, and Leonard Bernstein.

979   _____. GREAT MEN OF AMERICAN POPULAR SONG: THE HISTORY OF THE AMERICAN POPULAR SONG TOLD THROUGH THE LIVES, CAREERS, ACHIEVEMENTS, AND PERSONALITIES OF ITS FOREMOST COMPOSERS AND LYRICISTS--FROM WILLIAM BILLINGS TO THE REVOLUTIONARY WAR THROUGH BOB DYLAN, JOHNNY CASH, BURT BACHARACH. Englewood Cliffs, N.J.: Prentice Hall, 1972. 404 p.

980   _____. THE LIFE AND DEATH OF TIN PAN ALLEY: THE GOLDEN AGE OF AMERICAN POPULAR MUSIC. New York: Funk and Wagnalls, 1964. 380 p. Song list, lyricist and composer list, bibliog., index.

Account of the songs, composers, publishers, promoters, and performers during the heyday of Tin Pan Alley.

981 _____. MEN OF POPULAR MUSIC. New York: Ziff-Davis, 1944.
Reprint. Freeport, N.Y.: Books for Libraries Press, 1972. 213 p. Illus.

> Biographical and career essays on King Oliver, Irving Berlin,
> Louis Armstrong, W.C. Handy and Meade Lux Lewis, Duke
> Ellington, Paul Whiteman and Ferde Grofé, George Gershwin,
> Jerome Kern, Rodgers and Hart, Cole Porter, Benny Goodman,
> and Raymond Scott.

982 _____. NEW COMPLETE BOOK OF THE AMERICAN MUSICAL THE-
ATER: A GUIDE TO MORE THAN 300 PRODUCTIONS OF THE AMERI-
CAN MUSICAL THEATER FROM THE BLACK CROOK (1886) TO THE
PRESENT, WITH PLOT, PRODUCTION HISTORY, STARS, SONGS,
COMPOSERS, LIBRETTISTS, AND LYRICISTS. Rev. ed. New York:
Holt, Rinehart and Winston, 1970. 800 p.

983 Feather, Leonard Geoffrey. THE BOOK OF JAZZ--FROM THEN TILL
NOW: A GUIDE TO THE ENTIRE FIELD. New York: Bonanza Books,
1965. 280 p. Notes, index.

> After a brief discussion of background, origins, and race, the
> author discusses the performers associated with the basic in-
> struments, then provides an anatomy of improvisation and a
> discussion of the future of jazz.

984 _____. THE ENCYCLOPEDIA OF JAZZ IN THE SIXTIES. New York:
Horizon, 1966. 312 p. Photos, award lists, bibliog.

> Career notes on jazz performers; includes tour information,
> brief assessment, recording notes, and home address.

985 _____. NEW EDITION OF THE ENCYCLOPEDIA OF JAZZ. New
York: Horizon Press, 1960. 527 p.

> New edition of the encyclopedia of jazz; completely re-
> vised, enlarged and brought up to date; appreciations by
> Duke Ellington, Benny Goodman and John Hammond.

986 _____. THE PLEASURES OF JAZZ: LEADING PERFORMERS ON THEIR
LIVES, THEIR MUSIC, THEIR CONTEMPORARIES. New York: Horizon,
1976. 200 p.

> Career sketches of forty-three jazz artists, with quoted material.

987 Feather, Leonard Geoffrey, and Gitler, Ira. THE ENCYCLOPEDIA OF
JAZZ IN THE SEVENTIES. New York: Horizon Press, 1976. 393 p.

> Continues the coverage begun in THE ENCYCLOPEDIA OF
> JAZZ (1960) and continued in THE ENCYCLOPEDIA OF
> JAZZ IN THE '60S (1966). Includes polls, education, films,
> recommended recordings and a bibliography, 1966-1975.

988   Finkelstein, Sidney. COMPOSER AND NATION: THE FOLK HERITAGE
       OF MUSIC. New York: International Publishers, 1960. 333 p. Name
       index.

          Broad interpretations of numerous thematic aspects of folk
          music and its influence on the culture.

989   Foner, Philip S. AMERICAN LABOR SONGS OF THE NINETEENTH
       CENTURY. Music in American Life. Urbana: University of Illinois
       Press, 1975. 356 p. Illus., bibliog., index.

          The text provides thematic organization and continuity for
          reprinted songs of labor organizations and those arising as
          expressions of social protest.

990   Fox, William S., and Wince, Michael H. "Musical Taste Cultures and
       Taste Publics." YOUTH AND SOCIETY 7 (December 1975): 198–224.

          Gans's "taste culture" and "taste public" are tested with
          college students.

991   Fuld, James J. THE BOOK OF WORLD-FAMOUS MUSIC; CLASSICAL,
       POPULAR AND FOLK. Rev. ed. New York: Crown, 1971. 688 p.
       Illus., notes, index.

          Technical data on identifying, collecting, and preserving
          music with notes on terminology, arrangements, selection
          and biography. Included is a list of compositions with notes
          on origins, printing history, and other information about the
          songs and their composers.

992   Garland, Phyl. THE SOUND OF SOUL. Chicago: Henry Regnery,
       1969. 246 p. Index, discography.

          An informal discussion of the meaning of soul music, based
          on the author's personal experiences, her interviews with
          musicians, and on secondary research.

993   Garon, Paul. BLUES AND THE POETIC SPIRIT. Preface by Franklin
       Rosemont. London: Eddison Press, 1975. 178 p. Bibliog., index.

          Heavily illustrated with examples, the volume contains a
          bibliographical essay on blues scholarship, chapters on the
          psychology of enjoyment, race differences, motifs, and sym-
          bols and images.

994   Gentry, Linnell. A HISTORY AND ENCYCLOPEDIA OF COUNTRY,
       WESTERN, AND GOSPEL MUSIC. Nashville: McQuiddy Press, 1961.
       380 p.

          Reprints of articles from popular magazines, accounts of country music shows since 1924, checklists of songs for major performers, lists of singers, musicians, and comedians.

995 Gilbert, Douglas. LOST CHORDS: THE DIVERTING STORY OF AMERICAN POPULAR SONGS. New York: Cooper Square, 1970. 377 p.

A social history of the popular tune from the Civil War to World War II, focusing on mainstream songs through popular themes and motifs.

996 Gillett, Charlie. THE SOUND OF THE CITY: THE RISE OF ROCK AND ROLL. New York: Outerbridge and Dienstfrey, 1970. 375 p. Bibliog., discography, notes, index to artists.

One of the most useful histories of the stylistic patterns in music that led to contemporary rock and roll. Divided into four major parts, the volume traces rock from 1954 to 1958, the influence of rhythm and blues from 1945 to 1956, country and soul during 1958 to 1969, and the international and intercoastal influences from 1962 to 1969.

997 Godrich, John, and Dixon, Robert M.W. BLUES AND GOSPEL RECORDS, 1902-1942. London: Storyville Publications, 1969. 912 p.

An attempt to list all records containing "distinctively Negroid folk music" published before 1942. The volume contains brief notes on major labels, the listing with some notes on artists, and miscellaneous information on releases.

998 Goldberg, Isaac. TIN PAN ALLEY: A CHRONICLE OF THE AMERICAN POPULAR MUSIC RACKET. New York: John Day, 1930. 341 p. Illus., index.

A history and assessment of the products of Tin Pan Alley, from its roots in sentimental and minstrel songs through Sousa, De Koven, Victor Herbert, and others, with chapters on promotion, jazz, and motion pictures.

999 Gonzalez, Fernando L. DISCO-FILE: THE DISCOGRAPHICAL CATALOG OF AMERICAN ROCK AND ROLL AND RHYTHM AND BLUES VOCAL HARMONY GROUPS, 1902-1976. 2d ed. Flushing, N.Y.: Gonzalez, 1977. 486 p.

An extensive listing of the records of vocal groups that influenced and expressed rhythm and blues and rock and roll music.

1000 Gottfried, Martin. BROADWAY MUSICALS. New York: Harry N. Abrams, 1979. 352 p. Illus., index.

Lavishly illustrated with color and black and white photographs, the volume discusses book, music, lyrics, and design. Chapters on major directors, composers, ANNIE, and black musicals.

1001   Green, Abel, and Laurie, Joe, Jr. SHOW BIZ: FROM VAUDE TO VIDEO. New York: Henry Holt and Co., 1951. 613 p. Glossary, index.

A detailed account of the industry and personalities from 1905 to 1950.

1002   Green, Archie. ONLY A MINER: STUDIES IN RECORDED COAL-MINING SONGS. Urbana: University of Illinois Press, 1972. 504 p. Illus.

Examines the relationships between oral tradition and the practices of the recording industry.

1003   Green, Douglas B. COUNTRY ROOTS: THE ORIGINS OF COUNTRY MUSIC. New York: Hawthorn, 1976. 238 p. Chronology, discography, bibliog., illus., index.

Chapters cover old-time music, blues, comedy, singing cowboys, cajun, bluegrass, western swing, gospel, country rock, honky-tonk, country pop, and the Nashville sound.

1004   Greenfield, Robert. S.T.P.: A JOURNEY THROUGH AMERICA WITH THE ROLLING STONES. New York: Saturday Review Press/E.P. Dutton, 1974. 337 p.

A behind-the-scenes account of the 1972 Rolling Stones tour through the United States.

1005   Grossman, Loyd. A SOCIAL HISTORY OF ROCK MUSIC: FROM THE GREASERS TO GLITTER ROCK. New York: McKay, 1976. 150 p. Index.

An informal history of rock music and its milieu from 1954 through 1975, with emphasis on accompanying life-style changes.

1006   Haralambos, Michael. RIGHT ON: FROM BLUES TO SOUL IN BLACK AMERICA. New York: Drake, 1975. 187 p. Illus., bibliog., index, discography.

A useful study of the rise of the blues and its replacement by soul as the reflection of black society. The author correlates social and economic indicators with sales and performance.

1007   Havlice, Patricia Pate. POPULAR SONG INDEX. Metuchen, N.J.: Scarecrow Press, 1975. 933 p. Indexes.

Indexes 301 songbooks published during 1940–72, of folk songs, pop tunes, spirituals, hymns, children's songs, sea chanteys, and blues. The indexes are keyed to titles, first lines, first lines of choruses, composers, and lyricists.

1008   Hemphill, Paul. THE NASHVILLE SOUND: BRIGHT LIGHTS AND COUNTRY MUSIC. New York: Simon and Schuster, 1970. 289 p. Index.

An affectionate, informal account of electric country music based on interviews and a life in the South; the volume covers the styles, many performers, and the hype of "white soul" music.

1009   Hentoff, Nat. JAZZ COUNTRY. New York: Harper and Row, 1976. 146 p.

A novel of a young white male on the jazz scene.

1010   _____. JAZZ IS. New York: Random House, 1976. 288 p. Illus., bibliog., discography, index.

An informal attempt to define the range of jazz and its appeal through reminiscence, quotation, and thinking aloud.

1011   _____. THE JAZZ LIFE. New York: Dial, 1961. 255 p.

Reprinted material and fresh pieces explore the social, economic, and psychological aspects of modern jazz, including comments on Norman Mailer's THE WHITE NEGRO and such contemporaries as Charles Mingus, Count Basie, John Lewis, Miles Davis, Thelonious Monk, and Ornette Coleman.

1012   THE HISTORY OF MUSIC MACHINES. Ed. by Cynthia A. Hoover. Washington, D.C.: National Museum of History and Technology, Smithsonian Institution, 1971. Reprint. New York: Drake, 1975. 139 p. Illus., bibliog.

Notes on extensive illustrations covering nineteenth-century machines, music parlors, home machines, radio receivers, movies, jukeboxes, high fidelity, and electronic instruments.

1013   Hixon, Donald. MUSIC IN EARLY AMERICA: A BIBLIOGRAPHY OF MUSIC IN EVANS. Metuchen, N.J.: Scarecrow Press, 1970. 607 p.

An annotated compilation of items, with biographical sketches and indexes to composers and compilers, titles, and Evans's numbers.

1014   Horn, David. THE LITERATURE OF AMERICAN MUSIC IN BOOKS AND FOLK MUSIC COLLECTIONS: A FULLY ANNOTATED BIBLIOGRAPHY.

Metuchen, N.J.: Scarecrow Press, 1977. 556 p. Index.

Annotated items on bibliography, history, women in music, vocal music, church music, musical life, the cultivated tradition, Indian music, folk music, hillbilly and country music, black music, blues, jazz, and popular genres.

1015 Hunst, Jack. NASHVILLE'S GRAND OLE OPRY. New York: Abrams, 1975. 404 p. Illus., discography, index.

A lavishly illustrated history and celebration of the Grand Ole Opry and its performers.

1016 Ivey, Donald. SONG: ANATOMY, IMAGERY, AND STYLES. New York: Free Press, 1970. 273 p. Bibliog., index.

An analysis of the relationships between lyrics and music in traditional songs in Western cultures, with discussion of the synthesis in imagery, and a chronological treatment of styles.

1017 Jones, Francis Arthur. FAMOUS HYMNS AND THEIR AUTHORS. London: Hodder and Stoughton, 1902. Reprint. Detroit: Singing Tree Press, 1970. 337 p. Illus., index.

Divided into sections on morning and evening, Advent, Christmas, New Year, Passion, Easter, processional, Communion, matrimony, sea, missions, funeral, harvest, All Saints' Day, children's and general hymns, the accounts provide biographical and historical anecdotes.

1018 Jones, Robert M., ed. "Popular Music: A Survey of Folios, with an Index to Recently Reviewed Recordings." NOTES: THE QUARTERLY JOURNAL OF THE MUSIC LIBRARY ASSOCIATION 30 (March 1974): 616-33.

1019 Kahn, Kathy. HILLBILLY WOMEN. Garden City, N.Y.: Doubleday, 1973. 230 p. Illus., organization list.

Interviews with nineteen southern mountain women active in or sympathetic to various human rights and regional issues.

1020 Karshner, Roger. THE MUSIC MACHINE. Los Angeles: Nash Publishing, 1971. 196 p.

An informal account of the popular music industry, particularly those aspects which are exploitative, shady, or simply dishonest.

1021 Keil, Charles. URBAN BLUES. Chicago: University of Chicago Press, 1966. 231 p.

The transformation of southern blues singers by the recording industry.

1022 Kennington, Donald. THE LITERATURE OF JAZZ--A CRITICAL GUIDE. Chicago: American Library Association, 1971. 142 p. 2d rev. ed. 1980. 236 p. Bibliog., filmography, index.

Background essays with partially annotated chapter bibliographies on history, biography, criticism, reference books, periodicals, organizations, and fiction. With a brief section on jazz films.

1023 Kinkle, Roger D. THE COMPLETE ENCYCLOPEDIA OF POPULAR MUSIC AND JAZZ, 1900-1950. Vol. 1: MUSIC YEAR BY YEAR, 1900-1950. New Rochelle, N.Y.: Arlington House, 1974.

Contains the apparatus for the series, together with an annual listing of Broadway (and movie) musicals, "popular songs," representative recordings arranged by performer for popular music and jazz.

1024 ____. THE COMPLETE ENCYCLOPEDIA OF POPULAR MUSIC AND JAZZ, 1900-1950. Vol. 2: BIOGRAPHIES A THROUGH K. New Rochelle, N.Y.: Arlington House, 1974.

Biographies and credits for musicians.

1025 ____. THE COMPLETE ENCYCLOPEDIA OF POPULAR MUSIC AND JAZZ, 1900-1950. Vol. 3: BIOGRAPHIES L THROUGH Z. New Rochelle, N.Y.: Arlington House, 1974.

Biographies of musicians, with credits.

1026 ____. THE COMPLETE ENCYCLOPEDIA OF POPULAR MUSIC AND JAZZ, 1900-1950. Vol. 4: INDEXES AND APPENDICES. New Rochelle, N.Y.: Arlington House, 1974.

Appendixes: DOWN BEAT and METRONOME poll winners, 1937-1972; release dates of record series numbers by major companies; Oscar nominees and winners, 1934-1972; a note on record collecting; numerical listing of records for major companies, mid-1920s to early 1940s; personal name index; Broadway musical index; movie musical index; popular song index, bibliography.

1027 Klamkin, Marian. OLD SHEET MUSIC: A PICTORIAL HISTORY. New York: Hawthorn, 1975. 214 p. Illus., index.

A thematic portrayal, with interpretive text, of hundreds of examples of artists' conceptions of songs.

1028 Kreuger, Miles. SHOW BOAT: THE STORY OF A CLASSIC AMERICAN MUSICAL. New York: Oxford University Press, 1977. 246 p. Illus., discography, index.

An illustrated history of the musical, with chapters on the novel, the Ziegfeld productions and the film versions. Appendixes identify production information for media.

1029 Lawless, Ray McKinley. FOLKSINGERS AND FOLKSONGS IN AMERICA: A HANDBOOK OF BIOGRAPHY, BIBLIOGRAPHY, AND DISCOGRAPHY. New York: Duell, Sloan and Pearce, 1965. 750 p.

Brief essays on the definition and status of folk song, biographical sketches of numerous singers, reference materials and collections; folklore societies and folk festivals, a checklist of song titles, discography, with a supplement on recent singers, instruments, scholarship, and other matters.

1030 Leadbitter, Mike. DELTA COUNTRY BLUES. Bexhill-on-Sea, Engl.: Blues Unlimited, 1969. 47 p. Illus., index.

An account of the blues performers who were recorded in the Mississippi area during the 1950s.

1031 Leadbitter, Mike, and Shuler, Eddie. FROM THE BAYOU: THE STORY OF GOLDBAND RECORDS. Bexhill-on-Sea, Engl.: Blues Unlimited, 1969. 62 p.

An account of the history of this small company in Lake Charles, Louisiana.

1032 Leadbitter, Mike, and Slaven, Neil. BLUES RECORDS, JANUARY 1943 TO DECEMBER 1966. New York: Oak Publications, 1968. 381 p.

A listing by artist of blues records that continues (without gospel listings) the volume by John Godrich and Robert M.W. Dixon, BLUES AND GOSPEL RECORDS, 1902-1942 (1942).

1033 Leigh, Robert. INDEX TO SONG BOOKS: A TITLE INDEX TO OVER 11,000 COPIES OF ALMOST 6,800 SONGS IN 111 SONG BOOKS PUBLISHED BETWEEN 1933 AND 1962. Stockton, Calif.: Robert Leigh, 1964. 237 p.

An updating of Sears's 1934 supplement to SONG INDEX (see no. 1086).

1034 Leonard, Neil. JAZZ AND THE WHITE AMERICANS: THE ACCEPTANCE OF A NEW ART FORM. Chicago: University of Chicago Press, 1962. 215 p. Notes, bibliog., index.

A study in the rapid change in audience taste for jazz between World War I and World War II, with emphasis on quality and the artist-audience gap.

1035   Leverence, John. "Promoting TOMMY." JOURNAL OF POPULAR
       CULTURE 8 (Winter 1974): 465-76.

       Summary of the marketing considerations for the promotion of
       the film, TOMMY. Underlines the continuing saturation of
       record-stage musical-film activity.

1036   Levy, Lester S. FLASHES OF MERRIMENT: A CENTURY OF HUMOR-
       OUS SONGS IN AMERICA, 1805-1905. Norman: University of Okla-
       homa Press, 1971. 370 p. Illus., bibliog., index.

       An account of comic narrative songs, the sexes, dialect,
       nonsense, humorous history, animal songs, drink, the Currier
       sheet music covers, and novelty songs.

1037   _____. GIVE ME YESTERDAY: AMERICAN HISTORY IN SONG, 1890-
       1920. Norman: University of Oklahoma Press, 1975. 420 p. Illus.,
       bibliog., index.

       Accounts of the songs of the period about show business,
       being footloose, the rich and powerful, suffragettes, states
       and regions, athletes and sports, murder and tragedy, enter-
       tainment, progress, and social issues.

1038   _____. GRACE NOTES IN AMERICAN HISTORY: POPULAR SHEET
       MUSIC FROM 1820-1900. Norman: University of Oklahoma Press, 1967.
       410 p. Illus., bibliog, index.

       Divided into sections on history and mores, costume, minstrels,
       drinking, UNCLE TOM'S CABIN, games, social movements,
       Indians, events, politics, disasters, and transportation.

1039   Limbacher, James L. THE SONG LIST, A GUIDE TO CONTEMPORARY
       MUSIC FROM CLASSICAL SOURCES. Ann Arbor, Mich.: Pierian Press,
       1973. 229 p.

       Identifies classical composer and work for popular songs in
       ballets, theme songs for radio and television shows, dance
       bands, and films. Includes contemporary title, arranger,
       original composer, and original title.

1040   Longstreet, Stephen. SPORTIN' HOUSE: A HISTORY OF THE NEW
       ORLEANS SINNERS AND THE BIRTH OF JAZZ. Los Angeles: Sher-
       bourne Press, 1965. 293 p. Sketches.

       Based on documents, memoirs, reminiscences, and personal
       observations, the volume provides insight into the milieu for
       early jazz forms.

1041   Lowens, Irving. A BIBLIOGRAPHY OF SONGSTERS PRINTED IN AMERICA

BEFORE 1821. Worcester, Mass.: American Antiquarian Society, 1976. 229 p. Index, tables, bibliog.

An annotated descriptive bibliography of 649 songsters, with locations, chronologies, and geographical listings for origins.

1042 Lumpkin, Ben Gray, and McNeil, Norman L. FOLK-SONGS ON REC- ORDS. Denver: Alan Swallow, 1950-- . Annual. Bibliog., index.

A listing of over seven hundred records containing folk songs, ballads, spirituals, work songs, American Indian songs, and folk dance songs.

1043 Lydon, Michael. BOOGIE LIGHTNING. New York: Dial, 1974. 229 p. Photos.

Developments in recent black music through interviews with John Lee Hooker, Bo Diddley, Aretha Franklin, and Ray Charles.

1044 Lyttleton, Humphrey. THE BEST OF JAZZ: BASIN STREET TO HARLEM: JAZZ MASTERS AND MASTERPIECES, 1917-1930. New York: Taplinger, 1979. 214 p. Illus., bibliog., discography, index.

Essays on the Original Dixieland Jazz Band, James P. John- son, King Oliver, Sidney Bechet, Bessie Smith, Jelly Roll Morton, Fletcher Henderson, Louis Armstrong, Bix Beiderbecke, Duke Ellington, the Chicagoans, Johnny Dodds and Jimmy Noone, Louis Armstrong and Earl Hines, and Luis Russell.

1045 Mabey, Richard. THE POP PROCESS. London: Hitchinson Educational, 1969. 190 p. Notes, bibliog.

An essay on the English rock music scene, with emphasis on musical style and life-styles of the audience and performers; a chapter on protest music is included.

1046 McCarthy, Albert J. BIG BAND JAZZ. New York: Putnam, 1974. 368 p. Photos., notes, index.

Traces big jazz bands from early syncopated bands through developments in Chicago and New York, regional and white bands, the swing era, influences on European music, Duke Ellington, and the decline of the style in the late 1940s.

1047 _____ . THE DANCE BAND ERA: THE DANCING DECADES FROM RAGTIME TO SWING: 1910-1950. Philadelphia: Chilton Book Co., 1971. 176 p. Illus., discography, bibliog., index.

An informal history from about 1910 to after World War II for the United States and England, with chapters on business and European dance music.

1048   McCarthy, Albert J.; Morgan, Alun; Oliver, Paul; and Harrison, Max. JAZZ ON RECORD: A CRITICAL GUIDE TO THE FIRST FIFTY YEARS: 1917-1967. New York: Oak Publications, 1968. 416 p. Index.

        Selected encyclopedic entries on performers, with attached discographies. Further sections treat jazz periods, other creative personnel, festivals and concerts, and related genres.

1049   McCue, George, ed. MUSIC IN AMERICAN SOCIETY, 1776-1976: FROM PURITAN HYMN TO SYNTHESIZER. New Brunswick, N.J.: Transaction Books, 1977. 201 p. Index.

        Essays on Americanism in music, hymns, black music, Indian music, folk song collecting, popular music, jazz, musical theatre, and musical corporations.

1050   Malone, Bill C., and McCulloh, Judith, eds. STARS OF COUNTRY MUSIC: UNCLE DAVE MACON TO JOHNY RODRIGUEZ. Urbana: University of Illinois Press, 1975. 476 p. Illus., bibliog., notes, index.

        Career biographies based on interviews and secondary material for nineteen country and western performers, with chapters on early pioneers and stars since World War II.

1051   Marks, Edward B. THEY ALL HAD GLAMOUR: FROM THE SWEDISH NIGHTINGALE TO THE NAKED LADY. New York: J. Messner, 1944. Reprint. Westport, Conn.: Greenwood Press, 1972. 448 p. Appendixes, bibliog., index.

        Accounts of singers and the musical theater in the mid-nineteenth century, with miscellaneous information on favorite songs, music teachers, New York critics, actor families, and collo-quialisms.

1052   Merriam, Alan P. A BIBLIOGRAPHY OF JAZZ. Bibliographical Series, vol. 4. Philadelphia: American Folklore Society, 1954. 145 p. Index.

        The volume contains 3,324 items and a checklist of 113 jazz magazines.

1053   Middleton, Richard. POP MUSIC AND THE BLUES: A STUDY OF THE RELATIONSHIP AND ITS SIGNIFICANCE. London: Victor Gollancz, 1972. 271 p. Glossary, bibliog., index.

        A musician's interpretation of the relationship between blues and popular music, with an account of the move of country blues to the city, the transformation of urban blues, the emergence of blues-related popular music, and the attempts to synthesize blues and rock in the work of Bob Dylan and the Merseyside Beat.

1054   Morton, Marian J., and Conway, William P.   "Cowboy Without a Cause:
       His Image in Today's Popular Music."   ANTIOCH REVIEW   35 (Spring-
       Summer 1977):   193-204.

       The figure is infused with nostaliga in the music of the late
       sixties and early seventies, when he declines as a significant
       mythic figure who may be revived when national self-confidence
       returns.

1055   Murray, Albert.   STOMPING THE BLUES.   New York: McGraw-Hill
       Book Co., 1976.   264 p.   Illus., index.

       Essay with numerous illustrations on the relationship between
       the blues and dancing.

1056   MUSIC INDEX.   Detroit: Information Coordinators, 1949-- .   Monthly.

       The volume for 1979 (1980) lists over three hundred periodicals,
       indexed, with annual cumulations.   Popular music in a variety
       of media are available through cross-indexed subject headings.

1057   Nanry, Charles, with Berger, Edward.   THE JAZZ TEXT.   New York:
       Van Nostrand Reinhold, 1979.   276 p.   Index.

       A useful introductory textbook on jazz that clarifies terms,
       provides a brief history, and discusses the origins of styles.
       Chapter 7 is a student's guide to research sources, and chap-
       ter 8 surveys a sociological approach to the study of jazz.

1059   Nettl, Paul.   THE STORY OF DANCE MUSIC.   New York: Philosophi-
       cal Library, 1947.   370 p.   Illus., index.

       A general history of dance music from primitive times through
       modern dance, with some treatment of social dancing, espe-
       cially of the waltz.

1060   Nite, Norm N.   ROCK ON: THE ILLUSTRATED ENCYCLOPEDIA OF
       ROCK N'ROLL; THE SOLID GOLD YEARS.   New York: Thomas Y.
       Crowell, 1974.   676 p.   Illus.

       Encyclopedia of performers "on the charts" from about 1950
       through the early sixties.   Brief anecdotal entries, many with
       publicity photographs, followed by a chronological list of
       recordings with publisher.

1061   Oliver, Paul.   ASPECTS OF THE BLUES TRADITION.   New York: Oak
       Publications, 1970.   294 p.   Notes, index.

       A continuation of Oliver's thematic analysis of blues (see
       below), with sections on Christmas motifs, religion, the piano,
       social issues, Joe Louis and John Henry, motifs, censorship,
       and classification.

1062 _____. CONVERSATION WITH THE BLUES. New York: Horizon Press, 1965. 217 p. Illus., discography, index.

An exploration of the blues based on interviews with blues singers throughout the South and West. Brief biographical sketches of singers.

1063 _____. THE STORY OF THE BLUES. Philadelphia: Chilton, 1969. 176 p. Photos., bibliog., index.

A history and photographic essay of the blues tradition, focusing on roots, tent shows, informal bands, regional expression, radio exposure, and contemporary variations.

1064 Ord-Hume, Arthur W.J.G. CLOCKWORK MUSIC: AN ILLUSTRATED HISTORY OF MECHANICAL MUSICAL INSTRUMENTS FROM THE MUSICAL BOX TO THE PIANOLA: FROM AUTOMATON LADY VIRGINAL PLAYERS TO ORCHESTRION. New York: Crown, 1973. 334 p. Illus., appendix, index.

A history from antiquity of automaton displays, musical boxes, tin discs, automatic orchestras, organettes and self-playing organs, player pianos, gramophones, and other devices.

1065 Orloff, Katherine. ROCK'N ROLL WOMAN. Los Angeles: Nash, 1974. 199 p. Illus.

Interviews with Bonnie Raitt, Grace Slick, Maria Muldar, Rita Coolidge, Linda Ronstadt, and Carly Simon.

1066 Otis, Johnny. LISTEN TO THE LAMBS. New York: W.W. Norton, 1968. 256 p.

Autobiography of a white jazz and rock musician who identified with and was accepted into the black community.

1067 Palmer, Tony. ALL YOU NEED IS LOVE: THE STORY OF POPULAR MUSIC. New York: Grossman, Viking, 1976. 323 p. Illus., index.

An illustrated survey of ragtime, jazz, blues, vaudeville and music halls, Tin Pan Alley, musicals, swing, rhythm and blues, country, war and protest, rock and roll, the Beatles, "sour rock," and glitter rock.

1068 Pease, Esther E., ed. COMPILATION OF DANCE RESEARCH, 1901-1964. Washington, D.C.: American Association for Health, Physical Education, and Recreation, 1964. 52 p. Topical index.

A bibliography of 704 items on dance research.

1069   Pitts, Michael R., and Harrison, Louis H. HOLLYWOOD ON RECORD:
THE FILM STARS' DISCOGRAPHY. Metuchen, N.J.: Scarecrow Press,
1978. 411 p.

> Lists LPs and representative 45 rpm recordings of motion
> picture performers.

1070   Pleasants, Henry. THE GREAT AMERICAN POPULAR SINGERS. New
York: Simon and Schuster, 1974. 384 p. Glossary, name index.

> An appreciative analysis of the contributions of twenty-two
> popular singers from Al Jolson through Barbra Streisand. The
> introduction compares and contrasts popular and classical sing-
> ing, and a brief chapter notes the characteristics of popular
> song styling.

1071   Pollock, Bruce. IN THEIR OWN WORDS: LYRICS AND LYRICISTS,
1955-1974. New York: Macmillan, 1975. 231 p. Illus.

> Interviews with twenty pop lyricists.

1072   Price, Steven D. OLD AS THE HILLS: THE STORY OF BLUEGRASS
MUSIC. New York: Viking, 1975. 110 p. Illus., notes.

> An introduction to the genre, with chapters on the roots,
> modern innovations, and featured performers.

1073   Rabson, Carolyn. SONGBOOK OF THE AMERICAN REVOLUTION.
Peaks Island, Maine: NEO Press, 1974. 112 p. Bibliog., index,
music, lyrics.

> Brief notes introduce ballads, hymns, and national songs.

1074   Redd, Lawrence N. ROCK IS RHYTHM AND BLUES: THE IMPACT OF
MASS MEDIA. East Lansing: Michigan State University Press, 1974.
167 p.

> Analysis of the two forms, together with interviews of blues
> performers.

1075   Reid, Jan. THE IMPROBABLE RISE OF REDNECK ROCK. Austin, Tex.: Hei-
delberg Publishers, 1974. Reprint. New York: DaCapo, 1977. 342 p. Illus.

> An informal account of the background, personalities, good
> times, and music of country rock.

1076   Reisner, Robert George, comp. THE LITERATURE OF JAZZ: A SELEC-
TIVE BIBLIOGRAPHY. 2d ed. New York: New York Public Library,
1959. 63 p.

> A checklist of books and periodicals.

1077   Roehl, Harvey. PLAYER PIANO TREASURY: THE SCRAPBOOK HISTORY OF THE MECHANICAL PIANO IN AMERICA AS TOLD IN STORY, PIC-TURES, TRADE JOURNAL ARTICLES AND ADVERTISING. 1961. 2d ed. Vestal, N.Y.: Vestal Press, 1973. 251 p. Illus.

A documentary history of piano and violin playing machines.

1078   Rowe, Mike. CHICAGO BREAKDOWN. New York: Drake Publishers, 1975. 226 p. Illus., discography, index.

A history of Chicago blues, through discussion of the musicians, record entrepreneurs, night clubs, and social life.

1079   Roxon, Lillian. LILLIAN ROXON'S ROCK ENCYCLOPEDIA. 1969. New York: Grosset and Dunlap, 1978. 565 p. Illus.

Entries are primarily of performers, with a few subjective entries on styles; entries on performers include albums and dates with cuts listed, plus singles through about 1968. An appendix contains a chronological listing of CASH BOX top selling albums (1960-68) and singles (1949-68), as well as a list of BILLBOARD top weekly singles (1950-67).

1080   Russell, Tony. BLACKS, WHITES AND BLUES. London: Studio Vista, 1970. 112 p. Illus., bibliog., index, discography.

A brief topical account of the blues from minstrelsy through white response, with chapters on regional variations.

1081   Rust, Brian A.L. THE AMERICAN DANCE BAND DISCOGRAPHY: 1917-1942. 2 vols. New Rochelle, N.Y.: Arlington House, 1975. 2,066 p.

A seemingly exhaustive compilation from recording company files and catalogs, which lists releasing company, date of release, songs, artists, and catalog numbers.

1082   _____. THE AMERICAN RECORD LABEL BOOK. New Rochelle, N.Y.: Arlington House, 1978. 336 p. Glossary.

An authoritative listing, with descriptions of company activi-ties, of record labels in effect through 1942.

1083   _____. THE DANCE BANDS. London: Ian Allan, 1972. 160 p. Illus., index.

A survey of American dance bands in the United States and England from about 1919 to about 1944.

1084   Sarlin, Bob. TURN IT UP!: (I CAN'T HEAR THE WORDS); THE BEST OF THE NEW SINGER/SONGWRITERS. New York: Simon and Schuster, 1974. 222 p. Photos.

A tribute to song poets such as Bob Dylan, Joni Mitchell, Randy Newman, Van Morrison, Laura Nyro, Don McLean, and Robert Hunter.

1085 Schafer, William J., and Riedel, Johannes. THE ART OF RAGTIME: FORM AND MEANING OF AN ORIGINAL BLACK AMERICAN ART. Baton Rouge: Louisiana State University Press, 1973. 249 p. Illus., bibliog., index, appendixes.

A history and analysis of ragtime as an original popular form, with emphasis on the musical qualities, performance, and thematic variations.

1086 Sears, Minnie Earl. SONG INDEX: AN INDEX TO MORE THAN 12,000 SONGS IN 177 SONG COLLECTIONS, COMPRISING 262 VOLUMES. New York: Shoe String Press, 1967.

An index which includes both the original 1926 volume and the 1934 supplement. Contains an alphabetical list of titles, composers, authors, first lines, references, and in many cases, voice; with a classified list of collections indexed, and a directory of publishers.

1087 _____, comp. STANDARD CATALOG FOR PUBLIC LIBRARIES, FINE ARTS SECTION: AN ANNOTATED LIST OF 1200 TITLES, INCLUDING BOOKS ON COSTUME AND AMUSEMENTS, WITH A FULL ANALYTICAL INDEX. New York: H.W. Wilson, 1928. 191 p.

An analytical index of items in the 700-799 classification of the Dewey decimal system, together with 391 (costume).

1088 Shapiro, Nat. POPULAR MUSIC: AN ANNOTATED INDEX OF AMERI-CAN POPULAR SONGS. 6 vols. New York: Adrian Press, 1964-73. Vol. 1, 1950-59; vol. 2, 1940-49; vol. 3, 1960-64; vol. 4, 1930-39; vol. 5, 1920-29; vol. 6, 1965-69.

Yearly listings by title. Other information includes title variations, author, composer, current publisher, and the medium in which the song was introduced.

1089 Shapiro, Nat, and Hentoff, Nat, eds. HEAR ME TALKIN' TO YA: THE STORY OF JAZZ AS TOLD BY THE MEN WHO MADE IT. New York: Rinehart, 1955. Reprint. New York: Dover, 1966. 429 p. Index.

Anecdotes of New Orleans and its musicians, and of the various personalities and styles associated with jazz as told by over one hundred musicians.

1090 _____. THE JAZZ MAKERS. New York: Rinehart, 1957. 368 p. Illus., index.

> Essays on Jelly Roll Morton, Warren "Baby" Dodds, Louis Armstrong, Jack Teagarden, Earl Hines, Bix Beiderbecke, Pee Wee Russell, Bessie Smith, "Fats" Waller, Art Tatum, Coleman Hawkins, Benny Goodman, Duke Ellington, Charlie Parker, Fletcher Henderson, William "Count" Basie, Lester Young, Billie Holiday, Roy Eldridge, Charlie Christian, and John "Dizzy" Gillespie.

1091 Shaw, Arnold. THE ROCKIN' '50S: THE DECADE THAT TRANSFORMED THE POP MUSIC SCENE. New York: Hawthorn Books, 1974. 296 p. Discography, illus., bibliog., index.

> Accounts of the major singers and groups from the end of the Tin Pan Alley era through the emergence of rock and roll, with interviews with Frankie Lane, Johnnie Ray, Jerry Wexler, Ahmet Ertegun, B.B. King, Bo Diddley, Bill Haley, Jerry Lee Lewis, Paul Anka, and Della Reese.

1092 Shelton, Robert, and Goldblatt, Burt. THE COUNTRY MUSIC STORY: A PICTORIAL HISTORY OF COUNTRY AND WESTERN MUSIC. Secaucus, N.J.: Castle Books; New Rochelle, N.Y.: Arlington House, 1966. 256 p. Illus., discography, index.

> Traces country and western music from its emergence in media through contributions by major figures and institutions. Some rare photographs.

1093 Shemel, Sidney, and Krasilovsky, M. William. THIS BUSINESS OF MUSIC. New York: Billboard Publications, 1964. 426 p. Appendixes, index.

> An extensive survey of typical business arrangements and legal agreements among industry parties. The volume covers artist contracts, foreign recording agreements, independents, record clubs, agents, payola, counterfeiting, regulation, copyright, contracts, organizations' mechanical rights, arrangements and abridgments, privacy, and protection. Appendixes reprint extensive trade agreements and standard contract forms.

1094 Shestack, Melvin. THE COUNTRY MUSIC ENCYCLOPEDIA. New York: Thomas Y. Crowell, 1974. 410 p. Photos., index.

> Entries average one column or less and are primarily of performers, often with photographs. Lists include the Country Music Association's list of radio stations in the United States, Puerto Rico, and Canada; a discography of available recordings; and a brief sample of sheet music facsimiles.

1095 Simon, George T. THE BIG BANDS. New York: Macmillan, 1967.
537 p. Illus., index.

A consideration of the milieu for the bands, profiles of
several hundred bands, and key personnel.

1096 Spaeth, Sigmund. THE FACTS OF LIFE IN POPULAR SONG. New
York: Whittlesey House, 1934. 148 p.

A light, though often pithy examination of numerous popular
songs of the thirties, with emphasis on the innuendoes in
those of the Tin Pan Alley variety. Spaeth discusses as well
rhyming patterns, the simplification of grammar in songs, torch
singers, nostalgic tendencies, novelty songs, and domestic and
nature imagery.

1097 _____. A HISTORY OF POPULAR MUSIC IN AMERICA. New York:
Random House, 1948. 729 p. Song lists, bibliog., index.

A standard history of popular music which features a wealth
of detail for each decade. A chapter is devoted to the
emergence of ragtime and jazz.

1098 Stambler, Irwin. ENCYCLOPEDIA OF POP, ROCK AND SOUL. New
York: St. Martin's Press, 1974. 609 p. Bibliog., award lists, illus.

Brief factual entries on contemporary performers from about
the early sixties to the early seventies, with commentaries
by Johnny Otis, Michael Ochs, and a brief history by
Stambler. Appendixes include Gold Record Awards from
1958-73, Grammy winners from 1958-73, Oscar nominees and
winners for the best song and scoring from 1965-73.

1099 _____. ENCYCLOPEDIA OF POPULAR MUSIC. New York: St. Martin's
Press, 1965. 359 p. Illus., bibliog., discography.

More conservative than his ENCYCLOPEDIA OF POP, ROCK
AND SOUL (see entry above), this volume covers several
decades prior to the publication date. Articles include tips
on tape recorders and stereophonic sound, together with Hal
Levy's "The Popular Song." Appendixes include a list of
the National Academy of Recording Arts and Sciences Achievement Awards, 1958-1964; a list of four musicals awarded the
Pulitzer Prize for drama; Oscar nominees and winners for best
song and scoring, 1934-1964; and the Recording Industry Association of America Gold Record awards from 1958-1965. Discographies for performers, composers, and musicals are included.

1100 Stambler, Irwin, and Landon, Grelun. ENCYCLOPEDIA OF FOLK,

COUNTRY AND WESTERN MUSIC. New York: St. Martin's Press, 1969. 396 p. Bibliog., discography.

Brief encyclopedic entries on performers and some institutions and styles. Special articles on folk and country music and the relationship between country and popular music. Appendixes include a list of NARAS Grammy Awards, 1958-1968; RIAA Gold Record Awards, 1958-1968; Country Music Hall of Fame Members, 1961-68; Country Music Association Awards, 1967-1968; Academy of Country Music and Western Music Awards, 1965-1967.

1101   Steane, J.B. THE GRAND TRADITION: SEVENTY YEARS OF SING-ING ON RECORD. New York: Scribners, 1974. 628 p. Illus., bibliog., index.

A Art and classical songs.

1102   Stearns, Marshall. THE STORY OF JAZZ. New York: Oxford, 1956. 367 p. Illus., notes, bibliog., index.

A history that begins with African and West Indian roots, tours New Orleans, considers folk and blues traditions, and traces the development of jazz into the 1950s.

1103   Stokes, Geoffrey. STAR-MAKING MACHINERY: THE ODYSSEY OF AN ALBUM. New York: Bobbs, 1976. 234 p. Illus.

Travelling with Commander Cody and the Lost Planet Airmen, Stokes chronicles the problems of making and selling music.

1104   Tassin, Myron, and Henderson, Jerry. FIFTY YEARS AT THE GRAND OLE OPRY. Foreword by Minnie Pearl. Introduction by Mother May-belle Carter. Gretna, La.: Pelican, 1975. 112 p. Illus.

A pictorial history.

1105   Tawa, Nicholas E. SWEET SONGS FOR GENTLE AMERICANS: THE PARLOR SONG IN AMERICA, 1790-1860. Bowling Green, Ohio: Bowling Green University Popular Press, 1980. 273 p. Bibliog., illus., notes, index.

An extensive examination of this influential form, with chapters on its acceptance, ballad singers, minstrel songs, economics, subject matter, musical characteristics, and its role in music education.

1106   Thurman, Howard. DEEP RIVER: REFLECTIONS ON THE RELIGIOUS INSIGHT OF CERTAIN NEGRO SPIRITUALS. New York: Harper, 1945. Reprint. Port Washington, N.Y.: Kennikat Press, 1969. 93 p.

An inspirational interpretation of spirituals based on the author's experiences and his reading of other interpretations.

1107 Titon, Jeff Todd. EARLY DOWNHOME BLUES: A MUSICAL AND CULTURAL ANALYSIS. Urbana: University of Illinois Press, 1977. 296 p. Illus., bibliog., index.

An analysis of the cultural and musicological aspects of blues, with consideration of records, the song-producing system, formulaic structure of lyrics, race record advertisements, patterns of listening, and related matters.

1108 Truzzi, Marcello. "The 100% American Song-Bag: Conservative Folk-songs in America." WESTERN FOLKLORE 28, no. 1 (1969): 27-40.

Folk songs and quasi-folk songs in the past frequently identi-fied their sentiments with the status quo. Examples are lyrics that are antiunion, southern pro-slave, oppressed Negro, anti-revolutionist. Criteria for collection of songs should be his-torical accuracy, not propaganda. If present bias in collect-ing continues, the "cultural diversity" of American song will be the last consideration of future historians.

1109 Tudor, Dean, and Biesenthal, Linda. ANNUAL INDEX TO POPULAR MUSIC RECORD REVIEWS. Metuchen, N.J.: Scarecrow Press, 1972-- Index.

Indexes reviews of about fifty-seven hundred records of rock, mood and pop, country, old time music and bluegrass, folk and ethnic, jazz, blues, soul, reggale and salsa, popular religious music, show and humor, and anthologies and con-certs; with a directory of labels, specialty stores.

1110 Tudor, Dean, and Tudor, Nancy. GRASS ROOTS MUSIC. Littleton, Colo.: Libraries Unlimited, 1979. 367 p. Indexes.

Essentially an expanded and extensively annotated discography with appropriate apparatus for identifying and collecting re-corded folk and country music, the volume contains a brief history and discussion of related genres as well. Included are descriptions of ethnic background material, British and Ameri-can folk traditions, American folk revivals, old time music, and bluegrass, southwestern, country, sacred, and troubador music as it has been preserved on discs in anthologies and performers' major works. Indexes to book and periodical citations, di-rectories of labels and specialized record dealers, and artist index.

1111 _____. POPULAR MUSIC PERIODICALS INDEX. Metuchen, N.J.: Scarecrow Press, 1973-- . Annual.

Subject index of forty-seven popular music periodicals and selective index of nineteen.

1112   Ulanov, Barry. A HANDBOOK OF JAZZ. New York: Viking, 1957. 248 p. Bibliog., chronology, index.

An introduction to jazz, with brief biographical notes on performers.

1113   _____. A HISTORY OF JAZZ IN AMERICA. New York: Viking, 1952. Reprint. New York: DaCapo, 1972. 382 p. Glossary, index.

The DOWN BEAT columnist's informal history of personalities, city scenes, and styles.

1114   Ullman, Michael. JAZZ LIVES: PORTRAITS IN WORDS AND PICTURES. Washington, D.C.: New Republic Books, 1980. 244 p. Illus., discography.

Career sketches of twenty-three jazz musicians.

1115   Vassal, Jacques. ELECTRIC CHILDREN: ROOTS AND BRANCHES OF MODERN FOLKROCK. New York: Taplinger Publishing Co., 1976. 270 p. Illus., bibliog., discography, index.

A Frenchman's account of the growth of rock music, beginning with the contributions of blacks, whites, and by inference, Indians. Chapters on Guthrie, Dylan, urban folk festivals, new consciousness, and British contributions.

1116   VICTORIAN SHEET MUSIC COVERS. By Ronald Pearsall. Detroit: Gale Research Co., 1972. 116 p. Illus., index.

Victorian sheet music covers are a fascinating mirror of an age, a special kind of ephemera that reflects the times with more clarity and insight than academic pictures of the period. Pearsall presents fifty-seven prime examples of covers created by important graphic artists who depicted the musicians and performers of the great music halls as well as scenes inspired by the popular music. He discusses the printing techniques, the artists, and the events and personalities, portrayed.

1117   Walton, Oritz M. MUSIC: BLACK, WHITE, AND BLUE: A SOCIO-LOGICAL SURVEY OF THE USE AND MISUSE OF AFRO-AMERICAN MUSIC. New York: William Morrow and Co., 1972. 180 p.

History of Afro-American music and critique of the situation of Afro-American music in the contemporary music industry.

1119   Whitcomb, Ian. AFTER THE BALL: POP MUSIC FROM RAG TO ROCK. New York: Simon and Schuster, 1972. 312 p. Index.

A history of popular music from the nineteenth century through contemporary rock, with the author's British experiences woven in as a commentary on contemporary practices. Sections cover the development of Tin Pan Alley, innovations in styles and technology between World War I and II, Britain from World War II, and the emergence of rock in America and Britain.

1120   Whiteman, Paul, and McBride, Mary Margaret.   JAZZ.   New York: J.H. Sears, 1926.   Reprint.   New York: Arno Press, 1974.   298 p. Illus.

Autobiography and history of big band jazz.

1121   Wolfe, Richard J.   SECULAR MUSIC IN AMERICA, 1801-1825:   A BIBLIOGRAPHY.   3 vols.   New York: New York Public Library, 1964. 1,238 p.   Index, illus.

A descriptive bibliography of published music, arranged alphabetically by composer.

DANCE

1122   Ames, Jerry, and Siegelman, Jim. THE BOOK OF TAP: RECOVERING AMERICA'S LONG LOST DANCE. New York: David McKay Co., 1977. 178 p. Instructions, bibliog., index.

    A celebration and history of tap dancing from its roots in diverse informal dancing styles to contemporary studios.

1123   Beaumont, Cyril W. A BIBLIOGRAPHY OF DANCING. London: The Dancing Times, 1929. Reprint. New York: Benjamin Blom, 1963. 228 p. Index.

    An annotated bibliography of books on all aspects of popular, art, folk, ceremonial, and other forms of dance.

1124   Chujoy, Anatole, and Manchester, P.W., comp. and ed. THE DANCE ENCYCLOPEDIA. New York: A.S. Barnes, 1949. Rev. ed. New York: Simon and Schuster, 1967. 546 p. Bibliog., discography, illus.

    Arranged alphabetically by subject, the volume contains references to personalities, topics, and previous publications, with brief signed articles on major subjects.

1125   Cressey, Paul G. THE TAXI-DANCE HALL: A SOCIOLOGICAL STUDY IN COMMERCIALIZED RECREATION AND CITY LIFE. Chicago: University of Chicago, 1932. 300 p. Index.

    A description of the world, dancers, patrons, problems, prospects for reform, and attendant matters oriented to dance halls.

1126   Dannett, Sylvia G.L., and Rachel, Frank R. DOWN MEMORY LANE: ARTHUR MURRAY'S PICTURE STORY OF SOCIAL DANCING. New York: Greenberg, 1954. 191 p. Illus.

    Essentially a series of captioned photographs, cartoons, illustrations and other ephemera.

1127   Franks, A.H. SOCIAL DANCE: A SHORT HISTORY. London: Routledge and Kegan Paul, 1963. 233 p. Bibliog., index.

      After a chapter on ancient origins, the volume focuses on centuries, from the fifteenth through the middle twentieth, with international coverage. Appendixes include a section from THE CHRONICLES OF FROISSART (1393), an essay from March 23, 1844, edition of THE ILLUSTRATED LONDON NEWS on the polka, two extracts from DANCING (1895), an excerpt from Irene and Vernon Castle's MODERN DANC- ING (1914), and an excerpt from Gladys Beattie Crozier's THE TANGO AND HOW TO DANCE IT (1913).

1128   Gonos, George. "Go-Go Dancing: A Comparative Frame Analysis." URBAN LIFE 5 (July 1976): 189-220.

      Sociological analysis of the entertainment popular in bars during the 1960s and early 1970s.

1129   Hanna, Judith Lynne. TO DANCE IS HUMAN: A THEORY OF NON- VERBAL COMMUNICATION. Austin: University of Texas, 1979. 327 p. Appendixes, notes, illus., bibliog., index.

      An examination of the bases of dancing in psychology, social intercourse, social structure, somatic expression, with atten- tion to dance in religion, politics, ethnic groups, and modern urban societies.

1130   Highwater, Jamake. DANCE: RITUALS OF EXPERIENCE. New York: A and W Publishers, 1978. 223 p. Illus., bibliog., index.

      A ritual analysis of modern dance, with consideration of dance as a separate reality and synopses of ten dances.

1131   Jones, Bessie, and Hawes, Bess Lomax. STEP IT DOWN: GAMES, PLAYS, SONGS, AND STORIES FROM THE AFRO-AMERICAN HERITAGE. New York: Harper and Row, 1972. 233 p. Notes, bibliog., discog- raphy, index.

      An attempt to capture, through recordings of Jones's and the Georgia Sea Island Singers' performances and cross-checking of standard sources, the authentic heritage of Afro-American children's outdoor games, songs, musical accompaniments, and other forms of play.

1132   Kinney, Troy, and Kinney, Margaret West. SOCIAL DANCING OF TO-DAY. New York: Frederick A. Stokes, 1914. 49 p. Illus.

      Illustrated instructions for performing variations on the one step, the Boston, the hesitation waltz, and the Argentine tango.

1133   Lange, Roderyk. THE NATURE OF DANCE: AN ANTHROPOLOGICAL
        PERSPECTIVE. New York: International Publications Service, 1976.
        142 p. Illus., notes, bibliog., index.

        Considers origins, rhythm, movement, art, spiritual qualities,
        function and form, and dance as a component of human culture.

1134   Magriel, Paul David, comp. A BIBLIOGRAPHY OF DANCING: A
        LIST OF BOOKS AND ARTICLES ON THE DANCE AND RELATED SUB-
        JECTS. New York: H.W. Wilson, 1936. Reprint. New York:
        Benjamin Blom, 1966. 229 p. Index.

        Covers history, criticism; folk, national, and ethnological
        dancing; art, ballet, mime and pantomime, masques, costume,
        social dancing, and music. Includes supplements.

1135   _____, ed. CHRONICLES OF AMERICAN DANCE. New York:
        H. Holt, 1948. 268 p. Notes.

        Essays on Shaker ritual dance, minstrelsy, early musicals,
        ballroom dancing, and such notable dancers as John Durang,
        Mary Ann Lee, Augusta Maywood, George Washington Smith,
        Isadora Duncan, Loie Fuller, Maud Allen, and Martha Graham.

1136   Marks, Joseph E. III. AMERICA LEARNS TO DANCE: A HISTORICAL
        STUDY OF DANCE EDUCATION IN AMERICA BEFORE 1900. New
        York: Exposition Press, 1957. 133 p. Notes, index.

        A history of dance education from the seventeenth through
        the nineteenth century, with attention to books, the emergence
        of dancing masters, and formalized education in dance, ex-
        cluding ballet and stage dancing.

1137   Meerloo, Joost Abraham Maurito. THE DANCE, FROM RITUAL TO
        ROCK AND ROLL--BALLET TO BALLROOM. Philadelphia: Chilton,
        1960. 92 p. Illus., bibliog.

        Illustrations, with brief notes on types of dance and dance-
        like forms of expression.

1138   Nye, Russel B. "Saturday Night at the Paradise Ballroom: or, Dance
        Halls in the Twenties." JOURNAL OF POPULAR CULTURE 7 (Summer
        1973): 14-22.

        Concise analysis of the formative years of dance halls as
        an extremely popular form of socialization and entertainment.

1139   Rowe, Patricia A., and Stodelle, Ernestine, eds. DANCE RESEARCH
        COLLAGE: A VARIETY OF SUBJECTS EMBRACING THE ABSTRACT AND

THE PRACTICAL. New York: Congress on Research in Dance, 1979. 287 p. Illus., notes.

Essays on dance theories, human action sign and semasiology, symbolism and the meaning of movement, and related matters.

1140 Stearns, Marshall, and Stearns, Jean. JAZZ DANCE: THE STORY OF AMERICAN VERNACULAR DANCE. New York: Macmillan, 1968. 464 p. Notes, bibliog., filmography, illus., dance notation, index.

A history and analysis of Afro-American dance and its diffusion throughout American popular culture, with chapters on the beginnings, vernacular development in acts, Tin Pan Alley, Broadway, technical innovations, specialties, acrobatics, class acts, and the jitterbug, through the mid-1960s.

1141 Terry, Walter. THE DANCE IN AMERICA. New York: Harper and Row, 1956. 248 p. Illus., index.

A history of dance from colonial times to the 1950s, with chapters on innovators such as Isadora Duncan, Loie Fuller, Ruth St. Denis, Ted Shawn, Martha Graham, and Doris Humphrey. A survey of contemporary activities includes information on ballet, ethnic dances, dance in the media (film, theater, and television), recreational dancing, and archival work.

PUBLIC ART

1142 Ainsworth, Ed. THE COWBOY IN ART. New York: World Publishing Co., 1968. 242 p. Illus., index.

> An illustrated topical account of the cowboy in songs, paintings, sculpture, cartoons, children's art, and other forms.

1143 Battersby, Martin. THE DECORATIVE TWENTIES. New York: Walker and Co., 1969. 216 p. Illus., bibliog., index.

> Divided into sections on the decorative arts in France and those in England and America, the volume covers interior decoration, the industry, furniture, wallpaper, ceramics and glass, textiles, posters, and decorative painting.

1144 Bishop, Robert. AMERICAN FOLK SCULPTURE. New York: E.P. Dutton, 1974. 392 p. Illus., notes, bibliog., index.

> An illustrated discussion of gravestones, signs, weathervanes, figureheads, scrimshaw, statues, religious artifacts, pottery, carousel sculpture, circus artifacts, decoys, and toys.

1145 Cockcroft, Eva; Weber, John; and Cockcroft, James. TOWARD A PEOPLE'S ART: THE CONTEMPORARY MURAL MOVEMENT. New York: Dutton, 1977. 292 p. Illus., list of organizations, bibliog., index.

> A history and examination of contemporary murals painted by collectives or individual artists working in cooperation. Chapters cover various communities, funding, aesthetics, and cooperative projects.

1146 Davis, Douglas. ART AND THE FUTURE. New York: Praeger, 1973. 208 p.

> Argues that traditional art is dead and that a new classless art is emerging.

1147   Fundaburk, Emma Lila, and Davenport, Thomas G., comps. ART IN PUBLIC PLACES IN THE UNITED STATES. Bowling Green, Ohio: Bowling Green University Popular Press, 1975. 384 p. Photos., indexes.

       A collection of articles, with illustrations, by twenty-three contributors on a wide range of public art topics. The volume is divided into two parts: illustrated essays by artists and architects; and photographs of museums, schools, structures, and outdoor areas.

1148   Greif, Martin. DEPRESSION MODERN: THE THIRTIES STYLE IN AMERICA. New York: Universe Books, 1975. 192 p. Illus., index.

       An informal appreciation through illustrations of the functional machine art of modernism in contrast to art deco.

1149   Hemphill, Herbert W., Jr., and Weissman, Julia. TWENTIETH-CENTURY AMERICAN FOLK ART AND ARTISTS. New York: E.P. Dutton, 1974. 237 p. Illus., bibliog., index.

       A more or less chronological discussion of "folk artists" and their art from 1900 to the early 70s.

1150   Hull, John. ART DECO. San Francisco: Troubador Press, 1975. 47 p. Illus.

       Brief introduction with illustrations of designs for art deco projects in a dozen media.

1151   Lipman, Jean. AMERICAN FOLK DECORATION. 1951. New York: Dover, 1972. 163 p. Illus., bibliog., index.

       Illustrated informal essays with practical tips on furniture, tinware, fabrics, signs, and architectural decoration.

1152   Logan, Ian, and Henry Nield. CLASSY CHASSY. New York: A and W Visual Library, 1977. 82 p.

       An illustrated volume of reproductions of the pinup artwork on World War II, Korean War airplanes, and flight jackets.

1153   Marzio, Peter C. THE ART CRUSADE: AN ANALYSIS OF AMERICAN DRAWING MANUALS, 1820-1860. Washington, D.C.: Smithsonian Institution Press, 1976. 94 p. Notes, illus., bibliog.

       Examines the social effort to democratize art in 145 drawing manuals.

1154   Rossi, Paul A., and Hunt, David C. THE ART OF THE OLD WEST. New York: Alfred A. Knopf, 1971. 335 p. Illus., bibliog.

       A topical illustrated survey of western art.

1155   Schnier, Jacques. SCULPTURE IN MODERN AMERICA. Berkeley: University of California Press, 1948. Reprint. Westport, Conn.: Greenwood Press, 1972. 224 p. Illus., bibliog., index.

Traces sculpture from the formative period through modern expressionism with plates organized into heads, figures, animals, reliefs, and variant forms.

1156   Sommer, Robert. STREET ART. New York: Links Books, 1975. 66 p. Photos., bibliog.

A good brief introduction to amateur and professional outdoor murals, with emphasis on the late 1960s in the United States.

1157   Walters, Thomas, ART DECO. New York: St. Martin's Press, 1974. 87 p. Illus., index.

Brief introduction and notes for illustrations of art deco designs.

ADVERTISING

1158 Bauer, Raymond A.; Greyser, Stephen A.; et al. ADVERTISING IN AMERICA: THE CONSUMER VIEW: A REPORT AND INTERPRETATION OF THE AMERICAN ASSOCIATION OF ADVERTISING AGENCIES' STUDY ON THE CONSUMER JUDGMENT OF ADVERTISING. Boston: Harvard University, Division of Research, Graduate School of Business Administration, 1968. 473 p. Charts, tables, appendixes.

An interpretation of questionnaire data and discussion of traditional issues regarding public reactions to advertising, questions of deception, effectiveness of ads.

1159 Buzzi, Giancarlo. ADVERTISING: ITS CULTURAL AND POLITICAL EFFECTS. Translation by B. David Garmize. Minneapolis: University of Minnesota Press, 1968. 147 p. Notes, index.

Exploration of the cultural, political, and moral effects of advertising and their endemic relationships to capitalist marketing.

1160 Clinton, Katherine B. "The New West: Themes in Nineteenth Century Urban Promotion, 1815-1880." BULLETIN: MISSOURI HISTORICAL SOCIETY 30 (January 1974): 75-88.

Urban promoters used pitches with three primary elements to attract; natural advantages, Divine Providence, and quasi-scientific appeals.

1161 Cohen, Dorothy. ADVERTISING. New York: Wiley, 1972. 689 p. Illus., bibliog., index.

A textbook on advertising processes, social context, administration, creation, and communication, with study questions.

1162 Dispenza, Joseph E. ADVERTISING THE AMERICAN WOMAN. Dayton, Ohio: Pflaum, 1975. 181 p. Illus.

Notes on 285 advertisements for women's products that emphasize the implicit assumptions about stereotypical images.

1163   Ewen, Stuart. THE CAPTAINS OF CONSCIOUSNESS: ADVERTISING
        AND THE SOCIAL ROOTS OF CONSUMER CULTURE. New York:
        McGraw-Hill, 1977. 261 p. Notes, bibliog., index.

> Analysis of the ideology of consumer capitalism through exam-
> ination of the words of its spokesperson. Divided into three
> parts, "Advertising as Social Production," "The Political
> Ideology of Consumption," and "Toward a Modern Architec-
> ture of Daily Life," Ewen develops his argument through
> consideration of such topics as the self as commodity and the
> images of family members in advertising.

1164   Fowles, Jib. MASS ADVERTISING AS SOCIAL FORECAST: A METHOD
        FOR FUTURES RESEARCH. Westport, Conn.: Greenwood Press, 1976.
        153 p. Bibliog., illus., index, tables.

> Attempts to provide a methodology for forecasting the future
> through examination of advertisements.

1165   Freeman, William M. THE BIG NAME. New York: Printers' Ink Books,
        1957. 237 p. Illus., index.

> An informal survey of the use of testimonials with a wide
> range of products.

1166   Goffman, Erving. GENDER ADVERTISEMENTS. Cambridge, Mass.:
        Harvard University Press, 1979. 84 p. Illus., bibliog.

> An important contribution not only to the study of the depic-
> tion of male and female imagery, but also to the broad range
> of photographic portrayal and its effects on acquired perceptual
> tendencies.

1167   Heighton, Elizabeth, and Cunningham, Don R. ADVERTISING IN THE
        BROADCAST MEDIA. Belmont, Calif.: Wadsworth, 1976. 349 p.
        Illus., bibliog., index.

> A textbook of marketers, with sections on history, campaign
> development, buying and selling time, and social responsi-
> bility.

1168   Hower, Ralph Merle. HISTORY OF AN ADVERTISING AGENCY: N.W.
        AYER AND SON AT WORK 1869-1949. Rev. ed. Cambridge, Mass.:
        Harvard University Press, 1949. 647 p. Notes, portraits, index.

> A detailed history of one of the most successful, as well as
> earliest agencies in America.

1169   Langholz Leymore, Varda. HIDDEN MYTH: STRUCTURE AND SYM-
BOLISM IN ADVERTISING. New York: Basic Books, 1975. 208 p.
Notes, charts, appendixes, index.

A structural examination of magazine and television advertising
for a limited range of products over a brief span of time, focusing on the application of methodology.

1170   McLuhan, Marshall. THE MECHANICAL BRIDE: FOLKLORE OF IN-
DUSTRIAL MAN. New York: Vanguard Press, 1951. 157 p.

An attempt to discuss advertising and other imagery by presenting reproductions and discussing their features, together with
their place in context. There are useful observations on
comics, manners, popular values, celebrities, and other matters; a provocative potpourri of insights.

1171   Millum, Trevor. IMAGES OF WOMAN: ADVERTISING IN WOMEN'S
MAGAZINES. Totowa, N.J.: Rowan and Littlefield, 1975. 206 p.
Illus., bibliog., index.

An analysis of 1969 women's magazines in Britain, with a
useful survey of approaches to visual analysis, together with
chapters on interpretation of advertising.

1172   Noble, Valerie. THE EFFECTIVE ECHO: A DICTIONARY OF ADVER-
TISING SLOGANS. New York: Special Libraries Association, 1970.
165 p. Bibliog.

A brief introduction to slogans, with a cross-indexed list of
over two thousand slogans arranged by subject.

1173   Packard, Vance Oakley. THE HIDDEN PERSUADERS. New York:
David McKay, 1957. 275 p. Index.

A popular critique of psychological strategies in advertising
and politics.

1174   Paletz, David L.; Pearson, Roberta E.; and Willis, Donald. POLITICS
IN PUBLIC SERVICE ADVERTISING ON TELEVISION. New York:
Praeger, 1977. 116 p. Notes, index.

An investigation into the creation, promotion, and effects of
public service advertisements that attempts to weigh the in-
tent and influence of some forty-seven billion impressions
annually. PSAs are selectively funded to circumscribe alternative points of view and foster "pseudo-participation."

1175   Pease, Otis A. THE RESPONSIBILITIES OF AMERICAN ADVERTISING:
PRIVATE CONTROL AND PUBLIC INFLUENCE, 1920-1940. New Haven,

Conn.: Yale University Press, 1958. Reprint. New York: Arno Press, 1976. 232 p. Notes, bibliog., essay, index.

An examination of the record of advertising's concepts of public responsibility and the attitude of segments of the industry toward the consumer and problems between advertisers and consumers. A well documented study. The chapter on the development of persuasive techniques is especially useful. Covers newspaper and magazine advertising.

1176   Pollay, Richard W., ed. INFORMATION SOURCES IN ADVERTISING HISTORY. Westport, Conn.: Greenwood Press, 1979. 330 p. Index.

An annotated sources on advertising, with bibliographic essays on economic data, commercial and professional sources, and the trade press. Of interest are sources on history, psychology and sociology, case histories, and fiction.

1177   Presbrey, Frank. THE HISTORY AND DEVELOPMENT OF ADVERTISING, WITH MORE THAN THREE HUNDRED AND FIFTY ILLUSTRATIONS. Garden City, N.Y.: Doubleday, 1929. 642 p. Illus., index.

A history which includes information on ancient notices and British development, but which emphasizes American practices from colonial times through the 1920s. Chapters focus on key innovators, shifts in practice, and adaptation to new technologies.

1178   Preston, Ivan L. THE GREAT AMERICAN BLOW UP: PUFFERY IN ADVERTISING AND SELLING. Madison: University of Wisconsin Press, 1975. 368 p. Notes, table, index.

A study of "advertising statements which are not illegal though they cannot be proven to be true." The author traces the kinds and influence of this form of legal deception.

1179   Ramond, Charles. ADVERTISING RESEARCH: THE STATE OF THE ART. New York: Association of National Advertisers, 1976. 148 p. Bibliog., index, tables.

A review of current research on how advertising communicates and sells, theme research, target audiences, copy research, frequency, media research, budget research, and the future of such research.

1180   Rosefsky, Robert S. FRAUDS, SWINDLES, AND RACKETS: A RED ALERT FOR TODAY'S CONSUMERS. Chicago: Follett Publishing Co., 1973. 338 p.

A survey of the gimmicks and get-rich-quick schemes that pervade the American scene. Chapters cover mail-order schemes, home improvement rackets, land swindles, easy credit, other swindles, and suggestions for caution. Lists of consumer protection agencies.

1181   Rowsome, Frank, Jr. THEY LAUGHED WHEN I SAT DOWN: AN IN-FORMAL HISTORY OF ADVERTISING IN WORDS AND PICTURES. New York: Bonanza Books, 1959. 181 p. Illus.

A history of trends and themes in advertising from around 1900 through the 1940s.

1182   Schrank, Jeffrey. DECEPTION DETECTION: AN EDUCATOR'S GUIDE TO THE ART OF INSIGHT. Boston: Beacon Press, 1975. 154 p.

A handy little volume for teachers that includes chapters on standard deceptive practices, nonverbal communication, media deception, creativity training, and visual awareness.

1183   Selden, Joseph S. THE GOLDEN FLEECE: SELLING THE GOOD LIFE TO AMERICANS. New York: Macmillan, 1963. Reprint. New York: Arno Press, 1976. 305 p. Index.

Examines the central place of advertising in American society, and argues that by understanding advertising it is possible to better understand the culture. Chapters trace the development of advertising, the proliferation of goods, built-in obsolescence, packaging, media, the use of psychological techniques, and the "corruption of science."

1184   Tyler, Poyntz, ed. ADVERTISING IN AMERICA. New York: H.W. Wilson, 1959. 214 p. Bibliog.

Essays from popular magazines and trade periodicals are collected into sections on the world of agencies, media, and social and economic effects.

1185   Vries, Leonard de, and Amstel, Ilonka van, comps. THE WONDERFUL WORLD OF AMERICAN ADVERTISEMENTS, 1865–1900. Chicago: Follett, 1972. 143 p. Illus.

A collection of advertisements drawn from twelve popular magazines.

1186   Wagner, Charles L.H. THE STORY OF SIGNS: AN OUTLINE HISTORY OF THE SIGN ARTS FROM EARLIEST RECORDED TIMES TO THE PRESENT "ATOMIC AGE." Boston: Arthur MacGibbon, 1954. 123 p. Illus.

Immodestly described in the title, though coverage is spotty.

1187   Ward, Scott; Wackman, Daniel B.; and Wartella, Ellen. HOW CHIL-

DREN LEARN TO BUY: THE DEVELOPMENT OF CONSUMER INFORMA-
TION-PROCESSING SKILLS. Beverly Hills, Calif.: Sage Publications,
1977. 271 p. Bibliog., appendixes, index, charts.

Based on 615 interviews, the study attempts to isolate the
influence of both television commercials and parental attitudes as determinants of information processing.

1188 Watkins, Julian Lewis. ONE HUNDRED GREATEST ADVERTISEMENTS:
WHO WROTE THEM AND WHAT THEY DID. New York: Dover Publications, 1959. 234 p. Index.

There are 113 ads, each with a brief account of how they
originated and were promoted.

1189 Wight, Robin. THE DAY THE PIGS REFUSED TO BE DRIVEN TO MAR-
KET: ADVERTISING AND THE CONSUMER REVOLUTION. New York:
Random House, 1974. 230 p. Illus.

Argues that a transformation of the relationship between business and the consumer is taking place.

1190 Wood, James Playsted. THE STORY OF ADVERTISING. New York:
Ronald Press, 1958. 512 p. Bibliog., illus., index.

A history of advertising, with emphasis on significant changes.
Beginning with street vending, the volume traces newspaper
and magazine advertising, agencies, innovative businesses,
rhyming and the use of slogans and folk figures, radio, propaganda, and public complaints.

THEATER

1191   Anderson, John. THE AMERICAN THEATRE AND THE MOTION PICTURE
IN AMERICA. New York: Dial Press, 1938. 430 p. Illus., bibliog.,
index.

A brief critical history of American stage drama from 1787. Film
section by Rene Fülöp Miller (Zurich, Switz.: Amaltheaverlag,
1931).

1192   Blum, Daniel C. GREAT STARS OF THE AMERICAN STAGE: A PIC-
TORIAL RECORD. New York: Greenberg, 1952. 305 p. Index, illus.

A collection of portraits of 150 stars, with brief biographical
sketches.

1193   _____. A PICTORIAL HISTORY OF THE AMERICAN THEATRE, 1860-
1976. Enl. and rev. by John Willis. New York: Crown, 1977. 448 p.
4th ed.

The volume contains fifty pages of pre-1900 history and yearly
pictorial coverage from 1900 to 1976.

1194   Cartmell, Van Henry, and Cerf, Bennett, comps. FAMOUS PLAYS OF
CRIME AND DETECTION; FROM "SHERLOCK HOLMES" TO "ANGEL
STREET." Philadelphia: Blakiston Co., 1946. 910 p.

A collection of thirteen plays of crime and detection produced from 1899 to 1939.

1195   Charney, Maurice. COMEDY HIGH AND LOW: AN INTRODUCTION
TO THE EXPERIENCE OF COMEDY. New York: Oxford University
Press, 1978. 203 p. Illus., notes.

An extensive discussion of the language and rhetoric of comedy,
comic characters and their conventions, comic structure, such
forms as farce, tragic farce, burlesque, comedy of manners,
satire, and festive comedy; and seven aspects of the comic
hero.

1196   Churchill, Allen. THE GREAT WHITE WAY: A RE-CREATION OF
        BROADWAY'S GOLDEN ERA OF THEATRICAL ENTERTAINMENT. New
        York: Dutton, 1962. 310 p. Illus., bibliog., index.

    An account of Broadway hits from 1900 to 1919.

1197   Coad, Oral Sumner, and Mims, Edward, Jr. THE AMERICAN STAGE.
        New Haven, Conn.: Yale University Press, 1929. 362 p. Illus., index.

    A survey of theatrical development throughout the United
    States, the stars, producers, and stagecraft.

1198   Crawford, Mary Caroline. THE ROMANCE OF THE AMERICAN THEATRE.
        2d ed. Boston: Little, Brown, 1925. 508 p. Illus., notes, index.

    An account of major performers, with material on audiences
    and a chapter on the growth of minstrelsy.

1199   DiMeglio, John E. VAUDEVILLE, U.S.A. Bowling Green, Ohio:
        Bowling Green University Popular Press, 1974. 259 p. Bibliog., notes,
        illus., index.

    A study of background, key personalities, variety acts, the
    audience, censorship, performers, amateur nights, black per-
    formers, the geographical settings, and theater practices re-
    garding experimentation and conventionality.

1200   Disher, M. Willson. MELODRAMA: PLOTS THAT THRILLED. New
        York: Macmillan, 1954. 210 p. Illus.

    Illustrated examination of international melodrama in plays
    and films through the discussion of twenty-eight types. In-
    dexes to plays, films, individuals, and theaters.

1201   Elsom, John. EROTIC THEATER. New York: Taplinger, 1974. 269 p.
        Illus.

    The author compares social attitudes from 1890 to 1910 with
    those from 1950 to 1973.

1202   Engel, Lehman. THE AMERICAN MUSICAL THEATER. New York: Mac-
        millan, 1975. 266 p. Rev. ed. Discography, list of sources, bibliog.,
        index.

    An excellent introduction to the musical theater, especially
    its effective production, by one of Broadway's most knowledge-
    able musicians.

1203   _____. THE CRITICS. New York: Macmillan, 1976. 332 p. Index.

    An assessment of newspaper and magazine drama criticism and

reviews, focusing on contemporary critics and their contributions to the theater and its public.

1204 _____. THE MAKING OF A MUSICAL. New York: Macmillan, 1977. 157 p. Index.

A step-by-step analysis of the elements comprising musical shows, based on the author's musical theater workshop curriculum.

1205 _____. WORDS WITH MUSIC. New York: Macmillan, 1972. 358 p. Bibliog., index.

A study of the basic principles common to musicals in contrast to plays, with consideration given to operettas, operas, musical comedy, and similar genres.

1206 Eustis, Morton. BROADWAY INC! THE THEATRE AS A BUSINESS. New York: Dodd, Mead, 1934. Reprint. New York: Benjamin Blom, 1970. 356 p.

Commercial aspects of professional theater in America, from the costs of set building to the financial problems of the acting profession.

1207 Ewen, David. NEW COMPLETE BOOK OF THE AMERICAN MUSICAL THEATER. New York: Holt, Rinehart and Winston, 1970. 800 p. Illus., chronology, songlist, index.

Encyclopedic entries on musical shows, librettists, lyricists, and composers.

1208 _____. THE STORY OF AMERICA'S MUSICAL THEATRE. Philadelphia: Chilton Book Co., 1968. 278 p. Index.

An informal history of the music, primarily in the twentieth century, of burlesque, extravaganzas, revues, and musical comedies, with emphasis on composers and lyricists.

1209 Gilbert, Douglas. AMERICAN VAUDEVILLE: ITS LIFE AND TIMES. New York: McGraw-Hill, 1940. Reprint. New York: Dover, 1963. 428 p. Illus., list of acts, index.

An informal history from about 1880 to 1932 of halls and acts, with chapters on stock characters, performers, managers, and types of acts.

1210 Green, Stanley. ENCYCLOPEDIA OF THE MUSICAL THEATRE. New York: Dodd, Mead and Co., 1976. 488 p. Award list., bibliog., discography.

An encyclopedic guide to major personalities, productions, and songs regarding musical comedy, musical plays, musical farce, musical spectacle, revues, operettas, and commercial opera.

1211 _____. RING BELLS! SING SONGS! BROADWAY MUSICALS OF THE 1930S. New Rochelle, N.Y.: Arlington House, 1971. 385 p. Illus., credits, index.

An enthusiastic year-by-year account of 175 productions of the decade, including musical comedies, musical plays, revues, operettas, and operas.

1212 Grimsted, David. MELODRAMA UNVEILED: AMERICAN THEATRE AND CULTURE, 1800-1850. Chicago: University of Chicago Press, 1968. Bibliog., index.

Analysis of the cultural ideas embodied in melodrama through examination of the audiences, stages, performers, the variety of plays and entertainments, playwrights, the heritage of earlier plays, the structure of melodrama, and the themes and motifs found in the plays. Includes appendixes on popularity and the frequency of types.

1213 Harvey, Ruth. CURTAIN TIME. Boston: Houghton Mifflin, 1949. 310 p.

Reminiscences of Harvey's experiences in the theater.

1214 Havens, Daniel F. THE COLUMBIAN MUSE OF COMEDY: THE DEVELOPMENT OF A NATIVE TRADITION IN EARLY AMERICAN SOCIAL COMEDY, 1787-1845. Carbondale: Southern Illinois University Press, 1973. 181 p. Notes, bibliog., index.

A study of the emergence of American comic drama, focusing on Royall Tyler's THE CONTRAST (1787), William Dunlap's THE FATHER (1789), James Nelson Barker's TEARS AND SMILES (1807), Robert Montgomery Bird's THE CITY LOOKING GLASS (1828), Mowatt's FASHION (1845), and other comedies of manners.

1215 Heilman, Robert Bechtold. TRAGEDY AND MELODRAMA: VERSIONS OF EXPERIENCE. Seattle: University of Washington Press, 1968. 326 p. Notes.

Extended essay on the early forms of the genres, with attention to the perspectives they engender and the characteristic responses their audiences have for them.

1216 Hermassi, Karen. POLITY AND THEATER IN HISTORICAL PERSPECTIVE. Berkeley and Los Angeles: University of California Press, 1977. 222 p. Notes, bibliog., index.

A study of the relation of drama and political thought in ancient Greek, Elizabethan, and contemporary times, with the contemporary focus on Bertolt Brecht's dramas.

1217 Hodge, Francis. YANKEE THEATRE: THE IMAGE OF AMERICA ON THE STAGE, 1825–1850. Austin: University of Texas Press, 1964. 320 p. Illus., notes, bibliog., index.

A study of the emergence of the American vernacular characters and their relationship to American social history.

1218 Hopkins, Albert. MAGIC: STAGE ILLUSIONS AND SCIENTIFIC DIVERSIONS. New York: Benjamin Blom, 1897. Reprint. New York: Dover, 1976. 556 p. Illus., bibliog.

Late nineteenth-century stage tricks and machines, with a broad survey of the whole history of legerdemain, ventriloquism, and shadowgraphy.

1219 Hornblow, Arthur. A HISTORY OF THE THEATRE IN AMERICA. 2 vols. Philadelphia: J.B. Lippincott, 1919. Reprint. Philadelphia: Benjamin Blom, 1965. 729 p. Illus., notes, index.

A general history of major figures, theaters, and production to about 1910.

1220 Hoyt, Harlowe R. TOWN HALL TONIGHT. New York: Bramball House, 1955. 292 p. Illus., index.

The story of country theaters from 1880 to 1900, with emphasis on the stock companies and plays that kept them alive.

1221 Hughes, Glenn. A HISTORY OF THE AMERICAN THEATRE, 1700–1950. New York: Samuel French, 1951. 562 p. Illus., bibliog., index.

Especially useful are items on stars, promotion, commercialism, and the activities at various playhouses.

1222 Hummel, David. THE COLLECTOR'S GUIDE TO THE AMERICAN MUSICAL THEATRE. Grawn, Mich.: D.H. Enterprises, 1978. 238 p.

A discography and tape source for musicals that updates the 1955 edition. Covers original cast albums, studio cast albums, demonstration recordings, backer's auditions, foreign versions of American musicals, and private live performance tapes. Film and television musicals are cited only when the musical was also performed on stage.

1223 Inchbald, Mrs. Elizabeth, ed. A COLLECTION OF FARCES AND OTHER AFTERPIECES. 7 vols. London: Longman, Hurst, Rees, and Orme, 1809. Reprint. New York: Benjamin Blom, 1970. Illus.

Sixty-three plays that represent some of the most popular
theatrical entertainments of the end of the eighteenth century.

1224   Larson, Carl F.W.   AMERICAN REGIONAL THEATRE HISTORY TO 1900:
A BIBLIOGRAPHY.   Metuchen, N.J.:   Scarecrow Press, 1979.   187 p.
Indexes.

Contains published items arranged by state and city, with
regional listings for more general sources, miscellaneous
items, and bibliographies.   Indexes to foreign language
theater, persons, and authors.

1225   Laurie, Joe Jr.   VAUDEVILLE: FROM THE HONKY-TONKS TO THE
PALACE.   New York: Henry Holt, 1953.   561 p.   Index.

Accounts of personalities and types of acts that made vaudeville entertainment so popular.

1226   Lewis, Philip C.   TROUPING: HOW THE SHOW CAME TO TOWN.
New York: Harper and Row, 1973.   266 p.   Illus., index, notes.

Drama on the road from New York through the hinterlands
in 1905.   Photographs, play schedules.

1227   McLean, Albert F., Jr.   AMERICAN VAUDEVILLE AS RITUAL.   Lexington: University of Kentucky Press, 1965.   250 p.   Illus., notes, index.

A study of the symbolic and ritual expressions of vaudeville
in the manner of Cassirer's thesis, as an expression of "his-
torically significant value judgments upon life in an expanding industrial democracy."   The author sees vaudeville as a
bridge, from 1885-1930, by which secular ritual linked an
older pluralistic culture to modern mass culture.

1228   Mates, Julian.   THE AMERICAN MUSICAL STAGE BEFORE 1800.   New
Brunswick, N.J.:   Rutgers University Press, 1962.   331 p.   Notes,
bibliog., index.

Focusing on William Dunlap and Benjamin Carr's THE ARCHERS
(1796), the author explores the development of conventions
that form the basis for modern productions.

1229   Mayer, David, and Richards, Kenneth, eds.   WESTERN POPULAR
THEATRE.   London: Methuen, 1977.   277 p.   Illus., notes.

A collection of essays on international popular theater, with
useful studies of the Wild West exhibitions as drama of civilization, American burlesque, entertainment posters, and theory
of popular theater.

1230   Meserve, Walter J. AN EMERGING ENTERTAINMENT: THE DRAMA
        OF THE AMERICAN PEOPLE TO 1828. Bloomington: Indiana University
        Press, 1977. 342 p. Bibliog., index, notes.

   Useful study of early American drama, with chapters on
   moralities, melodramas and farces, and the influence of
   politics and nationalism in the plays.

1231   Moody, Richard. AMERICA TAKES THE STAGE: ROMANTICISM IN
        AMERICAN DRAMA AND THEATRE, 1750-1900. Bloomington: Indiana
        University Press, 1955. 322 p. Illus., notes, bibliog., list of plays,
        index.

   An exploration of the Romantic spirit in drama, indicating
   the significance of such native themes and characters as the
   Negro, Indian, Yankee, wars, frontier, folk and Negro minstrelsy; with chapters on the influence of Romance on acting,
   scene design, and the development of panoramas.

1232   Mordden, Ethan. BETTER FOOT FORWARD: A NEW HISTORY OF AMER-
        ICAN MUSICAL THEATRE. New York: Grossman, Viking, 1976.
        369 p. Bibliog., index.

   After a brief chapter on nineteenth-century backgrounds, the
   author explores revues, comic opera, operetta, book musicals,
   a history of developments by decades, and major productions.

1233   Morris, Lloyd. CURTAIN TIME: THE STORY OF THE AMERICAN
        THEATER. New York: Random House, 1953. 380 p. Illus., index.

   An informal history from the early nineteenth century to
   1953, with emphasis on the development of regional theaters,
   travelling performers, and the major productions throughout
   the nineteenth century.

1234   Mosedale, John. THE MEN WHO INVENTED BROADWAY: DAMON
        RUNYON, WALTER WINCHELL AND THEIR WORLD   New York: Richard
        Marek, 1981. 321 p. Illus., bibliog., index.

   An account of the friendship between Runyon and Winchell
   and of their influence on Broadway's emergence and style.

1235   Nathan, Hans. DAN EMMETT AND THE RISE OF EARLY NEGRO MIN-
        STRELSY. Norman: University of Oklahoma Press, 1962. 496 p. Illus.,
        documents, index.

   A useful study of the impersonations, early Negro bands, and
   minstrel groups, and the career of Emmett.

1236   Newton, Henry Chance. CRIME AND THE DRAMA: OR DARK DEEDS

DRAMATIZED. London: S. Paul, 1927. Reprint. Port Washington, N.Y.: Kennikat Press, 1970. 284 p. Illus., index.

An informal, often personal, account of stage thrillers.

1237 Paskman, Dailey. "GENTLEMEN BE SEATED!": A PARADE OF AMERI-CAN MINSTRELS. New York: Clarkson N. Potter, 1976. 253 p. Illus., index.

A light account with extensive examples of the content, places of origin, and major performers of minstrelsy.

1238 Quinn, Arthur Hobson. A HISTORY OF AMERICAN DRAMA FROM THE BEGINNINGS TO THE CIVIL WAR. New York: Harper, 1923. Reprint. New York: Appleton-Century-Crofts, 1964. 432 p. Checklist of plays, bibliog., index.

Gives the background, revolutionary drama, comedy, melo-drama, history plays, and major figures in production and writing that shaped the early history of the American theater.

1239 _____. A HISTORY OF AMERICAN DRAMA FROM THE CIVIL WAR TO THE PRESENT DAY. Rev. ed. New York: Appleton-Century-Crofts, 1951. Illus., bibliog., playlist, index.

Emphasis on playwrights and their contributions to realism, character types, frontier drama, Romance, manners, social comedy, protest, spectacle, passion, and melodrama.

1240 Rahill, Frank. THE WORLD OF MELODRAMA. University Park and London: Pennsylvania State University Press, 1967. 334 p. Bibliog., index.

Examines the production of France, England, and America through discussions of major themes.

1241 Richards, Stanley, ed. THE MOST POPULAR PLAYS OF THE AMERICAN THEATRE: TEN OF BROADWAY'S LONGEST-RUNNING PLAYS. New York: Stein and Day, 1979. 703 p.

Contains LIFE WITH FATHER; TOBACCO ROAD; ABIE'S IRISH ROSE; HARVEY; MARY, MARY; BAREFOOT IN THE PARK; ARSENIC AND OLD LACE; SAME TIME, NEXT YEAR; ANGEL STREET; and CACTUS FLOWER.

1242 Sampson, Henry T. BLACKS IN BLACKFACE: A SOURCE BOOK ON EARLY BLACK MUSICAL SHOWS. Metuchen, N.J.: Scarecrow, 1980. 552 p. Illus., index.

Chapters on the history of early black musical shows, pro-ducers and financial backers, theaters, comedy shows (1900-

1940), and biographical sketches of performers. Appendixes reproduce the TOBA (Theater Owners Booking Association) show contract, and partial lists of black musical shows and black newspapers, 1900–1940.

1243 Smith, Cecil. MUSICAL COMEDY IN AMERICA. New York: Theatre Arts Books; Robert M. MacGregor, 1950. 374 p. Illus., index.

An informal critical history from 1864 to 1950, focusing on major productions and personalities, with brief chapters on changes in style and formulas.

1244 Sobel, Bernard. A PICTORIAL HISTORY OF VAUDEVILLE. New York: Citadel Press, 1961. 224 p. Illus., picture index.

A brief general history with numerous publicity stills of the vaudeville era.

1245 Steele, William Paul. THE CHARACTER OF MELODRAMA: AN EXAMI-NATION THROUGH DION BOUCICAULT'S THE POOR OF NEW YORK, INCLUDING THE TEXT OF THE PLAY. University of Maine Studies, Second Series, no. 87. Orono: University of Maine Press, 1968. 111 p. Bibliog.

Outline of the features of melodrama, a brief discussion of the text together with a chart of actions and consequences.

1246 Stevenson, Isabelle, ed. THE TONY AWARD: A COMPLETE LISTING WITH A HISTORY OF THE AMERICAN THEATRE WING. New York: Crown, 1980. 165 p. Award regulations, theater list, Tony winners, index.

A brief history of American Theatre Wing and Antoinette Perry Awards is followed by a year-by-year list of winners in each category from 1947 to 1979.

1247 Stoddard, Richard, ed. THEATRE AND CINEMA ARCHITECTURE: A GUIDE TO INFORMATION SOURCES. Performing Arts Information Guide Series, vol. 5. Detroit: Gale Research Co., 1979. 368 p.

1248 Taubman, Howard. THE MAKING OF THE AMERICAN THEATRE. New York: Coward-McCann, 1967. 402 p. Illus., index.

The NEW YORK TIMES drama critic's informal history from about 1750 to the mid-1960s.

1249 Toll, Robert C. BLACKING UP: THE MINSTREL SHOW IN NINETEENTH-CENTURY AMERICA. New York: Oxford University Press, 1974. 310 p. Illus., notes, chronology, bibliog., index.

A perceptive examination of the cultural significance of

minstrel shows, with chapters on the emergence of a "common man's culture," the early shows, images of Negroes, Civil War content, post-Civil War transformation, social commentary, black minstrels, and the content of black minstrel shows.

1250 _____. ON WITH THE SHOW: THE FIRST CENTURY OF SHOW BUSINESS IN AMERICA New York: Oxford University Press, 1976. 361 p. Bibliog. essay, chronology, index.

Excellent introduction to popular entertainments through the early twentieth century in America. Covers early popular drama, P.T. Barnum, the circus, minstrel shows, Negroes in show business, nineteenth-century popular drama, musicals, strip tease, impersonators, vaudeville, and the Ziegfeld follies.

1251 Vernon, Grenville, comp. YANKEE DOODLE-DOO: A COLLECTION OF SONGS OF THE EARLY AMERICAN STAGE. New York: Payson and Clarke, 1927. Reprint. Detroit: Gale Research Co., 1978. 165 p. Illus., notes.

A collection of songs representative of plays from 1767 to 1840.

1252 Wilmeth, Don B., ed. THE AMERICAN STAGE TO WORLD WAR I: A GUIDE TO INFORMATION SOURCES. Performing Arts Information Guide Series, vol. 4. Detroit: Gale Research Co., 1978. 269 p.

Bibliography of materials on the American stage published from the late eighteenth century to the present.

1253 Wilson, Garff B. A HISTORY OF AMERICAN ACTING. Bloomington: Indiana University Press, 1966. 310 p. Illus., notes, index.

Emphasis is on performers, with chapters on heroic, classic, emotional, and personality schools, the comic stage, motion picture, radio and television acting, and the new theater.

1254 Young, William C. AMERICAN THEATRICAL ARTS: A GUIDE TO MANUSCRIPTS AND SPECIAL COLLECTIONS IN THE UNITED STATES AND CANADA. Chicago: American Library Association, 1971. 166 p. Index.

A descriptive listing of 136 collections in the United States and Canada.

1255 _____. FAMOUS AMERICAN PLAYHOUSES. 2 vols. Documents of American Theater History. Chicago: American Library Association, 1973. 624 p. Illus., bibliog., indexes.

Historical and architectural sketches of 199 playhouses from 1716 to 1771.

ENTERTAINMENTS

1256   Alexander, H.M. STRIP TEASE: THE VANISHED ART OF BURLESQUE.
New York: Knight Publishers, 1938. 124 p. Illus., glossary.

       Informal report of the business with a brief glossary of slang.

1257   Barnum, P.T. STRUGGLES AND TRIUMPHS: OR, FORTY YEARS' REC-
OLLECTIONS OF P.T. BARNUM WRITTEN BY HIMSELF. Hartford,
Conn.: J.B. Burr, 1869. Reprint. New York: Macmillan, 1930.
577 p.

       Barnum's autobiography from birth through age fifty-nine.

1258   Berger, Phil. THE LAST LAUGH: THE WORLD OF THE STAND-UP
COMICS. New York: William Morrow and Co., 1975. 377 p. Illus.

       Comedians from the fifties to the present through anecdotes.

1259   Bouissac, Paul. CIRCUS AND CULTURE: A SEMIOTIC APPROACH.
Bloomington: Indiana University Press, 1976. 206 p. Illus., notes,
index.

       One of the most useful applications of semiotics to popular
culture, the study considers acrobatic acts, horse acts, jugglers
and magicians, clown performances, circus posters, and the
poetics and ritual characteristics of animal acts.

1260   Burns, Thomas A., and Burns, Inger H. DOING THE WASH: AN EX-
PRESSIVE CULTURE AND PERSONALITY STUDY OF A JOKE AND ITS
TELLERS. Norwood, Pa.: Norwood Editions, 1976. 359 p. Bibliog.,
notes.

       A study of folk communications based on the selection and
telling of jokes by various tellers to particular audiences,
with various tests administered in order to determine psychological profiles and attitudes.

1261 Cahn, William. THE LAUGH MAKERS: A PICTORIAL HISTORY OF AMERICAN COMEDIANS. New York: G.P. Putnam's Sons, 1957. 192 p. Illus., notes.

Includes comic performers and comedians from 1787 to the early 1950s. Brief informal notes to a large collection of photographs.

1262 Caputi, Anthony. BUFFO: THE GENIUS OF VULGAR COMEDY. Detroit: Wayne State University, 1978. 263 p. Illus., notes, bibliog., index.

A discussion of the origins, development and contemporary manifestations of folk and popular comedy, with chapters on antiquity, carnival, May Festival, wooing revels, the Feast of Fools, revue plays, Plautine plays, and modern expressions of the form.

1263 Chapman, Antony J., and Foot, Hugh C., eds. IT'S A FUNNY THING, HUMOUR. New York: Pergamon Press, 1977. 507 p. Illus., bibliog.

A collection of essays on the nature of humor, comedy and laughter, methodology, humor as therapy, cross-cultural humor, children's humor, ethnic humor, humor and communication, individual differences in humor, comic humor, and further assorted essays. Contributions are primarily from psychologists and sociologists.

1264 Christopher, Milbourne. THE ILLUSTRATED HISTORY OF MAGIC. New York: Thomas Y. Crowell, 1973. 452 p. Illus., bibliog., index.

A general history that focuses on major events and personalities, with chapters on magic in the colonies, American Indian conjuring, vaudeville specialists, television productions, and other matters.

1265 Claflin, Edward. STREET MAGIC: AN ILLUSTRATED HISTORY OF WANDERING MAGICIANS AND THEIR CONJURING ARTS. Garden City, N.Y.: Dolphin, 1977. 156 p. Brief annotated bibliog., subject index.

Good, light history. Brief chapters on tribal origins, and Eastern and Western influences, with overall emphasis on contemporary American practices.

1266 Corio, Ann, with DiMona, Joseph. THIS WAS BURLESQUE. New York: Madison Square Press; Grosset and Dunlap, 1968. 197 p. Illus.

Informal pictorial history with speculations on the origins of the striptease and the use of comic routines on stage and television.

1267 Cox, Samuel S. WHY WE LAUGH. New York: Harper and Brothers, 1876. Reprint. New York: Benjamin Bloom, 1969. 387 p.

> An informal discussion of American humor in general, with particular attention to political humor, wit, anecdotes, burlesque, evasions, and related types found among politicians.

1268 Durant, John, and Durant, Alice. PICTORIAL HISTORY OF THE AMERI-CAN CIRCUS. New York: A.S. Barnes, 1957. 328 p. Index, bibliog.

> Traces the origins of the American circus from Old World roots through P.T. Barnum, summer quarters, and road seasons. Contains a list, with brief notes, of slightly over one hundred circuses.

1269 Eastman, Max. THE SENSE OF HUMOR. New York: Charles Scribner's Sons, 1921. Reprint. New York: Octagon, 1972. 257 p. Notes.

> A survey of the types of humor and their characteristic forms, with brief discussions of various attempts to understand how and why it works for people.

1270 Esar, Evan. THE COMIC ENCYCLOPEDIA: A LIBRARY OF THE LITERA-TURE AND HISTORY OF HUMOR CONTAINING THOUSANDS OF GAGS, SAYINGS, AND STORIES. Garden City, N.Y.: Doubleday, 1978. 831 p. Name index.

> Definitions of terms, styles, motifs, and themes in humor, with extensive examples.

1271 Feibleman, James. IN PRAISE OF COMEDY: A STUDY IN ITS THEORY AND PRACTICE. New York: Russell and Russell, 1962. 284 p. Notes, index.

> Chapters survey the history of comedy through the nineteenth century, classical theories of comedy, contemporary theories, and provide a discussion of the meaning of comedy. A final section examines types of comedy with illustrations from the Marx Brothers, James Joyce, Gertrude Stein, Charlie Chaplin, "Prince" Romanoff, surrealism, Will Rogers, and Charlie McCarthy.

1272 Finch, Christopher. THE ART OF WALT DISNEY: FROM MICKEY MOUSE TO THE MAGIC KINGDOMS. New York: H.N. Abrams, 1975. 458 p. Illus., bibliog., award list, index.

> An illustrated history of Disney Enterprises from early efforts through feature animation, live-action films, and the amusement parks.

1273 Fischer, Heinz-Dietrich, and Melnik, Stefan Reinhard, eds. ENTER-
TAINMENT: A CROSS-CULTURAL EXAMINATION. Humanistic Studies
in the Communication Arts. New York: Hastings House, 1979. 330 p.
Notes, bibliog., index.

> American popular culture is not directly treated in depth,
> but essays on entertainment as communication, studio audiences
> for television situation comedies, romantic fiction, news read-
> ing, advertising, theory of leisure, best-sellers, radio music,
> and other topics are thoughtfully treated and useful for com-
> parative purposes.

1274 Ford, Corey. THE TIME OF LAUGHTER. Boston: Little, Brown, 1967.
232 p. Index, bibliog., illus.

> A rambling autobiographical and historical sketch of New
> York and Hollywood in the 1920s and early 1930s.

1275 Fox, Charles Philip, and Kelley, F. Beverly. THE GREAT CIRCUS
STREET PARADE IN PICTURES. New York: Dover, 1978. 127 p. Illus.

> An illustrated history and topical discussion of circus parades
> through about 1939, with notes on variations of wagons,
> musical units, special features, and related matters.

1276 Franklin, Joe. JOE FRANKLIN'S ENCYCLOPEDIA OF COMEDIANS.
Secaucus, N.J.: Citadel, 1979. 349 p.

> A brief historical introduction is followed by biographical
> sketches of several hundred comedians and comedy terms.

1277 Fry, William F., Jr., M.D., and Allen, Melanie. MAKE 'EM LAUGH:
LIFE STUDIES OF COMEDY WRITERS. Palo Alto, Calif.: Science and
Behavior Books, 1975. 202 p. Illus., bibliog.

> Interviews with and interpretations of the humor of Norman
> Lear, Jack Elinson, Ruth Flippen, Bob Henry, Billy Barnes,
> Arnie Rosen, and Herbie Baker.

1278 Funnell, Charles E. BY THE BEAUTIFUL SEA: THE RISE AND HIGH
TIMES OF THAT GREAT AMERICAN RESORT, ATLANTIC CITY. New
York: Alfred A. Knopf, 1975. 208 p. Notes, bibliog., index.

> A social history of Atlantic City through some of the current
> nineteenth-century themes (machines and the city, nature,
> morality, and pleasure). The volume covers the period from
> 1890 to around 1908, during the heyday of the beach's de-
> velopment.

1279 Gill, Robert. MAGIC AS A PERFORMING ART: A BIBLIOGRAPHY OF
CONJURING. New York: Bowker, 1976. 252 p. Index.

An excellent annotated bibliography of books on all aspects of performance, with subject, name, and title indexes.

1280   Gordon, George N. EROTIC COMMUNICATIONS: STUDIES IN SEX, SIN, AND CENSORSHIP. New York: Hastings House, 1980. 338 p. Illus., notes, index.

An examination of the communication of erotica in print, pictures, moving pictures, and the marketplace, with chapters on censorship, "the sin market," the dynamics of prurience, the relationships of pornography and technoculture, and the future of the trade.

1281   Griffin, Al. "STEP RIGHT UP, FOLKS!" Chicago: Henry Regnery, 1974. 257 p. Park lists, illus., index.

The most authoritative book available on amusement parks, with chapters on rides, concessions, traditional amusement parks by geographical area, kiddielands, and theme parks.

1282   Grotjahn, Martin. BEYOND LAUGHTER: HUMOR AND THE SUBCON-SCIOUS. 1957. New York: McGraw-Hill, 1966. 285 p. Illus., notes, bibliog., index.

A psychoanalytic study of humor, with an introduction to Freud's perspective, and chapters on child development, comedy, clowns, burlesque queens, the circus, fantasy and art, Halloween, mystery stories, Westerns, Kilroy jokes, Ferdinand the Bull and Mickey Mouse, and ALICE IN WONDERLAND.

1283   Harris, Neil. HUMBUG: THE ART OF P.T. BARNUM. Boston: Little, Brown, 1973. 337 p. Illus., notes, index.

A corrective biography of Barnum that focuses on his public role as a symbol of change in the newly emerging democratic milieu of the nineteenth century.

1284   Jennings, Gary. PARADES! CELEBRATIONS AND CIRCUSES ON THE MARCH. Philadelphia: J.B. Lippincott, 1966. 150 p. Bibliog., index.

A celebration of parades from ancient times to the twentieth century. The illustrated volume features seasonal parades, heroic and funeral parades, military parades, parades associated with particular cultures and events, circus parades, and parade music.

1285   KIDDIELANDS: A BUSINESS WITH A FUTURE. North Tonawanda, N.Y.: Allan Herschell Co., n.d. 95 p. Illus.

Brief history of small midways for children, with hints for development and locations of kiddielands and their equipment.

1286 Kirby, E.T. "Popular Entertainments." DRAMA REVIEW 28 (March 1974): 5-15.

Traces the origins back to tribal rites of juggling, mime conjuring, fire eating, and other entertainments.

1287 Kniffen, Fred. "The American Agricultural Fair: Time and Place." ANNALS OF THE ASSOCIATION OF AMERICAN GEOGRAPHER 41 (March 1951): 42-57.

Diffusion of the fair.

1288 Kyriazi, Gary. THE GREAT AMERICAN AMUSEMENT PARKS: A PICTORIAL HISTORY. Secaucus, N.J.: Citadel Press, 1976. 256 p. Park index.

Essentially a guide to amusement parks, with a chapter on their growth. Major parks, such as Coney Island, Steeplechase Park, Luna Park, and Dreamland include historical sketches; less lavish parks are given collective treatment, while a chapter is devoted to Disneyland and other theme parks. Contains a brief annotated list of parks identified by state, with address and phone number.

1289 Levine, Jacob, ed. MOTIVATION IN HUMOR. New York: Atherton Press, 1969. 182 p. Notes, index.

Fourteen essays by contributors in various disciplines discuss humor and anxiety, as disturbing stimulus, psychological correlates of humor preferences, aggression and the need for social approval and humor, repression and insight as related to reactions to cartoons, clowning, and children's humor.

1290 Linn, Edward A. BIG JULIE OF VEGAS. New York: Walker, 1974. 217 p.

Biography of Julie Weintraub, a tour guide for the Dunes Hotel in Las Vegas.

1291 McGhee, Paul E., and Chapman, Antony J., eds. CHILDREN'S HUMOUR. New York: John Wiley and Sons, 1980. 322 p. Bibliog., index.

Essays on humor, play and self-regulation of arousal; imagination, interest and joy; the development of linguistic humor; children's literary development; creative aspects; humor, laughter and social interaction; individual differences; the sense of humor over time; humor and learning; the clinical use of

humor; and an overview of the research on children's humor
by psychologists.

1292 McKechnie, Samuel. POPULAR ENTERTAINMENTS THROUGH THE
AGES. Reprint. London: S. Low, Marston & Co., 1931. New
York: Benjamin Blom, 1969. 240 p. Illus.

Includes histories of mimes, minstrels, strolling players, fairs,
the comedy of masks, Punch and Judy, pantomime, music
halls, the cinematograph and the circus, primarily of England.

1293 Mangels, William F. THE OUTDOOR AMUSEMENT INDUSTRY: FROM
EARLIEST TIMES TO THE PRESENT. New York: Vantage Press, 1952.
206 p. Illus., association list.

Brief chapters trace the history of resorts, parks, carnivals,
Coney Island, devices, carrousels, merry-go-round music,
roller coasters, centrifugal pleasure railways, wheels, water
rides, mechanical swings, flat rides, towers, world's fairs,
fun houses, menageries, dance halls, lighting, fireworks,
and miscellaneous attractions.

1294 Marin, Louis. "Disneyland: A Degenerate Utopia." GLYPH I, pp. 50-66.
Johns Hopkins Textual Studies. Baltimore: Johns Hopkins University, 1977.

A structural analysis of the determining effects of the design,
iconology, and management perspectives of the amusement
park.

1295 Meyer, Robert, Jr. FESTIVALS U.S.A. AND CANADA. New York:
Ives Washburn, 1967. 280 p. List of annual events, index.

Extensive report on festivals oriented to agriculture, arts,
beauty, community, crafts, dance, drama, fairs, film, fish,
flora, folk, forest, holidays, Indians, music, sports, and
winter activities.

1296 Pieper, Josef. IN TUNE WITH THE WORLD: A THEORY OF FESTIVITY.
Translation from the German by Richard Winston and Clara Winston. New
York: Harcourt, Brace and World, 1965. 81 p.

A provocative argument for the understanding of festival in
its traditional sense through its inversion in modern societies.

1297 Ritchey, David. "Columbia Garden: Baltimore's First Pleasure Garden."
SOUTHERN SPEECH COMMUNICATION JOURNAL 39 (Spring 1974):
241-47.

The first transplanted English pleasure garden lasted from
1805 to 1807 and provided drinking, dining, theater, and
conversation for the wealthy.

1298   Rust, Brian A.L., and Debus, Allen G. THE COMPLETE ENTERTAIN-
MENT DISCOGRAPHY, FROM THE MID 1890S TO 1942. New Rochelle,
N.Y.: Arlington House, 1973. 677 p.

>Artists of American birth who worked in minstrel, vaudeville,
radio, film and drama; excluding jazz and blues musicians,
commercial dance bands, and artists known primarily through
records.

1299   Samuels, Charles. THE MAGNIFICENT RUBE: THE LIFE AND GAUDY
TIMES OF TEX RICKARD. New York: McGraw-Hill, 1957. 301 p.
Illus.

>Biography of the turn-of-the-century promoter and conspicuous
consumer extraordinaire.

1300   Samuels, Charles, and Samuels, Louise. ONCE UPON A STAGE: THE
MERRY WORLD OF VAUDEVILLE. New York: Dodd, Mead and Co.,
1974. 278 p. Illus., index.

>Informal history of vaudeville from secondary sources.

1301   Schickel, Richard. THE DISNEY VERSION. New York: Simon and
Schuster, 1968. 384 p. Bibliog., index.

>A critical history of Disney creation and merchandising ex-
ploits from Walt Disney's early films to the development of
an international commercial empire.

1302   Snow, Robert E., and Wright, David E. "Coney Island: A Case Study
in Popular Culture and Technical Change." JOURNAL OF POPULAR
CULTURE 9 (Spring 1976): 960-75.

>Coney Island went through numerous changes during its history,
often utilizing the latest technology.

1303   Sobel, Bernard. BURLEYCUE: AN UNDERGROUND HISTORY OF
BURLESQUE DAYS. New York: Farrar and Rinehart, 1931. 284 p.

>Brief chapters on features, circuits, houses, comics, acts,
management, strippers and posers, and miscellaneous information.

1304   Starbuck, James C. THEME PARKS: A PARTIALLY ANNOTATED BIB-
LIOGRAPHY OF ARTICLES ABOUT MODERN AMUSEMENT PARKS.
Council of Planning Librarians Exchange Bibliography, no. 953. Monti-
cello, Ill.: M. Vance, 1976. 20 p.

>Items are exclusively from popular magazines and technical
journals.

1305   Toole-Scott, Raymond. CIRCUS AND ALLIED ARTS: A WORLD BIB-
        LIOGRAPHY, 1500-1970; BASED MAINLY ON CIRCUS LITERATURE IN
        THE BRITISH MUSEUM, THE LIBRARY OF CONGRESS, THE UNIVERSI-
        TEITSBIBLIOTHEEK VAN AMSTERDAM, THE BIBLIOTHEQUE NATIONALLE
        AND ON HIS OWN COLLECTION. 4 vols. [Title varies slightly].
        Derby, Engl.: Harpur and Sons, 1958. 1,203 p. Index, illus., appendixes.

        Identifies, often with annotations, over fourteen thousand
        items on all aspects of the circus, with additional references
        on toys, prints, dime novels, juvenilia; dramas, novels and
        other art forms with circus orientation; and numerous miscel-
        laneous items related to circus, acts, performers, carnivals,
        expositions, and shows.

1306   Weaver, Robert B. AMUSEMENTS AND SPORTS IN AMERICAN LIFE.
        Chicago: University of Chicago Press, 1939. 195 p. Illus., bibliog.

        History of colonial amusements and sports, amusements follow-
        ing the revolutionary war, miscellaneous recreations of mid-
        century, frontier amusements, post Civil War amusements and
        sports, notes on movies and theater, and brief histories of
        selected sports.

1307   Wilde, Larry. THE GREAT COMEDIANS TALK ABOUT COMEDY. New
        York: Citadel Press, 1968. 382 p.

        Interviews with Woody Allen, Jack Benny, Milton Berle,
        Shelley Berman, Joey Bishop, George Burns, Johnny Carson,
        Maurice Chevalier, Phillis Diller, Jimmy Durante, Dick
        Gregory, Bob Hope, George Jessel, Jerry Lewis, Danny
        Thomas, and Ed Wynn.

1308   _____. HOW THE GREAT COMEDY WRITERS CREATE LAUGHTER.
        Chicago: Nelson-Hall, 1976. 285 p.

        Interviews with Goodman Ace, Norman Lear, Art Buchwald,
        Neil Simon, Mel Brooks, Abe Burrows, Bill Dana, Selma
        Diamond, Jack Douglas, Hal Kanter, Carl Reiner.

1309   Wilmeth, Don B., ed. AMERICAN AND ENGLISH POPULAR ENTER-
        TAINMENT: A GUIDE TO INFORMATION SOURCES. Performing Arts
        Information Guide Series, no. 7. Detroit: Gale Research Co., 1980.
        465 p. Index, appendixes.

        An annotated bibliography of 2,478 items on backgrounds, ex-
        hibitions, circus, animal acts, clowns, amusements, fairs, popu-
        lar museums, medicine shows, minstrel shows, vaudeville,
        burlesque and striptease, magic, illusions, musical theatre
        and related areas; with appendixes on periodicals, collections
        and museums, and organizations.

1310   Wilson, Christopher P. JOKES: FORM, CONTENT, USE AND FUNC-
TION. European Monographs in Social Psychology, no. 16. New York:
Academic Press, 1979. 252 p. Illus., bibliog., index.

An interdisciplinary attempt to provide a general explanation
of humor, particularly of jokes, partially based on original
experiments. The author discusses prior theories, amusement,
arousal hypotheses, joke content, taboo content, sexual content, derision and amusement, joking mechanisms, abuse,
filth, and personal and social functions.

1311   Yates, Norris Wilson. THE AMERICAN HUMORIST: CONSCIENCE OF
THE TWENTIETH CENTURY. Ames: Iowa State University Press, 1964.
410 p. Illus., bibliog.

Discussion of humor in the 1890s, the declining image of the
common man, John Kendrick Bangs, George Ade, Finley Peter
Dunne, Kin Hubbard, Will Rogers, Irvin S. Cobb, H.L.
Mencken, Ring Lardner, Don Marquis, Clarence Day, Jr.,
Robert Benchley, Dorothy Parker, James Thurber, E.B. White,
Will Cuppy, and S.J. Perleman.

1312   Zehnder, Leonard E. FLORIDA'S DISNEY WORLD: PROMISES AND
PROBLEMS. Tallahassee: Peninsular Publishing Co., 1975. 360 p.
Index, illus., bibliog.

A case history of the impact of tourism on central Florida
through the establishment of Walt Disney World. Emphasis
is on official sources.

LITERATURE

GENERAL WORKS

1313 Atkinson, Frank. DICTIONARY OF LITERARY PSEUDONYMS: A SELECTION OF POPULAR MODERN WRITERS IN ENGLISH. 2d ed. Hamden, Conn.: Linnet, 1977. 248 p.

Contains lists of real names and pseudonyms, some 8,000, without acknowledgment of sources.

1314 Austin, James, and Koch, Donald A., eds. POPULAR LITERATURE IN AMERICA: A SYMPOSIUM IN HONOR OF LYON N. RICHARDSON. Bowling Green, Ohio: Bowling Green University Popular Press. 1972. 205 p.

Essays on definition, popular taste in Cleveland, Ohio, detective fiction, southern mountain feud fiction, native themes in early nineteenth-century fiction, historical fiction, Westerns, colonial satire, Sut Lovingood, dialect sermons, burlesque skits in the mid-nineteenth century, reform fiction, Benjamin Flower's THE ARENA, post-Civil War writers, and television in American life.

1315 Bennett, James O'Donnell. MUCH LOVED BOOKS: BEST SELLERS OF THE AGES. New York: Liveright, 1927. 461 p. Bibliog.

Informal essays, with excerpts, on forty literary works, including such popular classics as TREASURE ISLAND, THE THREE MUSKETEERS, and others.

1316 Berman, Neil David. PLAYFUL FICTIONS AND FICTIONAL PLAYERS: GAME, SPORT, AND SURVIVAL IN CONTEMPORARY AMERICAN FICTION. Port Washington, N.Y.: Kennikat Press, 1981. 112 p. Notes, bibliog., index.

Essays on FAT CITY, NORTH DALLAS FORTY, END ZONE, ONE ON ONE, and THE UNIVERSAL BASEBALL ASSOCIATION.

1317   Berry, Thomas Elliott. THE NEWSPAPER IN THE AMERICAN NOVEL, 1900-1969. Metuchen, N.J.: Scarecrow, 1970. 170 p. Index.

        Examination of relevant fiction for conclusions about the newspaper in American culture, concluding that the picture is sketchy.

1318   Bibby, [Harold] Cyril. THE ART OF THE LIMERICK. Hamden, Conn.: Archon Books, 1978. 276 p. Illus., notes, bibliog., index.

        A general discussion of the limerick from Edward Lear's popularization of the form through contemporary efforts within the tradition.

1319   Blackburn, Alexander. THE MYTH OF THE PICARO: CONTINUITY AND TRANSFORMATION OF THE PICARESQUE NOVEL, 1554-1954. Chapel Hill: University of North Carolina Press, 1979. 267 p. Notes, bibliog., index.

        Includes chapters on the soul's dark journey, conversion of the natural man, the symbolic confidence man, and the tragicomedy of self-creation.

1320   Blake, Fay M. THE STRIKE IN THE AMERICAN NOVEL. Metuchen, N.J.: Scarecrow Press, 1972. 292 p. Bibliog., annot. bibliog. of novels, index.

        A chronology of the treatment of the strike from 1870 to 1945, with references to earlier works.

1321   Brown, Herbert Ross. THE SENTIMENTAL NOVEL IN AMERICA, 1789-1860. Durham, N.C.: Duke University Press, 1940. 407 p. Bibliog., index.

        An examination of the "social trends, forces, creeds, movements, and literary fashions" found in sentimental novels, beginning with a discussion of Richardson, Sterne, seduction, sentimentality and sex; with a discussion of the sentimental formula and several categories of it including temperance, emancipation, domestic, inspirational and other variations of the formula.

1322   Burns, Rex. SUCCESS IN AMERICA: THE YEOMAN DREAM AND THE INDUSTRIAL REVOLUTION. Amherst: University of Massachusetts Press, 1976. 212 p. Illus., bibliog., index.

        The dream of success in popular literature up to the twentieth century.

1323   Cady, Edwin H. THE LIGHT OF COMMON DAY: REALISM IN AMERI-

CAN FICTION. Bloomington: Indiana University, 1971. 224 p. Index.

> Chapters on the realist sensibilities, early literary influences, native humor and travel literature, Twain, Hawthorne, Howells, Crane, and Owen Wister.

1324 Cawelti, John G. "The Writer as a Celebrity: Some Aspects of American Literature as Popular Culture." STUDIES IN AMERICAN FICTION 5 (Spring 1977): 161-74.

> This essay distinguishes between fame and celebrity, and identifies several models for the notion of contemporary celebrity in Dickens, Byron, and others. The process for creating writer-celebrities, beginning in the nineteenth century, is traced to the present, with observations of the functions of the author in contemporary society.

1325 Coan, Otis W., and Lillard, Richard G. AMERICA IN FICTION: AN ANNOTATED LIST OF NOVELS THAT INTERPRET ASPECTS OF LIFE IN THE UNITED STATES, CANADA, AND MEXICO. 5th ed. Palo Alto, Calif.: Pacific Books, 1967. 232 p. Index.

> An annotated bibliography of fiction depicting pioneering, farm and village life, industrial life, politics and institutions, religion, and minority and ethnic groups.

1326 Cohen, Sarah Blacher, ed. COMIC RELIEF: HUMOR IN CONTEMPORARY AMERICAN LITERATURE. Urbana: University of Illinois, 1978. 339 p. Bibliog.

> Essays on science fiction humor, college humor, the urban tall tale, fiction dreck, and contemporary writers.

1327 CONTEMPORARY LITERARY CRITICISM. Detroit: Gale Research Co., 1973-- . Annual.

> Includes numerous mystery writers as well as other genre writers.

1328 CONTEMPORARY NOVELISTS. Edited by James Vinson. New York: St. Martin's Press, 1976. 1,600 p.

> Contains lists of authors' works, critical comments, and biographical notes. Despite its length many popular writers have been omitted.

1329 Cook, Sylvia Jenkins. FROM TOBACCO ROAD TO ROUTE 66: THE SOUTHERN POOR WHITE IN FICTION. Chapel Hill: University of North Carolina Press, 1976. 208 p. Notes, bibliog., index.

> A lucid examination of the image of the poor white from folk to literary figure in fiction and journalism during the

1930s, with discussion of Faulkner, Caldwell, Mary Heaton
Vorse, Fielding Burke, Myra Page, Grace Lumpkin, Sherwood
Anderson, William Rollins, James Agee, John Steinbeck, and
others.

1330   CUMULATED FICTION INDEX. Comp. by various contributors.   London:
        Association of Assistant Librarians, 1945–60.

        A subject index to authors and titles in several thousand
        categories.

1331   Dataller, Roger. THE PLAIN MAN AND THE NOVEL. London and
        New York: T. Nelson and Sons, 1940. Reprint. Port Washington,
        N.Y.: Kennikat Press, 1970. 185 p. Index.

        Published originally under the name of Arthur Archibald
        Eaglestone, this critical work was aimed at the average
        reader. Chapters cover detective, propaganda, historical,
        autobiographical, industrial, sea, rural, and social fiction,
        with discussion of the sex motif and literary reputations.

1332   Davis, David Brian. HOMICIDE IN AMERICAN FICTION, 1798–1860:
        A STUDY IN SOCIAL VALUES. Ithaca, N.Y.: Cornell University
        Press, 1957. 346 p. Bibliog.

        Data on early novelists who wrote murder and detective
        stories in the nineteenth century.

1333   Deegan, Dorothy Yost. THE STEREOTYPE OF THE SINGLE WOMAN IN
        AMERICAN NOVELS: A SOCIAL STUDY WITH IMPLICATIONS FOR THE
        EDUCATION OF WOMEN. New York: King's Crown Press, 1951. Reprint.
        New York: Octagon, 1969. 252 p. Appendixes, notes, bibliog., index.

        A sociopsychological study of the fictional portrayal of "the
        woman '30 years of age or older' who has not married" to
        1935, with references to later fiction and conclusions.

1334   Dettelbach, Cynthia Golomb. IN THE DRIVER'S SEAT: THE AUTO-
        MOBILE IN AMERICAN LITERATURE AND POPULAR CULTURE. Con-
        tributions to American Studies, no. 25. Westport, Conn.: Greenwood
        Press, 1976. 139 p. Notes, illus., bibliog., index.

        The dream-nightmare aspects of the American automobile as
        metaphor of innocence and experience, of freedom and con-
        straint of success and failure, of possession and being possessed.

1335   Dietrichson, Jan W. THE IMAGE OF MONEY IN THE AMERICAN
        NOVEL OF THE GILDED AGE. New York: Humanities Press, 1969.
        417 p. Notes, bibliog., index.

        The focus is primarily on the work of Henry James and William
        Dean Howells, with a brief chapter devoted to regional writers.

1336   Donald, Miles. THE AMERICAN NOVEL IN THE TWENTIETH CENTURY.
        New York: Barnes and Noble, 1978. 215 p. Bibliog., index.

>   Chapter 5 contains weak reviews, but useful critiques of
>   examples of science fiction and detective fiction, with notes
>   on generic features.

1337   Donelson, Ken. "The Trouble with 'Read Only the Best.'" MEDIA
        AND METHODS 14 (March 1978): 32-33, 68, 70.

>   Refers to his own childhood reading and observes that people
>   must find their own ways in reading; this means that their
>   tastes must have more freedom than narrow strictures often
>   allow.

1338   Downs, Robert Bingham. FAMOUS AMERICAN BOOKS. New York:
        McGraw-Hill, 1971. 377 p.

>   An examination of the influence, rather than the popularity,
>   of fifty books circulating in America, including works by
>   Mason Weems, James Fenimore Cooper, Horatio Alger, Fannie
>   Farmer, Owen Wister, Emily Post, and others.

1339   Dunlap, George A. THE CITY IN THE AMERICAN NOVEL, 1789-1900.
        Philadelphia: University of Pennsylvania Press, 1934. Reprint. New
        York: Russell and Russell, 1965. 187 p. Bibliog.

>   A study of American novels portraying contemporary condi-
>   tions in New York, Philadelphia, and Boston.

1340   Eichelberger, Clayton L., comp. A GUIDE TO CRITICAL REVIEWS OF
        UNITED STATES FICTION, 1870-1910. 2 vols. Metuchen, N.J.:
        Scarecrow, 1971-74. 766 p. Index.

>   Includes many minor writers.

1341   Emrich, Duncan, ed. AMERICAN FOLK POETRY: AN ANTHOLOGY.
        Boston: Little, Brown, 1974. 831 p.

>   Bibliography of folk song by Joseph C. Hickerson. Includes
>   songs, poems, ballads arranged under subject headings.

1342   FICTION CATALOGUE. New York: H.W. Wilson Co., 1908-- .
        Annual.

>   Reprints quarterly cumulations of reviews of books arranged
>   by author and indexed according to titles and subjects.

1343   Fiedler, Leslie A. THE RETURN OF THE VANISHING AMERICAN.
        New York: Stein and Day, 1968. 192 p. Index.

>   Essays on regionalism, images of America before it was dis-
>   covered, four basic American myths, and images of the West, of

Indians, and of sentiment in the imagination.

1344   Fiedler, Leslie A., and Zeiger, Arthur, eds. O BRAVE NEW WORLD:
AMERICAN LITERATURE FROM 1600 TO 1840: A CRITICAL ANTHOLOGY
OF AMERICAN LITERATURE. Vol. 1. New York: Dell, 1968. Notes,
index.

A useful collection, with notes, of early American popular
literature arranged into sections on myth, sentiment, and
melancholy in literature. Included are selections on cap-
tivity narratives and other encounters, stereotypes, race,
patriotic heroes, the West, nature, the domestic scene,
Calvinism, the general cult of death, seduction and suicide,
and the gothic mode.

1345   Filler, Louis. A QUESTION OF QUALITY: POPULARITY AND VALUE
IN MODERN CREATIVE WRITING. Bowling Green, Ohio: Bowling
Green University Popular Press, 1976. 264 p. Index.

A collection of eighteen essays on Erich Segal, Ring Lardner,
Erskine Caldwell, James Gould Cozzens, James T. Farrell,
Irving Wallace, Henry James and Dashiell Hammett, John
Dos Passos, Vachel Lindsay, Meyer Levin, B. Traven, Stephen
Vincent Benet, Norman Mailer, Edna St. Vincent Millay,
Ross Lockridge, Jr., John Steinbeck, and Ben Hecht.

1346   Fine, David M. THE CITY, THE IMMIGRANT AND AMERICAN FIC-
TION, 1880-1920. Metuchen, N.J.: Scarecrow Press, 1977. 182 p.

An extensive examination of major and minor works of fiction
responding to and arising out of the conditions of city (especially ghetto) life. Chapters treat the cultural melieu, the
heritage found in key works, native American fiction, and
the novels of the immigrants themselves.

1347   Gardner, Frank M. SEQUELS; INCORPORATING ALDRED AND
PARKER'S SEQUEL STORIES. 6th ed. London: Association of Assistant Librarians, 1974. 291 p.

Lists twenty thousand titles keyed to authors, including genre
writers and writers of juvenile series.

1348   Gove, Philip Babcock. THE IMAGINARY VOYAGE IN PROSE FIC-
TION: A HISTORY OF ITS CRITICISM AND A GUIDE FOR ITS
STUDY, WITH AN ANNOTATED CHECKLIST OF 215 IMAGINARY
VOYAGES FROM 1700 TO 1800. New York: Columbia University
Press, 1961. 445 p. Notes, short title index, bibliog., and index.

An introduction to the definition and critical history of the
genre, with chapters on the influence of ROBINSON CRUSOE
and on the genre's relationship to other forms of prose fiction.

1349   Hackett, Alice Payne, and Burke, James Henry. EIGHTY YEARS OF BEST
       SELLERS, 1895–1975. New York: R.R. Bowker, 1977. 265 p. Bibliog.,
       index.

       A brief history, with lists of hardbound and paperback best-
       sellers; children's books, cookbooks, crime and suspense, do-
       it yourself and gardening, poetry, reference, and religion;
       an annotated chronology includes the ten best-sellers per year
       from 1895 to 1975, with a chapter on early best-sellers.

1350   Haight, Anne Lyon, and Grannis, Chandler B. BANNED BOOKS: 387
       B.C. TO 1978 A.D. INFORMAL NOTES ON SOME BOOKS BANNED
       FOR VARIOUS REASONS AT VARIOUS TIMES AND IN VARIOUS PLACES.
       Rev. ed. New York: R.R. Bowker, 1978. 196 p. Bibliog., index.

       A bibliography of banned books arranged according to author,
       with notes on the circumstances and appendixes which identify
       trends in censorship, statements on freedom of the press, ex-
       cerpts from court decisions and official reports, and lists of
       laws.

1351   Harap, Louis. THE IMAGE OF THE JEW IN AMERICAN LITERATURE:
       FROM EARLY REPUBLIC TO MASS IMMIGRATION. Philadelphia:
       Jewish Publication Society of America, 1975. 586 p. Index, bibliog.

       Through 1917, by genre and chronology.

1352   Hart, James D. THE POPULAR BOOK: A HISTORY OF AMERICA'S
       LITERARY TASTE. New York: Oxford, 1950. 351 p. Chapter notes,
       chronology of books discussed, index.

       The most influential book on the American best-seller tradi-
       tion, this social history of major trends provides a valuable
       introduction to the literary imagery of the middle classes
       from the Puritans to the organization man. Hart discusses
       religious works in the early colonial period, political and
       practical works in the early eighteenth century, the emerg-
       ing influence of sentiment, historical romances, domestic
       fiction, poetry, fiction and accounts of the West, post-Civil
       War fiction, nostalgia for Medievalism in fiction, best-sellers
       at the turn of the century, and an excursion through the fiction
       of the thirties and forties, with a postscript on success books.

1353   Havlice, Patricia Pate. INDEX TO AMERICAN AUTHOR BIBLIOGRA-
       PHIES. Metuchen, N.J.: Scarecrow Press, 1971. 204 p. Index.

       Identifies 2,225 bibliographies published in periodicals.

1354   Howarth, Patrick. PLAY UP AND PLAY THE GAME: THE HEROES OF POP-
       ULAR FICTION. London: Eyre Methuen, 1973. 178 p. Bibliog., note.

A historical examination of popular British fiction with attention to penny dreadfuls, schoolboy stories, historical adventure fiction, colonial fiction, mystery and spy stories, war
stories, and other popular themes.

1355   Hubert, Karen M. TEACHING AND WRITING POPULAR FICTION:
HORROR, ADVENTURE, MYSTERY AND ROMANCE IN THE AMERICAN
CLASSROOM. New York: Virgil Books, 1976. 235 p.

A genre approach to fiction for high school teachers, which
emphasizes the nature and content of popular fiction and contains practical suggestions for stimulating student writing ideas.

1356   Inglehart, Babette F., and Mangione, Anthony R. THE IMAGE OF
PLURALISM IN AMERICAN LITERATURE: AN ANNOTATED BIBLIOGRA-
PHY ON THE AMERICAN EXPERIENCE OF EUROPEAN ETHNIC GROUPS.
New York: Institute on Pluralism and Group Identity of the American
Jewish Committee, 1974. 73 p.

Contains 403 annotated books, oriented to the literature of
eleven ethnic groups and concerned with pluralistic experience.

1357   Kerr, Elizabeth Margaret. BIBLIOGRAPHY OF THE SEQUENCE NOVEL.
Minneapolis: University of Minnesota Press, 1950. 126 p.

A brief introduction with an extensive world bibliography of
sequence novels.

1358   Kerr, Howard. MEDIUMS AND SPIRIT-RAPPERS, AND ROARING RADI-
CALS: SPIRITUALISM IN AMERICAN LITERATURE, 1850-1900. Urbana:
University of Illinois Press, 1972. 261 p. Bibliog., index.

An overview of spiritualism, humorous responses, occult fiction, satire, Howells, Twain, and James.

1359   Koehmstedt, Carol L. PLOT SUMMARY INDEX. Metuchen, N.J.:
Scarecrow Press, 1973. 312 p. Bibliog., index.

Covers 1952 to 1971. Indexes the sources for finding plot
summaries.

1360   Koontz, Dean R. WRITING POPULAR FICTION. 1972. Cincinnati:
Writer's Digest Books, 1979. 232 p. Index.

On writing genre fiction, with chapters on science fiction and
fantasy, suspense, mysteries, gothic romance, Westerns, erotica.
Concluding chapters answer questions on marketing and other
practical matters for would-be writers.

1361   Loshe, Lillie Deming. THE EARLY AMERICAN NOVEL, 1789-1830.

New York: Columbia University Press, 1907. Reprint. New York: Ungar, 1966. 131 p. Chronology of fiction, index.

Contains chapters on sentimental, gothic, historical, and Indian novels, novels of the Revolution, and James Fenimore Cooper and his contemporaries.

1362 Lynn, Kenneth. THE DREAM OF SUCCESS: A STUDY OF THE MODERN AMERICAN IMAGINATION. Boston: Little, Brown, 1955. 269 p. Index.

A study of the impact of the success myth on the consciousnesses of Theodore Dreiser, Jack London, David Graham Philips, Frank Norris, and Robert Herrick.

1363 Madden, David. A PRIMER OF THE NOVEL: FOR READERS & WRITERS. Metuchen, N.J.: Scarecrow, 1980. 454 p. Chronology, bibliog., index.

Includes a brief section on background, followed by descriptions of about seventy types of novels, a discussion of techniques, close analyses of techniques represented in key passages novels, and a chronology of the development of the novel.

1364 May, John R. TOWARD A NEW EARTH: APOCALYPSE IN THE AMERICAN NOVEL. Notre Dame, Ind.: Notre Dame University Press, 1972. 254 p. Notes, index, bibliog.

A study of the apocalyptic theme in Hawthorne, Melville, Twain, Faulkner, West, O'Connor, Ellison, Baldwin, Wright, Barth, Pynchon, and Vonnegut, with emphasis on the elements of judgment, catastrophe, and renewal in the works.

1365 Mott, Frank Luther. GOLDEN MULTITUDES. New York: Macmillan, 1947. Reprint: New York: R.R. Bowker, 1960. 357 p. Index.

A standard history of the best-seller from colonial times to the 1940s. The volume contains chapters on definition, methodology, children's books, sentimental fiction, political fiction, poetry, popular editions of Shakespeare, history and biography, Walter Scott's influence, Irving and Cooper, pirated editions of Dickens, UNCLE TOM'S CABIN, dime novels, inspirational fiction, mysteries, bibles and school books, frontier fiction and other material. Appendixes list best- and better-seller chronologies.

1366 Myers, Carol Fairbanks. WOMEN IN LITERATURE: CRITICISM OF THE SEVENTIES. Metuchen, N.J.: Scarecrow Press, 1976. 256 p. Index.

Keyed to authors, with a bibliography of "comprehensive" works on genre, psychological, sociological, and philosophi-

cal backgrounds; author entries are oriented to women characters in relation to other characters, women as myth and symbol,
biographical and critical works on women authors, interviews,
selected reviews, and feminist criticism.

1367   Noel, Mary. VILLAINS GALORE: THE HEYDAY OF THE POPULAR
        STORY WEEKLY. New York: Macmillan, 1954. 320 p. Illus., index.

        An informal account of the origins and development of story
        papers, with their skeptical editors and gullible, semiliterate
        readers who were nourished on sweetness and violence.

1368   Omrcanin, Margaret Stewart. THE NOVEL AND POLITICAL INSURGENCY:
        A STUDY OF AMERICAN POLITICS AND POLITICIANS AS PORTRAYED
        IN SOME NOVELS OF THE LATE NINETEENTH AND EARLY TWENTI-
        ETH CENTURIES. Philadelphia: Dorrance, 1973. 119 p. Notes,
        bibliog.

        A survey of politics and the novel, with attention to THE
        HONORABLE PETER STIRLING; THE BOSS; J. DEVLIN,
        BOSS; THE MAN HIGHER UP; THE 13TH DISTRICT; and THE
        PLUM TREE.

1369   Overton, Grant. THE WOMEN WHO MAKE OUR NOVELS. New York:
        Moffet, Yard, 1918. Reprint. New York: Dodd, Mead, 1928. Reprint.
        Freeport, N.Y.: Books for Libraries, 1967. 393 p. Author checklists.

        Informal career biographies of thirty-five women writers, in-
        cluding Mary Roberts Rinehart, Gene Stratton-Porter, Mary
        Johnston, Anna Katharine Green, Edna Ferber, among other
        popular writers.

1370   Papashvily, Helen Waite. ALL THE HAPPY ENDINGS: A STUDY OF
        THE DOMESTIC NOVEL IN AMERICA, THE WOMEN WHO WROTE IT,
        THE WOMEN WHO READ IT, IN THE NINETEENTH CENTURY. New
        York: Harper and Brothers, 1956. 231 p. Bibliog., index.

        Excellent informal topical study of the popular domestic novel
        in America from about 1848 to the late 1880s.

1371   Pattee, Fred Lewis. THE FEMININE FIFTIES. New York: D. Appleton
        Century, 1940. Reprint. Port Washington, N.Y.: Kennikat Press, 1966.
        339 p. Index, illus.

        A survey and interpretation of the domestic romances, humor,
        major writers, and themes of the period.

1372   Rajec, Elizabeth M. THE STUDY OF NAMES IN LITERATURE: A
        BIBLIOGRAPHY. New York: K.G. Saur, 1978. 261 p. Index.

        Partially annotated bibliography of 1,346 items arranged
        according to authors.

1373 Reginald, Robert, and Burgess, M.R., eds. CUMULATIVE PAPERBACK INDEX, 1939-1959: A COMPREHENSIVE BIBLIOGRAPHIC GUIDE TO 14,000 MASS-MARKET PAPERBACK BOOKS OF 33 PUBLISHERS ISSUED UNDER 69 IMPRINTS. Detroit: Gale Research Company, 1973. 362 p. Title index.

Arranged according to authors, with a section on publisher specifications.

1374 Rollock, Barbara. THE BLACK EXPERIENCE IN CHILDREN'S BOOKS. New York: New York Public Library, 1974. 122 p. Index.

This briefly annotated bibliography, portraying elements of the black experience in stories considered suitable for children, is arranged according to types of stories, with coverage of the United States, Central and South America, the Carribean, Africa, and England.

1375 Rupp, Richard H. CELEBRATION IN POSTWAR AMERICAN FICTION, 1945-1967. Coral Gables, Fla.: University of Miami Press, 1970. 232 p. Notes, index.

Based on Josef Pieper's views on festivity, the author explores the expression of celebration in ten contemporary novelists.

1376 Smith, Herbert F. THE POPULAR AMERICAN NOVEL, 1865-1920. Boston: Twayne, 1980. 192 p. Notes, bibliog., index.

A useful contribution to studies of popular American literature, with chapters on success stories, sentimental fiction, New England novels, popular southern fiction, social satire, utopian and Western romances, political fiction, and writers who developed new techniques.

1377 Spengemann, William C. THE ADVENTUROUS MUSE: THE POETICS OF AMERICAN FICTION, 1789-1900. New Haven, Conn.: Yale University Press, 1977. 290 p. Notes, bibliog., index.

An exploration of the relationship among New World travel writing, European literature, Romantic aesthetics and their effects on American fiction, with a chapter on the domestic romance and its impact on travel writing, resulting in the American gothic.

1378 Spiegel, Alan. FICTION AND THE CAMERA EYE: VISUAL CONSCIOUSNESS IN FILM AND THE MODERN NOVEL. Charlottesville: University Press of Virginia, 1976. 203 p. Notes, index.

The origins and development of "cinematrographic form" in novels from the middle of the nineteenth century to contemporary works, especially as expressed in Zola, James, Conrad, Faulkner, Nabokov, Robbe-Grillet, and others.

1379   Staehelin-Wackernagel, Adelheid. THE PURITAN SETTLER IN THE AMERI-
CAN NOVEL BEFORE THE CIVIL WAR. Bern, Switz.: A. Francke,
1961. 165 p. Notes, bibliog., index.

> An examination of the figure of the Puritan in American
> literature from 1820 to 1860, with emphasis on Cooper,
> Hawthorne, and historical romances.

1380   Stevens, George. LINCOLN'S DOCTOR'S DOG AND OTHER FAMOUS
BEST SELLERS. Philadelphia: J.B. Lippincott, 1938. 77 p. Illus.

> On publishing tactics used to market Hervey Allen's ANTHONY
> ADVERSE in 1933, and on later best sellers, with remarks on
> THE READER'S DIGEST.

1381   Strelka, Joseph P., ed. THEORIES OF LITERARY GENRE. Yearbook of
Comparative Criticism, Vol. 8. University Park: Pennsylvania State University Press, 1978. 281 p. Notes, index.

> Fourteen essays on basic theoretical problems, special aspects,
> and contemporary genre criticism.

1382   Turner, Robert. SOME OF MY BEST FRIENDS ARE WRITERS, BUT I
WOULDN'T WANT MY DAUGHTER TO MARRY ONE. Los Angeles:
Sherbourne Press, 1970. 253 p.

> Turner's reminiscences as a writer of pulp and slick fiction.

1383   Utter, Robert Palfrey, and Needham, Gwendolyn Bridges. PAMELA'S
DAUGHTERS. New York: Macmillan, 1936. Reprint. New York:
Russell and Russell, 1972. 512 p. Illus., notes, index.

> A discussion of romances through the Victorian era, especially
> such topics as economic obstacles to love, prudery, emotion-
> ality, literary fainting, the heroine's delicate air, the old
> maid, sinning, the virtuous working girl, the new woman as
> heroine, and the end of the Victorian era in fiction.

1384   Veeder, William. HENRY JAMES--THE LESSONS OF THE MASTER:
POPULAR FICTION AND PERSONAL STYLE IN THE NINETEENTH
CENTURY. Chicago: University of Chicago, 1975. 287 p. Illus.,
notes, index.

> An exploration of debts James had to popular fiction and
> the innovations of style and character he achieved by draw-
> ing on popular themes.

1385   Wasserstrom, William. HEIRESS OF ALL THE AGES: SEX AND SENTI-
MENT IN THE GENTEEL TRADITION. Minneapolis: University of
Minnesota, 1959. 157 p. Notes, index.

A study of genteel images of women from the early nineteenth century through about 1920, with emphasis on the social milieu of the fiction.

1386 White, George Abbott, and Newman, Charles. LITERATURE IN REVOLU-
TION. New York: Holt, Rinehart and Winston, 1972. 640 p.

Twenty-one essays explore the relationship of literature to politi-
cal and social change. The subjects range from Thoreau to
"underground" comics; the contributors include Noam Chomsky,
Frederick Crews, Carlos Fuentes, Carl Oglesby, Harry Levin,
Conor Cruise O'Brien, Aileen Ward, Raymond Williams, Sol
Yurick, Leo Marx, John Seelye.

1387 Wisse, Ruth R. THE SCHLEMIEL AS MODERN HERO. Chicago: University of Chicago Press, 1971. 134 p. Bibliog., index.

An examination of the schlemiel in Yiddish and American
literature, from the figure's roots in European folklore through
his particular appropriateness for survival in the modern world.

1388 Witham, W. Tasker. THE ADOLESCENT IN THE AMERICAN NOVEL,
1920-1960. New York: Frederick Ungar, 1964. 345 p. Notes, index,
bibliog., chronological checklist.

Chapters cover background, sexual awakening, revolt from
the family, adjustment to school and college, vocations and
inspiration, the community, special problems of adolescents,
and the styles and themes of the novels.

1389 Zweig, Paul. THE ADVENTURER: THE FATE OF ADVENTURE IN THE
WESTERN WORLD. New York: Basic Books, 1974. 275 p. Notes,
index.

An analysis of the genre from classical times; includes discussion of Providence literature, Robinson Crusoe, Casanova,
the gothic novel, Poe, and Nietzsche.

DETECTIVE, CRIME, MYSTERY, AND SPY FICTION

1390 Adams, Donald, ed. THE MYSTERY AND DETECTION ANNUAL.
Beverly Hills: D. Adams, 1972-- . Annual.

Essays, poetry, fiction, reviews and "notes and queries."

1391 Allen, Dick, and Chacko, David, eds. DETECTIVE FICTION: CRIME
AND COMPROMISE. New York: Harcourt Brace Jovanovich, 1974.
481 p.

Contains a wide selection of stories and seven theoretical essays, together with topics for writing and research.

1392 Ball, John, ed. THE MYSTERY STORY. San Diego: University Extension, University of California in cooperation with Publisher's Inc., 1976. 390 p. Bibliog.

A fine collection of essays by various writers, this volume is especially useful for James Sandoe's expanded list of annotated titles of best hardboiled novels, Waugh on the police procedural, Yates on the locked room story, Hubin on the series detective, Penzler on the great crooks, Nevins' list of pseudonyms and Briney's annotated bibliography.

1393 Barnes, Melvyn. BEST DETECTIVE FICTION: A GUIDE FROM GODWIN TO THE PRESENT. Hamden, Conn.: Shoe String Press, 1975. 121 p. Bibliog., index.

A lively annotated bibliography of some 250 authors in "the classic puzzle form" and those emphasizing how or why murders were committed. It is exclusive of many novels often considered important expressions of the detective genre.

1394 BEST DETECTIVE STORIES OF THE YEAR. New York: E.P. Dutton, 1945-- . Annual. Bibliog. award lists, necrology.

A collection of stories, with encapsulated news of interest to readers and writers.

1395 Borowitz, Albert. INNOCENCE AND ARSENIC: STUDIES IN CRIME AND LITERATURE. New York: Harper and Row, 1977. 170 p.

Essays on accounts of actual crimes in which writers and musicians are involved in some aspect of the crime, and on crimes that are the subject of great literary works. Includes discussion of the Moors murder case that interested C.P. Snow and Pamela Hansford Johnson; Robert Louis Stevenson's DR. JEKYLL AND MR. HYDE; Thackeray's interest in a hanging; Charles Dickens' THE MYSTERY OF EDWIN DROOD; Salieri and the legend of his murder of Mozart; a critique of the attempts to identify Jack the Ripper; Cicero's defense of Cluentius; Aldo Braibanti's alleged "psychological kidnapping" of two young men through his writings; Clarisse Manson's memoir of her testimony in the Joseph-Bernardin Fualdes murder case; a concluding chapter explains how the author goes about his research.

1396 Briney, Robert E., and Nevins, Francis M., Jr., eds. MULTIPLYING VILLAINIES: SELECTED MYSTERY CRITICISM, 1942-1968. By Anthony Boucher. Salem, Mass.: A Bouchercon Book, 1973. 136 p.

Collection of Boucher's criticism together with his reviews
of detective fiction from the NEW YORK TIMES BOOK
REVIEW.

1397 Champigny, Robert. WHAT WILL HAVE HAPPENED: A PHILOSOPHI-
CAL AND TECHNICAL ESSAY ON MYSTERY STORIES. Bloomington:
Indiana University Press, 1977. 183 p. Notes, bibliog., index.

An inquiry into the narrative structure of detective stories,
with discussion of elements of adventure, viewpoint, legend,
atmosphere, destiny, justice, necessity, probability, individu-
ation, clues and pseudonarratives.

1398 Eames, Hugh. SLEUTHS, INC.: STUDIES OF PROBLEM SOLVERS:
DOYLE, SIMENON, HAMMETT, AMBLER, CHANDLER. Philadelphia:
J.B. Lippincott, 1978. 228 p. Notes, bibliog.

A series of essays on sleuths and the art of sleuthing, the
backgrounds for the authors' fiction, and asides on historical
detectives and agencies.

1399 Gribbin, Lenore S. WHO'S WHODUNIT: A LIST OF 3218 DETECTIVE
STORY WRITERS AND THEIR 1100 PSEUDONYMS. Library Studies Num-
ber 5. Chapel Hill: University of North Carolina Library, 1968. 174 p.
Bibliog.

Provides a primary list of authors' names and pseudonyms with
birth and death dates when available, and sources for the
information.

1400 Hagen, Ordean A. WHO DONE IT? A GUIDE TO DETECTIVE,
MYSTERY AND SUSPENSE FICTION. New York: R.R. Bowker Co.,
1969. 834 p. Index.

Contains an author bibliography of mystery fiction from 1841
to 1967, a subject guide in twenty-nine categories with information on films, drama, location, anthologies and collections, awards, and criticism. An appendix contains information on various other aspects.

1401 Haining, Peter. MYSTERY! AN ILLUSTRATED HISTORY OF CRIME
AND DETECTIVE FICTION. London: Souvenir Press, 1977. 176 p.
Illus.

Heavily illustrated with black and white color plates, the
volume traces crime illustrations from Newgate prison accounts
through penny dreadfuls, pulps, and various thematic topics.

1402 Harper, Ralph. THE WORLD OF THE THRILLER. Cleveland: Case
Western Reserve University, 1969. 139 p. Notes.

An analysis of twentieth-century spy novels.

1403   Hartman, Geoffrey H. THE FATE OF READING AND OTHER ESSAYS.
Chicago: University of Chicago Press, 1975. 352 p. Notes, index.

Collected essays on contemporary literary criticism, reading
and the analysis of texts. Of particular interest are essays
on reading, communication, and the detective story.

1404   Haycraft, Howard, ed. THE ART OF THE MYSTERY STORY: A COL-
LECTION OF CRITICAL ESSAYS. New York: Simon and Schuster, 1946,
565 p. Index.

Some fifty-three essays from 1883 to the mid-1940s explore
the genre's definition, writing, humor, criticism, fiction versus
real life, collecting and related topics.

1405   _____. MURDER FOR PLEASURE: THE LIFE AND TIMES OF THE DE-
TECTIVE STORY. 1941. Reprint. New York: Appleton-Century,
1968. 409 p. Illus., bibliog.

The most comprehensive history of the detective story written
in America. Contains an excellent introduction by Nicholas
Blake, "The Detective Story--Why?"

1406   Indiana University, Lilly Library. THE FIRST HUNDRED YEARS OF DE-
TECTIVE FICTION, 1841-1941, BY ONE HUNDRED AUTHORS ON THE
HUNDRED THIRTIETH ANNIVERSARY OF THE FIRST PUBLICATION IN
BOOK FORM OF EDGAR ALLAN POE'S "THE MURDERS IN THE RUE
MORGUE." PHILADELPHIA, 1843. Bloomington: 1973. 64 p. Index,
illus.

Annotated list of 132 volumes of Poeiana, editions of Doyle,
Gaboriau and others from France, England, America.

1407   J. & S. Graphics. DETECTIVE FICTION: MYSTERIES AND CRIME.
Chicago: J. & S. Graphics, 1972. 340 p. Illus.

A catalog of 4,561 items, with variant editions noted in
many cases, and some reproductions of dust jackets.

1408   Lacassin, Francis. MYTHOLOGIE DU ROMAN POLICIER: TOME II.
Paris: Union generale d'editions, 1974. 317 p. Bibliog.

The volume discusses and provides checklists of the appearances of the work of Dashiell Hammett, Raymond Chandler,
Kenneth Fearing, Frederic Brown, Chester Himes, and others
in various media.

1409   LaCour, Tage, and Morgensen, Harold. THE MURDER BOOK: AN
ILLUSTRATED HISTORY OF THE DETECTIVE STORY. Translation from
Danish by Roy Duffell. London: Allen and Unwin, 1971. 192 p.
Bibliog., illus., index.

An excellently illustrated account of detective fiction's history and major personalities, which covers books, pulps, films from Poe to Bond, hundreds of photographs and illustrations.

1410   Lambert, Gavin. THE DANGEROUS EDGE. London: Barrie and Jenkins, 1975. 272 p. Bibliog.

Essays on Wilkie Collins, Arthur Conan Doyle, G.K. Chesterton, John Buchan, Eric Ambler, Graham Greene, Georges Simenon, Raymond Chandler, and Alfred Hitchcock.

1411   Layman, Richard. DASHIELL HAMMETT: A DESCRIPTIVE BIBLIOGRAPHY. Pittsburgh: University of Pittsburgh Press, 1979. 185 p. Index.

Includes bibliographical descriptions of first editions, collections, first-appearance in periodicals, newspapers, public letters and petitions signed by Hammett, movies and other matters. Appendixes cite ad copy written by Hammett, together with citations of radio, film, television and stage plays based on the author's work, with notes by the compiler and selected references.

1412   Mundell, E.H., and Rausch, G. Jay. THE DETECTIVE SHORT STORY: A BIBLIOGRAPHY AND INDEX. Manhattan: Kansas State University Library, 1974. 493 p. Index.

Bibliography of detective short stories and first appearances of stories in book form. Includes sections listing espionage stories, problem and puzzle stories, detective experiences, detective lists and author index. Covers 1,400 collections and 7,500 short stories.

1413   Murch, Alma Elizabeth. THE DEVELOPMENT OF THE DETECTIVE NOVEL. New York Philosophical Library, 1958. Reprint. Port Washington, N.Y.: Kennikat Press, 1968. 272 p. Notes, bibliog., index.

Chapters on early sources, detective themes in Continental literature, Poe, English novels, Dickens and Collins, the roman policier, women writers, Holmes, and twentieth-century development.

1414   Mystery Writers of America. THE MYSTERY WRITER'S HANDBOOK: A HANDBOOK ON THE WRITING OF DETECTIVE, SUSPENSE, MYSTERY AND CRIME STORIES. Edited by Herbert Brean. New York: Harper and Brothers Publishers, 1956. 268 p.

Contributions by many writers on writing and publishing crime novels, together with several useful sections on clichés, money, and other miscellanea on writing.

1415   Nevins, Francis M. THE MYSTERY WRITER'S ART. Bowling Green, Ohio: Popular Press, 1971. 338 p.

A collection of previously published essays on detective fiction, authors and several films, organized in sections featuring appreciations, taxonomy, and speculations and critiques.

1416   Palmer, Jerry. THRILLERS: GENESIS AND STRUCTURE OF A POPULAR GENRE. London: E. Arnold, 1978. 232 p. Notes, bibliog., index.

An examination of the thriller formula which provides sections on heroes and villains, ideology and excitement, historical perspective, and a sociological perspective. Palmer provides a useful critique of genre theory in earlier analyses.

1417   Penzler, Otto, ed. THE GREAT DETECTIVES. Boston: Little, Brown, 1978. 281 p. Author checklist, filmography.

Twenty-six authors explain the origins of their fictional detectives.

1418   Ruehlmann, William. SAINT WITH A GUN: THE UNLAWFUL AMERICAN PRIVATE EYE. New York: American University Presses, 1974. 155 p. Notes, bibliog.

An exploration of the detective figure as avenger and the American detective story as a metaphorical expression of violence.

1419   Smith, Myron J., Jr. CLOAK-AND-DAGGER BIBLIOGRAPHY: AN ANNOTATED GUIDE TO SPY FICTION, 1937-1975. Metuchen, N.J.: Scarecrow Press, 1976. 225 p. Index.

Includes an author list of 1,675 spy novels, together with a title index and symbols designating original paperbacks, juveniles and those with low sex content or with an emphasis on humor.

1420   Steinbrunner, Chris, et al. DETECTIONARY: A BIOGRAPHICAL DICTIONARY OF LEADING CHARACTERS IN DETECTIVE AND MYSTERY FICTION, INCLUDING FAMOUS AND LITTLE-KNOWN SLEUTHS, THEIR HELPERS, ROGUES BOTH HEROIC AND SINISTER, AND SOME OF THEIR MOST MEMORABLE ADVENTURES, AS RECOUNTED IN NOVELS, SHORT STORIES, AND FILMS. Compiled by Otto Penzler, Chris Steinbrunner, et al. Woodstock, N.Y.: Overlook Press, 1977. 299 p. Index.

1421   Stewart, R.F. . . . AND ALWAYS A DETECTIVE: CHAPTERS ON THE HISTORY OF DETECTIVE FICTION. London: David and Charles, 1980. 351 p. Notes, bibliog., index.

Essays on definition, history, origins, sensational fiction in
the nineteenth century, detective characters, Emile Gaboriau's
influence on Doyle and others.

1422   Thomson, H. Douglas. MASTERS OF MYSTERY: A STUDY OF THE
DETECTIVE STORY. London: W. Collins, 1931. Reprint. Folcroft,
Pa.: Folcroft Library Editions, 1973. 288 p. Index.

Though primarily concerned with the English detective novel,
the volume contains numerous references to and a chapter on
American crime fiction and one on Poe. Other chapters cover
French stories; Holmes; domestic, realistic and orthodox stories;
thrillers; and favorite reading.

GOTHIC FICTION

1423   Howells, Coral Ann. LOVE, MYSTERY, AND MISERY: FEELING IN
GOTHIC FICTION. London: Athlone Press, 1978. 199 p. Selective
checklist, notes, index.

An examination of the portrayal and innovative explorations
of the fiction of Radcliffe, Lewis, Austen, Maturin, Brontë,
Roche and the Minerva Press fiction, with a chapter on gothic
themes, values and techniques.

1424   MacAndrew, Elizabeth. THE GOTHIC TRADITION IN FICTION. New
York: Columbia University Press, 1979. 289 p. Notes, bibliog., index.

Much useful information on the conventions of the genre as
it evolved primarily in the high literature of England, but
with some international references. An epilog deals with
twentieth-century literature.

1425   McNutt, Dan J. THE EIGHTEENTH-CENTURY GOTHIC NOVEL: AN
ANNOTATED BIBLIOGRAPHY OF CRITICISM AND SELECTED TEXTS.
New York: Garland, 1975. 330 p. Index.

An annotated list of publications on bibliography and research,
aesthetic background, literary background; psychological,
social and scientific background; general studies, works on
the eighteenth-century gothic, and the genre's influence on
literature and film; with material for the study of Horace
Walpole, Clara Reeve, Charlotte Smith, Ann Radcliffe,
Matthew Gregory Lewis, and William Beckford.

1426   Radcliffe, Elsa J. GOTHIC NOVELS OF THE TWENTIETH CENTURY:
AN ANNOTATED BIBLIOGRAPHY. Metuchen, N.J.: Scarecrow Press,
1979. 272 p. Index.

A partially annotated bibliography of 1,973 novels, with an

introduction that distinguishes among historical, sentimental, horror, exotic, and whimsical gothics; and provides eight common elements of the gothic.

1427   Sieman, Fred, comp. GHOST STORY INDEX: AN AUTHOR-TITLE INDEX TO MORE THAN 2,200 STORIES OF GHOSTS, HORRORS AND THE MACABRE APPEARING IN 190 BOOKS AND ANTHOLOGIES. San Jose, Calif.: Library Research Associates, 1967. 141 p. Bibliog., index.

A listing arranged according to authors and titles, keyed to anthologies.

1428   Scarborough, Dorothy. THE SUPERNATURAL IN MODERN FICTION. New York: G.P. Putnam, 1917. Reprint. New York: Octagon Books, 1977. 329 p. Notes, index.

An exploration of the supernatural theme in gothic romances, ghost stories, folk tales, religion and science stories. The original edition was published as THE SUPERNATURAL IN MODERN ENGLISH FICTION.

1429   Summers, Montague. A GOTHIC BIBLIOGRAPHY. London: Fortune Press, 1941. 621 p. Illus.

Annotated bibliography of gothic romances listed first according to authors, then according to titles. Reference is made to some French and German works, and to plays.

1430   _____. THE GOTHIC QUEST: A HISTORY OF THE GOTHIC NOVEL. London: Fortune Press, 1938. Reprint. New York: Russell and Russell, 1964. 443 p. Plates, notes, index.

An exploration of the gothic romance, particularly the works of Matthew Gregory Lewis, with a useful discussion of the literary and cultural backgrounds of Romance, publishers and circulating libraries, and foreign influences.

JUVENILE FICTION

1431   Bakerman, Jane S. "Gene Stratton-Porter: What Price the Limberlost?" THE OLD NORTHWEST 3 (June 1977): 173-84.

Examination of FRECKLES (New York: Grosset and Dunlap, 1904) and A GIRL OF THE LIMBERLOST (New York: Grosset and Dunlap, 1909) reveals that the wilderness is a place for evolving popular urban values, rather than presenting a set of alternatives to them.

1432   Blount, Margaret. ANIMAL LAND: THE CREATURES OF CHILDREN'S

FICTION. New York: William Morrow, 1975. 336 p. Illus., bibliog., index.

> Divided into sections on the animal fable, animal fantasy, and three animal edens, Blount's clever volume includes consideration of story types such as the fable, moral tale and satire, mythical beasts, dressed animals, mouse stories, pet stories, humanized nature stories, and other types.

1433 Cadogan, Mary, and Craig, Patricia. YOU'RE A BRICK, ANGELA! A NEW LOOK AT GIRL'S FICTION FROM 1839 TO 1975. London: Victor Gollancz, 1976. 397 p. Illus., bibliog., index.

> A study of fiction for British girls, with some examination of American fiction which became popular in England, and which provided prototypes for or parallels to British fiction.

1434 Fisher, Margery. WHO'S WHO IN CHILDREN'S BOOKS: A TREASURY OF THE FAMILIAR CHARACTERS OF CHILDHOOD. New York: Holt, Rinehart and Winston, 1975. 399 p. Illus., index.

> Guide to characters in children's books with indexes to authors and titles.

1435 Gardner, Martin, and Nye, Russel B. THE WIZARD OF OZ & WHO HE WAS. East Lansing: Michigan State University Press, 1957. 208 p. Illus., notes, bibliog.

> An appreciation by Nye, biographical sketch of the author by Gardner, and test by Baum.

1436 Garis, Roger. MY FATHER WAS UNCLE WIGGILY. New York: McGraw-Hill, 1966. 217 p.

> Reminiscences of the son of Howard R. Garis, whose 15,000 Uncle Wiggily stories sold over 18 million books, and who wrote over 700 additional volumes under various pen names.

1437 GIRLS' SERIES BOOKS: A CHECKLIST OF HARDBACK BOOKS PUBLISHED 1900-1975. Minneapolis: Children's Literature Research Collections, University of Minnesota Libraries, 1978. 121 p. Bibliog.

> Series checklist, with author, publisher, and chronological indexes.

1438 Halsey, Rosalie V. FORGOTTEN BOOKS OF THE AMERICAN NURSERY: A HISTORY OF THE DEVELOPMENT OF THE AMERICAN STORY-BOOK. Boston: C.E. Goodspeed, 1911. Reprint. Detroit: Singing Tree Press, 1969. 243 p. Index, illus.

> Chapters on the English playbooks, Newberry books, patriotic

printers, child and book, toy books, American writers, and English critics.

1439 Hoffman, Miriam, and Samuels, Eva, eds. AUTHORS AND ILLUSTRATORS OF CHILDREN'S BOOKS: WRITINGS ON THEIR LIVES AND WORKS. New York and London: R.R. Bowker, 1972. 471 p. Checklists, notes.

Biographical and autobiographical sketches of fifty authors of children's books.

1440 Hudson, Harry K. A BIBLIOGRAPHY OF HARD-COVER BOYS' BOOKS. Rev. ed. Tampa, Fla.: Data Print, 1977. 280 p.

Arranged according to series title, with author, number of volumes, dates, story type, title list, format, number of illustrations, artist's name, description of dust jacket, notes. Covers 1900 to 1975.

1441 Kelly, R. Gordon. MOTHER WAS A LADY: SELF AND SOCIETY IN SELECTED AMERICAN CHILDREN'S PERIODICALS, 1865-1890. Contributions in American Studies, no. 12. Westport, Conn.: Greenwood, 1974. 233 p. Illus., bibliog., notes, index.

A study of the social values of genteel republicanism embodied in the literature of popular children's magazines, with chapters on publishing practices, the "ordeal" and "change of heart" formulas for the youthful audience, and the relationship of reassuring stories to an age of insecurity.

1442 Kirkpatrick, Daniel. TWENTIETH CENTURY CHILDREN'S WRITERS. New York: St. Martin's Press, 1977. 1,507 p.

Contains brief biography, bibliography, and critical essay on some 630 English-language writers of children's fiction, poetry and drama, together with an appendix on influential nineteenth-century authors and a supplementary essay on modern writers widely available in English translation.

1443 Kujoth, Jean Spealman. BEST-SELLING CHILDREN'S BOOKS. Metuchen, N.J.: Scarecrow Press, 1973. 305 p.

A partially annotated listing of 958 books that are currently in print and have sold more than 100,000 copies, organized according to author, title, illustrator, year of publication, number of copies sold, genre, type, and age level. Many series books are omitted.

1444 MacCann, Donnarae, and Woodard, Gloria. THE BLACK AMERICAN IN BOOKS FOR CHILDREN: READINGS IN RACISM. Metuchen, N.J.: Scarecrow Press, 1972. 228 p. Notes, index.

A collection of previously published essays on the black perspective, racism in Newberry Prize books and others, and publishing.

1445 McFarlane, Leslie. GHOST OF THE HARDY BOYS: AN AUTOBIOGRAPHY. New York: Two Continents, 1976. 211 p.

On McFarlane's life and his stories for the Stratemeyer writing syndicate.

1446 MacLeod, Anne Scott. A MORAL TALE: CHILDREN'S FICTION AND AMERICAN CULTURE 1820-1860. Hamden, Conn.: Archon, Shoe String Press, 1975. 196 p. Notes, bibliog., index.

An examination of conventional adult attitudes in tales for children, particularly the creation of early self-definition as a form of coping with the perceived hazards of life.

1447 Mason, Bobbie Ann. THE GIRL SLEUTH: A FEMINIST GUIDE. Old Westbury, N.Y.: Feminist Press, 1975. 144 p. Notes.

Investigation into the Honey Bunch series, Bobbsey Twins, Nancy Drew, Dana Girls, Judy Bolton, and other guides into the middle class.

1448 Meacham, Mary. INFORMATION SOURCES IN CHILDREN'S LITERATURE: A PRACTICAL REFERENCE GUIDE FOR CHILDREN'S LIBRARIANS, ELEMENTARY SCHOOL TEACHERS, AND STUDENTS OF CHILDREN'S LITERATURE. Contributions in Librarianship and Information Science, No. 24. Westport, Conn.: Greenwood Press, 1978. 256 p. Illus., appendixes, index.

An expanded bibliographical essay on basic collections, reference materials, special fields, illustrators, authors, awards, reading, and technical processes.

1449 Monson, Dianne L., and Peltola, Bette J., comps. RESEARCH IN CHILDREN'S LITERATURE: AN ANNOTATED BIBLIOGRAPHY. Newark, Del.: International Reading Association, 1976. 96 p. Index.

Three hundred thirty-two items, including dissertations, ERIC documents, articles, monographs and books on studies of content, racial and ethnic characterization, value systems, attitude change, and literary influence on readers below tenth-grade level.

1450 Quayle, Eric. THE COLLECTOR'S BOOK OF BOYS' STORIES. London: Studio Vista, 1973. 160 p. Illus., bibliog., index.

A survey of boys' books, covering Westerns, R.M. Ballantine's frontier stories, treasure stories, Twain, adventure, the public school, sagas, and science fiction.

1451 Smith, Lillian H. UNRELUCTANT YEARS: A CRITICAL APPROACH TO CHILDREN'S LITERATURE. Chicago: American Library Association, 1953. 193 p. Bibliog., index.

A critical survey of major contributions to children's literature, with chapters on critical perspective, fairy tales, myths, epics and sagas, poetry, picture books, stories, fantasy, historical fiction, and books of knowledge.

1452 Sutherland, Zena. THE BEST IN CHILDREN'S BOOKS: THE UNIVERSITY OF CHICAGO GUIDE TO CHILDREN'S LITERATURE, 1973-1978. Chicago: University of Chicago, 1980. 547 p. Publisher list, indexes.

Reviews of the books based on evaluations of the Advisory Committee of the Center for Children's Books of the University of Chicago, with indexes to titles, developmental values, curricular use, reading level, subjects and types.

1453 Turner, E.S. BOYS WILL BE BOYS: THE STORY OF SWEENEY TODD, DEADWOOD DICK, SEXTON BLAKE, BILLY BUNTER, DICK BARTON, ET AL. London: Michael Joseph, 1976. 277 p. Illus., index.

Intended to "transport the sentimental reader back to the heyday of popular British boys' fiction," from the mid-nineteenth century to the 1950s. Much of the fiction was popular on both sides of the Atlantic and a fair amount of it originated in the United States.

1454 White, Virginia L., and Schulte, Emerita S., comps. BOOKS ABOUT CHILDREN'S BOOKS: AN ANNOTATED BIBLIOGRAPHY. Newark, Del.: International Reading Association, 1979. 48 p.

Includes post-1967 bibliographies, biographies, criticism, histories, indexes, research, teaching methodology, and textbooks.

1455 WOMEN ON WORDS AND IMAGES. DICK AND JANE AS VICTIMS: SEX STEREOTYPING IN CHILDREN'S READERS. 2d ed. Princeton: Women on Words and Images, 1975. 80 p. Illus., charts, bibliog.

Content analyses of school readers, with statistical summaries of active mastery, second sex themes, adult role models, biographies and occupations.

SCIENCE, FANTASY, AND UTOPIAN FICTION

1456   Aldiss, Brian. BILLION YEAR SPREE: THE TRUE HISTORY OF SCIENCE FICTION. New York: Doubleday, 1973. 339 p. Chapter notes, brief critical bibliog., index.

> An informative general history of the genre from Mary Shelley through the fiction of the sixties. The volume includes chapters on Shelley, Poe, Lucien, and other antecedents; Victorian contributions; H.G. Wells, Edgar Rice Burroughs, John W. Campbell's ASTOUNDING, and an outline history of work from the thirties through the sixties.

1457   Aldiss, Brian W., and Harrison, Harry, eds. HELL'S CARTOGRAPHERS: SOME PERSONAL HISTORIES OF SCIENCE FICTION WRITERS. New York: Harper and Row, 1975. 246 p. Checklists.

> Autobiographical sketches by Robert Silverberg, Alfred Bester, Harry Harrison, Damon Knight, Frederik Pohl, and Brian Aldiss, with notes on working habits.

1458   Aquino, John. FANTASY IN LITERATURE. Washington, D.C.: National Education Association, 1977. 63 p. Notes, selected bibliog.

> An introduction to the study and teaching of literary fantasy, with brief chapters on fantasy as an activity of the mind, fantasy literature, teaching, characteristics of fantasy literature, and suggested readings in myths, fairy tales, and pure fantasy.

1459   Armytage, W.H.G. YESTERDAY'S TOMORROWS: A HISTORICAL SURVEY OF FUTURE SOCIETIES. Toronto: University of Toronto Press, 1968. 288 p. Extensive notes, index.

> Essential background for the serious study of science fiction, the volume covers the major intellectual explorations of the future from classical times through the mid-twentieth century in capsule form.

1460   Ash, Brian. FACES OF THE FUTURE: THE LESSONS OF SCIENCE FICTION. New York: Taplinger Publishing Co., 1975. 213 p. Bibliog., index.

> An informal exploration of the history and themes of science fiction.

1461   _____. WHO'S WHO IN SCIENCE FICTION. London: Hamish Hamilton, Elm Tree, 1976. 220 p. Bibliog.

> Brief career biographies, with checklists of major science

fiction writers, with a descriptive list of two dozen themes
and writers associated with them.

1462 _____, ed. VISUAL ENCYCLOPEDIA OF SCIENCE FICTION. London:
Pan Books, 1977. 352 p. Illus., index, chronological checklist.

Essays on themes, science fiction as literature, recurrent
concepts, fandom, science fiction art, magazines, and media.
Lavish color illustrations.

1463 Ashley, Michael, ed. THE HISTORY OF THE SCIENCE FICTION MAGA-
ZINE. London: New English Library, 1975. 349 p. Author checklists,
table of magazine issues, editor list, cover artist, bibliog.

Introduction, with ten stories.

1464 Ashley, Michael. WHO'S WHO IN HORROR AND FANTASY FICTION.
New York: Taplinger, 1978. 240 p. Title guide, magazine price
guide, anthology list, award list, bibliog., chronology.

Brief biographical and plot notes on about four hundred
selected writers of fantasy, a genre whose events happen
"contrary to accepted scientific laws and observations."
The author divides fantasy into supernatural, heroic, and
humorous fantasy. The main body of the work is an alpha-
betized author listing with appended chronology, index to
key works, checklist of weird fiction anthologies with notes
on contents, a similar list of magazines, and a list of award
winners. Brief checklist of reference works.

1465 Bleiler, E[verett].F. THE CHECKLIST OF SCIENCE-FICTION AND SUPER-
NATURAL FICTION. Glen Rock, N.J.: Firebell Books, 1978. 266 p.

An author checklist with category designations, together
with a title index.

1466 Bretnor, Reginald, ed. THE CRAFT OF SCIENCE FICTION: A SYM-
POSIUM ON WRITING SCIENCE FICTION AND SCIENCE FANTASY.
New York: Harper and Row, 1976. 321 p. Index.

Divided into sections on sources, creativity, and trade secrets,
this collection of original essays by major science fiction
writers considers basic plots, the uses of science, and writing
technique.

1467 _____. MODERN SCIENCE FICTION: ITS MEANING AND ITS
FUTURE. New York: Coward-McCann, 1953. 294 p.

Original essays on publishing, criticism, science fiction's

relation to mainstream writing, social science fiction, science fiction and morality, and science fiction as preparation for the space age; includes a survey of science fiction in film, radio, and TV by Don Fabren.

1468   Briney, Robert E., and Wood, Edward. SCIENCE-FICTION BIBLIOGRA-PHIES: AN ANNOTATED BIBLIOGRAPHY OF BIBLIOGRAPHICAL WORKS ON SCIENCE FICTION AND FANTASY FICTION. Chicago: Advent Publishers, 1972. 49 p. Index.

An annotated bibliography of magazine indexes, author bibliography of magazine indexes, author bibliographies, general indexes, checklists, and foreign-language bibliographies.

1469   Carter, Paul A. THE CREATION OF TOMORROW: FIFTY YEARS OF MAGAZINE SCIENCE FICTION. New York: Columbia University Press, 1977. 318 p. Index.

A useful examination of a number of themes in magazine science fiction. Chapters cover moon travel stories, interplanetary pastorals, time travel, dictatorial leaders, evolutionary motifs, the feminine mystique, post-utopian ideas, descent into barbarity, and the scope of the genre. A final essay on collections and anthologies completes the volume.

1470   Clareson, Thomas. SCIENCE FICTION CRITICISM: AN ANNOTATED CHECKLIST. The Serif Series: Bibliographies and Checklists, No. 23. Kent, Ohio: Kent State University Press, 1972. 225 p. Indexes.

An excellent reference bibliography that includes a wide range of books, journals, magazine, and newspaper articles. Covers general works, literary studies, reviews, visual arts, futurology and utopian (as well as distopian) works, classroom and library aids, publishing resourse materials, and contemporary activities in the field. Indexes to fiction authors and to the authors of the items noted in the bibliography.

1471   _____, ed. SCIENCE FICTION: THE OTHER SIDE OF REALISM: ESSAYS ON MODERN FANTASY AND SCIENCE FICTION. Bowling Green, Ohio: Bowling Green University Popular Press, 1971. 356 p.

A solid collection of essays on definition, technique, themes, individual writers and works, and science fiction film. Brief checklists of award-winning novels, criticism, journals, and collections.

1472   _____, ed. VOICES FOR THE FUTURE. Bowling Green, Ohio: Popular Press, 1976. 283 p. Bibliog.

Collection of essays on science fiction authors, including

Jack Williamson, Olaf Stapledon, Clifford D. Simak, Issac
Asimov, Robert A. Heinlein, Theodore Sturgeon, Ray Bradbury, Kurt Vonnegut, Arthur C. Clarke, and others.

1473 Clarke, I.F. THE TALE OF THE FUTURE, FROM THE BEGINNING TO
THE PRESENT DAY: AN ANNOTATED BIBLIOGRAPHY OF THOSE
SATIRES, IDEAL STATES, IMAGINARY WARS AND INVASIONS, COM-
ING CATASTROPHES AND END-OF-WORLD STORIES, POLITICAL
WARNINGS AND FORECASTS, INTERPLANETARY VOYAGES AND
SCIENTIFIC ROMANCES--ALL LOCATED IN AN IMAGINARY FUTURE
PERIOD--THAT HAVE BEEN PUBLISHED IN THE UNITED KINGDOM
BETWEEN 1644 AND 1976. London: Library Association, 1978. 357 p.
Illus., bibliog.

A chronological list, often with brief notes, together with
short-title and author indexes; many U.S. authors are included.

1474 Contento, William. INDEX TO SCIENCE FICTION ANTHOLOGIES
AND COLLECTIONS. Boston: G.K. Hall, 1978. 608 p. Indexes.

Contains a checklist of books indexed, author and story indexes, and coding symbols.

1475 Crawford, Joseph H., Jr.; Donahue, James J.; and Grant, Donald M.,
eds. "333": A BIBLIOGRAPHY OF THE SCIENCE-FANTASY NOVEL.
New York: Arno Press, 1975. 80 p.

Annotated bibliography of 333 novels, which are identified
as gothic romance, weird tale, science fiction, fantasy, lost
race, fantastic adventure, unknown world, oriental novel, or
associational novel.

1476 Day, Bradford M. CHECKLIST OF FANTASTIC LITERATURE IN PAPER-
BOUND BOOKS. New York: Arno Press, 1975. 128 p.

Author and title listings with dates and publisher.

1477 de Camp, L. Sprague. LITERARY SWORDSMEN AND SORCERERS: THE
MAKERS OF HEROIC FANTASY. Introduction by Lin Carter. Sauk City,
Wis.: Arkham House, 1976. 313 p.

A brief history, chapters on ten writers, and a chapter on
minor writers make up the volume. Writers discussed include
such influential authors as William Morris, Lord Dunsany,
H.P. Lovecraft, E.R. Eddison, Robert E. Howard, Fletcher
Pratt, Clark Ashton Smith, Jr., J.R.R. Tolkien, and T.H.
White.

1478 Eastman, Mary Huse. INDEX TO FAIRY TALES, MYTHS, AND LEGENDS.

Useful Reference Series, no. 26. 1915. Boston: F.W. Faxon, 1926.
2d rev. ed. 610 p. SUPPLEMENT. 2 vols. Useful Reference Series,
nos. 61, 82. Boston: F.W. Faxon, 1937-1952.

A subject index to stories and tales in anthologies and collections, with author and title lists, geographical and ethnic
indexes, subject index, and directory of publishers.

1479 Elliott, Robert C. THE SHAPE OF UTOPIA: STUDIES IN A LITERARY
GENRE. Chicago: University of Chicago Press, 1970. 158 p. Notes,
index.

A consideration of the genre and of individual utopias in a
series of essays. Themes are satire, fear, and the aesthetics
of utopias; individual utopias include UTOPIA, THE BLITHE-
DALE ROMANCE, WALDEN TWO and ISLAND.

1480 Hall, H.W., ed. SCIENCE FICTION BOOK REVIEW INDEX, 1923-
1973. Detroit: Gale Research Co., 1975. 438 p. Indexes.

Author checklists, with title checklist and magazine directory.
Annual updates.

1481 Ireland, Norma Olin. INDEX TO FAIRY TALES, 1949-1972, INCLUD-
ING FOLKLORE, LEGENDS, AND MYTHS, IN COLLECTIONS. Useful Reference Series, no. 101. Westwood, Mass.: Faxon, 1973. 741 p.

Covers material in 406 anthologies. Supplements through 1977.

1482 Knight, Damon. IN SEARCH OF WONDER: ESSAYS ON MODERN
SCIENCE FICTION. Introduction by Anthony Boucher. Chicago:
Advent, 1967. Rev. and enl. ed. 306 p. Bibliog., index.

Perceptive analyses of science fiction and the writing process,
with much essential advice for both writers and critics. Chapters on Campbell, van Vogt, Heinlein, Asimov, Bradbury,
Sturgeon, Kuttner and Moore, Kornbluth, Blish, Pratt, Mosko-
witz and others, with notes on style.

1483 Knight, Damon Francis, ed. TURNING POINTS: ESSAYS ON THE
ART OF SCIENCE FICTION. New York: Harper and Row, 1977.
303 p. Notes.

Twenty-three essays on writing and conceptualizing science
fiction--the history of the genre, criticism, science, as
prophecy, and related matters. Excellent collection by the
writers themselves.

1484 Locke, George. VOYAGES IN SPACE: A BIBLIOGRAPHY OF INTER-
PLANETARY FICTION, 1801-1914. London: Ferret Fantasy, 1975.
80 p. Charts, index.

Brief introduction, with an annotated bibliography of 263
items, and a postscript on frequency of appearance.

1485 Lundwall, Sam J. SCIENCE FICTION: WHAT IT'S ALL ABOUT. Introduction by Donald A. Wollheim. New York: Ace, 1971. 256 p. Notes,
brief bibliog., index.

First published in Sweden, this is a delightful, often thoughtful, sometimes nonsensical introduction to many of the themes
of science fiction, with discussion of major and minor contributions. Included are chapters on definition, early contributions, utopian influences, anti-utopian nightmares, fantasy, adventure, female characters, comics, magazine fiction,
fandom, and the "New Wave" writers.

1486 McGhan, Barry, comp. SCIENCEFICTION AND FANTASY PSEUD-
ONYMS. N.p.: Misfit Press, 1976. 70 p. Bibliog.

Alphabetical listing.

1487 Menville, Douglas, and Reginald, R., eds. ANCESTRAL VOICES: AN
ANTHOLOGY OF EARLY SCIENCE FICTION. New York: Arno Press,
1975. Var. pag.

Ten English and American stories in facsimile, collected from
the period 1887 to 1915.

1488 Moore, Patrick. SCIENCE AND FICTION. London: G.G. Harrap,
1957. 192 p. Notes, index.

Traces the roots of science fiction to antiquity in a brief
chapter, then provides an outline of Verne and Wells, considers BEMs, magazine fiction, juveniles, mutants and robots,
time travel, disembodied minds, the media, and social science
fiction.

1489 Mullen, R.D., and Suvin, Darko, eds. SCIENCE-FICTION STUDIES:
SELECTED ARTICLES ON SCIENCE FICTION 1976-1977. 2d ser. Introduction by Marc Angenot. Boston: Gregg Press, 1978. 355 p.

The volume contains thirty-six essays and a bibliography on
paraliterature and sociology by Marc Angenot. Essays are
divided into science fiction before Wells; Morris, Wells,
and London; science fiction since Wells; and the sociology
of science fiction. Most of the essays focus on single authors
or works, though there are several more general pieces included. All essays first appeared in the journal SCIENCE
FICTION STUDIES.

1490 Negley, Glenn. UTOPIAN LITERATURE: A BIBLIOGRAPHY, WITH A

SUPPLEMENTARY LISTING OF WORKS INFLUENTIAL IN UTOPIAN THOUGHT. Lawrence: The Regents Press of Kansas, 1977. 228 p. Short title index and chronological index.

A basic international source for identifying and locating utopian literature and works influential in utopian thought, with locating keys for twelve libraries.

1491 Nicholls, Peter, ed. THE SCIENCE FICTION ENCYCLOPEDIA. Garden City, N.Y.: Doubleday, 1979. 672 p.

An excellent reference work with entries on authors, themes, films, magazines, illustrators, editors, critics, filmmakers, publishers, series, television programs, anthologies, comics, terms, awards, fanzines, with further notes on pseudonyms and international science fiction. Entries range from very brief notes to entries of more than three columns; each is detailed and unusually accurate.

1492 Parrinder, Patrick, ed. SCIENCE FICTION: A CRITICAL GUIDE. New York: Longman, 1979. 238 p. Index.

Critical essays on background, Jules Verne, H.G. Wells, utopias, science, the cold war, religion, and characterization, as these topics concern science fiction. Includes chapters on American science fiction since 1960, British science fiction, and European science fiction.

1493 Rabkin, Eric S. THE FANTASTIC IN LITERATURE. Princeton, N.J.: Princeton University Press, 1976. 234 p. Notes, index.

A useful examination of fantasy, escape, perspective, genre criticism, literary history in relation to the fantastic, with a chapter on the scope of fantasy. Of particular interest for the study of popular culture is the chapter on genre criticism, where the author is concerned with the qualities and categories of science fiction.

1494 Reginald, Robert, ed. SCIENCE FICTION AND FANTASY LITERATURE: A CHECKLIST FROM EARLIEST TIMES TO 1974 WITH CONTEMPORARY SCIENCE FICTION AUTHORS II. 2 vols. Detroit: Gale Research Co., 1979. 1,141 p. Illus.

Volume 1 contains author, title, series, awards, Ace and Belmont Doubles indexes; volume 2 contains biographical sketches and vital statistics of authors, along with a pictorial history of dust jackets.

1495 Rock, James A., comp. WHO GOES THERE: A BIBLIOGRAPHIC DICTIONARY: BEING A GUIDE TO THE WORKS OF AUTHORS WHO

HAVE CONTRIBUTED TO THE LITERATURE OF FANTASY AND SCIENCE
FICTION, AND WHO HAVE PUBLISHED SOME OR ALL OF THEIR
WORK PSEUDONYMOUSLY. Bloomington, Ind.: James A. Rock, 1979.
202 p. Illus., bibliog., index.

An author checklist, with notes on collecting.

1496   Roemer, Kenneth M. THE OBSOLETE NECESSITY: AMERICAN UTOPIAN
WRITINGS: 1888-1900. Kent, Ohio: Kent State University Press, 1976.
239 p. Annot. bibliog., notes, index.

An examination of 160 fictional and nonfictional utopian,
anti-utopian and partially utopian works during the period,
with emphasis on ideas and attitudes, the relevancy of
utopian reforms and speculation, and what such utopias re-
veal about American society of the time.

1497   Rottensteiner, Franz. THE FANTASY BOOK: THE GHOSTLY, THE
GOTHIC, THE MAGICAL, THE UNREAL. London: Thames and Hudson,
1978. 160 p. Illus., bibliog., index.

A thematic history of gothic origins, authors, themes and
characters, and ghost and horror stories in the United States
and other countries, with discussion of subgenres.

1498   Scholes, Robert. STRUCTURAL FABULATION: AN ESSAY ON FICTION
OF THE FUTURE. Notre Dame: University of Notre Dame Press, 1975.
111 p. Brief critical bibliog. and index.

The volume, based on the author's four Ward-Phillips lectures
for 1974, constitutes a brief introduction to the critical vision
of science fiction, a generic theory and historical framework,
the varieties of science fiction through a discussion of bound-
ary cases, and considerable attention to the work of Ursula K.
LeGuin.

1499   Scholes, Robert, and Rabkin, Eric S. SCIENCE FICTION: HISTORY,
SCIENCE AND VISION. New York: Oxford University Press, 1977.
258 p. Annotated bibliog., index.

A solid introduction to the genre, the volume contains an
outline history, science fiction in media, the uses of science
in the fiction, forms and themes related to the genre, and a
discussion of ten representative novels. Useful for classroom.

1500   Shurter, Robert Le Fevre. THE UTOPIAN NOVEL IN AMERICA, 1865-
1900. New York: AMS Press, 1973. 302 p.

A study of utopian fiction that considers classifications of
utopias, historical background from 1865 to 1900, American
and British predecessors to Edward Bellamy, and focuses on
Bellamy's LOOKING BACKWARD (1888).

1501 Slusser, George E.; Guffey, George R.; and Rose, Mark, eds. BRIDGES TO SCIENCE FICTION. Carbondale and Edwardsville: Southern Illinois University, 1980. 168 p. Notes, index.

Essays on science and fiction, Platonic science fiction in the Middle Ages, empirical views of God, aliens, the search for transcendence, fairy tales and science fiction, science fiction as truncated epic, gothic parallels, the nature of science fictional worlds, and the history of science fiction.

1502 Suvin, Darko. METAMORPHOSES OF SCIENCE FICTION: ON THE POETICS AND HISTORY OF A LITERARY GENRE. New Haven, Conn.: Yale University Press, 1979. 317 p. Notes, bibliog., index.

Essays on the poetics, history, and structure of science fiction.

1503 Tuck, Donald H. THE ENCYCLOPEDIA OF SCIENCE FICTION AND FANTASY. 2 vols. Chicago: Advent, 1974, 1978. Illus.

Volume 1 covers "Who's Who and Works A-L," consisting of an alphabetical listing of authors, editors, artists, and so forth, with biographical information and compilations of their fantasy-science fiction works, in most cases covering all known forms and editions, including foreign translations. Volume 2 covers M-Z, with a title list. A third volume is projected and will cover magazines, paperbacks, pseudonyms, series stories, films, and other matters.

1504 Tymn, Marshall B., and Schlobin, Roger C. THE YEAR'S SCHOLARSHIP IN SCIENCE FICTION AND FANTASY: 1972-1975. Serif Series, No. 36. Kent, Ohio: Kent State University Press, 1979. 222 p. Indexes to authors and titles.

Annotated bibliography of general studies, bibliographical and reference material, author studies, and teaching and visual aids.

1505 Tymn, Marshall B.; Zahorski, Kenneth J.; and Boyer, Robert H. FANTASY LITERATURE: A CORE COLLECTION AND REFERENCE GUIDE. New York: R.R. Bowker, 1979. 273 p. Publisher's directory, index.

Arranged into parts listing primary works and research aids, the guide identifies adult fantasy, scholarship, periodicals, organizations, awards, and collections.

1506 Tymn, Marshall B.; Schlobin, Roger C.; and Currey, L.W., comps. and eds. A RESEARCH GUIDE TO SCIENCE FICTION STUDIES: AN ANNO-TATED CHECKLIST OF PRIMARY AND SECONDARY SOURCES FOR FANTASY AND SCIENCE FICTION. New York: Garland, 1977. 165 p. Short title index.

Includes sections on preliminary sources, sources for primary materials, (nonarchival), secondary materials, author studies, periodicals and further sources; bibliography of doctoral dissertations by Douglas R. Justus; some film coverage.

1507　Versins, Pierre. ENCYCLOPEDIE DE L'UTOPIE, DES VOYAGES EXTRAORDINAIRES, ET DE LA SCIENCE FICTION. Lausanne: Editions L'Age d'Homme, 1972. 997 p. Illus.

An extensive encyclopedia of utopias, fantastic voyages and science fiction appearing in a variety of media and even as themes in ephemera.

1508　Waggoner, Diana. THE HILLS OF FARAWAY: A GUIDE TO FANTASY. New York: Atheneum, 1978. 326 p. Indexes.

Excellent introduction to and bibliography of fantasy, with appendixes on chronology, award winners, illustration, and subgenres.

1509　Warrick, Patricia. THE CYBERNETIC IMAGINATION IN SCIENCE FICTION. Cambridge: MIT Press, 1980. 282 p. Notes, index, bibliog.

Discusses myths, early automata, Frankenstein, Asimov, the robot as metaphor, distopias, man-machine symbiosis and open systems, and Philip K. Dick's robots.

1510　Wells, Stuart W. III, comp. THE SCIENCE FICTION AND HEROIC FANTASY AUTHOR INDEX. Duluth, Minn.: Purple Unicorn Books, 1978. 185 p.

An attempt to identify science fiction and heroic fantasy published since 1945, resulting in 5,000 titles of over 1,000 authors.

1511　Wollheim, Donald D. THE UNIVERSE MAKERS: SCIENCE FICTION TODAY. New York: Harper and Row, 1971. 122 p. Name and title index.

An informal survey of contemporary science fiction from the perspective of a knowledgeable editor and publisher. Of particular interest is Wollheim's observations about the appeal of various popular works.

WAR FICTION

1512　Aichinger, Peter. THE AMERICAN SOLDIER IN FICTION, 1880-1963:

A HISTORY OF ATTITUDES TOWARD WARFARE AND THE MILITARY ESTABLISHMENT. Ames: Iowa State University, 1975. 143 p. Notes, bibliog., index, checklist.

A topical history, with chapters on war as metaphor, civilian soldiers and officers, Jews in war novels, blurring distinctions between civilian and military organizations, the absurd, non-heroes, black humor, and the war novel as pop art.

1513 Cooperman, Stanley. WORLD WAR I AND THE AMERICAN NOVEL. Baltimore: Johns Hopkins Press, 1967. 271 p. Bibliog., notes, index.

An examination of the novels of prewar propaganda, the war, heroes, antiheroes, limbo; with emphasis on themes and major novels.

1514 Jones, Peter G. WAR AND THE NOVELIST: APPRAISING THE AMERI-CAN WAR NOVEL. Columbia: University of Missouri Press, 1976. 260 p. Notes, bibliog., index.

An analysis of the themes of education, the relationships of sexuality and violence, developing attitudes toward com-manders, and the psychology of combat in war novels pub-lished between 1944 and 1968, with a chapter on Vonnegut.

1515 Lively, Robert A. FICTION FIGHTS THE CIVIL WAR: AN UNFINISHED CHAPTER IN THE LITERARY HISTORY OF THE AMERICAN PEOPLE. Chapel Hill: University of North Carolina, 1957. Reprint. Westport, Conn.: Greenwood Press, 1973. 230 p. Notes, bibliog., index.

An examination of 512 popular novels of the Civil War, with attention to chronology, themes, differentiation among novels focusing on the North and South, novelistic techniques, and the relationships between fiction and history.

1516 Miller, Wayne Charles. AN ARMED AMERICA--ITS FACE IN FICTION: A HISTORY OF THE AMERICAN MILITARY NOVEL New York: New York University, 1970. 294 p. Notes, bibliog., index.

A survey of the military novel from Cooper and Melville through the major wars, the military elite, CATCH-22, and the nuclear age.

1517 Smith, Myron J. WAR STORY GUIDE: AN ANNOTATED BIBLIOG-RAPHY OF MILITARY FICTION. Metuchen, N.J.: Scarecrow, 1980. 437 p. Index.

An annotated bibliography arranged into chronological group-ings of 3,917 novels and other fictional accounts of war ex-perience, from the dawn of literature to 1978, with an index to pseudonyms.

1518 Waldmeir, Joseph J. AMERICAN NOVELS OF THE SECOND WORLD WAR. The Hague: Mouton Publishers, 1971. 180 p. Bibliog., index.

> A study of American novels depicting war and committed ideologically to it, with chapters comparing World War I and II novels, the archetypal THE CRUSADERS (Boston: Little, Brown, 1948), faces of villainy, dissenting voids, and styles of commitment.

WESTERNS

1519 Cawelti, John G. THE SIX GUN MYSTIQUE. Bowling Green, Ohio: Bowling Green University Popular Press, 1971. 138 p. Lists of titles in several media, bibliography.

> Cawelti's is the first book-length study of the Western formula in fiction and film. Includes discussion of the importance of setting, complex of characters, types of situations and patterns of action, the dramatic structure of the Western and the relationships of formula to culture.

1520 Etulain, Richard W. WESTERN AMERICAN LITERATURE: A BIBLIOGRAPHY OF INTERPRETIVE BOOKS AND ARTICLES. Vermillion, S.D.: Dakota Press, 1972. 137 p.

> A checklist of critical pieces on some two hundred authors, with additional entries identifying anthologies, bibliographies, general works, and three topics--The Beats, local color and regionalism, and popular Western fiction.

1521 Etulain, Richard W., and Marsden, Michael T., eds. THE POPULAR WESTERN: ESSAYS TOWARD A DEFINITON. Bowling Green, Ohio: Bowling Green University Popular Press, 1974. 111 p. Illus., bibliog., notes.

> A collection of essays, with introduction and afterword, on the revenge theme in the dime novel, B.M. Bower, Zane Grey, Clay Fisher, Luke Short, Jack Schaefer, the history of Westerns, and literary criticism of Westerns.

1522 Folsom, James K. THE AMERICAN WESTERN NOVEL. New Haven, Conn.: College and University Press, 1966. 224 p. Notes, bibliog., index.

> A study of the influence of James Fenimore Cooper on the imaginative creation of the West, fiction about the settling of the West, the hero in Westerns, depiction of Indians, and characteristic themes of Westerns.

1523 _____, ed. THE WESTERN: A COLLECTION OF CRITICAL ESSAYS.

Englewood Cliffs, N.J.: Prentice-Hall, 1979. 177 p. Brief chronology and bibliography.

> Ten essays by various writers on the cowboy hero, dime novels, Andy Adams, Owen Wister, THE OX-BOW INCIDENT (1940) and Vardis Fisher on the writing of fiction; included are comparisons of the American Western with gaucho fiction and the English version of the Western. Richard Etulain discusses the rise of critical attention to the Western.

1524   Gaston, Edwin W., Jr. THE EARLY NOVEL OF THE SOUTHWEST. Albuquerque: University of New Mexico Press, 1961. 318 p. Bibliog., index.

> Includes a survey of novels from 1789 to 1914, chapters on plots and techniques, character portrayal, geography, intellectual concepts and notes on authors.

1524a   Jones, Daryl. THE DIME NOVEL WESTERN. Bowling Green, Ohio: Popular Press, 1978. 186 p. Notes, checklist, bibliog.

> Discusses the origin, setting, heroic types, later settings, plot and structure, and unifying vision.

1525   Milton, John R. THE NOVEL OF THE AMERICAN WEST. Lincoln: University of Nebraska, 1980. 341 p. Bibliog., index.

> After having "chastised" the popular Western, Milton discusses the writer's West, the evolution of the Western novel, Vardis Fisher, A.B. Guthrie, Frederick Manfred, Walter Tan Tilburg Clark, Harvey Fergusson, Frank Waters, and variations on Western realism.

1526   _____. THREE WEST: CONVERSATIONS WITH VARDIS FISHER, MAX EVANS AND MICHAEL STRAIGHT. Vermillion: University of South Dakota, 1970. 166 p.

> Interviews with the authors on writing and aspects of Western writing, based on KUSD-TV tapes.

1527   Pilkington, William T. CRITICAL ESSAYS ON THE WESTERN AMERICAN NOVEL. Boston: G.K. Hall, 1980. 275 p. Notes, index.

> General essays cover early critical statements, history and theory of the popular and literary Western novel, and provide an overview of fiction about the American West. The bulk of the book is comprised of essays on Emerson Hough, Owen Wister, Vardis Fisher, A.B. Guthrie, Louis L'Amour, Walter Van Tilburg Clark, Frederick Manfred, Jean Stafford, Michael Straight, William Eastlake, Edward Abbey, Larry McMurtry, N. Scott Momaday, and Rudolfo Anaya.

1528   Sonnichsen, C.L. FROM HOPALONG TO HUD: THOUGHTS ON WESTERN FICTION. College Station: Texas A & M University, 1978. 201 p. Notes, bibliog., index.

>Arguing that Westerns provide an index to America, the author examines the fantasy West, the Wyatt Earp syndrome, Tombstone in fiction, images of the Apache and Mexican-Americans, the unheroic cowboy, Susan Shubrick Pinckney, images of the sharecropper in fiction, love and sex in Westerns, and suggestions for further examination of the fiction.

1529   Steeves, Harrison R. "The First of the Westerns." SOUTHWEST REVIEW 53, no. 1 (1968): 74-83.

>Claims that the writer of the first "western"--a fictional account of the suppression of outlawry--was a German, Friedrich Gerstäcker, who spent about ten months in Texas in 1838-39. When he returned to Germany he wrote THE REGULATORS IN ARKANSAS (1845) and numerous other fictional and nonfictional accounts.

1530   VanDerhoof, Jack. A BIBLIOGRAPHY OF NOVELS RELATED TO AMERICAN FRONTIER AND COLONIAL HISTORY. Troy, N.Y.: Whitston, 1971. 501 p.

>A checklist of 6,439 novels whose settings are clearly in the colonial period or the frontier regardless of historical time. Novels dealing with the Civil War are not included.

OTHER FICTION

1531   Bacon, Daisy. LOVE STORY WRITER. New York: Hermitage House, 1954. 172 p. Index.

>A former writer and editor explains what the love story is, how to write it, what editors want, basic plots and themes, and how to sell the story.

1532   Butterfield, H. THE HISTORICAL NOVEL: AN ESSAY. Cambridge: The University Press, 1924. Reprint: Folcroft, Pa.: Folcroft Library Editions, 1971. 113 p.

>An attempt to find a critical approach to the use of fiction to understand the past.

1533   Collett, Dorothy. WRITING THE MODERN CONFESSION STORY. Boston: The Writer, 1971. 185 p.

>A how-to book for aspiring writers, with chapters on the market, technique, and discussion of one of the author's own stories.

1534 Day, Bradford M. BIBLIOGRAPHY OF ADVENTURE: MUNDY, BUR-
ROUGHS, ROHMER, HAGGARD. Rev. ed. New York: Arno Press,
1978. 125 p.

Checklists, with brief biographical sketches, of the four
British writers, all of whom became enormously popular in
the United States.

1535 Dickinson, A.T., Jr. AMERICAN HISTORICAL FICTION. 3d ed.
Metuchen, N.J.: Scarecrow, 1971. 380 p. Author and short title
indexes.

An annotated bibliography of 2,440 items arranged in periods
from colonial times through the 1960s, with a section on
chronicles.

1536 Ezell, Macel D. UNEQUIVOCAL AMERICANISM: RIGHT-WING
NOVELS IN THE COLD WAR ERA. Metuchen, N.J.: Scarecrow Press,
1977. 152 p. Notes, appendix, bibliog., index.

Analysis of the content of right-wing novels and those judged
to be objectionable to this faction, together with a discussion
of recurring themes in right-wing novels and criticism. An
appendix discusses contemporary right-wing book clubs.

1537 Fiedler, Leslie A. THE INADVERTENT EPIC: FROM UNCLE TOM'S
CABIN TO ROOTS. New York: Touchstone, 1980. 85 p.

A reinterpretation of UNCLE TOM'S CABIN, THE KLANS-
MEN (and BIRTH OF A NATION), GONE WITH THE WIND,
and Alex Haley's ROOTS.

1538 Harlequin Enterprises. THE FIRST THIRTY YEARS OF THE WORLD'S
BEST ROMANCE FICTION. Toronto: Harlequin, 1979. 286 p.
Illus., checklists, index.

Brief historical account of the house, with chronological
series checklists, author notes and some autobiographical
sketches.

1539 Irwin, Leonard B., comp. A GUIDE TO HISTORICAL FICTION FOR
THE USE OF SCHOOLS, LIBRARIES, AND THE GENERAL READER.
10th ed. Brooklawn, N.J.: McKinley, 1971. 255 p. Author and
title indexes.

Briefly annotated items arranged alphabetically by author
according to period and/or locale, with separate sections on
juvenile novels. The bibliography contains only fiction published after 1940, and which was given critical approval.

1540 Jones, Robert Kenneth. THE SHUDDER PULPS: A HISTORY OF THE WEIRD MENACE MAGAZINES OF THE 1930S. West Linn, Oreg.: Fax Collectors, 1975. 238 p. Illus., index.

> A thematic history of the subgenre "in which the villain perpetrated seemingly supernatural deviltries, which were logically explained at the end."

1541 Leisy, Ernest E. THE AMERICAN HISTORICAL NOVEL. 1950. Norman: University of Oklahoma, 1962. 280 p. Chronological checklist, index, notes.

> Chapters on topical aspects of the colonial period, the Revolution, the westward movement, the Civil War and Reconstruction, and national expansion.

1542 Levin, David. IN DEFENSE OF HISTORICAL LITERATURE: ESSAYS ON AMERICAN HISTORY, AUTOBIOGRAPHY, DRAMA AND FICTION. New York: Hill and Wang, 1967. 144 p. Notes, index.

> A collection of essays on how formal history should be criticized, and on the criticism of biography, historical fiction, and historical drama, with emphasis on the hazing of Cotton Mather, Franklin's AUTOBIOGRAPHY, the Salem Witchcraft trials, Hawthorne, and Faulkner's ABSALOM, ABSALOM!

1543 McGarry, Daniel D., and White, Sarah Harriman. HISTORICAL FICTION GUIDE: ANNOTATED CHRONOLOGICAL, GEOGRAPHICAL AND TOPICAL LIST OF FIVE THOUSAND SELECTED HISTORICAL NOVELS. New York: Scarecrow Press, 1963. 628 p. Index.

> The United States section includes a list of about 140 pages covering five periods from the beginnings to 1900 to novels written up to about 1960.

1544 Male, Roy R. ENTER, MYSTERIOUS STRANGER: AMERICAN CLOISTRAL FICTION. Norman: University of Oklahoma, 1979. 128 p. Checklist of fiction, index.

> An examination of the story of "the quest or the picaresque turned inside out ('outside in' would be better)" in which a mysterious stranger who is a potential savior or destroyer enters an isolated setting and conducts a transaction with the point-of-view character(s).

1545 Schweitzer, Darrell. CONAN'S WORLD AND ROBERT E. HOWARD. The Milford Series, Popular Writers of Today, vol. 17. San Bernardino, Calif.: R. Reginald/Borgo Press, 1978. 64 p. Bibliog.

> A balanced critical assessment of Howard's work.

1546 Smith, Myron J., Jr., and Weller, Robert C. SEA FICTION GUIDE. Metuchen, N.J.: Scarecrow Press, 1976. 256 p. Bibliog., index.

A partially annotated bibliography of 2,525 novels and anthologies, with an additional index to pseudonyms and joint authors.

1547 Smith, Pauline. CONFESS FOR CASH: THE INSIDE STORY OF HOW TO WRITE AND SELL CONFESSION STORIES. New York: Pilot, 1960. 32 p. Periodical list.

Practical advice on the genre, editors, readers, and manuscript preparation.

1548 STRASBOURG'S CATALOGUE AND GUIDE TO THE ROMANCES. Redondo Beach, Calif.: Strasbourg's Publishing Co., 1978. 245 p.

A listing of 5,000 romance paperbacks by series with some author lists, notes on authors, and pseudonyms.

1549 Van Derhoof, Jack. A BIBLIOGRAPHY OF NOVELS RELATED TO AMERICAN FRONTIER AND COLONIAL HISTORY. Troy, N.Y.: Whitston, 1971. 501 p. Bibliog.

A bibliography of titles with key phrases.

POPULAR NONFICTION

1550 Carpenter, Charles. HISTORY OF AMERICAN SCHOOLBOOKS. Philadelphia: University of Pennsylvania Press, 1963. 322 p. Illus., bibliog., index.

A subject history of the most influential textbooks, with brief chapters on early American schools, primers and readers, and progress in publishing.

1551 Cirino, Robert. DON'T BLAME THE PEOPLE: HOW THE NEWS MEDIA USE BIAS, DISTORTION AND CENSORSHIP TO MANIPULATE PUBLIC OPINION. Los Angeles: Diversity Press, 1971. 341 p.

Though the author's discussion of the techniques of manipulation is not innovative, his use of extensive examples makes a strong case for the built-in biases of news media, and especially of their conservative owners and editorial heads.

1552 Harrison, John M., and Stein, Harry H., eds. MUCKRAKING: PAST, PRESENT AND FUTURE. University Park: Pennsylvania State University Press, 1974. 165 p. Notes, index.

Essays on background, Midwest muckrakers, race relations,

law and justice, contemporary best-sellers (Cawelti), the
aesthetics of muckraking, reform journalism, and the future
of the craft.

1553 Kittredge, George L. THE OLD FARMER AND HIS ALMANACK: BEING
SOME OBSERVATIONS OF LIFE AND MANNERS IN NEW ENGLAND A
HUNDRED YEARS AGO. Boston: Horace E. Ware, 1904. Reprint.
Cambridge: Harvard University Press, 1920. 402 p. Illus., index.

An investigation into the contents of eighteenth century
almanacs, particularly those of Robert Bailey Thomas, with
attention to astrology, artwork, wit and wisdom, natural
history, murder accounts, sensational reports, amusements
and entertainments, Indian talk, reading, travel, and other
topical matters.

1554 Klein, Frederick C., and Prestbo, John A. NEWS AND THE MARKET.
Chicago: H. Regnery, 1974. 228 p. Bibliog., index.

The effect of news stories on the stock market.

1555 McDade, Thomas M. THE ANNALS OF MURDER: A BIBLIOGRAPHY
OF BOOKS AND PAMPHLETS ON AMERICAN MURDERS FROM COLO-
NIAL TIMES TO 1900. Norman: University of Oklahoma Press, 1961.
360 p. Location symbols, index.

Contains 1,126 annotated items.

1556 Minnich, Harvey C. WILLIAM HOLMES McGUFFEY AND HIS READERS.
New York: American Book Co., 1936. 203 p. Illus., bibliog., index.

The origin, sources, rise in influence, social content, and
illustrations of the readers, with a biographical sketch of
McGuffey.

1557 Nietz, John A. THE EVOLUTION OF AMERICAN SECONDARY SCHOOL
TEXTBOOKS: RHETORIC AND LITERATURE, ALGEBRA, GEOMETRY,
NATURAL HISTORY, (ZOOLOGY), BOTANY, NATURAL PHILOSOPHY
(PHYSICS), CHEMISTRY, LATIN AND GREEK, FRENCH, GERMAN,
AND WORLD HISTORY AS TAUGHT IN AMERICAN LATIN GRAMMAR
SCHOOLS, ACADEMIES, AND EARLY HIGH SCHOOLS BEFORE 1900.
Rutland: Charles E. Tuttle, 1966. 265 p. Illus., notes, bibliog.,
index.

1558 _____. OLD TEXTBOOKS: SPELLING, GRAMMAR, READING,
ARITHMETIC, GEOGRAPHY, AMERICAN HISTORY, CIVIL GOVERN-
MENT, PHYSIOLOGY, PENMANSHIP, ART, MUSIC, AS TAUGHT IN
THE COMMON SCHOOLS FROM COLONIAL DAYS TO 1900. Pitts-
burgh: University of Pittsburgh, 1961. 364 p. Illus., notes, index.

1559   Roche, John P., et al. "Lo the Poor Quidnunc." THE ANTIOCH RE-
VIEW 35 (Spring-Summer 1977): 132-70.

> A series of brief articles responding to the question: in a
> world of news overkill, how does the conscientious citizen
> manage his quest for an understanding of what's happening?
> The answers reveal some sparkling examples and many useful
> suggestions.

1560   Rutland, Robert A. THE NEWSMONGERS: JOURNALISM IN THE LIFE
OF THE NATION, 1690-1972. Two Centuries of American Life. New
York: Dial, 1973. 430 p. Bibliog.

> Despite amazing technological advances, "the basic product
> only costs more," with dubious improvement. An unconven-
> tional history of American journalism, focussing on the profit-
> making instinct that has often smothered the social reformers
> and achieved goals opposite from those sought by the founding
> fathers.

1561   Stott, William. DOCUMENTARY EXPRESSION AND THIRTIES AMERICA.
New York: Oxford, 1973. 361 p. Bibliog., photos., index.

> Definition and extensive discussion of documentary expression
> through rhetoric, arts such as painting, dance, fiction, theater,
> radio, picture magazines; in popular thought, education, ad-
> vertising, case worker reports, social science writing, exposés
> and workers' narratives.

1562   Weber, Ronald. THE LITERATURE OF FACT: LITERARY NONFICTION
IN AMERICAN WRITING. Athens: Ohio University Press, 1980. 181 p.
Notes, bibliog., index.

> An examination of literary nonfiction through an examination
> of the various forms which journalistic prose has taken since
> Truman Capote's IN COLD BLOOD, the background of the
> form, and the styles and topics of major writers of the genre.

MEDIA

1563   Altheide, David. CREATING REALITY: HOW TV NEWS DISTORTS
EVENTS. Sage Library of Social Research, vol. 33. Beverly Hills,
Calif.: Sage Publications, 1976. 220 p. Bibliog.

>Based on observation of practices and other sources, the
>author discusses television news and everyday life, the com-
>mercial basis of news programming, division of labor in the
>newsroom, local news, political coverage, the Eagleton and
>Watergate stories; with a critical conclusion and methodologi-
>cal notes.

1564   ASPEN HANDBOOK ON THE MEDIA, 1977-79 EDITION: A SELECTIVE
GUIDE TO RESEARCH, ORGANIZATIONS AND PUBLICATIONS IN
COMMUNICATIONS. Edited by William L. Rivers, Wallace Thompson,
and Michael J. Nyhan. New York: Praeger Publishers, 1977. 438 p.

>Annotated lists of communication research programs, support-
>ing organizations, communications organizations, action
>groups, policymaking bodies, law curricula, international
>organizations.

1565   Barnouw, Eric. A TOWER IN BABEL: A HISTORY OF BROADCASTING
IN THE UNITED STATES. Vol. 1, TO 1933. New York: Oxford, 1966.
344 p. Illus., chronology, notes, bibliog., index.

>The standard history of broadcasting, focusing on the techni-
>cal, legal, and social history of radio.

1566   _____. THE GOLDEN WEB: A HISTORY OF BROADCASTING IN
THE UNITED STATES. Vol. 2, 1933-53. New York: Oxford, 1968.
391 p. Illus., chronology, notes, bibliog., index.

1567   _____. THE IMAGE EMPIRE: A HISTORY OF BROADCASTING IN
THE UNITED STATES. Vol. 3, FROM 1953. New York: Oxford, 1970.
396 p. Illus., chronology, notes, bibliog., index.

>Concludes the history at about 1969.

1568 Barslag, Karl. ROBBERY BY MAIL: THE STORY OF THE U.S. POSTAL INSPECTORS. New York: Farrar and Rinehart, 1938. 324 p.

An informal topical history of rackets, swindles, and frauds perpetrated through the mails, featuring numerous famous cases.

1569 Blum, Eleanor. BASIC BOOKS IN THE MASS MEDIA: AN ANNO-TATED, SELECTED BOOKLIST COVERING GENERAL COMMUNICA-TIONS, BOOK PUBLISHING, BROADCASTING, EDITORIAL JOUR-NALISM, FILM, MAGAZINES, AND ADVERTISING. Urbana: University of Illinois, 1980. 427 p. Index.

A bibliography of 1,179 pithily annotated items on books and book publishing, broadcasting, editorial journalism, film, magazines, advertising, and public relations.

1570 Boyd, Malcolm. CHRIST AND CELEBRITY GODS: THE CHURCH IN MASS CULTURE. Greenwich, Conn.: Seabury Press, 1958. 145 p. Bibliog., index.

A Christian assessment of the effects of the mass media through chapters on celebrity cult, the religious movie, Cecil B. DeMille's THE TEN COMMANDMENTS, Christian realism, and Christian witness.

1571 Brown, Charlene J.; Brown, Trevor R.; and Rivers, William L. THE MEDIA AND THE PEOPLE. New York: Holt, Rinehart and Winston, 1978. 472 p. Bibliog., index.

A useful summary of the media and American society that updates THE MASS MEDIA AND MODERN SOCIETY, by William L. Rivers, Theodore Peterson, and Jay W. Jensen (San Francisco: Rinehart Press, 1971). The bulk of the volume is concerned with the intellectual environment of media, and particularly with government's use and misuse of its powers. One brief section deals with entertainment.

1572 Budd, Richard W., and Ruben, Brent D. BEYOND MEDIA: NEW APPROACHES TO MASS COMMUNICATION. Rochelle Park, N.J.: Hayden, 1979. 292 p. Illus., bibliog., index.

Theory and critique of contemporary media with notes toward a reformulation; discussion of libraries, museums, religion, political campaigning, architecture, Sardi's restaurant, Broadway, and the visual arts.

1573 Čelebonovic, Aleksá. THE HEYDAY OF SALON PAINTING: MASTER-PIECES OF BOURGEOIS REALISM. London: Thames and Hudson, 1974. 200 p. Biogr. notes, bibliog., illus., index.

Arranged according to themes: religion, mythology, and antiquity, legend and history, Orientalism, social and family life, and portraits. Excellent plates.

1574 Ceynar, Marvin E., ed. CREATIVITY IN THE COMMUNICATIVE ARTS: A SELECTIVE BIBLIOGRAPHY 1960-1970. Compiled by Dorothy Jorstad et al. Troy, N.Y.: Whitston, 1975. 134 p.

Listing of 1,256 items on creativity in advertising, art, education, fiction, films, group communication, mass media, music, poetry, speech, and theatre.

1575 Chisholm, Margaret E. MEDIA INDEXES AND REVIEW SOURCES. College Park: University of Maryland, School of Library and Information Services, 1972. 84 p. Index.

A review essay on sources of reviews and similar information, with an annotated list of sources for reviews of media, primarily for educational purposes.

1576 Cirino, Robert. DON'T BLAME THE PEOPLE: HOW THE NEWS MEDIA USE BIAS, DISTORTION AND CENSORSHIP TO MANIPULATE PUBLIC OPINION. Los Angeles: Diversity Press, 1971. 341 p. Notes, bibliog., index.

A textbook survey of the ways in which news events may be biased by media. Numerous examples of the events that have or have not received coverage are included, with a series of "myths" people generally believe about media that are not true.

1577 _____. WE'RE BEING MORE THAN ENTERTAINED. Honolulu: Lighthouse Press, 1977. 224 p. Bibliog., illus., notes.

A critique of "Kojak," "All My Children," "Let's Make A Deal," "Tournament of Thrills," "Sesame Street," "Guardians of the Galaxy," television news and host shows, PLAYBOY magazine, and other entertainment.

1578 Daily, Jay E. THE ANATOMY OF CENSORSHIP. Books in Library and Information Science, vol. 6. New York: Marcel Dekker, 1973. 403 p. Notes, index.

A librarian's defense of publications of all forms without respect to content.

1579 Davis, Robert Edward. RESPONSE TO INNOVATION: A STUDY OF POPULAR ARGUMENT ABOUT NEW MASS MEDIA. New York: Arno Press, 1976. 725 p. Bibliog., index.

An examination of the controversy over the effects of radio, film, and television as it appeared in magazines from 1891

to 1955. Focus is on the rhetorical arguments used by critics
and proponents in some one thousand articles from seventy magazines.

1580   Gerbner, George, ed. MASS MEDIA POLICIES IN CHANGING CUL-
TURES. New York: John Wiley and Sons, 1977. 291 p. Notes,
index.

Divided into three parts--"International Trends," "New Directions," and "Developments in Theory and Research"--this
collection of essays provides a succinct scholarly review of
contemporary knowledge about, particularly, the American
role in international production and distribution.

1581   Gordon, George N. COMMUNICATIONS REVOLUTION: A HISTORY
OF MASS MEDIA IN THE UNITED STATES. New York: Hastings House,
1977. 338 p. Bibliog., index.

A history of print, press freedom, the penny press, giant
dailies, cinema, magazines, the growth of television, changes
in media.

1582   Halberstam, David. THE POWERS THAT BE. New York: Alfred A.
Knopf, 1979. 771 p. Bibliog., index.

An informal, but extensive review of the rise of broadcasting
through a discussion of the political influence of key industry
personalities. Halberstam traces the developing influence of
CBS, the LOS ANGELES TIMES, Time Incorporated, the
WASHINGTON POST and related corporations and their
connections to contemporary political powers, based on research and interviews with corporate personnel and others.

1583   Haney, Robert W. COMSTOCKERY IN AMERICA: PATTERNS OF CEN-
SORSHIP AND CONTROL. Boston: Beacon Press, 1960. 199 p. Bibliog.

Concerned with the emergence and practices of various re-
formist groups who have sought to censor public reading
matter.

1584   Hawes, William. THE PERFORMER IN MASS MEDIA: IN MEDIA PRO-
FESSIONS AND IN THE COMMUNITY. New York: Hastings House,
1978. 350 p. Illus., glossary, notes, bibliog., index.

Divided into sections on the performer and the performer's
environment, the text covers appearance, voice, movement,
talent, abnormalities, intangibles, the studio, preparation,
rehearsals, careers, media professionals and community experts, with emphasis on practical aspects of media production.

1585   Herman, Lewis Helmar, and Herman, Marguerite Shalett. MANUAL OF
       AMERICAN DIALECTS FOR RADIO, STAGE, SCREEN AND TELEVISION.
       Chicago: Ziff-Davis, 1947. 291 p.

> Phonetic pronunciations for performers, oriented to regional
> variations.

1586   Jacobs, Norman, ed. CULTURE FOR THE MILLIONS? MASS MEDIA
       IN MODERN SOCIETY. Princeton, N.J.: Van Nostrand, 1961. Re-
       print: Boston: Beacon Press, 1964. 200 p. Bibliog.

> A collection of essays in the mass culture tradition of the
> dangers and ideals of mass culture, on mass culture and the
> intellectual, conservative, artist, composer, and alarmist;
> with mediating voices.

1587   Jones, Barbara, and Howell, Bill. POPULAR ARTS OF THE FIRST
       WORLD WAR. New York: McGraw-Hill Book Co., 1972. 175 p.
       Illus., index.

> Toys, decorations, illustration, some advertisement, cartoons,
> and statuettes, such as middle- or upper-class person might
> own or see.

1588   Kahn, E.J., Jr. FRAUD: THE UNITED STATES POSTAL INSPECTION
       SERVICE AND SOME OF THE FOOLS AND KNAVES IT HAS KNOWN.
       New York: Harper and Row, 1973. 321 p.

> Accounts of famous cases of mail fraud and other crimes in-
> volving the postal service.

1589   Kendrick, Alexander. PRIME TIME: THE LIFE OF EDWARD E. MUR-
       ROW. Boston: Little, Brown, 1969. 548 p. Illus., bibliog., index.

> A career biography.

1590   Key, Wilson Bryan. MEDIA SEXPLOITATION. Englewood Cliffs, N.J.:
       Prentice-Hall, 1976. 220 p. Illus., bibliog., index.

> A continuation of his psychological critique of the hidden
> persuaders in advertising, packaging, and marketing imagery.
> Key argues that it is common practice to embed such images
> as skulls, sex organs, and other matter in the ground of
> illustrations in order to bypass conscious awareness.

1591   Kuhns, William. THE ELECTRIC GOSPEL: RELIGION AND MEDIA.
       New York: Herder and Herder, 1969. 173 p. Notes, bibliog.

> A perceptive critique of the imagery and influence of mass
> media in America. Chapters treat the mythic nature of
> media experience, heroes and celebrities, sin, ritualization

of viewing, advertising as magic, the substitution of fantasy for faith, and the problems these matters pose for religion.

1592 Lillard, Richard G. "Through the Disciplines with Sparticus: The Uses of a Hero in History and the Media." AMERICAN STUDIES (University of Kansas) 16 (Fall 1975): 15–28.

A consideration of the various stage and film portrayals from a critical perspective.

1593 Limbacher, James L. HAVEN'T I SEEN YOU SOMEWHERE BEFORE? REMAKES, SEQUELS AND SERIES IN MOTION PICTURES AND TELE-VISION, 1896–1978. Ann Arbor, Mich.: Pierian Press, 1979. 279 p. Bibliog.

A listing, with cross-indexed title entries.

1594 LITERARY TASTE, CULTURE, AND MASS COMMUNICATION: MASS MEDIA AND MASS COMMUNICATION. Vol. 2. Edited by Peter Davison, Rolf Meyersohn, and Edward Shils. Teaneck, N.J.: Somerset House, 1978. 348 p.

Thirty-one sociological essays previously published in various journals over the past forty years on media and cultural criticism. Oriented to a British audience, the essays deal with general issues related to the influence of mass media.

1595 LITERARY TASTE, CULTURE, AND MASS COMMUNICATION: THE USES OF LITERACY: MEDIA. Vol. 9. Edited by Peter Davison, Rolf Meyersohn, and Edward Shils. Teaneck, N.J.: Somerset House, 1978. 299 p.

Twenty-four sociological essays previously published in a variety of journals, divided into sections on the uses of literacy, the press, magazines (with an essay on comics), film, radio, and television. The essays are oriented to a British audience, but deal with American subjects as well. Publication dates range from 1935 through the early 1970s.

1596 Lyon, Peter. SUCCESS STORY. THE LIFE AND TIMES OF S.S. McCLURE. New York: Scribner, 1963. 433 p. Bibliog., index.

A career biography of McClure, who introduced syndication to newspapers, invented the Sunday supplement, published the first cheap magazines, supported muckrakers, introduced many new authors to wide circulation and many major writers to American audiences.

1597 McLuhan, H. Marshall. THE GUTENBERG GALAXY: THE MAKING OF TYPOGRAPHIC MAN. Toronto: University of Toronto Press, 1962. 293 p. Bibliog.

The author's exploration of the complex environmental impact
of the emergence of print, in which manifestations become
apparent through comparisons with oral cultures and modern
media cultures.

1598 Marzio, Peter C. THE MEN AND MACHINES OF AMERICAN JOUR-
NALISM: A PICTORIAL ESSAY FROM THE HENRY R. LUCE HALL OF
NEWS REPORTING. Washington, D.C.: National Museum of History
and Technology, Smithsonian Institution, 1973. 144 p. Illus., bibliog.,
index.

A potpourrie of brief notes on topics such as the first newspaper,
earliest editorial cartoons, first illustrations in newspapers,
advertisements, penny papers, newsboys, and personalities.

1599 THE MASS MEDIA: ASPEN INSTITUTE GUIDE TO COMMUNICATION
INDUSTRY TRENDS. Edited by Christopher H. Sterling and Timothy R.
Haight. New York: Praeger Publishers, 1977. 457 p. Bibliog.,
charts, graphs, index.

Sections on growth, ownership and control, economics, em-
ployment and training, content trends, size and characteristics
of audiences, and media industries abroad. Primarily data
and interpretive notes.

1600 MEDIA REVIEW DIGEST. Ann Arbor, Mich.: Pierian Press, 1973–74–– .
Annual.

Indexes reviews of films, video tapes, filmstrips, miscellaneous media, film awards, and "mediagraphies" appearing
in over one hundred trade, general, and film periodicals.

1601 Pember, Don R. MASS MEDIA IN AMERICA. 3d ed. Chicago: Science Research Associates, 1981. 433 p. Bibliog., illus., index.

A textbook on media history, newspapers, radio, television,
movies; with chapters on relationships of government, economics, social fragmentation, and the future.

1602 Phelan, John M. DISENCHANTMENT: MEANING AND MORALITY
IN THE MEDIA. Humanistic Studies in the Communication Arts. New
York: Hastings House, 1980. 191 p. Bibliog., index.

A social history and interpretation of issues surrounding
media control and effects, with consideration of the American character, censorship and other forms of control, technological determinism, and other topics.

1603 _____. MEDIAWORLD: PROGRAMMING THE PUBLIC. New York:
Seabury Press, 1977. 167 p.

Discusses a discourse in the media he calls melodoxy (from melos—song; and doxa—uninformed opinion), which communicates the form of the "homogenized form-assumptive MEDIA-WORLD." By providing a common background for mobile people lacking a common heritage, packaging ideas and events in "brief, colorful, blandly controversial" envelopes, and viewing the audience as consumers, industry has given people a false sense of the world.

1604   RAISON PRESENTE, no. 50, April–June 1979, entire issue.

Devoted to the ideology of American media.

1605   Read, William H. AMERICA'S MASS MEDIA MERCHANTS. Baltimore: Johns Hopkins University Press, 1976. 209 p. Notes, index.

An extensive study of the marketing of U.S.-made media throughout the world, with statistical support.

1606   Rissover, Frederic, and Birch, David C., eds. MASS MEDIA AND THE POPULAR ARTS. 2d ed. New York: McGraw-Hill, 1977. 494 p. Directory, bibliog., index.

An anthology of brief essays and other material for college students. Sections are devoted to advertising, journalism, cartoons and comic strips, popular print, radio and television, photography and films, popular music, and education. A thematic table of contents, and study aids are also included.

1607   Root, Wells. WRITING THE SCRIPT: A PRACTICAL GUIDE FOR FILMS AND TELEVISION. New York: Holt, Rinehart and Winston, 1979. 210 p. Index.

A primer on the practical aspects of writing scripts that sell, and how to see that they do sell.

1608   Rowan, Bonnie G. SCHOLARS' GUIDE TO WASHINGTON, D.C. FILM AND VIDEO COLLECTIONS. Washington, D.C.: Smithsonian Institution Press, 1980. 282 p. Bibliog., appendixes, index.

Descriptions of 186 collections, referral services and academic programs; with lists of media organizations, films, in a Washington setting, and notes on government paper records, available services, and related information.

1609   Schrank, Jeffrey. UNDERSTANDING MASS MEDIA. Skokie, Ill.: National Textbook Co., 1975. 260 p.

A high school text that includes sections on television, advertising, film, comics and cartoons, news, newspapers, magazines, radio, records, media control, imagery, and "future casting."

1610 Seldes, Gilbert. THE SEVEN LIVELY ARTS. 1924. Rev. ed. New York: Sagamore Press, 1962. 306 p.

A broad range of essays on Keystone, Chaplin, popular music, Ring Lardner, the Ziegfeld follies, Negro musicals, Jolson, "Krazy Kat" and other comic strips, vaudeville, burlesque, dance, circuses and clowns, film magnates, bogus arts, and painting.

1611 Silverman, Kenneth. A CULTURAL HISTORY OF THE AMERICAN REVOLUTION. 3 vols. New York: Thomas Y. Crowell, 1976. 699 p. Illus., bibliog., index.

Primarily concerned with elite arts, though with some discussion of illustration, broadsides, cartoons, verse, reprints of popular British books, song books, some ephemera.

1612 Snyder, Gerald. THE RIGHT TO BE INFORMED: CENSORSHIP IN THE UNITED STATES. New York: Julian Mesner, 1976. 191 p. Illus., bibliog., index.

An overview of the issues in censorship of books, television, movies, the press, and students' rights.

1613 Sobel, Robert. THE MANIPULATORS: AMERICA IN THE MEDIA AGE. Garden City, N.Y.: Anchor Press, 1976. 458 p. Notes, bibliog., index.

An ambitious exploration of the emergence of the mass audience and major figures in the media, with emphasis on the creation and dissemination of ideas as products for mass consumption. The book is divided into three parts: "Genesis," "Development," and "Maturation," which cover the emergence, key points in the development, and contemporary impact of journalism, higher education, political ideologies, film, radio, and television. The volume informally treats materials and information available from standard sources.

1614 Sommer, Robert. STREET ART. New York: Links, 1975. 64 p., with 84 p. color photos. Notes, bibliog.

A useful introduction to the new mural movement, with chapters on forms of street art, politics, Emeryville mudflats, people's art, and opportunities for creating street art.

1615 Stanley, Robert H., and Steinberg, Charles S. THE MEDIA ENVIRONMENT: MASS COMMUNICATIONS IN AMERICAN SOCIETY. New York: Hastings House, 1976. 296 p. Bibliog., index.

A survey of media and background information on communication processes. Chapters include summaries of print, with emphasis on newspapers and magazines; film (history, Holly-

wood, and self-regulation); the history of broadcasting,
broadcasting law, commercial television, self-regulation,
noncommercial television, noncommercial video; Supreme
Court decisions; global communication; minorities; public
relations and advertising; and the impact of cable and
satellite technologies.

1616   Steel, Ronald.   WALTER LIPPMANN AND THE AMERICAN CENTURY.
Boston: Little, Brown and Atlantic Monthly, 1980. 669 p. Illus.,
notes, bibliog., index.

A personal and career biography of Lippmann, with emphasis
on the reception of his work.

1617   Stewart, Douglas J.   "Pornography, Obscenity, and Capitalism."
ANTIOCH REVIEW 35 (Fall 1977): 389–425.

The author illustrates the relationships between FANNY HILL
(1749) and THE WEALTH OF NATIONS (1776) and shows the
need for a new understanding of pornography and obscenity.

1618   STUDIES IN COMMUNICATIONS: A RESEARCH ANNUAL.   Edited by
Thelma McCormack. Greenwich, Conn.: Aijai Press, 1980-- . Annual.
Index, notes.

Contains studies on culture and communication, mass media
in Latin America, feminism and pornography, differential
effects of television on boys and girls, analytical methodologies, media effects, and the formulation of news stories.

1619   Theall, Donald F.   THE MEDIUM IS THE REAR VIEW MIRROR: UNDER-
STANDING McLUHAN. Montreal: McGill-Queen's University Press,
1971. 261 p. Bibliog.

A forceful critique of McLuhan as superficial and derivative.

1620   Tuchman, Gaye.   MAKING NEWS: A STUDY IN THE CONSTRUCTION
OF REALITY. New York: Free Press, 1978. 244 p. Illus., bibliog.,
index.

Approaches the presentation of reality in news through examination of the constraints and resources of news work, professional journalists' practices, and newsroom organizational
structures. A valuable study with much useful insight.

1621   Voelker, Francis H., and Voelker, Ludmila A., eds.   MASS MEDIA:
FORCES IN OUR SOCIETY. 3d ed. New York: Harcourt Brace
Jovanovich, 1978. 470 p. Bibliog., study questions, index.

An anthology, for mass communication students, of brief
essays on print and electronic media, news, entertainment,

persuasion, and theory; case studies on the Daniel Schorr
revelations, violence, free and accessible media, social
issues, and comics.

1622 Weibel, Kathryn. MIRROR MIRROR: IMAGES OF WOMEN REFLECTED
IN POPULAR CULTURE. Garden City, N.Y.: Anchor Press, Doubleday,
1977. 256 p. Bibliog., index.

Images of women in television, fiction, movies and women's
magazines, with a chapter on women's fashions and an epilogue
on the influences women may exert on their images.

1623 THE WORKING PRESS OF THE NATION. Issued in 5 vols. Burlington,
Iowa: National Research Bureau, 1949-- . Annual. Title and publisher vary.

Volumes include NEWSPAPER DIRECTORY, listing personnel
of over four thousand daily and weekly newspapers; MAGA-
ZINE DIRECTORY, listing addresses, management, and editorial personnel for over thirty-five hundred magazines; RADIO/
TV DIRECTORY, listing major television stations in the United
States and Canada, as well as personnel for about seven
thousand radio and twenty-five hundred television stations;
FREE-LANCERS DIRECTORY, listing free-lance writers and
their specialties and credits; and HOUSE MAGAZINE DIREC-
TORY, listing editors and titles for house magazines in over
forty-five subject areas.

BOOKS

1624 Bleiler, E.F. EIGHT DIME NOVELS. New York: Dover Publications,
1974. 190 p. Illus.

Contains: THE BRADYS AND THE GIRL SMUGGLER; FRANK
JAMES ON THE TRAIL; SCYLLA, THE SEA ROBBER (Nick
Carter Story, 1905); DEADWOOD DICK, THE PRINCE OF
THE ROAD (first Deadwood Dick story); ADVENTURES OF
BUFFALO BILL FROM BOYHOOD TO MANHOOD (by
Prentice Ingraham); THE HUGE HUNTER, OR THE STEAM
MAN OF THE PRAIRIES (Edward Ellis); FRANK MERRIWELL'S
NOBILITY (Burt L. Standish); ADRIFT IN NEW YORK (Horatio
Alger).

1625 Faxon, Frederick Winthrop. LITERARY ANNUALS AND GIFT BOOKS,
AMERICAN AND ENGLISH: A BIBLIOGRAPHY. Bulletin of Bibliography, V:4-VI:8. Westwood, Mass.: Faxon Co., January 1908-July
1911. Monthly installments. Reprint: Pinner, Engl.: Middlesex, 1973.

A bibliography, with a chapter on English drawing room
annuals (VI:4).

1626   Haldeman, Julius Emanuel. THE FIRST HUNDRED MILLION. New York: Simon and Schuster, 1928. Reprint. New York: Arno, 1974. 340 p.

      Career autobiography of the publisher of the Little Blue Book series, with extensive explanation of promotion, sales, distribution through the mails, and other matters regarding publication.

1627   Jackinson, Alex. THE BARNUM-CINDERELLA WORLD OF PUBLISHING. New York: Impact Press, 1971. 353 p.

      Essays on various aspects of publishing, publishers, writers, books, and readers. Covers such topics as writers' schools, best-sellers, writing to particular audiences, examples of successful books, and the vagaries of publishing.

1628   Lehmann-Haupt, Hellmut; Wroth, Lawrence C.; and Silver, Rollo G. THE BOOK IN AMERICA: A HISTORY OF THE MAKING AND SELLING OF BOOKS IN THE UNITED STATES. 1951. 2d ed. New York: Bowker, 1969. 493 p.

      Covers book productions, selling, distribution, book collecting and library history.

1629   O'Neal, David L. EARLY AMERICAN ALMANACS: THE PHELPS COLLECTION, 1679-1900. Peterborough, N.H.: Antiquarian Booksellers, n.d. 162 p. Illus., index.

      A descriptive catalog of 1,621 editions, many with notes, of early almanacs.

1630   Pearson, Edmund. DIME NOVELS: OR, FOLLOWING THE OLD TRAIL IN POPULAR LITERATURE. Boston: Brown, Little, Brown, 1929. Reprint. Port Washington, N.Y.: Kennikat, 1968. 280 p. Illus., index.

      A discussion of the origins, proprieties, authors, readers' recollections, didacticisms, ideals, and such categories as detective fiction, typical heroes, and the Merriwell series.

1631   Shove, Raymond Howard. CHEAP BOOK PRODUCTION IN THE UNITED STATES, 1870 TO 1891. Urbana: University of Illinois Library, 1937. 155 p. Notes, bibliog., index.

      A history of the cheap cloth and paperbound books, excluding dime novels but including popular reprint series by Harper, Alden, Lovell, Munro, Belford-Clark, Peterson, Worthington, Hurst, Donnelly-Lloyd, and others.

1632   Skallerup, Harry R. BOOKS AFLOAT AND ASHORE: A HISTORY OF BOOKS, LIBRARIES, AND READING AMONG SEAMEN DURING THE

AGE OF SAIL. Hamden, Conn.: Shoe String Press, Archon Books, 1974. 277 p. Navy lists, illus., notes, index.

A history of shipboard and shoreside libraries from the earliest days of print to the Civil War, with emphasis on navy and merchant marine collections, and on reading at sea.

1633 Smith, Roger H. PAPERBACK PARNASSUS: THE BIRTH, THE DEVELOP-MENT, THE PENDING CRISIS . . . OF THE MODERN AMERICAN PAPERBOUND BOOK. Boulder, Colo.: Westview Press, 1976. 111 p. Tables, index.

Based on his PUBLISHERS WEEKLY series, the author surveys mass-market paperbacks, particularly their distribution and sale, with examples of quickly printed editions and also a discussion of trade paperbacks.

1634 Stegner, Wallace. "The Book and the Great Community." LIBRARY JOURNAL, 1 October 1968, pp. 3513-16.

The article states there were twenty-five thousand books published per year in the 1960s in the United States. A total of 15 percent of all Americans read books (about thirty million people).

1635 Stern, Madeleine B. BOOKS AND BOOK PEOPLE IN 19TH-CENTURY AMERICA. New York: R.R. Bowker, 1978. 341 p. Illus., index.

Essays on colonial publishers, foreign influences on American publishers, Western publishers, the first Beadle dime novel, Louisa May Alcott, the Fowler family's mind science publications, G.W. Carleton's humorous and sensational publications, domestic novels, and other matters.

PERIODICALS

1636 Albrecht, Milton. "Does Literature Reflect Common Values?" AMERI-CAN SOCIOLOGICAL REVIEW 21, no. 6 (1956): 722-29.

A total of 153 short stories from magazines categorized according to "cultural level" were evaluated for themes corresponding to configurations of family values. The author concludes that while the particular results are not statistically significant, the method can be used to demonstrate quantitative approaches to questions of a qualitative nature.

1637 Aldiss, Brian. SCIENCE FICTION ART. New York: Bounty Books, Crown, 1975. 128 p. Illus., magazine checklist, index, artist list.

Contains examples of the work of thirty artists and about
seventy magazines, with such themes as catastrophes, space-
ships, planets, aliens, future cities, girls, machines, robots
and the usual development of the idea of the flying city and
H.G. Wells's THE WAR OF THE WORLDS.

1638   Bainbridge, John. LITTLE WONDER: OR, THE READER'S DIGEST AND
HOW IT GREW. New York: Reynal and Hitchcock, 1946. 177 p.

Based on the author's NEW YORKER articles, this informal
history also provides an assessment of the magazine's success
formula.

1639   Bernard, George. INSIDE THE NATIONAL ENQUIRER . . . CON-
FESSIONS OF AN UNDERCOVER REPORTER. Port Washington, N.Y.:
Ashley Books, 1977. 354 p. Illus.

The confessions are primarily of the author's adventures as a
reporter, along with photographs of him with celebrities.

1640   Boylan, James. "Survey Sample: 'Shelter' Magazines." COLUMBIA
JOURNALISM REVIEW 3 (Summer 1964): 32-33.

A brief survey which finds that leading American "home"
magazines are designed primarily to "increase consumer
appetites for the goods displayed."

1641   Brosseau, Ray, and Andrist, Ralph A. LOOKING FORWARD: LIFE IN
THE TWENTIETH CENTURY AS PREDICTED IN THE PAGES OF AMERI-
CAN MAGAZINES FROM 1895-1905. New York: American Heritage
Press, 1970. 352 p. Illus.

A miscellaneous collection of articles, advertisements, and
other material culled from a wide variety of magazines,
though many of the pieces do not appear to be looking
forward.

1642   Dennis, Everette E., and Rivers, William L. OTHER VOICES: THE
NEW JOURNALISM IN AMERICA. San Francisco: Canfield Press, 1974.
218 p. Notes, index, bibliog.

A perceptive survey of nonfiction stories and sketches, alternative journalism, journalism reviews, advocacy journalism,
counterculture journalism, alternative broadcasting, and pre-
cision journalism, with a chapter on the future of the form.

1643   Dygert, James H. THE INVESTIGATIVE JOURNALIST: FOLK HEROES
OF A NEW ERA. Englewood Cliffs, N.J.: Prentice-Hall, 1976. 282 p.
Index.

A survey of recent investigative journalism throughout the
United States.

1644　Ford, James L.C.　MAGAZINES FOR MILLIONS: THE STORY OF
SPECIALIZED PUBLICATIONS.　New Horizons in Journalism.　Carbondale:
Southern Illinois University Press, 1969.　320 p.　Illus.

Brief surveys of domestic magazines, how-to, juveniles, in-
house and service publications, and professional organizations
Emphasis on statistics of circulation.

1645　Gauvreau, Emile.　MY LAST MILLION READERS.　New York: E.P.
Dutton, 1941.　Reprint.　New York: Arno Press, 1974.　488 p.　Index.

Career autobiography of an inveterate writer and newspaper
editor with connections among pulp editors, exposé publishers,
and others after 1900.

1646　Goodstone, Tony, comp. and ed.　THE PULPS: FIFTY YEARS OF AMERI-
CAN POP CULTURE.　New York: Bonanza Books, 1970.　239 p.　Illus.

A collection of stories from the pulps with brief introductions
to sections of detective stories, science fiction, Westerns, and
spicey stories.

1647　Goulart, Ron.　CHEAP THRILLS: AN INFORMAL HISTORY OF THE
PULP MAGAZINES.　New Rochelle, N.Y.:　Arlington House, 1972.
192 p.　Illus.

Contains chapters on publishing, heroes, THE SHADOW, masked
heroes, DOC SAVAGE, special agents, detectives, Westerns,
Tarzan and other primitive heroes, science fiction, and reminiscences by authors.

1648　Gruber, Frank.　THE PULP JUNGLE.　Los Angeles:　Sherbourne Press,
1967.　189 p.

The autobiography of one of the more prolific of the pulp
writers.　The book gives something of the flavor of the pulp
world of the thirties.

1649　Hynds, Ernest C.　AMERICAN NEWSPAPERS IN THE 1980S.　2d ed.
Studies in Media Management.　New York: Hastings House, 1980.　383 p.
Notes, bibliog., index.

A general history from the colonial times, with contemporary
emphasis on business practices, content, categories, pressure
groups and legal restraints, electronic innovations, and notable
newspapers.

1650   Inglis, Ruth. "An Objective Approach to the Relationships Between Fiction and Society." AMERICAN SOCIOLOGICAL REVIEW 3, no. 4 (1938): 526-40.

Analysis of the economic and occupational attributes of popular magazine heroines over a thirty-five year period, concluding that fictional trends lag ten years behind occupational fluctuations.

1651   Iverson, William. THE PIOUS PORNOGRAPHERS. New York: W. Morrow, 1963. 214 p.

A tongue-in-cheek discussion of soft pornography in contemporary women's magazines, based on the author's series of articles in PLAYBOY.

1652   Jones, Robert Kenneth. THE SHUDDER PULPS: A HISTORY OF THE WEIRD MENACE MAGAZINES OF THE 1930S. West Linn, Oreg.: FAX Collector's Edition, 1975. 238 p. Index.

The peak of the pulp period. This volume concentrates on the publishing of pulps "in which the villain perpetrated seemingly supernatural deviltries, which were logically explained in the end."

1653   Kallan, Richard A. "Style and the New Journalism: A Rhetorical Analysis of Tom Wolfe." COMMUNICATION MONOGRAPHS 46 (March 1979): 52-62.

Wolfe employs third-person point of view, scene-by-scene construction, extensive dialog, and recording of status-life symbols, together with particular typography and punctuation, language qualities, syntax, and organizational tactics to achieve what is called a televisionic journalistic style.

1654   Lantos, Robert. "Lying for Fun and Profit." SATURDAY NIGHT (Canada), 88 (June 1973): 17-21.

Study of exposé magazines by an ex-writer.

1655   Lee, Alfred McClung. THE DAILY NEWSPAPER: THE EVOLUTION OF A SOCIAL INSTRUMENT. New York: Macmillan, 1937. Reprint. New York: Octagon Books, 1973. 797 p. Notes, appendix, bibliog., index, tables, maps, charts.

Covers all aspects of dailies, from business and labor through advertising, syndication, and wire services.

1656   Levin, Martin, ed. HOLLYWOOD AND THE GREAT FAN MAGAZINES. New York: Arbor House, 1970. 224 p. Illus.

A collection of about seventy articles and a dozen trivia items from PHOTOPLAY, SILVER SCREEN, SCREEN BOOK, SCREENLAND, MODERN SCREEN and MOTION PICTURE, with a brief introduction.

1657　McKerns, Joseph Patrick. "The History of American Journalism: A Bibliographical Essay." AMERICAN STUDIES INTERNATIONAL 15 (Fall 1976): 17-34.

A concise essay covering sources from the earliest period with brief information on electronic journalism and major themes.

1658　Mott, Frank Luther. AMERICAN JOURNALISM: A HISTORY, 1690-1960. 3d ed. New York: Macmillan, 1962. 901 p. Illus., notes, index.

A standard history of newspaper, magazine, and electronic journalism, with much incidental information on publishing and social history.

1659　_____. A HISTORY OF AMERICAN MAGAZINES. 5 vols. Vol. 1, 1741-1850; Vol. 2, 1850-65; Vol. 3, 1865-85; Vol. 4, 1885-1905; Vol. 5, 1905-1930. Cambridge, Mass.: Harvard University Press, 1938-68.

The most comprehensive history of magazines available, with coverage of content, specific major magazines, magazine categories, and styles.

1660　Murphy, James E. "The New Journalism: A Critical Perspective." JOURNALISM MONOGRAPHS, no. 34, May 1974, 38 p. Notes.

Analysis of subjectivism and sytlistic tendencies in new journalism leads the author to conclude that the form is a culmination of a journalistic tradition that employs dramatic and intensifying qualities as well as other techniques.

1661　Newton, Richard F., and Sprague, Peter L. THE NEWSPAPER IN THE AMERICAN HISTORY CLASSROOM. Reston, Va.: American Newspaper Publishers Association Foundation, 1974. 47 p. Illus., bibliog.

Fourteen lessons using newspaper materials to explore and discuss issues in American history on the high-school level.

1662　Nordin, Kenneth E. "The Entertaining Press: Sensationalism in Eighteenth-Century Boston Press." COMMUNICATION RESEARCH 6 (July 1979): 295-320.

Content analysis of sensationalism based on the newspaper for selected years from 1704 to 1784, with the purpose of correcting the view that sensationalism began with the penny press of the nineteenth century.

1663   Ryan, Martin. "Portrait of PLAYBOY." STUDIES IN PUBLIC COMMU-ICATION, Summer 1957, pp. 11-21.

        Useful early study of the PLAYBOY format.

1664   Sonenschein, David. "Love and Sex in the Romance Magazines." JOURNAL OF POPULAR CULTURE 4 (Fall 1970): 398-409.

        Points up the themes of pulp romances and suggests the extent of their juvenile readership.

1665   Tebbel, John. THE AMERICAN MAGAZINE: A COMPACT HISTORY. New York: Hawthorn Books, 1969. 279 p. Bibliog., index.

        A condensed history that draws on Peterson's MAGAZINES IN THE TWENTIETH CENTURY (1964) and Mott's A HISTORY OF AMERICAN MAGAZINES (see no. 1659), as well as the author's own experiences as writer and editor. Of interest are chapter 17 on the origin of the pulps and chapter 18 on the LADIES HOME JOURNAL and SATURDAY EVENING POST.

1666   Woodward, Helen. THE LADY PERSUADERS New York: Ivan Obolensky, 1960. 189 p.

        An informal account of women's magazines, their formulas, and the purposes they serve.

1667   Yates, Norris W. WILLIAM T. PORTER AND THE SPIRIT OF THE TIMES: A STUDY OF THE BIG BEAR SCHOOL OF HUMOR. Louisiana State University Press, 1957. Reprint. New York: Arno Press, 1977. 222 p. Illus.

        The new form of popular newspaper humor began in the New York SPIRIT OF THE TIMES in the early 1830s. Often written by amateurs, the humor drew heavily from oral materials.

1668   Zuilen, A.J. van. THE LIFE CYCLE OF MAGAZINES: A HISTORICAL STUDY OF THE DECLINE AND FALL OF THE GENERAL INTEREST MASS AUDIENCE MAGAZINE IN THE UNITED STATES DURING THE PERIOD 1946-1972. Uithoorn, Holland: Graduate Press, 1977. 338 p. Tables, charts, bibliog.

        An analysis of the economics of publishing, with special attention to COLLIER'S, POST, LOOK, and LIFE, and discussion of magazine life cycles, increasing media specialization, and a comparison of magazines and other media.

EPHEMERA

1669 Brady, J.J. "Postcards and History." HISTORY TODAY 19, no. 12 (1969): 848–56.

> Mostly on the British industry. Wide open area for research in American history. The first postcards generally date to the 1860s, achieving tremendous popularity in America by the turn of the century.

1670 Bunday, George. THE HISTORY OF THE CHRISTMAS CARD. London: Rockliff, 1954. 304 p. Bibliog., checklists, illus., index.

> A topical history, primarily of English cards, including chapters on the effects of the valentine, postcards, and other ephemera, and the influence of events on the cards.

1671 Chase, Ernest Dudley. THE ROMANCE OF GREETING CARDS: AN HISTORICAL ACCOUNT OF THE ORIGIN, EVOLUTION AND DEVELOPMENT OF CHRISTMAS CARDS, VALENTINES AND OTHER FORMS OF GREETING CARDS FROM THE EARLIEST DAYS TO THE PRESENT TIME. Dedham City, Mass.: Rust Craft Publishers, 1956. Reprint. Cambridge, Mass.: University Press, 1971. Illus., index.

> Originally published in 1926, the book was revised to cover the general history from 1843 and suggest antecedents up to 1971.

1672 Lee, Ruth Webb. A HISTORY OF VALENTINES. New York: Thomas Y. Crowell, 1952. 239 p. Illus., index.

> A topical history of American and English cards, with emphasis on those manufactured by major companies.

1673 Lesser, Robert. A CELEBRATION OF COMIC ART AND MEMORABILIA. New York: Hawthorn, 1975. 292 p. Illus., index.

> A history and description for collectors, of original graphic art for newspapers, comic books, comic-character toys and timepieces, Buck Rogers collectables, comic insert cards, and decoders.

1674 Lewis, John. PRINTED EPHEMERA: THE CHANGING USES OF TYPE AND LETTER-FORMS IN ENGLISH AND AMERICAN PRINTING. Ipswich, Suffolk: W.S. Cowell, 1962. 288 p. Illus.

> Illustrates a wide range of printed material used in advertising, labeling, identification and circulation, primarily from the nineteenth century or earlier.

1675   Miller, George, and Miller, Dorothy. PICTURE POSTCARDS IN THE
        UNITED STATES: 1893-1918. New York: Clarkson N. Potter, 1976.
        280 p. Illus., bibliog., index.

        A standard history of exposition, advertising, political, social,
        and view cards; with chapters on sets, signed artists, patriotics
        and greetings, and novelty cards.

1676   Neuburg, Victor E. CHAPBOOKS: A GUIDE TO REFERENCE MATERIAL
        ON ENGLISH, SCOTTISH AND AMERICAN CHAPBOOK LITERATURE OF
        THE EIGHTEENTH AND NINETEENTH CENTURIES. London: Woburn
        Press, 1972. 81 p. Indexes.

        The introduction establishes the classification and social con-
        tent of chapbooks, followed by a bibliography of 193 items.

1677   Patterson, Jerry E. AUTOGRAPHS: A COLLECTOR'S GUIDE. New
        York: Crown, 1973. 248 p. Illus., bibliog., dealer list, index.

        A vocabulary essay, with notes on collecting and maintenance,
        and chapters discussing prices of autographs in eleven cate-
        gories.

1678   Rawlings, Ray. THE GUINESS BOOK OF AUTOGRAPHS. Enfield,
        Engl.: Guiness Superlatives, 1977. 244 p. American title: THE
        STEIN AND DAY BOOK OF AUTOGRAPHS. Illus.

        A brief definition, with reproductions of and notes on famous
        signatures arranged in alphabetical order.

1679   Rollins, Hyder Edward, ed. THE PACK OF AUTOLYCUS: OR, STRANGE
        AND TERRIBLE NEWS OF GHOSTS, APPARITIONS, MONSTROUS BIRTHS,
        SHOWERS OF WHEAT, JUDGMENTS OF GOD, AND OTHER PRODIGIOUS
        AND FEARFUL HAPPENINGS AS TOLD IN BROADSIDE BALLADS OF
        THE YEARS, 1624-1693. Cambridge, Mass.: Harvard University Press,
        1927. Reprint. Port Washington, N.Y.: Kennikat Press, 1969. 269 p.
        Illus., notes, index.

        Ballads, with bibliographical descriptions and historical notes.

1680   Shephard, Leslie. THE HISTORY OF STREET LITERATURE: THE STORY
        OF BROADSIDE BALLADS, CHAPBOOKS, PROCLAMATIONS, NEWS-
        SHEETS, ELECTION BILLS, TRACTS, PAMPHLETS, COCKS, CATCH-
        PENNIES, AND OTHER EPHEMERA. Newton Abbot, Engl.: David
        and Charles, 1973. 238 p. Illus., notes, song list, glossary, bibliog.,
        index.

        A history of printing, peddlers, and influences on street litera-
        ture, with topical chapters on chapbooks, children's literature,
        handbills, almanacs, street notices, ballad and prose broad-
        sides, newspapers, verse news, execution sheets, the Irish
        question, and other matters, primary British.

1681   Staff, Frank. THE VALENTINE AND ITS ORIGINS. London: Lutterworth Press, 1969. 144 p. Illus., bibliog., index, directory of manufacturers.

A brief illustrated history and survey of valentines from Margery Brews' first mention of them in 1477 to the late 1960s.

CARTOONS

1682   Hess, Stephen, and Kaplan, Milton. THE UNGENTLEMANLY ART: A HISTORY OF AMERICAN POLITICAL CARTOONS. New York: Macmillan, 1968. 252 p. Bibliog., index.

An excellent study based on thorough research that covers various media from 1747 through 1968. The first chapter discusses features of the genre and traces significant aspects of its social history. Chapters 2 through 5 cover copper engraving and woodcut, 1747–1828; lithography and early magazines, 1828–1865; magazines, 1866–1896; and newspapers, 1884–1968. A special section of plates concludes the volume. All illustrations are carefully documented.

1683   Murrell, William. A HISTORY OF AMERICAN GRAPHIC HUMOR. Vol. 1, 1747–1865. New York: Whitney Museum of American Art, 1933. 245 p. Illus., bibliog., index.

This enduring volume begins with distinctions between sketches, humorous drawings, and caricatures, then provides a chapter by chapter examination of major contributions. A brief concluding chapter entitled "Reflections," provides a social perspective. Contains 237 illustrations.

1684   _____. A HISTORY OF AMERICAN GRAPHIC HUMOR. Vol. 2, 1865–1938. New York: Whitney Museum of American Art, 1938. 271 p.

Covering the years 1865 to the 1930s, the volume continues the excellent coverage of graphic humor.

1685   Paston, George [Symonds, Emily Morse]. SOCIAL CARICATURE IN THE EIGHTEENTH CENTURY. London: Methuen, 1905. Reprint. New York: Arno, 1968. 143 p. Illus., notes, index.

A history of the caricature in periodicals of some practices common among the upper classes during the century.

1686   Shaffner, Laurence Frederic. CHILDREN'S INTERPRETATIONS OF CARTOONS. New York: Teachers College Press, 1930. Reprint. New York: AMS Press, 1972. 73 p. Illus., tables, bibliog.

An analysis of the responses of several thousand students, grades 4–12, to ten editorial cartoons from various newspapers.

COMIC STRIPS

1687 Berger, Arthur Asa. THE COMIC STRIPPED AMERICAN: WHAT DICK TRACY, BLONDIE, DADDY WARBUCKS, AND CHARLIE BROWN TELL US ABOUT OURSELVES. New York: Walker and Co., 1973. 225 p.

Essays on "The Yellow Kid," "The Katzenjammer Kids," "Mutt and Jeff," "Krazy Kat," "Little Orphan Annie," "Buck Rogers," "Blondie," "Dick Tracy," "Flash Gordon," superheroes, Batman, Pogo, "Peanuts," MARVEL COMICS, erotic comics, and Mr. Natural.

1688 _____. LI'L ABNER: A STUDY IN AMERICAN SATIRE. New York: Twayne Publishers, 1970. 191 p. Notes, bibliog., index.

A perceptive study of Al Capp and his comic art.

1689 Blackbeard, Bill, and Williams, Martin, eds. THE SMITHSONIAN COLLECTION OF NEWSPAPER COMICS. Washington, D.C.: Smithsonian Institution, 1978. 336 p. Illus., bibliog., index.

Reproduction of 750 comic strips covering the last eighty years, with capsule summaries and biographical sketches.

1690 Couperie, Pierre, et al. A HISTORY OF THE COMIC STRIP. New York: Crown, 1968. 256 p. Illus., index.

A history, with additional chapters on production and distribution, the audience, the created world, narrative technique, aesthetic, and figuration.

1691 Galewitz, Herb, ed. GREAT COMICS SYNDICATED BY THE DAILY NEWS AND CHICAGO TRIBUNE. New York: Crown, 1972. 319 p. Illus.

A brief introduction, followed by black and white and color illustrations of the strips.

1692 Goulart, Ron. THE ADVENTUROUS DECADE: COMIC STRIPS IN THE THIRTIES. New Rochelle, N.Y.: Arlington House, 1975. 224 p. Index, source notes.

Topical history of "Wash Tubbs," "Tarzan," "Buck Rogers," "Gangbusters," airplane strips, "Terry and the Pirates," mischievous kids, muscle men, Westerns, and military strips.

1693 Horn, Maurice. WOMEN IN THE COMICS. New York: Chelsea House, 1977. 229 p. Illus., bibliog., index.

An illustrated, informal history, from 1897 to the mid-1970s, of the portrayal of women in comic strips and books.

1694 _____, ed. THE WORLD ENCYCLOPEDIA OF COMICS. New York: Chelsea House, 1976. 790 p. Illus., bibliog., glossary, appendixes, indexes to proper names, titles, and illus.

> Contains chapters on world comics, a chronology of signifi-
> cant developments, brief analysis of the medium, and an ac-
> count of newspaper syndication. The main body of the work
> contains subject entries on aspects of the comic industry.
> Appendixes reprint the Code of the Comics Magazine Associ-
> ation of America, provide a directory of comic book pub-
> lishers, list Reuben Award winners, and list newspaper syndi-
> cates.

1695 Kunzle, David. THE EARLY COMIC STRIP: NARRATIVE STRIPS AND PICTURE STORIES IN THE EUROPEAN BROADSHEET FROM C. 1450 TO 1825. History of the Comic Strip, vol. 1. Berkeley and Los Angeles: University of California Press, 1973. 471 p. Illus., notes, bibliog., index.

> The three parts cover political cartoon strips; crime, morality,
> marriage, rakes and harlots; and Hogarth's influence. Ex-
> cellent history.

1696 Perry, George, and Aldridge, Alan. THE PENGUIN BOOK OF COMICS. Harmondsworth, Middlesex, Engl.: Penguin Books, 1967. 256 p. Illus.

> A standard social history of the comics in England and Ameri-
> ca. Contains information not found elsewhere, but lacks the
> technical demonstration of Couperie's history (see no. 1690).

1697 Reitberger, Reinhold, and Fuchs, Wolfgang. COMICS: ANATOMY OF A MASS MEDIUM. Boston: Little, Brown, 1972. 264 p. Illus., chronology, notes, bibliog., index.

> Chapters on the medium, humor and everyday life, adventure
> and melodrama, super heroes, criticism and censorship, the
> portrayal of society, the relationship of comics to other media,
> European comics, sex and satire, comics as art, and recent
> trends.

1698 Robinson, Jerry. THE COMICS: AN ILLUSTRATED HISTORY OF COMIC STRIP ART. New York: G.P. Putnam's Sons, 1974. 256 p. Illus., index.

> A comic strip artist's history, with brief comments by creators
> on the decades' work.

1699 Sheridan, Martin. COMICS AND THEIR CREATORS: LIFE STORIES OF AMERICAN CARTOONISTS. Boston: Hale, Cushman, and Flint, 1942. Reprint. New York: Luna Press, 1971. 304 p. Index.

> Biographical sketches of artists, organized by title and

arranged under old standbys, married strips, adventure strips, girl strips, potpourri, fantastic strips, panel comics, animated cartoons, with notes on selling.

1700 Walker, Mort. BACKSTAGE AT THE STRIP. New York: Mason, Charter, 1975. 311 p. Index.

Creator of "Beetle Bailey," on writing and life of comic strips and writers. Anecdotal.

1701 Waugh, Coulton. THE COMICS. New York: Macmillan, 1947. Reprint. New York: Luna Press, 1974. 360 p. Illus., index.

A rough history of the strips from "The Yellow Kid" through the 1940s, with a chapter on comics.

1702 White, David Manning. THE COMIC STRIP IN AMERICA: A BIBLIOG-RAPHY. Boston: Boston University, School of Public Relations and Communication, 1961. 31 leaves.

Good checklist of criticism through about 1959. The 450 items include a short list of theses and dissertations on the subject.

1703 White, David Manning, and Abel, Robert H., eds. THE FUNNIES: AN AMERICAN IDIOM. New York: Free Press, 1963. 304 p. Illus., bibliog.

Useful collection of essays by those who write the comics as well as those who read them. Essays by Al Capp, Allen Saunders, and Walt Kelley.

1704 Young, William H., Jr. "The Serious Funnies: Adventure Comics During the Depression, 1929-1938." JOURNAL OF POPULAR CULTURE 3 (Winter 1969): 404-27.

A useful study of the way in which the comic strips avoided the important social and economic issues during the Depression, while supporting threatened family structures.

COMIC BOOKS

1705 Crawford, Herbert H. CRAWFORD'S ENCYCLOPEDIA OF COMIC BOOKS. Middle Village, N.Y.: Jonathon David, 1978. 438 p. Illus., chronology, index.

Publishing history of D-C Comics, Quality Comics, King Features, Fawcett, Fiction House, Dell, Gilberton, Gleason, E-C, Fox, Marvel, United Feature, Eastern Color, Street

and Smith, Whitman, Embee, Hillman, Harvey, Columbia,
Novelty, Aragon, Better Culture, Avon, Komos, with a note
on dime novels.

1706   Daniels, Les. COMIX: A HISTORY OF COMIC BOOKS IN AMERICA.
New York: Outerbridge and Dienstfrey, 1971. 198 p. Illus., bibliog.

Reasonably priced and amply illustrated, this is an excellent
introduction to the history of the comic book. Includes
coverage of underground comic books.

1707   Dorfman, Ariel, and Mattelart, Armand. HOW TO READ DONALD
DUCK: IMPERIALIST IDEOLOGY IN THE DISNEY COMIC. Translated
by David Kunzle. New York: International General, 1975. 112 p.
Illus. First published in Chile.

A Marxist analysis of the imagery in Disney comics, especially
as revealed in the treatment of Third World people, or "natives,"
in relationship to treasure hunting. The critics also use
Freudian analysis on the Disney family to gain insight into
imperialist ideology.

1708   Feiffer, Jules. THE GREAT COMIC BOOK HEROES. New York: Dial
Press, 1965. 189 p. Illus.

A nostalgic but important celebration of the origins of the
superheroes. Feiffer is able to contribute greatly to the
understanding of youthful fascination with comics.

1709   Fleisher, Michael L., and Lincoln, Janet E. THE ENCYCLOPEDIA OF
COMIC BOOK HEROES. Vol. 1, BATMAN. New York: Macmillan,
1976. 387 p. Illus.

Contains over one thousand entries on characters, themes,
iconology, and episodes arranged in alphabetical order.

1710   _____. THE ENCYCLOPEDIA OF COMIC BOOK HEROES. Vol. 2,
WONDERWOMAN. New York: Macmillan, 1976. 253 p. Illus.

About 510 entries on characters, iconology, themes, and
episodes arranged in alphabetical order.

1711   Horn, Maurice. COMICS OF THE AMERICAN WEST. New York:
Winchester Press, 1977. 224 p. Illus., bibliog., index.

History and development of strips, books, international contributions, and themes.

1712   O'Brien, Richard. THE GOLDEN AGE OF COMIC BOOKS, 1937-1945.
New York: Ballantine Books, 1977. 63 p. Illus., bibliog.

A brief history with forty full-page color illustrations of covers.

1713   Overstreet, Robert M. THE COMIC BOOK PRICE GUIDE. New York: Harmony Books, Crown, 1970-- . Annual.

Prices and descriptions for an extensive range of comic books and ephemera.

1714   Reitberger, R., and Fuchs, Wolfgang. COMICS: ANATOMY OF A MASS MEDIUM. Boston: Little, Brown, 1972. 264 p. Chronology, notes, bibliog., index.

Well illustrated and researched. Covers history, humor, sex and satire, heroes, adventure, and censorship.

1715   Steranko, Jim. THE STERANKO HISTORY OF COMICS. Reading, Pa.: Supergraphics, vol. 1, 1970; vol. 2, 1972. Projected six volumes. Illus.

Written by a practicing comic artist, this promises to be the most complete and authoritative study of the art and milieu of the comic book.

POSTERS AND ILLUSTRATIONS

1716   Breitenbach, Edgar. THE AMERICAN POSTER: A BRIEF HISTORY. New York: American Federation of Arts, 1967. 71 p. Illus., bibliog., index.

Brief historical chapter is followed by a catalog of the AFA traveling display of 1967-69.

1717   Dykes, Jeff. FIFTY GREAT WESTERN ILLUSTRATORS: A BIBLIOGRAPHIC CHECKLIST. Flagstaff, Ariz.: Northland, 1975. 457 p. Illus.

Comprehensive checklist of catalogs identifying works, publications, and various ephemera created by Western illustrators.

1718   Frewin, Anthony. ONE HUNDRED YEARS OF SCIENCE FICTION ILLUS-TRATION, 1840-1940. London: Jupiter Books, 1974. 128 p. Illus., bibliog.

Annotated collection of illustrations on science fiction themes, from books, magazines, and ephemera.

1719   Hornung, Clarence Pearson. TWO HUNDRED YEARS OF AMERICAN GRAPHIC ART: A RETROSPECTIVE SURVEY OF THE PRINTING ARTS AND ADVERTISING SINCE THE COLONIAL PERIOD. New York: George Braziller, 1976. 211 p. Illus., bibliog., notes, index.

Covering the years from 1640 to 1975, the volume displays examples of the printer's art with brief social and technical sketches of the times and practices of each period. The black and white reproductions cover illustrations, posters, typography, advertising, stock certificates, and engravings.

1720   Margolin, Victor. AMERICAN POSTER RENAISSANCE. New York: Watson-Guptill, 1975. 224 p. Illus., bibliog., index.

Brief discussion with excellent plates of styles, artists, and patrons; with examples from mass magazines, little magazines, books, newspapers, business, and exhibitions.

1721   Mayor, A. Hyatt. PRINTS AND PEOPLE: A SOCIAL HISTORY OF PRINTED PICTURES. New York: Metropolitan Museum of Art, 1972. Unpaged. Illus., index.

Arranged according to topics and artists, the volume contains 752 illustrations. Brief references to American art.

1722   Pierpont Morgan Library, New York. EARLY CHILDREN'S BOOKS AND THEIR ILLUSTRATION. New York and Boston: Pierpont Morgan Library, David R. Godine, c. 1975. 263 p. Illus., bibliog., index.

A survey of early illustrated editions of AESOP'S FABLES, bestiaries, courtesy books, ABC's, primers and readers, religious books, emblem books, proverbs, grammars and texts, PILGRIM'S PROGRESS, fairy tales and fables, moral and cautionary tales, Robinsonnades, GULLIVER'S TRAVELS, hymns, street cries, nursery rhymes and poetry, almanacs and albums, sports and games, and influential authors.

1723   Pitz, Henry C. A TREASURY OF AMERICAN BOOK ILLUSTRATIONS. New York: American Studio, Watson-Guptill, 1947. 128 p. Illus., index.

A brief nineteen-page survey, with extensive illustrations from numerous genres and artists.

1724   Reed, Walt, ed. THE ILLUSTRATOR IN AMERICA, 1900-1960'S. New York: Reinhold, 1966. 272 p. Illus., bibliog.

Brief career sketches with examples of the art of hundreds of illustrators. Chapters cover decades and are contributed by various writers and artists.

1725   Rennert, Jack. ONE HUNDRED POSTERS OF BUFFALO BILL'S WILD WEST. London: Hart-Davis, MacGibbon, 1976. 112 p.

Large format plates of ninety-five annotated posters from

1871 to 1910, with an introductory discussion of Cody and poster printing.

1726   ____. 100 YEARS OF CIRCUS POSTERS. New York: Avon, 1974. 112 p. Illus., notes.

Notes on 112 illustrations depicting promotional posters for circuses around the world.

1727   Rottensteiner, Franz. THE SCIENCE FICTION BOOK: AN ILLUSTRATED HISTORY. New York: Seabury Press, 1975. 160 p. Illus., bibliog.

A discussion of themes, media, authors, and related matters throughout the world.

1728   Schau, Michael. ALL AMERICAN GIRL: THE ART OF COLES PHILLIPS. New York: Watson-Guptill, 1975. 176 p. Illus.

Said to have created the ideal image of the American girl in his illustrations for magazines, advertisements, and romantic novels.

PHOTOGRAPHY

1729   Beaton, Cecil Walter Hardy. PHOTOBIOGRAPHY. Garden City, N.Y.: Doubleday, 1951. 255 p.

Informal biography of Beaton's personal history and interests, with general information on celebrities and others interspersed.

1730   Buckland, Gail. REALITY RECORDED: EARLY DOCUMENTARY PHOTOGRAPHY. London: David and Charles, 1974. 128 p. Illus., notes, bibliog., index.

An essentially British emphasis on photography around the mid-nineteenth century.

1731   Coe, Brian. THE BIRTH OF PHOTOGRAPHY: THE STORY OF THE FORMATIVE YEARS, 1800-1900. New York: Taplinger Publishing Co., 1977. 144 p. Illus., glossary, bibliog., index.

A brief history of the development of technique, the popular use, and artistic perspectives of early photography.

1732   Coe, Brian, and Gates, Paul. THE SNAPSHOT PHOTOGRAPH: THE RISE OF POPULAR PHOTOGRAPHY, 1888-1939. London: Ash and Grant, 1977, 144 p. Illus., glossary, appendix, index.

Discusses the development of the inexpensive and simple camera, then provides a thematic set of illustrations.

1733   Earle, Edward W., ed. POINTS OF VIEW: THE STEREOGRAPH IN AMERICA--A CULTURAL HISTORY. Rochester, N.Y.: Visual Studies Workshop Press, 1979. 119 p. Illus., notes, bibliog.

A chronology of events, cultural history, and samples of stereographs.

1734   THE ENCYCLOPEDIA OF PHOTOGRAPHY. 20 vols. New York: Greystone Press, 1964. 3,840 p. Illus., bibliog., index.

Extensive popular treatment of technical and commercial matters for photographers.

1735   Green, Jonathan, ed. and intro. THE SNAPSHOT. Millerton, N.Y.: Aperture, 1974. 126 p. Illus.

An attempt to capture the vitality and ambiguity of the home snapshot through the contributions of skilled photographers. Originally published as volume 19, issue 1 of APERTURE, the volume is essentially reproductions with brief comments, though the all-too-brief essays by Steven Halpern, John Kouwenhoven, and Judith Wechsler are valuable as well.

1736   Jussim, Estelle. VISUAL COMMUNICATION AND THE GRAPHIC ARTS: PHOTOGRAPHIC TECHNOLOGIES IN THE NINETEENTH CENTURY. New York: R.R. Bowker, 1974. 364 p. Illus., notes, glossary, bibliog., index.

A discussion of photography and its relationships to the graphic arts, particularly to representational codes in sketching, painting, engraving, and illustration. Essays treat the contributions of Howard Pyle, William Hamilton Gibson, Frederic Remington, and coverage of expositions.

1737   Lindquist-Cock, Elizabeth. THE INFLUENCE OF PHOTOGRAPHY ON AMERICAN LANDSCAPE PAINTING, 1839-1880. New York: Garland Publishing Co., 1977. 270 p. Illus., notes, bibliog.

The focus of the study is on photographic imagery, landscapes promoted by news photography in the American West, and key photographers.

1738   Rudsill, Richard. MIRROR IMAGE: THE INFLUENCE OF THE DA-GUERREOTYPE ON AMERICAN SOCIETY. Albuquerque: University of New Mexico, 1971. 342 p. Illus., notes, bibliog., index.

A study of the origins, use, documentary, and symbolic development, truth, and social consequences of the daguerreotype.

1740 Thomas, Alan. TIME IN A FRAME: PHOTOGRAPHY AND THE NINE-
TEENTH CENTURY MIND. New York: Schocken, 1977. 171 p.
Illus., notes, bibliog., index.

> A discussion of the cultural implications of the photograph
> through chapters on family, fashion, theater, scenes, and
> everyday life.

1741 Welling, William B. COLLECTOR'S GUIDE TO THE 19TH CENTURY
PHOTOGRAPHS. New York: Macmillan, 1976. 204 p. Illus.,
notes, bibliog., index.

> A discussion of cased photographs, tintypes, stereographs,
> card photographs, photographic prints.

1742 _____. PHOTOGRAPHY IN AMERICA: THE FORMATIVE YEARS:
1839-1900. New York: Thomas Y. Crowell, 1978. 431 p. Illus.,
bibliog., journal location list.

> A detailed year-by-year chronicle of technical and commer-
> cial developments during the period.

1743 Willsberger, Johann. THE HISTORY OF PHOTOGRAPHY: CAMERAS,
PICTURES, PHOTOGRAPHERS. Garden City, N.Y.: Doubleday, 1977.
Unpaged. Illus., notes.

> Essentially an annotated collection of photographs and re-
> productions of plates.

RADIO

1744 Buxton, Frank, and Owen, Bill. THE BIG BROADCAST, 1920-1950:
A NEW, REVISED, AND GREATLY EXPANDED EDITION OF RADIO'S
GOLDEN AGE, THE COMPLETE REFERENCE WORK. New York:
Viking Press, 1972. 301 p. Illus., bibliog.

> Credits and genre designation, often with brief notes, of
> programs.

1745 _____. RADIO'S GOLDEN AGE: THE PROGRAMS AND THE PER-
SONALITIES. New York: Easton Valley Press, 1966. 417 p. Illus.,
bibliog.

> Credits and notes on numerous radio programs, with talent
> lists.

1746 Cantril, Hadley. THE INVASION FROM MARS: A STUDY IN THE
PSYCHOLOGY OF PANIC, WITH THE COMPLETE SCRIPT OF THE

FAMOUS ORSON WELLES BROADCAST. Princeton, N.J.: Princeton University Press, 1940. 228 p. Index.

A questionnaire-based study of the background, social situation, experience, and individual reactions of people to the broadcast.

1747 Cantril, Hadley, and Allport, Gordon W. THE PSYCHOLOGY OF RADIO. New York: Harper, 1935. 276 p. Diagrams.

A psychological analysis of the radio experience, with its effect on mental life, program content, listeners' tastes and habits, the radio voice, sex differences of voices, natural and reproduced speech, listening versus reading, entertainment, advertising, and education.

1748 Dreyer, Sherman H. RADIO IN WARTIME. New York: Greenberg, 1942. 384 p.

Strategies for the use of radio in wartime, with coverage of the expedient lie and propaganda, morale, news reporting, discussion programs, drama programming, This is War series, and government programs.

1749 Dunning, John. TUNE IN YESTERDAY: THE ULTIMATE ENCYCLOPEDIA OF OLD-TIME RADIO, 1926-1976. Englewood Cliffs, N.J.: Prentice-Hall, 1976. 703 p. Illus., index.

Programs are arranged by title, with a discussion of the origins, content, cast, and running time following each. Each entry is an informal capsule history with anecdotes about performers and runs about a page in length.

1750 Fang, Irving E. THOSE RADIO COMMENTATORS! Ames: Iowa State University, 1977. 341 p. Illus., bibliog., index.

Career essays on H.V. Kaltenborn, Floyd Gibbons, Lowell Thomas, Father Coughlin, Boake Carter, Upton Close, Dorothy Thompson, Raymond Gram Swing, Elmer Davis, Fulton Lewis, Jr., Drew Pearson, Walter Winchell, Baukhage, Gabriel Heatter, and Edward R. Murrow.

1751 Gordon, George N., and Falk, Irving A. ON-THE-SPOT REPORTING: RADIO RECORDS HISTORY. New York: Julian Messner, 1967. 191 p. Illus., bibliog., index.

An informal history of reporters and reporting, with emphasis on innovations and major reporters.

1752 Hall, Claude, and Hall, Barbara. THIS BUSINESS OF RADIO PRO-
GRAMMING: A COMPREHENSIVE LOOK AT MODERN PROGRAMMING
TECHNIQUES USED THROUGHOUT THE RADIO WORLD. New York:
Billboard Publications, 1977. 360 p. Glossary, index.

  An extensive discussion of programming, the Bill Drake format,
  disc jockeys, voice styles, general managers, program directors,
  ratings, business research, radio promotions, music; with interviews with Bill Stewart, Chuck Blore, George Wilson, Ron
  Jacobs, Bill Drake, Charlie Tuna, Bruce Johnson, Gary Owens,
  Dwight Case, George Burns (of Burns Media Consultants), Don
  Imus, and Robert W. Morgan.

1753 Harmon, Jim. THE GREAT RADIO COMEDIANS. Garden City, N.Y.:
Doubleday, 1970. 195 p. Illus., index.

  Nostalgic discussion of radio comedy genres and comedians.

1754 _____. THE GREAT RADIO HEROES. New York: Doubleday, 1967.
263 p.

  Very nostalgic, but informative essays on such radio programs
  as "I Love a Mystery," "Gangbusters," "The Shadow," "Inner
  Sanctum Mysteries," "Superman," "Buck Rogers," "Dick Tracy,"
  "Little Orphan Annie," "Tom Mix," "The New Adventures of
  Sherlock Holmes," "Ellery Queen," "The Thin Man," "The
  Adventures of Sam Spade," "Big Town," "Crime Photographer,"
  "Stella Dallas" and other soap operas, "Lone Ranger," "Ser-
  geant Preston of the Yukon," "The Green Hornet," "Captain
  Midnight," "Jack Armstrong, the All-American Boy" and
  others.

1755 Hettinger, Herman S. A DECADE OF RADIO ADVERTISING. Chicago:
University of Chicago, 1933. Reprint. New York: Arno Press, 1971.
354 p. Tables, charts, bibliog., index.

  The first systemmatic study of radio advertising, covering the
  years from 2 November 1920, when KDKA in Pittsburgh initi-
  ated the first regular program service, through the end of the
  decade, the volume considers the extent and manner of radio
  advertising, trends in its structure, and radio's contribution
  to the public interest. Chapters consider the bases of the
  medium's popularity, its psychological adaptability to the
  advertising message, an audience analysis, the advertising
  chain, how advertising is used effectively, and related matters.

1756 Koch, Howard. THE PANIC BROADCAST: PORTRAIT OF AN EVENT.
Boston: Little, Brown, 1970. 163 p. Illus., script.

A scriptwriter recalls the making and aftermath of the 1938 "War of the Worlds" radio broadcast.

1757   Lazarsfeld, Paul F. RADIO AND THE PRINTED PAGE. New York: Duell, Sloan and Pearce, 1940. Reprint. New York: Arno, 1971. 354 p. Tables, charts, index.

A dated but still useful study of the impact of radio as an educational form, with a concern for building audiences. Of interest are chapters 2, "Why Do People Like a Program"; and 5, "Radio and the Printed Page as Sources of News."

1758   McCavitt, William E., comp. RADIO AND TELEVISION: A SELECTED, ANNOTATED BIBLIOGRAPHY. Metuchen, N.J.: Scarecrow Press, 1978. 229 p. Author index.

Brief annotations for about eleven hundred books, monographs, and articles published from 1920 to 1976. Divided into subject classifications.

1759   MacDonald, J. Fred. DON'T TOUCH THAT DIAL: RADIO PROGRAMMING IN AMERICAN LIFE FROM 1920-1960. Chicago: Nelson-Hall, 1979. 412 p. Illus., bibliog., notes, index.

Excellent interpretation of the relationships of radio to American listeners. Beginning with an extensive historical overview of broadcasting from 1920 to 1960, the volume covers radio comedy, detective programs, Westerns, soap operas, broadcast journalism, and the contributions of blacks.

1760   Passman, Arnold. THE DEEJAYS. New York: Macmillan, 1971. 320 p. Illus., index.

Open-ended essay on the disc jockey phenomenon in America, with numerous literary and historical references.

1761   Settel, Irving. A PICTORIAL HISTORY OF RADIO. New York: Grosset and Dunlap, 1967. 192 p. Illus., index.

Decade-by-decade survey of radio, with attention to stars and major programs.

1762   Taylor, Sherrill, ed. RADIO PROGRAMMING IN ACTION: REALITIES AND OPPORTUNITIES. New York: Hastings House, 1967. 183 p. Index.

Radio executives write about news and public service, modern music, country music, "beautiful" music, FM radio, and sports broadcasting.

1763 Wertheim, Arthur Frank. RADIO COMEDY. New York: Oxford University Press, 1979. 439 p. Notes, index.

The author details the evolution of radio comedy from the 1920s through the early 1950s, stressing the relationship between radio comedy and American values during the great Depression and World War II, and focusing on major programs.

TELEVISION

1764 Adams, William, and Schreibman, Fay, eds. TELEVISION NETWORK NEWS: ISSUES IN CONTENT RESEARCH. Washington, D.C.: George Washington University, Television and Politics Study Program, School of Public and International Affairs, 1978. 231 p. Bibliog., index.

Ten essays on current bibliography, monitoring, news criticism, archives, content analysis, visual analysis, and future directions in research.

1765 Alley, Robert S. TELEVISION: ETHICS FOR HIRE? Nashville: Abingdon, 1977. 192 p. Notes.

A survey of television morality, with special attention to medical drama, shows with strong violent content, humorous shows, sports programming, and the relationship between series and movies.

1766 Anderson, Kent. TELEVISION FRAUD: THE HISTORY AND IMPLICATIONS OF THE QUIZ SHOW SCANDALS. Contributions in American Studies, no. 39. Westport, Conn.: Greenwood Press, 1978. 226 p. Bibliog., index.

An examination of the quiz shows as an entertainment that fell victim to the pressures of ratings.

1767 Arlen, Michael [J]. THE LIVING ROOM WAR. New York: Viking, 1969. 242 p.

A series of essays which first appeared in THE NEW YORKER on coverage of the Vietnam War by television.

1768 _____. THIRTY SECONDS. New York: Farrar, Straus and Giroux, 1980. 211 p.

A series of anecdotes about the making of television advertisements, the personnel involved, and the workaday world of the advertising business.

1769 _____. THE VIEW FROM HIGHWAY 1. New York: Farrar, Straus and Giroux, 1976. 293 p.

Contains Arlen's controversial essays on television criticism which appeared in the NEW YORKER.

1770 Baggaley, Jon. PSYCHOLOGY OF THE TV IMAGE. Westmead, Farnborough, Hants, Engl.: Gower, 1980. 189 p. Tables, notes, bibliog., index.

An analysis of the television image, based on investigations of such visual aspects as camera angle, visual background detail, editing techniques, studio seating positions, subtitles, antocue, and styles of performance. Dubbed music is also considered.

1771 Baggaley, Jon, and Duck, Steve. DYANMICS OF TELEVISION. Farnborough Hants, Engl.: Saxon House, 1976. 180 p. Illus.

One of the few book-length studies that attempts to explain the correspondence between perceptual and social processes in television viewing, the volume considers the mediums' technical dimensions, the message, viewing, experience, physical and perceptual imagery, persuasion, education, and control.

1772 Barcus, Francis Earle, and Wolkin, Rachael. CHILDREN'S TELEVISION: AN ANALYSIS OF PROGRAMMING AND ADVERTISING. New York: Praeger, 1977. 218 p. Tables, appendixes.

Statistical study of the content variables found in children's television on Saturday and Sunday mornings during April 1975 and after-school hour programming for the young found in ten independent stations across the United States. Concludes that, "for the most part, the economic security of one-dimensional characters who lack depth of feeling and who offer the child a monotonous litany of cliches" is typical of the fare.

1773 Barnouw, Erik. THE SPONSOR: NOTES ON A MODERN POTENTATE. New York: Oxford University Press, 1978. 220 p. Notes, index.

Divided into sections dealing with the rise of sponsorship in radio and television, the impact of sponsorship in television programming, and prospects for the future, Barnouw provides a hard, informed look at the vast influences sponsors have had in shaping contemporary American culture.

1774 _____. TUBE OF PLENTY: THE EVOLUTION OF AMERICAN TELEVISION. New York: Oxford University Press, 1975. 518 p. Illus., bibliog., notes, chronology, index.

A brief chapter on radio and the early experiments with

television are followed by a social, technological, and
economic history of television.

1775   Berger, Arthur Asa. TELEVISION AS AN INSTRUMENT OF TERROR:
ESSAYS ON MEDIA, POPULAR CULTURE, AND EVERYDAY LIFE. New
Brunswick, N.J.: Transaction Books, 1980. 214 p. Illus.

A collection of essays on method, comics, television, advertising, humor, fads, food, artifacts, British popular culture.

1776   _____ . THE TV-GUIDED AMERICAN: WHAT "ALL IN THE FAMILY,"
"KUNG FU," "MISSION IMPOSSIBLE," " RHODA" AND OTHER PRO-
GRAMS TELL US ABOUT OURSELVES. New York: Walker, 1976.
194 p. Illus.

Essays on situation comedies, the 1974 Frank Sinatra Spec-
tacular, "Mission Impossible," "Kung Fu," commercials,
"Rhoda," "Chico and the Man," children's television, "Iron-
side," "Star Trek," news, television, football, "Gunsmoke,"
"Upstairs-Downstairs," humor, and a conclusion.

1777   Blair, Karin. MEANING IN STAR TREK. Chambersburg, Pa.: Anima
Books, 1977. 157 p. Illus., index.

Jungian analysis of the television series.

1778   Bluem, A. William. DOCUMENTARY IN AMERICAN TELEVISION:
FORM, FUNCTION, METHOD. New York: Hastings House, 1965.
311 p. Illus., checklist, bibliog., index.

A brief history of the documentary in photography, film, and
radio, is followed by discussion of news documentaries, theme
documentaries, innovations; commentary by documentarists and
a newsman.

1779   _____ . RELIGIOUS TELEVISION PROGRAMS: A STUDY OF RELEVANCE.
New York: Hastings House, 1969. 220 p. Illus., bibliog., station
list, index.

A discussion of the variety of programs, programming from
1964 to 1966, local programs, guidelines for program plan-
ners, and related matters.

1780   Bluem, A. William, and Manvell, Roger, eds. TELEVISION, THE
CREATIVE EXPERIENCE: A SURVEY OF ANGLO-AMERICAN PROGRESS.
New York: Hastings House, Communications Arts Books, 1967. 328 p.
Index.

Interviews with personnel involved in the creation and production of drama and comedy, themes, television journalism,
the arts on television.

1781   Blum, Richard A. TELEVISION WRITING: FROM CONCEPT TO CON-
       TRACT. New York: Hastings House, 1980. 184 p. Illus., bibliog.,
       index.

> A guide to writing program proposals, scripts, revisions; with
> tips on marketing and addresses for networks, studios, pro-
> duction companies, agencies, foundations, guilds, useful trade
> publications, agents, and courses.

1782   Brauer, Ralph. THE HORSE, THE GUN AND THE PIECE OF PROPERTY:
       CHANGING IMAGES OF THE TV WESTERN. Bowling Green, Ohio:
       Popular Press, 1975. 246 p. Bibliog.

> The most extensive examination of the television Western
> available, this study draws on Northrup Frye's insights on
> fables as well as other contemporary criticism to reveal
> cultural meanings in such programs as "F-Troop," "The Wild,
> Wild West," "Wagon Train," "Rawhide," and "Gunsmoke,"
> in Western stereotypes and in Nixon's Manson speech and
> Dylan's "John Wesley Harding."

1783   Brooks, Tim, and Marsh, Earle. THE COMPLETE DIRECTORY TO PRIME
       TIME NETWORK TV SHOWS, 1946-PRESENT. New York: Ballantine,
       1979. 848 p. Index.

> An alphabetical listing of night time network television series,
> with data on genre, dates of telecast, production data, star
> or brief casting information, and synopsis. Appendixes list
> prime time schedules, 1946-78, Emmy Award winners, top-
> twenty-five rated programs, longest running series, series on
> more than one network, and television song hits.

1784   Brown, Les. THE NEW YORK TIMES ENCYCLOPEDIA OF TELEVISION.
       New York: Times Books, 1977. 492 p. Illus., bibliog.

> Topical entries cover programs, personalities, and other sub-
> jects reviewed through 1 May 1977 in the NEW YORK TIMES.

1785   _____. TELEVI$ION: THE BUSINESS BEHIND THE BOX. New York:
       Harcourt Brace Jovanovich, 1971. 374 p. Index.

> An informal account of the 1969-70 season for television
> that remains one of the best sources for understanding the
> practical realities of decision making about money, ratings,
> and programming.

1786   Brown, Ray, ed. CHILDREN AND TELEVISION. Beverly Hills, Calif.:
       Sage Publications, 1976. 368 p. Index.

Quantitative studies of children's relationships to television in three parts which emphasize the extent of viewing in Britain and the United States, influences on children's viewing habits, and the effects of viewing.

1787 Cantor, Muriel G. THE HOLLYWOOD TELEVISION PRODUCER: HIS WORK AND HIS AUDIENCE. New York: Basic Books, 1971. 256 p. Notes, appendix, index.

An investigation into the training, coworkers, network personnel, and practices, which form producers' background and workaday world, with a chapter on creating for audiences.

1788 Cater, Douglas, and Adler, Richard. TELEVISION AS A SOCIAL FORCE: NEW APPROACHES TO TELEVISION CRITICISM. New York: Praeger, 1975. 171 p. Index.

An anthology of essays on television as communication and experience. Includes an essay by Cater, "Television and Thinking People," who argues that technology is progressing rapidly and that we must keep informed. Michael Novak argues that television changed the way people experience reality, Benjamin DeMott advocates informed television criticism, Richard Adler summarizes the literature on the impact of the medium, David Littlejohn discusses the difficulty of using the medium to create a dialog of ideas, Paul H. Weaver distinguishes between news in newspapers and on television, Michael J. Robinson examines opinions about politics and television, and Kas Kalba speculates on the video culture now and in the future. An appendix lists participants in the 1974 Aspen Workshop on Television.

1789 Chin, Felix. CABLE TELEVISION: A COMPREHENSIVE BIBLIOGRAPHY. New York: IFI/Plenum, 1978. 285 p. Appendixes.

Includes annotated entries for some seven thousand selected articles, studies, and reports published between 1950 and 1977, most after 1965. Appendixes list the fifty largest CATV systems, top fifty CATV companies, chronology of major decisions and actions affecting CATV, government agencies and committees, FCC section headings for rules, and a glossary.

1790 Cole, Barry G., ed. TELEVISION. New York: Free Press, 1970. 605 p. Bibliog.

A collection of seventy-nine articles from the 1959 to 1970 TV GUIDE on news, programming, censorship, audience, effects, and "the future."

1792 _____. TV SEASON. Phoenix, Oryx Press, 1976-- . Annual.

The best brief reference on current television programs. Includes main listing by show title, giving brief synopses, source of material when known, length, day appearing, and credits. Other lists include cancelled shows, new cancelled shows, summer shows, Emmy nominees and awards, and an index to persons identified in credits. Also includes a listing of shows by categories, identification of captioned shows, and a list of Peabody Awards.

1793 Diamant, Lincoln, Ed. THE ANATOMY OF A TELEVISION COMMERCIAL: THE STORY OF EASTMAN KODAK'S "YESTERDAYS." New York: Hastings House Publishers, 1970. 191 p. Illus.

Follows the step-by-step production of the commercial.

1794 Diamond, Edwin. GOOD NEWS, BAD NEWS. Cambridge: MIT Press, 1978. 263 p. Notes, index.

Influence of the media on candidates and vice versa, debates, presidential images, agenda setting, audience seduction, ratings, magazines, newspapers, coverage of busing in Boston, and Watergate.

1795 _____. THE TIN KAZOO: TELEVISION, POLITICS, AND THE NEWS. Cambridge: MIT Press, 1975. 269 p. Index.

Discussion of industry practices, the medium, audiences, network and local news, and specific cases including Vietnam coverage, psychojournalism, Watergate coverage, and general comments.

1796 Edmondson, Madeleine, and Rounds, David. FROM MARY NOBLE TO MARY HARTMAN: THE COMPLETE SOAP OPERA BOOK. New York: Stein and Day, 1976. 256 p. Illus., index.

An informal account of the stars, content, and history of the soaps with silent debts to Raymond Stedman and others.

1797 Feldman, David, and Wright, John L., eds. "In-Depth: TV." JOURNAL OF POPUALR CULTURE 7 (Spring 1974): 885-1014. Bibliog.

Collection of essays and an interview with television director Alan Rafkin. The essays are on the medium, program direction, British programs, nonfiction, violence, program structures, soap operas, mysteries, the "Mary Tyler Moore Show," and the future of television in culture. Introduction and Afterword by Wright and Feldman.

1798 Field, Stanley. THE MINI-DOCUMENTARY: SERIALIZING TV NEWS Blue Ridge Summit, Pa.: G/L Tab Books, 1975. 249 p. Illus., bibliog., index.

Based on local production practices, the volume includes a definition and brief history, traces practices in three network affiliates and an independent station, and surveys some notable successes.

1799   Galanoy, Terry. TONIGHT! Garden City, N.Y.: Doubleday, 1972. 229 p.

An informal history of "The Tonight Show."

1800   Gerani, Gary, and Schulman, Paul H. FANTASTIC TELEVISION. New York: Harmony, 1977. 192 p. Illus., credits, index.

Descriptive essays with credits and episode synopses for "Superman," "One Step Beyond," "Twilight Zone," "Thriller," "Outer Limits," Irwin Allen productions, "Batman," "Star Trek," "Invaders," "Prisoner," "Night Gallery," "Kolchak," and "Space 1999"; with brief essays on American and British "telefantasy," juvenile shows, and made-for-television movies.

1801   Gianakos, Larry. TELEVISION DRAMA SERIES PROGRAMMING: A COMPREHENSIVE CHRONICLE, 1959-1975. Metuchen, N.J.: Scarecrow Press, 1978. 794 p. Title index.

Time schedules for prime time, together with episode titles and dates for regular drama programs. Series entries typically provide a brief overview noting cast regulars, followed by the list of episodes.

1802   Hofstetter, C. Richard. BIAS IN THE NEWS: NETWORK TELEVISION COVERAGE OF THE 1972 ELECTION CAMPAIGN. Columbus: Ohio State University Press, 1976. 213 p. Charts, index.

A statistical interpretation of the coverage of the 1972 election campaign by the weekly news broadcasts. Concludes that differences in treatment were more likely to be ambiguous or neutral rather than favorable or unfavorable.

1803   Joslyn, James, and Pendleton, John. "The Adventures of Ozzie and Harriet." JOURNAL OF POPULAR CULTURE 7 (Summer 1973): 23-41.

Drawing on scripts, an interview and reruns, the authors find a formula incorporating comedy, honesty, integrity, and respect.

1804   Klaven, Eugene. TURN THAT DAMNED THING OFF: AN IRREVERENT LOOK AT TV'S IMPACT ON THE AMERICAN SCENE. Indianapolis: Bobbs-Merrill, 1972. 227 p.

A chatty, often witty, poke at the broadcasting business by
a New York radio personality.

1805   McCavitt, William E., comp.   RADIO AND TELEVISION: A SELECTED,
ANNOTATED BIBLIOGRAPHY.   Metuchen, N.J.: Scarecrow Press,
1978.   229 p.   Author index.

Contains eleven hundred annotated items, arranged according
to surveys, history, regulation, organization, programming,
production, minorities, responsibility, society, criticism,
public broadcasting, audience, cable, careers, technical
aspects, and research materials.

1806   McNeil, Alex.   TOTAL TELEVISION: A COMPREHENSIVE GUIDE TO
PROGRAMMING FROM 1948-1980.   New York: Penguin, 1980.   1,087 p.
Index.

Contains plot summaries and/or data for 3,400 series and
570 specials, with prime-time schedules, award winning programs, list of top-rated shows, and a list of series premiering
in early 1980.

1807   Melody, William.   CHILDREN'S TELEVISION: THE ECONOMICS OF
EXPLOITATION.   New Haven, Conn.: Yale University Press, 1973.
164 p.

Commissioned by the Action for Children's Television consumer
group, the study examines advertising control over children's
programming.   A history and analysis of current trends in
which children are exploited as premature consumers.

1808   Metz, Robert.   CBS: REFLECTIONS IN A BLODSHOT EYE.   Chicago:
Playboy Press, 1975.   428 p.   Illus., chronologies, bibliog., index,
photos.

A history of the organizational structure of CBS through primary sources and interviews with management personnel.
Metz recreates the situations in which decisions about public
and corporate issues were resolved or failed to be resolved.

1809   Meyer, Manfred, and Nissen, Ursula, comps.   EFFECTS AND FUNC-
TIONS OF TELEVISION: CHILDREN AND ADOLESCENTS: A BIBLIOG-
RAPHY OF SELECTED RESEARCH LITERATURE, 1970-1978.   Communication Research and Broadcasting, no. 27.   New York: K.G. Saur, 1979.
172 p.

An international bibliography of 914 items regarding general
studies, uses and functions, cognitive and emotional effects,
socialization, violence, series, news, and advertising.

1810 Miller, Merle, and Rhodes, Evan. ONLY YOU, DICK DARLING!
      OR HOW TO WRITE ONE TELEVISION SCRIPT AND MAKE $50,000,000:
      A TRUE-LIFE ADVENTURE. New York: William Sloane, 1964. 350 p.

> An informal account of the writing of the pilot film for the
> TV series, "Calhoun."

1811 Newcomb, Horace. TV: THE MOST POPULAR ART. Garden City:
      Anchor Press, Doubleday, 1974. 272 p. Bibliog., index.

> A genre approach to television criticism through the examina-
> tion of comedies, Westerns, mysteries, doctor and lawyer
> shows, adventures, soap operas, nonfiction, and current shows.
> Also contains an essay on television aesthetics.

1812 _____, ed. TELEVISION: THE CRITICAL VIEW. New York: Oxford
      University Press, 1979. 2d ed. 557 p. Graphs, bibliog.

> Essays on series, news, individual shows, commercials, and
> aesthetics.

1813 Parish, James Robert. ACTORS' TELEVISION CREDITS: 1950-1972.
      Metuchen, N.J.: Scarecrow, 1973. 869 p.

> Based primarily on TV GUIDE for the New York City market,
> the index lists appearances for all genres except repeats,
> theatrical films, and nonentertainment programming. The
> supplement includes corrections to the original volume.

1814 _____. ACTORS' TELEVISION CREDITS: SUPPLEMENT I. Metuchen,
      N.J.: Scarecrow Press, 1978. 423 p.

> Expands and adds credits through 1976 to the author's ACTORS'
> TELEVISION CREDITS (above entry).

1815 Powers, Ron. THE NEWSCASTERS. New York: St. Martin's Press,
      1977. 243 p. Index.

> Brief essays on various aspects of the news-producing agencies
> of television and the personalities and gimmicks used to ex-
> tend ratings.

1816 Quinlan, Sterling. THE HUNDRED MILLION DOLLAR LUNCH. Chicago:
      J. Philip O'Hara, 1974. 241 p.

> An anecdotal account of how the FCC decisions about various
> licenses are discussed and resolved, especially with respect
> to the case of WHDH-TV in Boston.

1817   Reed, Maxine K., ed. THE VIDEO SOURCE BOOK. Syosset, L.I., N.Y.: National Video Clearing House, 1979. 685 p. Index.

> Lists fifteen thousand program titles on video tape and disc culled from 153 catalogs, with items oriented to entertainment, information, and education. Entries note sources, type of program, length, and brief descriptions of contents.

1818   Sass, Lauren R., ed. TELEVISION: THE AMERICAN MEDIUM IN CRISIS. New York: Facts on File, 1979. 232 p. Illus., index.

> Reprinted editorials from newspapers about politics and television, regulation, behavior, programming, and public broadcasting.

1819   Schneider, Ira, and Korot, Beryl, eds. VIDEO ART: AN ANTHOLOGY. New York: Harcourt Brace Jovanovich, 1976. 286 p. Distributor list.

> Brief coverage of numerous artists working in video, with a collection of essays.

1820   Schorr, Daniel. CLEARING THE AIR. Boston: Houghton Mifflin Co., 1977. 333 p. Illus., bibliog., index.

> The account of Watergate from the perspective of the CBS reporter, based on fresh interviews and a concern for "information and perspective" with a minimum of "gossip and rancor."

1821   Sharp, Harold S., and Sharp, Marjorie Z., comps. INDEX TO CHARACTERS IN THE PERFORMING ARTS: PART IV--RADIO AND TELEVISION. Metuchen, N.J.: Scarecrow Press, 1973. 697 p.

> A finders' list for twenty thousand characters in twenty-five hundred major national programs to 1955 for radio and 1972 for television. Characters are listed alphabetically with cross-listings.

1822   Silverstone, Roger. "An Approach to the Structural Analysis of the Television Message." SCREEN 17 (Summer 1976): 9-40.

> Applies the analytical frameworks of Christian Metz, Vladimir Propp, and Algirdas Greimas in a tentative analysis of the television series, INTIMATE STRANGERS, shown on London Weekend Television between September 20 and December 13, 1974.

1823   Small, William. TO KILL A MESSENGER: TELEVISION NEWS AND THE REAL WORLD. New York: Hastings House, 1970. 302 p. Index.

> Beginning with Edward P. Murrow's criticisms, the author surveys the depth of television reporting, the portrayal of

blacks, violence, the Vietnam War, protest, politics, presidential debates, political conventions, and control of television.

1824   Smith, Craig R. "Television News as Rhetoric." WESTERN JOURNAL OF SPEECH COMMUNICATION 41 (Summer 1977): 147-59.

A well-documented study of the techniques used to manage viewers' responses to coverage of news, emphasizing the 1968 presidential campaign.

1825   Soares, Manuela. THE SOAP OPERA BOOK. New York: Harmony Books, 1978. 182 p. Illus.

A superficial but engaging volume that attempts to cover all aspects of the contemporary soap opera, with chapters on the craze, the new shows for the young, ideas about the appeal of the form, a survey of shows, styles, archetypes, sex, plots, family relationships and other images, production, audiences, character notes, and a list of favorites.

1826   Stein, Ben. THE VIEW FROM SUNSET BOULEVARD: AMERICA AS BROUGHT TO YOU BY THE PEOPLE WHO MAKE TELEVISION. New York: Basic Books, 1979. 156 p. Index.

An informal discussion of program topics and genres based on interviews with producers and others; with chapters on top shows, the talent, television businessmen, crime, police, America, the military, government, small towns, big cities, the rich, the poor, clergy, television fantasy life, and Hollywood attitudes.

1827   Steinberg, Cobbett S. TV FACTS. New York: Facts on File, 1980. 541 p. Charts, index.

Contains prime-time schedules from 1950 to 1980, lists of one hundred long-running programs, program costs, data on television households, ratings for the most popular shows, data on revenue and advertising, data on awards and polls, and a capsule economic history of stations and networks.

1828   Sterling, Christopher H., and Kittross, John M. STAY TUNED: A CONCISE HISTORY OF AMERICAN BROADCASTING. Belmont, Calif.: Wadsworth, 1978. 562 p. Chronology, illus., glossary, statistics, bibliog., index.

A general history with an alternate topical table of contents organized into technical innovations, stations, networks, education, advertising, programming, audiences, regulatory trends, and social effects.

1829   Terrace, Vincent. THE COMPLETE ENCYCLOPEDIA OF TELEVISION
        PROGRAMS, 1947-1979. 2 vols. New York: A.S. Barnes, 1979.
        Illus., index.

> Shows are arranged by title, with each characterized by
> genre. Information about programs includes a brief plot
> summary, cast of characters, length, running time, network
> affiliation, and notice of syndication. Does not include
> sports, religious programming, news, or specials that are
> not regular series.

1830   Whitfield, Stephen E., and Roddenberry, Gene. THE MAKING OF
        "STAR TREK." New York: Ballantine, 1968. 414 p.

> The origins, official biography of characters, production, and
> anecdotes of the television program through the 1966-68 seasons.

1831   Wilk, Max. THE GOLDEN AGE OF TELEVISION: NOTES FROM THE
        SURVIVORS. New York: Delacorte Press, 1976. 274 p. Illus., index.

> An informal survey of programming from 1947 to the mid-
> 1950s.

1832   Willener, Alfred; Milliard, Guy; and Ganty, Alex. VIDEOLOGY AND
        UTOPIA: EXPLORATIONS IN A NEW MEDIUM. London: Routledge
        and Kegan Paul, 1976. 171 p. Illus., bibliog., index.

> Sociological speculations and studies of the uses of video in
> a wide variety of situations.

1833   Winick, Charles; Williamson, Lorne G.; Chuzmir, Stuart F.; and Winick
        Mariann Pezella. CHILDREN'S TELEVISION COMMERCIALS: A CON-
        TENT ANALYSIS. New York: Praeger, 1973. 153 p. Charts, prod-
        uct list, notes, index.

> The analysis examines length, information, persuasion tech-
> niques, delivery, casts of characters, settings and story
> elements, authority figures and heroes, production techniques,
> language, age, and other aspects of selected commercials.

1834   Withey, Stephen B., and Abeles, Ronald P., eds. TELEVISION AND
        SOCIAL BEHAVIOR: BEYOND VIOLENCE AND CHILDREN: A RE-
        PORT OF THE COMMITTEE ON TELEVISION AND SOCIAL BEHAVIOR,
        SOCIAL SCIENCE RESEARCH COUNCIL. Hillsdale, N.J.: Lawrence
        Erlbaum Associates, 1980. 356 p. Appendixes, notes, index.

> Essays on effects, audiences and audience research, organi-
> zational approaches, the Surgeon General's Report's short-
> comings, social influence, the influence of television on
> personal decision making, research on children and television,
> Afro-American stereotypes and racism on television, and an
> overview of television research.

1835 Wyckoff, Gene. THE IMAGE CANDIDATES--AMERICAN POLITICS IN THE AGE OF TELEVISION. New York: Macmillan Co., 1968. 274 p. Illus., tables, index.

> Discusses the art of merchandising political personalities. Argues that voters seek reassuring clues to candidates' character in their appearance and demeanor; contains stories of Johnson, Reagan, Nixon, Romney, Lindsay, Percy and includes the complete scripts of successful campaign films about Lodge and Rockefeller. His book concludes with proposals for legislation to improve the use of political television.

1836 Yellin, David G. SPECIAL: FRED FREED AND THE TELEVISION DOCUMENTARY. New York: Macmillan, 1973. 289 p. Illus.

> Chronicles the development of the television documentary through the life and work of Fred Freed, pioneer in radio and television documentaries.

FILM

1837 Adams, Les, and Rainey, Buck. SHOOT-EM-UPS: THE COMPLETE REFERENCE GUIDE TO WESTERNS OF THE SOUND ERA. New Rochelle, N.Y.: Arlington House, 1978. 633 p. Illus., credits, index.

> Credits for 3,339 Westerns from 1903 to 1977, with an appended filmography of 133 continental Westerns from 1962 to 1977. The seven chronological divisions include production and thematic surveys.

1838 Alloway, Lawrence. VIOLENT AMERICA: THE MOVIES 1946-1964. New York: Museum of Modern Art, 1971. 95 p. Illus., notes.

> Based on a 1969 film series shown at the museum, the illustrated essay examines "the transformations of meaning undergone by set figures and set situations, revealed by the forms of movie violence under the pressure of the contemporary world" as found in the formula film of the times. Appendix of the films cited, with credits.

1839 Andrew, Dudley J. THE MAJOR FILM THEORIES: AN INTRODUCTION. New York: Oxford University Press, 1976. 278 p. Notes, bibliog., subject index.

> Interpretations of the work of Munsterberg, Arnheim, Eisenstein, Balazs, Kracauer, Bazin, Mitry, Metz, Ayfre, and Agel.

1840 Arijon, Daniel. GRAMMAR OF THE FILM LANGUAGE. New York: Focal Press, 1976. 624 p. Illus., index.

A handbook for filming narrative sequences to achieve optimal visual effects.

1841 Aros, Andrew A. AN ACTOR GUIDE TO THE TALKIES: 1965 THROUGH 1974. Metuchen, N.J.: Scarecrow Press, 1977. 771 p. Index.

A continuation of the work of Richard Dimmitt (see no. 1902). The volume identifies performers' roles according to film titles.

1842 _____. A TITLE GUIDE TO THE TALKIES! 1964 THROUGH 1974. Metuchen, N.J.: Scarecrow Press, 1977. 336 p. Index.

A continuation of the work of Richard Dimmitt (see no. 1903). The guide is arranged in alphabetical order according to title, and identifies the production company and the literary basis for the film.

1843 Atkins, Thomas R., ed. GRAPHIC VIOLENCE ON THE SCREEN. New York: Monarch Press, 1976. 96 p. Illus., bibliog., filmography.

Illustrated essays on the film noir, horror films from Hammer Studios, Kung Fu films and Italian Westerns, massacre films, and a memoir about death in contemporary films.

1844 _____. SEXUALITY IN THE MOVIES. Bloomington: Indiana University Press, 1975. 244 p. Illus., notes.

Essays on special values, censorship, genres, popular features, homosexuality, with pieces on I AM CURIOUS YELLOW, MIDNIGHT COWBOY, CARNAL KNOWLEDGE, DEEP THROAT, LAST TANGO IN PARIS, and CRIES AND WHIS-PERS.

1845 Balio, Tino, ed. THE AMERICAN FILM INDUSTRY. Madison: University of Wisconsin Press, 1976. 499 p. Illus., notes, bibliog., index.

A collection of essays on film technology, theaters, business, and social issues.

1846 Balshofer, Fred J., and Miller, Arthur C. ONE REEL A WEEK. Berkeley and Los Angeles: University of California Press, 1967. 218 p. Illus., index.

Two cameramen reminisce about early days in filmmaking with the facts and impressions as they remember them. An important contribution to the understanding of silent film.

1847 Barbour, Alan G. DAYS OF THRILLS AND ADVENTURE. New York: Collier-Macmillan, 1970. 168 p. Illus.

History of the sound serial from 1930 to 1956. The appendix lists films, with credits, and chapter titles.

1848   Barnouw, Erik. DOCUMENTARY: A HISTORY OF THE NON-FICTION
        FILM. New York: Oxford, 1974. 332 p. Illus., notes, bibliog.,
        index.

        A history of the genre from 1896 to 1971, featuring major
        filmmakers and influential films.

1849   Barris, Alex. HOLLYWOOD'S OTHER WOMEN. New York: A.S.
        Barnes, 1975. 211 p. Illus.

        A collection of career sketches of supporting actresses.

1850   _____. STOP THE PRESSES: THE NEWSPAPERMAN IN AMERICAN
        FILMS. South Brunswick, N.J.: A.S. Barnes, 1976. 211 p. Illus.,
        index.

        Accounts of films in which newspapermen are portrayed as
        crime busters, scandalmongers, crusaders, foreign correspon-
        dents, human beings, sob sisters, editors and publishers,
        villains and other types; with a chapter on the basic formula.

1851   Barsam, Richard M. NONFICTION FILM: A CRITICAL HISTORY. New
        York: Dutton, 1973. 332 p. Illus., bibliog., index.

        International coverage of documentaries with emphasis on
        English-language films. Chapters on Grierson, Flaherty,
        and World War II films. Appendixes identify production
        facts and awards.

1852   Batty, Linda. RETROSPECTIVE INDEX TO FILM PERIODICALS 1930-
        1971. New York: Bowker, 1975. 425 p.

        Indexes nineteen journals. Items arranged by films, subjects,
        and authors of reviewed books.

1853   Baxter, John. THE GANSTER FILM. New York: A.S. Barnes, 1970.
        160 p. Illus., index.

        Illustrated career sketches of 225 personalities involved in
        gangster films, with a brief introduction to the genre.

1854   _____. HOLLYWOOD IN THE SIXTIES. New York: A.S. Barnes,
        1972. 172 p. Illus.

        Survey of the themes, trends, and major films of the decade.

1855   _____. HOLLYWOOD IN THE THIRTIES. New York: A.S. Barnes,
        1968. 220 p. Illus.

        Informal survey of the themes, trends, and major films of
        the decade.

1856 _____ . SCIENCE FICTION IN THE CINEMA. New York: A.S. Barnes, 1970. 240 p. Illus., filmography, bibliog.

> Good basic history of the science fiction feature, with a chapter on the serial, through about 1968.

1857 _____ . STUNT: THE STORY OF THE GREAT MOVIE STUNT MEN. Garden City, N.Y.: Doubleday, 1974. Illus.

> Survey of the careers of these athletes of the film.

1858 Bazin, André. WHAT IS CINEMA? Vol. 1. Selected and translated by Hugh Gray. Berkeley and Los Angeles: University of California Press, 1967.

> Influential essays on the ontology of the photographic image, myth of total cinema, evolution of film language, qualities of montage, mixed cinema, film and theater, the stylistics of Robert Bresson, Charlie Chaplin, documentaries, and painting and film.

1859 _____ . WHAT IS CINEMA? Vol. 2. Essays selected and translated by Hugh Gray. Berkeley and Los Angeles: University of California, 1971. Index.

> Influential essays on Italian realism, LA TERRA TREMA, BICYCLE THIEF, DE SICA, UNBERTO D, Cabiria Rossellini, MONSIEUR VERDOUX, LIMELIGHT, the Western, the American pinup girl, THE OUTLAW, eroticism, and Jean Gabin.

1860 Bergman, Andrew. WE'RE IN THE MONEY: DEPRESSION AMERICA AND ITS FILMS. New York: New York University Press, 1971. 200 p. Filmography, illus., bibliog., index.

> Critical history of the films of the decade in relation to the social and economic milieu. Discusses genres, themes, and Hollywood production.

1861 Betancourt, Jeanne. WOMEN IN FOCUS. Dayton, Ohio: Pflaum Publishing, 1974. 186 p. Indexes, bibliog.

> An annotated film list and series of biographical sketches on women and men, selected for their treatment of women as subjects. Contains film and personality indexes, a brief thematic index, suggested film programs, a list of distributors, and an annotated bibliography by Madeline Warren.

1862 Bluem, A. William, and Squire, Jason E., eds. THE MOVIE BUSINESS: AMERICAN FILM INDUSTRY PRACTICE. Studies in Media Management. New York: Hastings House, 1972. 368 p. Index.

> Essays on developing the story and screenplay, financing and budgeting management, production, distribution, audiences,

and new technology; with appendixes on sponsored films and contracts.

1863 Blum, Daniel C. A NEW PICTORIAL HISTORY OF THE TALKIES. Rev. and enl. by John Kobal. New York: G.P. Putnam's Sons, 1973. 379 p. Illus., index.

A year-by-year pictorial account with brief capsule summaries of the high points.

1864 _____. A PICTORIAL HISTORY OF THE SILENT SCREEN. New York: G.P. Putnam's Sons, 1953. 334 p. Illus., index.

Pictorial account with brief historical inserts of the year-by-year productions of Hollywood.

1865 Bogle, Donald. TOMS, COONS, MULATTOES, MAMMIES, AND BUCKS: AN INTERPRETIVE HISTORY OF BLACKS IN AMERICAN FILMS. New York: Viking Press, 1973. 244 p. Photos., index.

A useful survey of the stereotypes inherited and developed by the movies, with discussion of the jesters of the 1920s, servants of the 1930s, problem people of the 1940s, black stars of the 1950s, and militants of the 1960s, with an epilogue on the early 1970s. The book contains many shrewd insights into Hollywood's attempts to capitalize on race relations within the context of the old types, without straining perceived audience values.

1866 Bohn, Thomas William. AN HISTORICAL AND DESCRIPTIVE ANALYSIS OF THE "WHY WE FIGHT" SERIES. New York: Arno Press, 1977. 359 p. Notes, bibliog.

A brief discussion of the documentary background, followed by a history of the series, its themes, sound, and visual style. Based on a 1968 University of Wisconsin dissertation.

1867 Bonko, Larry. SINNERS AND SHOW-OFFS. Virginia Beach, Va.: Donning Co., 1975. Illus. 236 p.

Interviews with various celebrities and personalities.

1868 Borde, Raymond, and Chaumeton, Etienne. PANORAMA DO FILM NOIR AMÉRICAIN: 1941-1953. Paris: Éditions de Minuit, 1955. Reprint. Éditions d'Aujourd'hui, 1975. 279 p. Bibliog., index.

The definition, background, major periods, stylistic sources and influence, together with fimographies of American and French films, and secondary bibliographies of the film noir popular from about 1940 to 1955.

1869   Braudy, Leo. THE WORLD IN A FRAME: WHAT WE SEE IN FILMS. Garden City, N.Y.: Anchor Press, Doubleday, 1976. 274 p. Index.

> Divided into three sections on visual coherence, genre, and acting and characterization, the study attempts to avoid mechanistic criticism and to provide a way of understanding film that goes beyond categorization.

1870   Brenner, Marie. GOING HOLLYWOOD: AN INSIDER'S LOOK AT POWER AND PRETENSE IN THE MOVIE BUSINESS. New York: Delacorte Press, 1978. 214 p. Illus.

> A collection of breezy articles on various Hollywood celebrities and power brokers, including Robert de Niro, Marthe Keller, Sue Mengers, Dino De Laurentiis, Lester Persky, and Tom Laughlin.

1871   Brosnan, John. FUTURE TENSE: THE CINEMA OF SCIENCE FICTION. London: Macdonald and Jane's, 1978. 320 p. Notes, annot. list of television programs, index.

> Covering the years 1900 to 1978, the volume attempts a critical history of the genre that argues for the viability of literate science fiction films.

1872   _____ . MOVIE MAGIC: THE STORY OF SPECIAL EFFECTS IN THE CINEMA. London: Macdonald, 1974. 285 p. Index, illus., notes, bibliog.

> An informal history of special effects, with emphasis on developments in Britain and the United States. Includes chapters on war films and science fiction. Appendixes contain notes on personalities and awards.

1873   Bruno, Michael. VENUS IN HOLLYWOOD: THE CONTINENTAL ENCHANTRESS FROM GARBO TO LOREN. New York: Lyle Stuart, 1970. 257 p. Bibliog., index of the stars.

> A brief history, with appendixes on the ten best films, the Production Code, name changes.

1874   Bukalski, Peter J., comp. FILM RESEARCH: A CRITICAL BIBLIOGRAPHY WITH ANNOTATIONS AND ESSAY. Boston: G.K. Hall and Co., 1972. 215 p.

> Annotated items appear on pages 29-38. Brief information on rental, purchase, periodicals, and various categories of information on subjects concerned with film study. Books only.

1875   Buscombe, Edward. "The Idea of Genre in the American Cinema."
       SCREEN 11 (March–April 1970): 33–45.

> Identification of many of the icons and motifs associated with
> the Western, together with an argument for further examina-
> tion of the relationships of genre to artistic creativity and
> social values.

1876   Butler, Ivan. THE HORROR FILM. New York: A.S. Barnes, 1967.
       176 p. Illus., filmography, bibliog., index.

> A brief survey of horror films which examines in some depth
> various classics of the genre.

1877   Byron, Stuart, and Weis, Elisabeth, eds. THE NATIONAL SOCIETY
       OF FILM CRITICS ON MOVIE COMEDY. New York: Grossman,
       Viking, 1977. 305 p. Index.

> Essays by film critics on directors, trends, and films of the
> silent era, sound era, contemporary themes, and European
> comedy. Essays cover underground comedy, Mel Brooks,
> Woody Allen, stud comedy, marriage; Nichols, May and
> Simon; black and apocalyptic comedy, and oddball heroes
> among contemporaries. European coverage includes France,
> Britain, Italy, Spain (Buñuel), and Sweden (Bergman).

1878   Calder, Jenni. THERE MUST BE A LONE RANGER: THE AMERICAN
       WEST IN FILM AND REALITY. London: Hamish Hamilton, 1974.
       Reprint. New York: McGraw-Hill, 1977. 241 p. Notes, filmography,
       index.

> An extensive examination of the Western myth and its rela-
> tionship to reality and the interpretation of the West through
> films.

1879   Cameron, Ian. ADVENTURE IN THE MOVIES. New York: Crescent
       Books, 1973. 152 p. Illus., index.

> Pictorial treatment of major themes in adventure films, in-
> cluding a section on the use of adventure for propaganda.

1880   Canham, Kingsley, et al. THE HOLLYWOOD PROFESSIONALS. New
       York: A.S. Barnes, 1973–76. 5 vols.

> Detailed essays on the directors, with filmographies and
> checklists of secondary sources. Volume 1 contains essays
> on Michael Curtiz, Raul Walsh, and Henry Hathaway; volume
> 2 covers Henry King, Lewis Milestone, and Sam Wood; volume
> 3 covers Howard Hawks, Frank Borzage, and Edgar G. Ulmer;
> volume 4 covers Tod Browning and Don Siegal; and volume 5
> covers King Vidor, John Cromwell, and Mervyn Le Roy.

1881   Carmen, Ira H.   MOVIES, CENSORSHIP, AND THE LAW.   Ann Arbor:
        University of Michigan Press, 1966. 339 p. Bibliog., index.

        A historical analysis of the actions of federal, state, and
        local courts and censorship boards, together with appendixes
        of interviews with individual censors, and a table of cases.

1882   Carroll, John M.   TOWARD A STRUCTURAL PSYCHOLOGY OF CINEMA.
        New York: Mouton, 1980. 227 p. Bibliog., charts.

        The author argues for a generative grammar of cinema through
        the discussion of the weaknesses of past theory, the findings
        of cognitive psychology, and a reworking of semiotics.

1883   Cawelti, John G.   ADVENTURE, MYSTERY, AND ROMANCE. Chicago:
        University of Chicago Press, 1976. 336 p. Bibliog., index.

        The most thorough available study of three basic popular
        genres and a variety of formulas most pervasive in fiction,
        television, and film.

1884   Cawkwell, Tim, and Smith, John M., eds. THE WORLD ENCYCLO-
        PEDIA OF FILM. New York: A and W Visual Library, 1972. 444 p.
        Illus., index.

        A substantial encyclopedia of personalities involved in film-
        making.

1885   Chicorel, Marietta, ed.   CHICOREL INDEX TO FILM LITERATURE.
        Chicorel Index Series, vols. 22 and 22A. New York: Chicorel Li-
        brary Publishing Corp., 1975. 914 p.

        Identifies books and arranges them into several dozen cate-
        gories.

1886   Clarens, Carlos.   AN ILLUSTRATED HISTORY OF THE HORROR FILMS.
        New York: Putnam, 1967. 256 p. Index, illus.

        Historical survey of international contributions to the genre,
        focused around an examination of major themes in horror
        films. The appendix provides credits for about four hundred
        films covered in the text.

1887   Cohn, Lawrence.   MOVIETONE PRESENTS THE TWENTIETH CENTURY.
        New York: Saint Martin's Press, 1976. 350 p. Illus.

        Stills, with a brief historical introduction.

1888   Collins, Richard.   "Genre: A Reply to Ed Buscombe." SCREEN 11
        nos. 4-5 (1970): 66-75.

Argues that Buscombe (see no. 1875) overemphasizes the iconography of the Western at the expense of seeing the form as an arbitrary collection of situations, antinomies, and motifs related to the American frontier from 1860 to 1890 which are used by directors to make particular statements.

1889 Conolly, L.W. "Pornography." DALHOUSIE REVIEW 54 (Winter 1974–75): 698–709.

Reviews recent investigations into the effects of pornography.

1890 Cook, David A. "Some Structural Approaches to Cinema: A Survey of Models." CINEMA JOURNAL 14 (Spring 1975): 41–54.

A useful analysis of the various structuralist and semiological perspectives on film drawing on Frederic Jameson's work on literature. The survey touches on Sol Worth after discussing the Eisenstein and Bazin approaches, and outlining the early development of semiology.

1891 Corliss, Richard. TALKING PICTURES: SCREENWRITERS IN THE AMERICAN CINEMA, 1927–1973. Woodstock, N.Y.: Overlook Press, 1974. 398 p.

Critical survey of the work of thirty-eight screenwriters.

1893 Cowie, Peter, ed. HOLLYWOOD, 1920–1970. New York and South Brunswick, N.J.: A.S. Barnes, 1977. 286 p. Illus., index.

This volume brings together the five separate volumes on the decades of American film written by David Robinson, John Baxter, Charles Higham, Joel Greenberg, and Gordon Gow. The illustrations are enlarged.

1893 _____. INTERNATIONAL FILM GUIDE. South Brunswick, N.J.: A.S. Barnes. 1964–– . Annual.

International film production, trends, people in filmmaking.

1894 Cripps, Thomas. BLACK FILM AS GENRE. Bloomington: Indiana University Press, 1978. 184 p. Bibliog., filmography, index.

Analysis of black films as a coherent genre through examination of six key films: THE SCAR OF SHAME, THE ST. LOUIS BLUES, THE BLOOD OF JESUS, THE NEGRO SOLDIER, NOTHING BUT A MAN, and SWEET SWEETBACK'S BAADASSSSS SONG. Contains chapters on the evolution of the genre and one on criticism.

1895   Cry, Helen W. A FILMOGRAPHY OF THE THIRD WORLD. Metuchen, N.J.: Scarecrow Press, 1976. 319 p. Index.

Brief credits and annotation for over two thousand films.

1896   Daniels, Les. LIVING IN FEAR: A HISTORY OF HORROR IN THE MASS MEDIA. New York: Charles Scribner's Sons, 1975. 248 p. Illus., index.

Affectionate collection of illustrations, photographs, comics, cartoons, and stories, interspersed among an extensive essay. Though the study is not intended to be exhaustive, it does contain a sensible introduction to the interpretation of horror and worthwhile historical information.

1897   Davis, Brian. THE THRILLER. London: Studio Vista, 1973. 159 p. Illus., index.

Survey of the detective, spy, and message thrillers, with chapters on the chase and the heist.

1898   Dawson, Bonnie, comp. WOMEN'S FILMS IN PRINT: AN ANNOTATED GUIDE TO 800 FILMS BY WOMEN. San Francisco: Booklegger Press, 1975. 165 p. Bibliog., index.

Lists the films of 370 filmmakers with brief annotations. Identifies distributors and some sources for further study.

1899   Dengler, Ralph S.J. "The Language of Film Titles." JOURNAL OF COMMUNICATION 25 (Summer 1975): 51-60.

The author applied the General Inquirer computer program to 7,590 film titles culled from various sources for the period from 1900 to 1968. Semantic clusters correlate with the industry and to the larger culture.

1900   Dick, Bernard F. ANATOMY OF FILM. New York: St. Martin's Press, 1978. 211 p. Bibliog., index.

An introduction to film for beginning students. Emphasis is on the construction of film and its perception by the audience.

1901   Di Lauro, Al, and Rabkin, Gerald. DIRTY MOVIES: AN ILLUSTRATED HISTORY OF THE STAG FILM, 1915-1970. Introduction by Kenneth Tynan. New York: Chelsea House, 1976. 160 p. Illus., bibliog., checklist of films.

Historical account of the stag film.

1902   Dimmitt, Richard Bertrand. AN ACTOR GUIDE TO THE TALKIES: A

COMPREHENSIVE LISTING OF 8,000 FEATURE-LENGTH FILMS FROM JANUARY 1949 UNTIL DECEMBER 1964. 2 vols. Metuchen, N.J.: Scarecrow Press, 1967-68.

Arranged according to film titles, the guide identifies actors' roles in most American and European films. Covers some thirty thousand actors.

1903 _____. A TITLE GUIDE TO THE TALKIES: A COMPREHENSIVE LISTING OF 16,000 FEATURE-LENGTH FILMS FROM OCTOBER 1927 UNTIL DECEMBER 1963. 2 vols. Metuchen, N.J.: Scarecrow Press, 1965. 2,133 p.

Identifies title, author, and genre for the source of some sixteen thousand feature-length films.

1904 Douglas, Drake. HORROR! New York: Macmillan, 1966. 309 p. Illus., bibliog., filmography, index.

Informative study of the horror story and film, with chapters on the vampire, werewolf, monster, mummy, walking dead, schizophrenic, phantom, and creators of horrible beings.

1905 Dowdy, Andrew. MOVIES ARE BETTER THAN EVER: WIDE-SCREEN MEMORIES OF THE FIFTIES. New York: William Morrow and Co., 1973. 242 p. Illus., index.

Survey of themes, fetishes, and motifs in popular films of the decade. Chapters cover the decline of audiences, blacklisting, three-dimensional films, public fears in films, censorship, soft pornography, youthful rebellion, science fiction, stars, adaptations, and the college audience.

1906 Druxman, Michael B. ONE GOOD FILM DESERVES ANOTHER. Cranbury, N.J.: A.S. Barnes, 1977. 175 p. Illus., filmography.

Survey of movie remakes.

1907 Durgnat, Raymond. THE CRAZY MIRROR: HOLLYWOOD COMEDY AND THE AMERICAN IMAGE. New York: Horizon Press, 1970. 280 p. Illus., bibliog., index.

Analysis of film comedy in a roughly historical context, both as surface realism and social fantasy.

1908 _____. FILMS AND FEELINGS. London: Faber and Faber, 1967. 288 p. Illus., bibliog., motif index, index.

A classic study of the psychology of popular film, with chapters on elements of style, creativity, production and the star system, the aesthetics of human interest, and the visual collages of film art. Particularly useful are Durgnat's comments on expressionism, science fiction films, and the industry's exploitation of conventional character and form.

1909 Dyment, Alan R. THE LITERATURE OF THE FILM: A BIBLIOGRAPHICAL GUIDE TO THE FILM AS ART AND ENTERTAINMENT, 1936-1970. London: White Lion Publishers, 1975. 398 p. Index.

Annotated bibliographies arranged according to history, aesthetics, personalities, screenplays, technique, genres and types, film and society, the industry, general works, and miscellany.

1910 Eberwein, Robert T. A VIEWER'S GUIDE TO FILM THEORY AND CRITICISM. Metuchen, N.J.: Scarecrow, 1979. 235 p. Bibliog., index.

A survey and interpretation of the film criticism of Vachel Lindsay, Hugo Münsterberg, Lev Kuleshov, Sergei Eisenstein, Béla Balázs, Rudolf Arnheim, André Bazin, Siegfried Kracauer, James Agee, Robert Warshow, Pauline Kael, Stanley Kauffmann, Andrew Sarris, Molly Haskell, Marjorie Rosen, Joan Mellen, Noël Burch, Christian Metz, and Peter Wollen.

1911 Edelson, Edward. VISIONS OF TOMORROW: GREAT SCIENCE FICTION FROM THE MOVIES. Garden City, N.Y.: Doubleday, 1975. 117 p. Illus.

A light treatment of science fiction films through the PLANET OF THE APES and THE ANDROMEDA STRAIN, with a chapter on television science fiction.

1912 Edmonds, I.G. BIG U: UNIVERSAL IN THE SILENT DAYS. South Brunswick, N.J.: A.S. Barnes and Co., 1977. 162 p. Illus., index.

Brief, but valuable, introduction to the early days of Universal Studios.

1913 Emmens, Carol A. FAMOUS PEOPLE ON FILM. Metuchen, N.J.: Scarecrow Press, 1977. 355 p. Filmography, index.

An international filmography of nonfiction films keyed to historical figures.

1914 Enser, A.G.S. FILMED BOOKS AND PLAYS: A LIST OF BOOKS AND PLAYS FROM WHICH FILMS HAVE BEEN MADE, 1928-1974. New York: Academic Press, 1974. 218 p.

Alphabetical film title index with production company and date, cross-indexed with author's names and title changes.

1915   Erens, Patricia, ed. 'SEXUAL STRATAGEMS: THE WORLD OF WOMEN
        IN FILM. New York: Horizon Press, 1979. 336 p. Illus., directors,
        filmographies, bibliog.

> Divided into male- and female-directed cinema, the volume
> includes essays on images of women as portrayed in individual
> films and those of particular directors, and feminist critical
> perspectives.

1916   Ernst, Morris L., and Lorentz, Pare. CENSORED: THE PRIVATE LIFE
        OF THE MOVIE. New York: Jonathan Cape and Harrison Smith,
        1930. 199 p.

> A satirical examination of some of the kinds of censorship
> that was being carried on in the late twenties by various
> censoring boards across the country.

1917   Everson, William K. THE BAD GUYS: A PICTORIAL HISTORY OF
        THE MOVIE VILLAIN. New York: Citadel Press, 1964. 241 p.
        Illus., index.

> An informal account, with numerous stills, of early villains,
> Noah Beery, brutes, good badmen, master criminals, outlaws,
> foreigners, gangsters, cads, monsters, the enemy, swashbucklers,
> hooded killers, comics, social villains, civilized villains,
> psychos, mad doctors, and bad girls.

1918   _____. CLASSICS OF THE HORROR FILM. Secaucus, N.J.: Citadel
        Press, 1974. 247 p. Illus.

> Brief, heavily illustrated chapters on individual films and
> subgenres.

1919   _____. THE DETECTIVE IN FILM. Secaucus, N.J.: Citadel Press,
        1972. 247 p. Illus., index.

> Accounts of detective films from the silents through the late
> 1960s, heavily illustrated and often impressionistic, with
> chapters on major series and films.

1920   Eyles, Allen. THE WESTERN: AN ILLUSTRATED GUIDE. New York:
        A.S. Barnes, 1975. 207 p. Index to films and names.

> Career sketches and filmographies of 358 persons associated
> with Westerns.

1921   Fadiman, William. HOLLYWOOD NOW. New York: Liveright, 1972.
        174 p. Bibliog., index.

> An attempt to provide a guide to occupational roles in
> Hollywood with chapters on the industry, agent, director,
> star, writer, producer, and the future.

1922 Farber, Stephen. THE MOVIE RATING GAME. Washington, D.C.:
Public Affairs Press, 1972. 128 p. Bibliog., notes.

Drawing from his experiences as an intern on the rating panel
and his subsequent experiences, Farber argues that the system
is hypocritical and arbitrary in its present form. Appendixes
include a reprint of the Motion Picture Alliance code ob-
jectives, studio contract stipulations, a list of typical ob-
jections, a list of appealed films with judgments, Dr. Aaron
Stern's rating definitions, and an extract from the original
Motion Picture Production code.

1923 Farren, Jonathan. "Cinema Et Rock N'Roll." CINÉMA, no. 200,
July and August 1975, pp. 18-54.

A collection of interviews, analyses, and an extensive
chronological filmography from 1956 to 1975.

1924 Faulkner, Robert R. HOLLYWOOD STUDIO MUSICIANS: THEIR WORK
AND CAREERS IN THE RECORDING INDUSTRY. Chicago: Aldine-
Atherton, 1971. 218 p. Bibliog., notes, index.

A sociological investigation through interviews of the job
situation for Hollywood musicians. The author is able to
identify characteristic types of musicians, consider styles
of coping by musicians, and adapt methodologies for examining
this type of occupation.

1925 Fell, John L. FILM: AN INTRODUCTION. New York: Praeger,
1975. 274 p. Illus.

Pages 245-49 discuss comics in relation to film. Introduction attacks the JOURNAL OF POPULAR FILM (1972--), but
the last sentence of the book calls for more of the kind of
study found in JPF.

1926 Fenin, George N., and Everson, William K. THE WESTERN: FROM
SILENTS TO THE SEVENTIES. New and expanded ed. New York:
Grossman, 1973. 396 p. Illus., index.

A detailed history of the Western, with brief chapters on
major directors, performers, films, and themes.

1927 Fernett, Gene. POVERTY ROW. Satellite Beach, Fla.: Coral Reef
Publications, 1973. 163 p. Illus.

Informal history of budget independent films from 1930 to
1950.

1928 Fielding, Raymond. THE AMERICAN NEWSREEL, 1911-1967. Norman:

University of Oklahoma Press, 1972. 392 p. Illus., notes, bibliog., index.

> A standard history of the newsreel, its evolving technique, social impact, critical assessment, and demise.

1929 _____. THE MARCH OF TIME, 1935-1951. New York: Oxford University Press, 1978. 359 p. Bibliog., index, filmography.

> Excellent historical and technical study of the series through interviews, examinations of the films, and secondary sources.

1930 _____. THE TECHNIQUES OF SPECIAL EFFECTS PHOTOGRAPHY. New York: Focal Press, 1972. 425 p. Illus., index.

> This bible of special effects cinematography covers cameras and other equipment, glass-shots, mirror-shots, mattes, optical printing, arial-image printing, rear- and front-projection, and miniatures. Essential reading for anyone interested in making films or teaching film technology.

1931 FILM DAILY YEAR BOOK OF MOTION PICTURES. New York: Film Daily. 1927-- . Annual. Title varies.

> Valuable compilation of statistics, credits, people in film, and other matters, as well as brief review articles on the year's films.

1932 THE FILM INDEX: A BIBLIOGRAPHY. New York: Museum of Modern Art Film Library and H.W. Wilson Co., 1941. 723 p.

> Important early annotated source for articles in popular magazines and other periodicals.

1933 FILM LITERATURE INDEX: A QUARTERLY AUTHOR-SUBJECT INDEX TO THE INTERNATIONAL LITERATURE OF FILM. Albany, N.Y.: Filmdex, 1973-- .

> Indexes articles on film from about 240 periodicals according to titles, films, and subjects.

1934 "Film III: Film Morality and Media Criticism." JOURNAL OF AESTHETIC EDUCATION 8 (January 1974): special issue.

> Essays on Jean Renoir as moralist, Antonioni's BLOW-UP, Kubrick's DR. STRANGELOVE, themes in contemporary novels and films, social context and creativity in mass communications, teaching evaluation of mass media, and commentaries.

1935 Finch, Christopher, and Rosenkrantz, Linda. GONE HOLLYWOOD. Garden City, N.Y.: Doubleday, 1979. 396 p. Illus.

Overview of Hollywood's industry and social life through its
personalities. The authors avoid discussing films as well as
filmmakers, though they do cover the contributions of cinema-
tographers, make-up artists, and costume designers to the
image of Hollywood. Topical chapters that provide an overview of the star system and studio system, the authors talk
about the people in the business end of the industry.

1936 Fordin, Hugh. THE WORLD OF ENTERTAINMENT! HOLLYWOOD'S
GREATEST MUSICALS. Garden City, N.Y.: Doubleday, 1975. 566 p.

Behind-the-scenes stories of the nearly fifty Arthur Freed
musicals for MGM, with credits for the films.

1937 Fox, Stuart. JEWISH FILMS IN THE UNITED STATES: A COMPRE-
HENSIVE SURVEY AND DESCRIPTIVE FILMOGRAPHY. Boston: G.K.
Hall, 1976. 359 p. Index.

Annotated bibliography of features, Yiddish features, news-
reels, documentaries, U.S. Army stock, films related to
Israel television shows, and Israel-produced films.

1938 French, Philip. WESTERNS: ASPECTS OF A MOVIE GENRE. New
York: Viking Press, 1977. 208 p. Illus., bibliog., index.

Useful exploration of the relationship between the Western
and political and cultural values through analysis of the
genre's iconology and characterization.

1939 Friar, Ralph E., and Friar, Natasha A. THE ONLY GOOD INDIAN
. . . THE HOLLYWOOD GOSPEL. New York: Drama Book Specialists,
1972. 332 p. Illus., index.

An extensive critique of the depiction and use of native
Americans in films, though some treatment of the literary
and dramatic heritage is also included. Appendixes identify
actors who have played Indians, and provide a motif index
to films dealing with characteristic plots involving Indian
themes.

1940 Froug, William. THE SCREENWRITER LOOKS AT THE SCREENWRITER.
New York: Dell, 1974. 352 p. Credits.

Interviews with Lewis John Carlino, William Bowers, Walter
Brown Newman, Jonathon Axelrod, Ring Lardner, Jr., I.A.L.
Diamond, Buck Henry, David Giler, Nunnally Johnson,
Edward Anhalt, Stirling Silliphant, and Fay Kanin. Writers'
credits and brief excerpts from scripts.

1941   Fry, Ron, and Fourzon, Pamela. THE SAGA OF SPECIAL EFFECTS. Englewood Cliffs: Prentice-Hall, 1977. 212 p. Illus.

        History of special effects.

1942   Gabree, John. GANGSTERS: FROM LITTLE CAESAR TO THE GOD-FATHER. New York: Galahad Books, 1973. 156 p. Illus., filmography, index.

        A heavily illustrated account of the gangster film, focusing on biographical gangsters, the 1930s films, detective films, and the fifties and sixties.

1943   Geduld, Harry, ed. AUTHORS ON FILM. Bloomington: Indiana University Press, 1972. 303 p. Index.

        Authors' comments on films, arranged into sections on silent film, the medium, screenwriting, the Hollywood experience, and movie stars.

1944   _____. THE BIRTH OF THE TALKIES: FROM EDISON TO JOLSON. Bloomington: Indiana University Press, 1975. 337 p. Notes, index.

        The technical history of sound from 1877 to about 1930, with excerpts of critical opinions, a list of 1,929 sound features, and patent information.

1945   _____, ed. FILM MAKERS ON FILM MAKING: STATEMENTS ON THEIR ART BY THIRTY DIRECTORS. Bloomington: Indiana University Press, 1967. 302 p.

        Interviews collected from various sources, with the editor's introduction.

1946   Glut, Donald. CLASSIC MOVIE MONSTERS. Introduction by Curt Siodmak. Metuchen, N.J.: Scarecrow Press, 1978. 442 p. Index.

        Examination and assessments of films based on such figures as the Wolf Man, Mr. Hyde, the Invisible Man, mummies, Quasimodo, phantoms, creatures, King Kong, and Godzilla.

1947   Goldman, Michael. "Actors." COLUMBIA FORUM 4 (Spring 1975): 10–18.

        Discusses the actor as public character.

1948   Gottesman, Ronald, and Geduld, Harry M. GUIDEBOOK TO FILM: AN ELEVEN-IN-ONE REFERENCE. New York: Holt, Rinehart and Winston, 1972. 230 p. Bibliog.

        Partially annotated lists of books and articles on various

aspects of film study, with lists of theses and dissertations, museums and archives, schools, equipment, distributors, book-stores and publishers, organizations, festivals, awards, and a glossary.

1949 _____, eds. THE GIRL IN THE HAIRY PAW: KING KONG AS MYTH, MOVIE, AND MONSTER. New York: Avon, 1976. 233 p. Illus.

A collection of serious essays, comic pieces, and illustrations on KING KONG and subsequent films in the genre.

1950 Gow, Gordon. HOLLYWOOD IN THE FIFTIES. New York: A.S. Barnes, 1971. 208 p. Illus.

Informal survey of the themes, genres, and major films of the decade.

1951 _____. SUSPENSE IN THE CINEMA. New York: A.S. Barnes, 1968. 167 p. Bibliog., filmography.

A useful discussion of the motifs and themes of the suspense film, particularly the irony, isolation, phobia, occult, acci-dent, psychosis, and related matters.

1952 Grant, Barry K., ed. FILM GENRE: THEORY AND CRITICISM. Metuchen, N.J.: Scarecrow Press, 1977. 249 p. Bibliog., index.

A collection of essays devoted to theoretical and critical perspectives, and to individual genres including screwball comedy, disaster, epic, gangster, horror, musical, monster, sport, and Western.

1953 Greenberg, Harvey R., M.D. THE MOVIES ON YOUR MIND. New York: Saturday Review Press, E.P. Dutton and Co., 1975. 273 p. Bibliog., index.

Psychological interpretations of THE WIZARD OF OX, THE TREASURE OF THE SIERRA MADRE, THE MALTESE FALCON, CASABLANCA, PSYCHO, 8-1/2, WILD STRAWBERRIES, and horror and science fiction films.

1954 Halas, John, and Manvell, Roger. THE TECHNIQUE OF FILM ANI-MATION. 4th ed. New York: Focal Press, 1976. 351 p. Illus., index, bibliog.

The most complete book available on animation techniques, written for practicing animators and advanced students. The volume covers all standard aspects of animation from concep-tion through specialized forms, with speculation on future development. An appendix contains opinions about the future of animation, mathematics, measurement tables, a list of films cited, a glossary, and a selected list of books.

1955   Halliwell, Leslie. THE FILMGOER'S COMPANION. 6th ed. New York: Hill and Wang, 1977. 825 p. Illus., checklist.

Each edition of this popular encyclopedia of film becomes more useful as a general reference. Entries on films, personalities and subjects are informal. Credit entries usually contain brief filmographies and there are some genre and theme entries. The entries are largely for English language material and people, and technical entries are sparse.

1956   Hanet, Kari. "Cinema Semiotics in English." SCREEN 16 (Autumn 1975): 125-28.

Introduction and bibliography of "the most important works" on visual imagery.

1957   Harmon, Jim, and Glut, Donald F. THE GREAT MOVIE SERIALS: THEIR SOUND AND FURY. Garden City, N.Y.: Doubleday, 1972. 384 p. Illus., index.

Informal history of the serials, with chapters on such genres as melodrama, science fiction, juveniles, biographical adventures, jungle stories, aviators, detectives, superheroes, Westerns, classics, and villains.

1958   Haskell, Molly. FROM REVERENCE TO RAPE: THE TREATMENT OF WOMEN IN THE MOVIES. New York: Holt, Rinehart and Winston, 1974. 388 p. Illus., index.

A feminist perspective on the female stereotypes and plot conventions that have reinforced male prejudices from the 1920s through the 1960s.

1959   Heath, Stephen. "Film and System: Terms of Analysis, Part I." SCREEN 16 (Spring 1975): 7-77.

Together with Part II (SCREEN 16 [Summer 1975]: 91-113), this is an ambitious attempt to analyze the text of A TOUCH OF EVIL in structural terms.

1960   Heinzkill, Richard. FILM CRITICISM: AN INDEX TO CRITICS' ANTHOLOGIES. Metuchen, N.J.: Scarecrow Press, 1975. 151 p. Index.

Index to forty-one critical anthologies by Renata Adler, James Agate, James Agee, Hollis Alpert, John Mason Brown, Judith Crist, Raymond Durgnat, Manny Farber, Otis Ferguson,

Penelope Gilliatt, Graham Greene, Pauline Kael, Stanley
Kauffmann, Caroline Lejeune, Dwight Macdonald, William
Pechter, Rex Reed, Andrew Sarris, Richard Schickel, Wilfred
Sheed, John Simon, Susan Sontag, Mark Van Doren, Robert
Warshow, Herman Weinberg, Richard Winnington, and Vernon
Young--through 1973. Arranged by film title with references
to critical works.

1961   Henderson, Brian. A CRITIQUE OF FILM THEORY. New York: E.P.
Dutton, 1980. 233 p. Notes.

A collection of essays, first published by the author in
FILM QUARTERLY, on traditional film theory and on film
semiotics and cine-structuralism.

1962   Heraldson, Donald. CREATORS OF LIFE: A HISTORY OF ANIMATION.
New York: Drake, 1975. 298 p. Illus., bibliog.

Informal introduction to the history, technical development,
and major contributors to animation. An appendix contains
how-to suggestions, lists Academy Awards, provides a brief
bibliography, and a list of suppliers.

1963   Higham, Charles, and Greenberg, Joel. HOLLYWOOD IN THE
FORTIES. New York: A.S. Barnes, 1968. 192 p. Illus.

Informal survey of the themes, trends, and major films of
the decade.

1964   Hochman, Stanley, comp. AMERICAN FILM DIRECTORS, WITH FILMOG-
RAPHIES AND INDEX OF CRITICS AND FILMS. New York: Ungar,
1974. 590 p.

Compilation of excerpts from reviews and commentary on the
work of sixty-five American directors, with filmographies and
an index to critics and films.

1965   Hunnings, Neville March. FILM CENSORS AND THE LAW. London:
George Allen and Unwin, 1967. 474 p. Bibliog., index, tables,
appendixes.

A comparative analysis of the practices of censors in England,
United States, India, Canada, Australia, Denmark, France,
Soviet Russia.

1966   Huss, Roy, and Ross, T.J., eds. FOCUS ON THE HORROR FILM.
Englewood Cliffs, N.J.: Prentice-Hall, 1972. 186 p. Filmography,
chronology, bibliog., index.

Twenty-five essays divided into "The Horror Domain"--to

provide an overview; "Gothic Horror"--FRANKENSTEIN and DRACULA; "Monster Terror"--KING KONG, BEAUTY AND THE BEAST, and others; and "Psychological Thriller"--various suspense and terror films.

1967   Huston, John. JOHN HUSTON: AN OPEN BOOK. New York: Alfred A. Knopf, 1980. 389 p. Illus., index.

        Recollections.

1968   INDEX TO CRITICAL FILM REVIEWS IN BRITISH AND AMERICAN FILM PERIODICALS, TOGETHER WITH INDEX TO CRITICAL REVIEWS OF BOOKS ABOUT FILM. 2 vols. Compiled and edited by Stephen E. Bowles. New York: Burt Franklin and Co., 1974.

        Indexes thirty-one film journals.

1969   INTERNATIONAL INDEX TO FILM PERIODICALS. Edited by Karen Jones, 1972-74; Frances Thorpe, 1975-- . New York: R.R. Bowker 1972-73; St. Martin's 1974-- . Annual.

        Annotated index of about ninety major film journals according to eleven subject categories, with subject, director, and author indexes.

1970   Jacobs, Lewis. THE MOVIES AS MEDIUM. New York: Octogon Books, 1970. 335 p. Illus., bibliog., index.

        Strong collection of essays on the effects of the physical properties of films and their manifestation through imagery. Divided into sections on image, movement, time and space, color and sound; with short chapters on directors' comments, film expression, and the "plastic structure." This has been an influential volume.

1971   _____ . THE RISE OF THE AMERICAN FILM, A CRITICAL HISTORY: WITH AN ESSAY: EXPERIMENTAL CINEMA IN AMERICA, 1921-1947. New York: Teachers College Press, 1968. 631 p. Illus., bibliog., index.

        A standard history of film in the United States through 1939, with chapters on Porter, Griffith, Chaplin, and other directors; chapters on business, story development, and themes.

1972   _____ , ed. THE DOCUMENTARY TRADITION: FROM NANOOK TO WOODSTOCK. New York: Hopkinson and Blake, 1971. 530 p. Illus., filmography, bibliog., index.

        Collection of essays focusing on key filmmakers and films from 1922 to 1970, with pieces on themes and trends during each decade.

1973   Jarvie, I.C. MOVIES AND SOCIETY. British title: TOWARDS A SOCIOLOGY OF THE CINEMA. New York: Basic Books, 1970. 394 p. Bibliog., index.

        Probably the best sociological study available. The volume contains a brief history, analysis of the audience, the experience of film genres (including Westerns, gangster films, spy films, and the musical), and the sociology of evaluation.

1974   _____. MOVIES AS SOCIAL CRITICISM: ASPECTS OF THEIR SOCIAL PSYCHOLOGY. Metuchen, N.J.: Scarecrow Press, 1978. 207 p. Bibliog., index.

        Analysis of film as an expression of collective behavior, with chapters on films about marriages and images of blacks in films.

1975   Johnson, William, ed. FOCUS ON THE SCIENCE FICTION FILM. Englewood Cliffs, N.J.: Prentice-Hall, 1972. 182 p. Filmography, illus., bibliog., index.

        Essays on science fiction films covering the beginnings to the present, with several essays on the issues, together with brief responses by several authors and filmmakers to questions about adaptations and production.

1976   Jowett, Garth. FILM: THE DEMOCRATIC ART. Boston: Little, Brown and Co., 1976. 518 p. Notes, tables, bibliog., index.

        The most useful general study of the social history of "moviegoing" available, if the most important consideration is the problem of control over the content of film. Written for social historians and others, the volume touches on most issues of film and society. Chapters cover early issues of film and society, early history, development of the industry, attempts to control and censor films and filmmakers, the war years, the impact of television, the Hollywood image, declining control, and contemporary issues. Appendixes document industry policies and audience characteristics.

1977   Kagan, Norman. THE WAR FILM: AN ILLUSTRATED HISTORY OF THE MOVIES. New York: Pyramid, 1974. 160 p. Illus., bibliog., filmography, index.

        A history of the genre which focuses on early efforts, films of the wars through the Vietnam War, comedy, antiwar films, and a mixture of related films.

1978   Kaminsky, Stuart M. AMERICAN FILM GENRES: APPROACHES TO A CRITICAL THEORY OF POPULAR FILM. Dayton, Ohio: Pflaum Publishing, 1974. 232 p. Filmographies, index.

Useful collection of essays on film genres and methodologies. The author approaches each genre with a different methodology in order to demonstrate critical perspectives. Included are an analysis of LITTLE CEASAR within the gangster genre, a comparison of the Samurai and Western genres, the adaptation of Hemingway's "The Killers," the theme of violence in the 1970s, various examples of the big caper film, the psychology of horror and science fiction, the musical as performance historical development and individual expression in comedy, Don Siegel as a genre director, and John Ford's use of character types.

1979 Kantor, Bernard R., ed. DIRECTORS AT WORK: INTERVIEWS WITH AMERICAN FILM MAKERS. New York: Funk and Wagnalls, 1970. 442 p. Film lists.

Interviews with Richard Brooks, George Cukor, Norman Jewison, Elia Kazan, Stanley Kramer, Richard Lester, Jerry Lewis, Elliot Silverstein, Robert Wise, and William Wyler.

1980 Karimi, A.M. TOWARD A DEFINITION OF THE AMERICAN FILM NOIR (1941-1949). New York: Arno Press, 1976. 255 p. Bibliog.

Includes a working definition, sources, pre- and postwar expression, and issues for further studies. The volume contains films listed according to directors, with an alphabetical list of films and review data. Based on a 1973 University of Iowa dissertation.

1981 Karpf, Stephen Louis. THE GANGSTER FILM: EMERGENCE, VARIATION, AND DECAY OF A GENRE, 1930-1940. New York: Arno Press, 1973. 299 p.

A detailed examination of the film of the period, with critical apparatus.

1982 Katz, Ephraim. THE FILM ENCYCLOPEDIA. New York: Thomas Y. Crowell, 1979. 1266 p.

More than seven thousand entries in alphabetical order on artistic, technical, and commercial aspects of American, British, and international film.

1983 Katz, John Stuart, ed. PERSPECTIVES ON THE STUDY OF FILM. Boston: Little, Brown and Co., 1971. 339 p. Bibliog., index.

Collection of essays by a wide range of contributors reprinted for the volume, arranged into sections on film study and education, the film as art and humanistic work, film as communications, environment and politics, and curriculum design.

1984 Kauffmann, Stanley, ed. AMERICAN FILM CRITICISM FROM THE BE-
GINNINGS TO CITIZEN KANE: REVIEWS OF SIGNIFICANT FILMS
AT THE TIME THEY FIRST APPEARED. New York: Liveright, 1972.
443 p. Notes, bibliog., index.

Brief pieces representing the newspaper and magazine reviews
and criticism of early short films, features, and sound films.

1985 Kay, Karyn, and Peary, Gerald, eds. WOMEN AND THE CINEMA:
A CRITICAL ANTHOLOGY. New York: Dutton, 1977. 464 p. Filmographies, index, bibliog.

Strong collection of essays divided into sections on feminist
perspectives, actresses, women in production, innovators,
political films, polemics, and feminist film theory.

1986 Kitses, Jim. HORIZONS WEST. Bloomington: Indiana University
Press, 1970. 176 p. Filmographies.

Illustrated essays on the Westerns of Anthony Mann, Budd
Boettcher, and Sam Peckinpah.

1987 Kolker, Robert Phillip. A CINEMA OF LONELINESS: PENN, KUBRICK,
COPPOLA, SCORSESE, ALTMAN. New York: Oxford, 1980. 395 p.
Illus., notes, filmography, index.

Discussions of the ways in which these filmmakers achieve
the independence of their art within the constrictions provided by the Hollywood system.

1988 Koszarski, Richard, ed. HOLLYWOOD DIRECTORS 1941-1976. New
York: Oxford University Press, 1977. 426 p. Index.

Collection of fifty previously printed essays by directors,
arranged in the order of the appearance of each director's
initial essay.

1989 Kowalski, Rosemary Ribich. WOMEN AND FILM: A BIBLIOGRAPHY.
Metuchen, N.J.: Scarecrow Press, 1976. 278 p. Index.

Divided into four major sections on women as performers, as
filmmakers, as columnists and critics, and images of women,
each section lists reference and historical works, catalogs
and "specific" works. The subject index is detailed.

1990 Krafsur, Richard, et al., eds. THE AMERICAN FILM INSTITUTE
CATALOGUE: FEATURE FILMS, 1961-1970. 2 vols. Washington, D.C.:
American Film Institute, 1976.

Volume 1 lists by title over 5,800 films exhibited in the
United States. Date includes country of origin, production

and distribution companies, date, and place of release,
length, Motion Picture Association of America rating; credits
for production, cast, and technical contributions; genre,
source material, plot synopsis, and subject classifications.
Volume 2 includes an index to credits, with credit biographies, an extensive subject index, literary and dramatic
source index, national production index listed by country.
Other volumes in this series cover shorts, nonfiction films,
and feature films throughout the history of American film.

1991   Lahue, Kalton C. CONTINUED NEXT WEEK: A HISTORY OF THE
MOVING PICTURE SERIAL. Norman: University of Oklahoma Press,
1964. 293 p. Illus.

History of the silent serial from 1914 to 1930. The appendix
lists serials from 1912 to 1930 and includes credits and chapter titles.

1992   _____. GENTLEMEN TO THE RESCUE: THE HEROES OF THE SILENT
SCREEN. South Brunswick, N.J.: A.S. Barnes, 1972. 244 p. Illus.

Brief illustrated career biographies of some thirty silent stars.

1993   _____. RIDERS OF THE RANGE: THE SAGEBRUSH HEROES OF THE
SOUND SCREEN. South Brunswick, N.J.: A.S. Barnes, 1973. 259 p.
Illus.

Accounts of Western performers, about twenty-eight in all.

1994   _____. WORLD OF LAUGHTER: THE MOTION PICTURE COMEDY
SHORT, 1910-1930. Norman: University of Oklahoma Press, 1966.
240 p. Illus., filmography, index.

Accounts of the short comedy films by major companies and
comedians.

1995   Lahue, Kalton C., and Gill, Samuel. CLOWN PRINCES AND COURT
JESTERS. South Brunswick, N.J.: A.S. Barnes, 1970. 406 p. Illus.

Biographies of several pages of fifty comics and comedy teams
appearing in films about 1915 to the late twenties.

1996   Lamb, Blaine P. "The Convenient Villain: The Early Cinema Views
the Mexican-American." JOURNAL OF THE WEST 14 (October 1975):
75-81.

Documented study of the stereotypes developed in American
film before World War I.

1997   Lee, Rohama, ed. THE FILM NEWS OMNIBUS OF FILM REVIEWS. New
York: Film News, 1939-- . Annual.

Reviews of fiction and nonfiction films, together with distribution data and awards. Subject index.

1998 Lee, Walt, and Warren, Bill, eds. REFERENCE GUIDE TO FANTASTIC
FILMS, SCIENCE FICTION, FANTASY AND HORROR. 3 vols. Los
Angeles: Chelsea Press, 1973. 691 p. Illus.

The most comprehensive filmography available for science
fiction, fantasy, and horror films.

1999 Levin, G. Roy. DOCUMENTARY EXPLORATIONS: FIFTEEN INTER-
VIEWS WITH FILMMAKERS. Garden City, N.Y.: Anchor Press, 1971.
420 p. Bibliog., index, illus.

Brief history of the documentary is followed by interviews
with Wright, Anderson, Cawston, Garnett, and Loach in
Britain; Franju and Rouch in France; Storck in Belgium; Van
Dyke, Leacock, Pennebaker, the Maysles, Barron, Wiseman,
Pincus, Shamberg, and Cort in the United States.

2000 Leyda, Jay. FILMS BEGET FILMS. New York: Hill and Wang, 1964.
176 p. Bibliog.

A history and interpretation of compilation films.

2001 _____, ed. VOICES OF FILM EXPERIENCE: 1894 TO THE PRESENT.
New York: Macmillan, 1977. 544 p. Index.

An alphabetically arranged pastiche of quotes by numerous
film personalities on their experiences.

2002 Limbacher, James L., comp. and ed. FILM MUSIC: FROM VIOLINS
TO VIDEO. Metuchen, N.J.: Scarecrow Press, 1974. 835 p. Index.

Divided into two parts, the first includes brief articles by
artists and others collected into sections on the early days,
theories and commentaries, techniques, scoring dramatic
films, film spectacles; arranging classical music for film,
and scoring animated films and comedies. The second part
amounts to a film list with dates; a chronology of films with
production company and composer(s); a composer checklist;
a discography.

2003 Lovell, Alan, and Hillier, Jim. STUDIES IN DOCUMENTARY. New
York: Viking, 1972. 176 p. Illus., filmographies, bibliog., sketches,
bibliog.

Studies of the films of John Grierson and Humphrey Jennings,
with notes on associated documentary filmmakers.

2004 Luhr, William, and Lehman, Peter. AUTHORSHIP AND NARRATIVE IN THE CINEMA: ISSUES IN CONTEMPORARY AESTHETICS AND CRITICISM. New York: Capricorn Books, G.P. Putnam's Sons, 1977. 320 p. Index, filmography.

Based on the authors' dissertations, this volume provides an analysis of the Westerns of John Ford (with emphasis on THE MAN WHO SHOT LIBERTY VALANCE and THE SEARCHERS) and the narrative heritage of film (with emphasis on THE STRANGE CASE OF DR. JEKYLL AND MR. HYDE).

2005 McArthur, Colin. UNDERWORLD USA. New York: Viking, 1972. 176 p. Illus., index.

An analysis of the gangster film and thriller from the early 1930s to about 1970. Chapters treat iconography, historical development, background, and individual directors, including Fritz Lang, John Huston, Jules Dassin, Robert Siodmak, Elia Kazin, Nicholas Ray, Samuel Fuller, Don Siegel, and Jean-Pierre Melville.

2006 MacBean, James Roy. FILM AND REVOLUTION. Bloomington: Indiana University Press, 1975. 339 p. Illus., notes, index.

An exposition of a Marxist theory of film based on the films of Jean-Luc Godard and Jean-Pierre Gorin, with a critique of post-Bazin criticism and the semiology of Christian Metz.

2007 McCaffrey, Donald W. THE GOLDEN AGE OF SOUND COMEDY: COMIC FILMS AND COMEDIANS OF THE THIRTIES. South Brunswick, N.J.: A.S. Barnes, 1973. 208 p. Illus., bibliog., index.

Informal account of the high points of comedy, illustrated with numerous stills.

2007a _____. THREE CLASSIC SILENT SCREEN COMEDIES STARRING HAROLD LLOYD. Rutherford, N.J.: Fairleigh Dickinson University Press, 1976. 264 p. Illus., bibliog., filmography, index.

Based on critical analysis and interviews with Lloyd, the author discusses GRANDMA'S BOY, SAFETY LAST, and THE FRESHMAN.

2008 MacCann, Richard Dyer. THE PEOPLE'S FILMS: A POLITICAL HISTORY OF U.S. GOVERNMENT MOTION PICTURES. New York: Hastings House, 1973. 238 p. Illus.

Chapters in the volume discuss documentary with regards to the needs of a democracy, U.S. government films, Pare Lorentz, the U.S. Film Service, films produced by the Office of War Information and the U.S. Armed Forces during World War II, films of the United States Information Agency, television programs originating with Congress and the White

House, and credibility in official documentaries.

2009   MacCann, Richard Dyer, and Perry, Edward S.   THE NEW FILM INDEX:
A BIBLIOGRAPHY OF MAGAZINE ARTICLES IN ENGLISH, 1930–1970.
New York: E.P. Dutton and Co., 1975. 522 p. Illus.

Follows the format of THE FILM INDEX (see no. 1932), with
subject categories and brief annotations for entries.

2010   McCarthy, Todd, and Flynn, Charles, eds.   KINGS OF THE BS:
WORKING WITHIN THE HOLLYWOOD SYSTEM: AN ANTHOLOGY
OF FILM HISTORY AND CRITICISM. New York: E.P. Dutton and
Co., 1975. 561 p. Illus.

Divided into four major sections and an extensive filmography,
this is the most useful collection of essays available on minor
films and directors. Contents include essays on attitudes
toward B films, various directors, films, film genres and
themes; interviews with major minor figures; and filmographies
of several hundred lesser known directors.

2011   McCarty, Clifford.   PUBLISHED SCREENPLAYS: A CHECKLIST. Kent,
Ohio: Kent State University Press, 1971. 127 p. Index.

Identifies the book and periodical sources for complete and
excerpted screenplays for 388 films.

2012   McConnell, Frank D.   THE SPOKEN SEEN: FILM AND THE ROMANTIC
IMAGINATION. Baltimore, Md.: Johns Hopkins University Press, 1975.
195 p. Index.

A significant contribution to the dialog on the nature of the
film experience, through a discussion of film forms, and the
basic "isomorphism between postromantic writing and film."
Chapters on film reality, language, politics of the medium,
genres, and film personas.

2013   Madsen, Axel.   THE NEW HOLLYWOOD: AMERICAN MOVIES IN
THE '70S. New York: Crowell, 1975. 183 p. Index.

Impressionistic view of contemporary film production, stars,
directors, publicity, with chapters on Peter Bogdanovich and
Francis Ford Coppola.

2014   Maltin, Leonard.   THE DISNEY FILMS. New York: Crown, 1973.
312 p. Illus., filmographies, index.

Accounts of the Disney films, with stills and credits.

2015   _____ .   OF MICE AND MAGIC: A HISTORY OF AMERICAN ANI-
MATED CARTOONS. New York: McGraw-Hill, 1980. 470 p.
Filmographies, glossary, purchase and rental sources, illus., index.

After a brief chapter on the silent era, Maltin traces the studio history of Walt Disney, Max Fleischer, Paul Terry and Terrytoons, Walter Lantz, Ub Iwerks, the Van Beuren Studio, Columbia, Warner Brothers, MGM, Paramount, Famous, and UPA.

2016   Mamber, Stephen. CINEMA VERITÉ IN AMERICA: STUDIES IN UN-CONTROLLED DOCUMENTARY. Cambridge: MIT Press, 1974. Filmographies, rental sources, course schedule, bibliog., index.

Essays on definition, style, and filmmakers which are oriented to classroom use. Included is material on Drew Associates, the Maysles Brothers, D.A. Pennebaker, Richard Leacock, and Frederick Wiseman.

2017   Manchel, Frank. AN ALBUM OF GREAT SCIENCE FICTION FILMS. New York: F. Watts, 1976. 96 p. Illus., bibliog., index.

A light, heavily illustrated history of the genre.

2018   _____. FILM STUDY: A RESOURCE GUIDE. Rutherford, N.J.: Fairleigh Dickinson University Press, 1973. 422 p. Indexes.

The most competent general guide. Contains eight sections of references identifying book and periodical items on film literature. Annotated filmographies and bibliographies for genres--war (exhaustive), gangster, musical, horror, science fiction, Western; stereotyping; themes--the self, conflict with society, family, adult roles, moral and philosophical aspects; literature and dramatic comparisons; the historical period, 1913-1919; film history; and a brief section of film study. Six appendixes: (1) critics and periodicals; (2) film distributors; (3) a list of cautions; (4) Motion Picture Code and Rating Program; (5) further sources: archives, libraries, bookstores, and sources for stills; and (6) selected dissertations.

2019   _____. YESTERDAY'S CLOWNS. New York: Franklin Watts, 1973. 154 p. Illus., bibliog., index.

After an introduction to early comedy, Manchel discusses the careers and films of Max Linder, Mack Sennett, Charles Chaplin, Buster Keaton, Harold Lloyd, and Harry Langdon.

2020   Manvell, Roger. THE ANIMATED FILM. London: Sylvan Press, 1954. 63 p. Illus.

A brief history of the development of animation techniques with illustrations drawn from ANIMAL FARM (1945).

2021   _____. FILMS AND THE SECOND WORLD WAR. South Brunswick, N.J.: A.S. Barnes, 1974. 388 p. Illus., bibliog.

An international survey of the films of the period.

2022 _____. THEATER AND FILM: A COMPARATIVE STUDY OF THE TWO FORMS OF DRAMATIC ART, AND OF THE PROBLEMS OF ADAPTATION OF STAGE PLAYS INTO FILMS. Rutherford, N.J.: Fairleigh Dickinson University Press, 1979. 303 p. Bibliog., index, lists of productions on film.

> Discussion of principles, practice, and distinctions between the media; with treatment of adaptations of fourteen plays.

2023 Manvell, Roger, and Jacobs, Lewis, eds. INTERNATIONAL ENCYCLO-PEDIA OF FILM. New York: Crown, 1972. 574 p. Illus., bibliog., index.

> More comprehensive than Cawkwell and Smith (see no. 1884), the volume includes a brief history, a chapter on color cinema-tography, and a chronological list of major films. The encyclo-pedia covers an extensive range of subjects in some depth. Checklist of title changes keyed to country of origin.

2024 Mapp, Edward. BLACKS IN AMERICAN FILMS: TODAY AND YESTER-DAY. Metuchen, N.J.: Scarecrow Press, 1971. 278 p. Illus., bibliog.

> History of the portrayal of blacks in film. Stills.

2025 Marcorelles, Louis. LIVING CINEMA: NEW DIRECTIONS IN CON-TEMPORARY FILM-MAKING. New York: Praeger, 1973. 155 p. Illus.

> Published by UNESCO in 1970, the volume provides a dis-missal of structural approaches to the cinema and an advoca-tion of the perceptions available through the direct cinema and concrete cinema of experimental filmmakers, with chap-ters on technique, aesthetics, styles, and individual film-makers.

2026 Maremaa, Thomas. "The Sound of Movie Music." NEW YORK TIMES MAGAZINE, 28 March 1976, 40 ff.

> Discusses the changes in contemporary film music with em-phasis on the compositions of John Williams.

2027 Mast, Gerald. FILM/CINEMA/MOVIE: A THEORY OF EXPERIENCE. New York: Harper and Row, 1977. 299 p. Illus., bibliog., index, notes.

> An eclectic theory of film that explores meaning in art, the effects of successive images, image classification, sound, and related matters.

2028 _____. A SHORT HISTORY OF THE MOVIES. New York: Pegasus, 1971. 463 p. Illus., bibliog., index.

A survey, with chapters on D.W. Griffith, Mack Sennett and Charles Chaplin, studio magnates, stars, the studio years, and development in world cinema.

2029 Mast, Gerald, and Cohen, Marshall. FILM THEORY AND CRITICISM: INTRODUCTORY READINGS. 2d ed. New York: Oxford University Press, 1979. 877 p. Illus., bibliog.

Selections from the work of about forty critics and scholars on reality and film, image and language, the medium, film and the other arts, genres, auteurs, and the audience.

2030 Mathis, Jack. VALLEY OF THE CLIFFHANGERS. Northbrook, Ill.: Jack Mathis Advertising, 1975. 448 p. Illus., index, credits.

An immaculately presented folio volume tribute to sixty-six Republic serials, with emphasis on production.

2031 May, Larry. SCREENING OUT THE PAST: THE BIRTH OF MASS CULTURE AND THE MOTION PICTURE INDUSTRY. New York: Oxford University, 1980. 304 p. Illus., appendixes, notes, index.

A social history of the American entertainment industry, with chapters on Victorian amusements, the decline of progress, urban progressivism and leisure, D.W. Griffith's aesthetics, the emergence of the star system from 1914 to 1918, the evolution of the theater palace from 1908 to 1929, Hollywood from 1914 to 1920, Cecil B. DeMille and the Consumer Ideal from 1918 to 1929, and a thoughtful epilogue on the relationship of movies to cultural change.

2032 Mayer, J.P. SOCIOLOGY OF FILM: STUDIES AND DOCUMENTS. London: Faber and Faber, 1946. 328 p. Illus., bibliog.

Interpretation of film's impact on children and adults, with testimonials from people on how films have affected them.

2033 MEDIA REVIEW DIGEST. Ann Arbor, Mich.: Pierian Press, 1970-- . Annual.

Indexes 167 periodicals; cites reviews of feature films, educational films, video tapes, filmstrips, records, audio tapes, and related materials. Also cites awards and prizes, book reviews, and mediagraphies dealing with film. Indexed according to alphabetical listing, classification and subject indicators, with LC headings and Dewey decimal numbers. Where applicable, information includes title, producer-distributor, release date, milimeter, number of frames, running time, sound and visual characteristics, summary, cataloging information, grade level, quality rating code, review source, excerpts, price.

2034 Mellen, Joan. BIG BAD WOLVES: MASCULINITY IN THE AMERICAN
FILM. New York: Pantheon Books, 1977. 365 p. Index.

Breezy psychohistorical survey of the image of masculinity
in American films.

2035 _____. WOMEN AND THEIR SEXUALITY IN THE NEW FILM. New
York: Horizon Press, 1973. 255 p. Illus.

Analysis of the bourgeois woman, lesbianism, Bergman and
women, sexual politics, Bertolucci's LAST TANGO IN PARIS,
the moral psychology of Rohmer's Fu Manchu stories, Mae
West, and other topics.

2036 Merritt, R.L. "The Bashful Hero in American Films of the Nineteen
Forties." QUARTERLY JOURNAL OF SPEECH 61 (April 1975): 129-39.

An interesting perspective on the characteristic hero represented by Bing Crosby, James Stewart, and others in the
romantic comedies and light social dramas of the period.

2037 Michael, Paul. THE AMERICAN MOVIES REFERENCE BOOK: THE
SOUND ERA. Englewood Cliffs, N.J.: Prentice-Hall, 1969. 629 p.
Bibliog., name index.

Chapter 1 is a brief history of the film through filmographic
histories of genres and other topics, while chapters 2 through
5 cover credits for players, films, directors, and producers;
chapter 6 lists awards.

2038 Miller, Don. B MOVIES: AN INFORMAL SURVEY OF THE AMERICAN
LOW-BUDGET FILM, 1933-1945. New York: Curtis Books, 1973.
350 p. Illus.

A useful background survey of the low-budget production
companies that flourished briefly before the Second World
War.

2039 Monaco, James. HOW TO READ A FILM: THE ART, TECHNOLOGY,
LANGUAGE, HISTORY, AND THEORY OF FILM AND MEDIA. New
York: Oxford, 1977. 502 p. Illus., bibliog., index.

A primer on film as art, technology, language and medium,
with sections on film history, theory, and other media. The
section on film language emphasizes semiotics, the history
section treats economics, social and psychological aspects,
and esthetics; a number of critics and theorists are surveyed,
including Lindsay, Münsterberg, Arnheim, Kracauer, Pudovkin,
Eisenstein, Balázs, Bazin, Godard, and Metz. Also noted are
print, electronic media, radio, records, and television.

2040   Monaco, Paul. CINEMA AND SOCIETY: FRANCE AND GERMANY
        DURING THE TWENTIES. New York: Elsevier, 1976. 174 p.
        Bibliog., index.

> A valuable analysis of the relationships between popular
> films and society through the analogy of films and dreams.
> This Freudian approach is used to analyze the motifs with
> respect to the historical milieu.

2041   Morella, Joe; Epstein, Edward Z.; Griggs, John. THE FILMS OF
        WORLD WAR II. Secaucus, N.J.: Citadel Press, 1973. 254 p. Illus.

> Brief introduction and afterword, frame credits, stills, and
> critical excerpts of some one hundred films with war themes
> produced from 1937 to 1946.

2042   Morin, Edgar. THE STARS. Translated by Richard Howard. Evergreen
        Profile Book, no. 7. New York: Grove Press, 1960. 191 p. Illus.,
        chronology.

> This is still the best general study of the emergence of the
> Hollywood stars, their cultural influence, and the relation-
> ship between stars and fans. Eight chapters cover Genesis,
> gods and goddesses, liturgy, Chaplin and James Dean, mer-
> chandising, performance, and audiences' relationships to stars.

2043   Morrow, James, and Suid, Murray. MOVIEMAKING ILLUSTRATED:
        THE COMIC-BOOK FILMBOOK. Rochelle Park, N.J.: Hayden Book
        Co., 1973. 150 p. Illus.

> A demonstration of film techniques through the use of comic
> imagery, this volume is designed for beginning filmmakers
> but is useful for demonstrating basic similarities between the
> two media.

2044   MOVIES FOR TV; 7393 RATINGS: THE RESULTS OF CONSUMER RE-
        PORTS CONTINUING MOVIE POLL, APRIL 1947-JANUARY 1974
        COVERING MORE THAN 5600 FILMS. Mount Vernon, N.Y.: Con-
        sumers Union, 1974. 60 p.

> Lists title, release date, and star(s), with Consumer Union
> and CONSUMER REPORTS reader quality ratings.

2045   Murray, Edward. THE CINEMATIC IMAGINATION: WRITERS AND
        THE MOTION PICTURES. New York: Frederick Ungar, 1972. 330 p.
        Notes, index.

> Divided into dramatists and novelists in relation to film,
> the volume includes essays on dramatists' and writers' dis-
> tinctions between drama, fiction and film, with comments

on innovations in drama and fiction resulting from film and related matters.

2046 _____. NINE AMERICAN FILM CRITICS: A STUDY OF THEORY AND PRACTICE. New York: Ungar, 1975. 248 p. Index.

Interpretative essays on James Agee, Robert Warshow, Andrew Sarris, Parker Tyler, John Simon, Pauline Kael, Stanley Kauffmann, Vernon Young, and Dwight Macdonald. Appendix includes brief responses by directors on critics.

2047 Nachbar, Jack [John G.], comp. FOCUS ON THE WESTERN Englewood Cliffs, N.J.: Prentice-Hall, 1974. 150 p. Chronology, bibliog., index.

Fourteen key essays on the origins, definition, cultural interpretation, and present state of the genre.

2048 _____. WESTERN FILMS: AN ANNOTATED CRITICAL BIBLIOGRAPHY. New York: Garland Publishing Co., 1975. 98 p. Index.

An extensively annotated bibliography of sources, divided into sections on reference materials, pre-1950 criticism, specific films, performers, directors, history, theory, audience, comparative studies, teaching, and selected periodicals.

2049 Naha, Ed. HORRORS FROM SCREEN TO SCREAM: AN ENCYCLOPEDIC GUIDE TO THE GREATEST HORROR AND FANTASY FILMS OF ALL TIME. New York: Avon, 1975. 306 p. Illus.

A fan's annotated list of horror films, personalities, and production companies. Film entries provide name of production company and year of release, followed by a synopsis. Personality items include birth and death dates with a brief biographical sketch.

2050 THE NATIONAL SOCIETY OF FILM CRITICS ON MOVIE COMEDY. Edited by Stuart Byron and Elisabeth Weis. New York: Grossman Publications, 1977. 308 p. Index.

Broad collection of excerpts by scholars and critics on most aspects of film comedy, including pieces on silent and sound comedy, contemporary comedy, sex and marriage, social satire, European comedy, and individual filmmakers.

2051 THE NEW YORK TIMES DIRECTORY OF THE FILM. New York: Arno Press, Random House, 1971. 1,243 p. Illus., index, award list.

The TIMES "ten best" list from 1924, New York Film Critics' Awards from 1935, together with portraits of two thousand

stars, and the original review of selected films from 1924
through 1970.

2052   Nichols, Bill, ed. MOVIES AND METHODS. Berkeley and Los Angels:
University of California Press, 1977. 640 p. Glossary, index.

A generally strong collection of articles arranged according
to critical perspective--political, genre, feminist, auteur,
mise-en-scène criticism; and theoretical approach--film theory,
and structuralism-semiology.

2053   Noble, Peter. THE NEGRO IN FILMS. New York: Arno Press, 1970.
288 p. Filmographies, index.

The portrayal of Negroes in American and European films,
with notes on song and dance, discussion of major performers,
and history from 1902 to 1948.

2054   NORTH AMERICAN FILM AND VIDEO DIRECTORY: A GUIDE TO
MEDIA COLLECTIONS AND SERVICES. Compiled by Olga S. Weber.
New York: R.R. Bowker Co., 1976. 283 p.

Includes sources reporting from the United States and Canada.
Information on libraries and other sources includes lending and
rental information on films and video tapes, the availability
of other media, budgets, expenditures, and staff.

2055   Null, Gary. BLACK HOLLYWOOD: THE NEGRO IN MOTION PIC-
TURES. Secaucus, N.J.: Citadel Press, 1975. 254 p. Index, illus.

History of blacks and blackface in films. Excellent reproductions of stills and some promotional material, though the
text is slight.

2056   Ogunbi, Adebayo, comp. BLACKS IN FILMS: A BIBLIOGRAPHY. East
Lansing: Michigan State University, Media Component, College of
Urban Development, 1974. 124 leaves.

Alphabetical checklist of books and articles about blacks in
films.

2057   O'Hara, Robert C. MEDIA FOR THE MILLIONS: THE PROCESS OF
MASS COMMUNICATION. New York: Random House, 1961. 421 p.
Bibliog.

Part 2 is basic reading on the formation and perpetuation of
stereotypes and certain formulas in mass media.

2058   THE OXFORD COMPANION TO FILM. Edited by Liz-Anne Bawden.
New York: Oxford University Press, 1976. 767 p.

An excellent source of brief references to films, filmmakers, technical terms, and related matters for major film producing countries. Some illustrations, including a brief section of color plates.

2059 Paine, Jeffrey Morton. THE SIMPLIFICATION OF AMERICAN LIFE: HOLLYWOOD FILMS OF THE 1930'S. New York: Arno Press, 1977. 305 p. Notes, bibliog.

An analysis of the Western, with discussion of the grammar of 30s films and a consideration of MR. SMITH GOES TO WASHINGTON (1939) in relation to the Victorian novel and the anticonventions of contemporary filmmakers. Based on a 1971 Princeton University dissertation.

2061 Parish, James Robert. THE GREAT MOVIE SERIES. South Brunswick, N.J.: A.S. Barnes, 1971. 333 p. Filmographies.

A useful illustrated survey of twenty-five series titles, including Andy Hardy, Blondie, Bomba, Boston Blackie, Bowery Boys, Charlie Chan, Crime Doctor, Dr. Christian, Dr. Kildare, Ellery Queen, the Falcon, Francis, Hopalong Cassidy, James Bond, Jungle Jim, Lone Wolf, Ma and Pa Kettle, Maisie, Matt Helm, Mr. Moto, Philo Vance, the Saint, Sherlock Holmes, Tarzan, and the Thin Man.

2062 _____. THE SLAPSTICK QUEENS. New York: Castle Books, A.S. Barnes, 1973. 298 p. Illus.

Light career biographies and credit filmographies for Margorie Main, Martha Raye, Joan Davis, Judy Canova, and Phyllis Diller.

2063 Parish, James Robert, and Leonard, William T. HOLLYWOOD PLAYERS: THE THIRTIES. New Rochelle, N.Y.: Arlington House, 1976. 576 p. Illus., index.

Career biographies of seventy-one performers whose careers began in the 1930s.

2064 Parish, James Robert, and Pitts, Michael R. FILM DIRECTORS: A GUIDE TO THEIR AMERICAN FILMS. Metuchen, N.J.: Scarecrow Press, 1974. 436 p. Illus.

Feature-length films (over 40 minutes) listed for about six hundred directors with production company and date noted.

2065 _____. THE GREAT GANGSTER PICTURES. Metuchen, N.J.: Scarecrow Press, 1976. 431 p. Illus.

Includes information on detective, procedural, and other
types as well as gangster films. Production information,
credits, usually with a plot summary, and often some indi-
cation of the film's reception.

2066 _____. THE GREAT SCIENCE FICTION PICTURES. Metuchen, N.J.:
Scarecrow Press, 1977. 382 p. Bibliog., indexes, checklists.

Synopses and credits for several hundred films, with brief
lists of science fiction programs on radio and television.

2067 _____. THE GREAT SPY PICTURES. Metuchen, N.J.: Scarecrow
Press, 1974. 585 p. Checklists.

This volume contains a brief history of the spy film, an
excellent filmography of 463 films with credits and plot
synopses; two weak lists of radio and television dramas;
and a good selective checklist of spy novels and one of
series novels by T. Allan Taylor.

2068 _____. THE GREAT WESTERN PICTURES. Metuchen, N.J.: Scarecrow Press, 1976. 457 p. Illus., bibliog.

Brief history of the genre, with credits and plot synopses
for three hundred films.

2069 Parish, James Robert, and Stanke, Don E. THE ALL-AMERICANS.
New Rochelle, N.Y.: Arlington House, 1977. 448 p. Index, illus.,
filmographies.

Career biographies with annotated filmographies on Gary
Cooper, Henry Fonda, William Holden, Rock Hudson, Fred
MacMurray, Ronald Reagan, and James Stewart.

2070 _____. THE LEADING LADIES. New Rochelle, N.Y.: Arlington
House, 1977. 526 p. Illus., index.

Accounts of the careers and personalities of Joan Blondell,
Joan Crawford, Bette Davis, Olivia de Havilland, Rosalind
Russell, and Barbara Stanwyck.

2071 _____. THE SWASHBUCKLERS. New Rochelle, N.Y.: Arlington
House, 1975. 672 p. Illus., notes, index.

Career biographies and credit filmographies of Douglas Fair-
banks, Sr., Ronald Colman, Tyrone Power, Errol Flynn,
Stewart Granger, Victor Mature, Cornel Wilde, and Tony
Curtis.

2072   Parker, David L., and Siegel, Esther, eds. GUIDE TO DANCE IN FILM: A CATALOG OF U.S. PRODUCTIONS INCLUDING DANCE SEQUENCES, WITH NAMES OF DANCERS, CHOREOGRAPHERS, DIRECTORS, AND OTHER DETAILS. Performing Arts Information Guide Series, vol. 3. Detroit: Gale Research Co., 1978. 220 p.

      Information on seventeen hundred dance performers in musical films, documentaries, and television specials. International coverage.

2073   Parkinson, Michael, and Jeavons, Clyde. A PICTORIAL HISTORY OF WESTERNS. London: Hamlyn, 1972. 217 p. Illus., index.

      A pictorial romp through the films, stars, character actors, directors, spaghetti Westerns, and television Westerns.

2074   Phillips, Gene D. THE MOVIE MAKERS: ARTISTS IN AN INDUSTRY. Chicago: Nelson-Hall, 1973. 249 p. Filmographies, bibliog.

      Essays covering the careers and individual films of American and British directors and cinematographer James Wong Howe.

2075   Phillips, Leona Rasmussen. SILENT CINEMA: ANNOTATED CRITICAL BIBLIOGRAPHY. Gordon Press Bibliographies for Librarians. New York: Gordon Press, 1978. 149 p.

      An extensively annotated bibliography of about one hundred books on silent films, with a brief discussion of films about the silents and lists of further sources.

2076   Poague, Leland A. "The Semiology of Peter Wollen: A Reconsideration." LITERATURE/FILM QUARTERLY 3 (Fall 1975): 309-15.

      Acknowledges Wollen's contributions to the understanding of auteur theory, but finds his semiology too mechanistic and fragmented, his references to Pierce and Levi-Strauss too glib and unsubstantiated. The author finds the ultimate weakness in Wollen's perspective to be a political one.

2077   Porfirio, Robert G. "No Way Out: Existential Motifs in the Film Noir." SIGHT AND SOUND 45 (Autumn 1976): 212-17.

      Perceptive essay on some of the themes and motifs in the film noir, with a discussion of the literary and philosophical background that pervades the form.

2078   Potamkin, Harry Alan. THE COMPOUND CINEMA: THE FILM WRITINGS OF HARRY ALAN POTAMKIN. Selected, arranged, and introduced by Lewis Jacobs. Studies in Culture and Communication. New York: Teachers College Press, 1977. 640 p. Bibliog., index.

The volume is arranged into sections on aesthetics, technique, film and society, international features, political aspects, and reviews.

2079   Powdermaker, Hortense. HOLLYWOOD THE DREAM FACTORY: AN ANTHROPOLOGIST LOOKS AT THE MOVIE-MAKERS. Boston: Little, Brown and Co., 1950. 342 p. Index.

Long one of the most influential studies of the Hollywood system and the relationships between film and the public imagination, the author covers most aspects of filmmaking and experiencing films in what appears to be a common sense, if circumspect way.

2080   Prawer, S.S. CALIGARI'S CHILDREN: THE FILM AS TALE OF TERROR. New York: Oxford University Press, 1980. 307 p. Illus., bibliog., index.

A consideration of the genre and its components, the uncanny and iconography of the horror film, together with detailed examination of DR JEKYLL AND MR. HYDE, VAMPYR, and THE CABINET OF DR. CALIGARI.

2081   Prédal, René. LE CINÉMA FANTASTIQUE. Paris: Éditions Seghers, 1970. 353 p. Chronology, filmography, illus., indexes, biogr. sketches.

An extensive survey of international contributions to fantastic cinema from Meliès to films of the late sixties, with sections on various monster figures, science fiction, literary adaptations, and critical commentary.

2082   Pye, Michael, and Myles, Lynda. THE MOVIE BRATS: HOW THE FILM GENERATION TOOK OVER HOLLYWOOD. New York: Holt, Rinehart and Winston, 1979. 273 p. Filmographies, bibliog.

A useful examination of the careers and peer influences of Francis Coppola, George Lucas, Brian DePalma, John Milius, Martin Scorsese, and Steven Spielberg. The volume opens with a discussion of the transformation of Hollywood production practices as they changed from the late 1940s through the mid-1970s. Career studies of the directors follow.

2083   Quirk, Lawrence J. THE GREAT ROMANTIC FILMS. Secaucus, N.J.: Citadel Press, 1974. 224 p. Illus.

Brief introduction followed by accounts of fifty films with romance, sentiment, and love.

2084   Rehrauer, George. CINEMA BOOKLIST. Metuchen, N.J.: Scarecrow Press, 1972. 473 p. Index. Supplement 1, 1974. 405 p. Supplement 2, 1977. 470 p.

The most useful guide to critical materials, listing some eighty-five hundred items with annotations.

2085 _____ . THE SHORT FILM: AN EVALUATIVE SELECTION OF FIVE-HUNDRED RECOMMENDED FILMS. New York: Macmillan Information, 1975. 199 p. Illus., bibliog., distributor list, index.

Annotated alphabetical filmography, noting genre, themes, length, appropriate audience, and review source.

2086 Renan, Sheldon. AN INTRODUCTION TO THE AMERICAN UNDER-GROUND FILM. New York: Dutton, 1967. 318 p. Bibliog., index.

Contains a brief history, biographical sketches of directors and some performers, a chapter on theaters and one on new directions. An appendix identifies distributors.

2087 Rilla, Wolf. THE WRITER AND THE SCREEN: ON WRITING FOR FILM AND TELEVISION. New York: William Morrow, 1974. 191 p. Index.

Practical discussion of the problems and possibilities of writing for film and television. Three sections deal with general orientation, component parts, and writing nonfiction scripts.

2088 Robinson, David. THE GREAT FUNNIES: A HISTORY OF FILM COMEDY. New York: Dutton, 1969. 160 p. Illus., index.

A heavily illustrated survey of film comedians with emphasis on silent films, beginning with early French efforts.

2089 _____ . HOLLYWOOD IN THE TWENTIES. New York: A.S. Barnes, 1968. 176 p. Index.

This is a useful introductory summary of the main features of film production in the 1920s. Chapters cover historical setting, the state of the industry, established personnel and newcomers, innovative producers, major directors, star performers, and the introduction of sound.

2090 Roffman, Peter, and Purdy, Jim. THE HOLLYWOOD SOCIAL PROBLEM FILM: MADNESS, DESPAIR, AND POLITICS FROM THE DEPRESSION TO THE FIFTIES. Bloomington: Indiana University, 1981. 364 p. Illus., notes, bibliog., filmography, index.

Examines themes in films, especially those characterizing the individual as victim from 1930 to 1933, the individual redeemed from 1933 to 1941, fascism and war, and the problems of the postwar period.

2091   Rohdie, Sam. "Who Shot Liberty Valance? Notes on Structures of Fabrication in Realist Film." SALMAGUNDI, no. 29, Spring 1975, pp. 159-71.

Semiotic analysis of the levels of deception built into FORT APACHE and THE MAN WHO SHOT LIBERTY VALANCE.

2092   Rosen, Marjorie. POPCORN VENUS: WOMEN, MOVIES AND THE AMERICAN DREAM. New York: Coward, McCann and Geoghegan, 1973. 416 p. Illus., notes, bibliog., index.

A history of the myths and social conventions regarding women incorporated into films from the beginnings through the early 70s.

2092a   Rosenblum, Ralph, and Karen, Robert. WHEN THE SHORTING STOPS . . . THE CUTTING BEGINS: A FILM EDITOR'S STORY. New York: Viking Press, 1979. 310 p. Index, illus.

Reminiscences on filmmaking by a veteran editor, with comments on the making of THE NIGHT THEY RAIDED MINSKY'S, THE PAWNBROKER, A THOUSAND CLOWNS, THE PRODUCERS, and the films of Woody Allen.

2093   Rotha, Paul and Griffith, Richard. THE FILM TILL NOW. New York: Funk and Wagnalls, 1949. 362 p. Rev. ed. New York: Twayne, 1960. 820 p. Bibliog.

Deals with the different movie trends in America in their historical context. Examples are discussed in the context of the gangster film and the Western. The question is raised concerning the effect of the film on society.

2094   Rovin, Jeff. FROM JULES VERNE TO STAR TREK. New York: Drake Publishers, 1977. 147 p. Illus., credits.

Brief accounts, many illustrated, of some one hundred films and television productions.

2095   _____. MOVIE SPECIAL EFFECTS. South Brunswick, N.J.: A.S. Barnes, 1977. 171 p. Illus., notes, index.

Historical introduction to special effects with discussion of contemporary films.

2096   _____. A PICTORIAL HISTORY OF SCIENCE FICTION FILMS. Secaucus, N.J.: Citadel Press, 1975. 204 p. Notes, illus., index.

History of special effects with chapters on science fiction, Disney, Harryhausen, and television.

2097 Rubenstein, Leonard. THE GREAT SPY FILMS. Secaucus, N.J.: Citadel Press, 1979. 223 p. Illus., filmography.

A discussion of themes in some fifty-five films, organized into sections on adventure, politics, loyalty, war, romance, paranoia, and humor.

2098 Ryall, Tom. "The Notion of Genre." SCREEN 11 (March–April 1970): 22–32.

Primarily a discussion of the Western, though with some references to the gangster film, the article is concerned with teaching the significance of genre imagery.

2099 Salt, Barry. "Film Style and Technology in the Forties." FILM QUARTERLY 31 (Fall 1977): 46–57.

Continuation of the author's consideration of technological developments and production techniques for the decade of the forties.

2100 _____. "Film Style and Technology in the Thirties." FILM QUARTERLY 30 (Fall 1976): 19–32.

Important consideration of technical developments and editing techniques in the production of feature films during the decade.

2101 Samples, Gordon. THE DRAMA SCHOLAR'S INDEX TO PLAYS AND FILMSCRIPTS: A GUIDE TO PLAYS AND FILMSCRIPTS IN SELECTED ANTHOLOGIES, SERIES, AND PERIODICALS. Metuchen, N.J.: Scarecrow Press, 1974. 448 p.

Locates sources for play scripts, filmscripts, critical essays, reviews, and biographical information in anthologies and periodicals. Arranged by author and title.

2102 _____. HOW TO LOCATE REVIEWS OF PLAYS AND FILMS: A BIBLIOGRAPHY OF CRITICISM FROM THE BEGINNINGS TO THE PRESENT. Metuchen, N.J.: Scarecrow Press, 1976. 114 p.

An annotated bibliography of guides, indexing services, checklists, periodicals, references for synopses, specialized publications, and sources for stills.

2103 Sampson, Henry T. BLACKS IN BLACK AND WHITE: A SOURCE BOOK ON BLACK FILMS. Metuchen, N.J.: Scarecrow Press, 1977. 333 p. Appendixes.

Excellent historical study of black film production, with brief credits and synopses for about two hundred films; biographical sketches of personalities. Appendixes include a filmography of all-black productions, black-cast film organizations, and credits for featured players.

2104   Samuels, Charles Thomas. MASTERING THE FILM AND OTHER ESSAYS. Edited by Lawrence Graver. Knoxville: University of Tennessee Press, 1977. 228 p. Notes, index.

Includes Samuels' essays on Carol Reed, Jean Renoir, Hitchcock, Fellini, BLOW-UP, BONNIE AND CLYCE, A CLOCKWORK ORANGE and other films; with much on film and fiction.

2105   Sands, Pierre Norman. A HISTORICAL STUDY OF THE ACADEMY OF MOTION PICTURE ARTS AND SCIENCES (1927-1947). New York: Arno Press, 1973. 262 p. Notes, bibliog., appendixes.

Dissertation on the history of the academy.

2106   Sarris, Andrew. THE AMERICAN CINEMA: DIRECTORS AND DIRECTIONS, 1929-1968. New York: E.P. Dutton, 1968. 383 p. Chronology, index.

An adaptation of the auteur approach to a collection of selected filmographies and brief impressions of directors arranged alphabetically within sections titled "Pantheon Directors," The Far Side of Paradise," "Expressive Esoterica," "Fringe Benefits," "Less Than Meets the Eye," and "Lightly Likable."

2107   _____, ed. HOLLYWOOD VOICES: INTERVIEWS WITH FILM DIRECTORS. Indianapolis: Bobbs-Merrill, 1971. 180 p. Illus., filmographies.

An introductory chapter on the rise and fall of the director is followed by interviews taken from various journals with George Cukor, Rouben Mamoulian, Otto Preminger, Preston Sturges, John Huston, Joseph Losey, Nicholas Ray, Abraham Polanski, and Orson Welles.

2108   _____. INTERVIEWS WITH FILM DIRECTORS. New York: Avon, 1967. 557 p.

Interviews with forty American and European directors reprinted from various sources. Included are Chaplin, Ford, Hawks, Huston, Lang, Losey, Lubitsch, Mamoulian, Peckinpah, Preminger, Ray, Sturges, and Welles.

2109   _____. THE JOHN FORD MOVIE MYSTERY. Bloomington: Indiana University Press, 1975. 192 p. Illus., filmography, bibliog.

A career biography and exploration of Ford's art.

2110 _____. POLITICS AND CINEMA. New York: Columbia University Press, 1978. 215 p. Index.

A collection of articles from VILLAGE VOICE and other periodicals on individual films, violence, pornography, reviewed books, and avant-garde films.

2111 Schickel, Richard. HIS PICTURE IN THE PAPERS: A SPECULATION ON CELEBRITY IN AMERICA BASED ON THE LIFE OF DOUGLAS FAIRBANKS, SR. New York: Charterhouse, 1974. 171 p. Illus., bibliog., index.

Light, engaging exploration of Fairbank's career and his relationship to his public, with provocative asides on contemporary stars.

2112 _____. THE MEN WHO MADE THE MOVIES: INTERVIEWS WITH FRANK CAPRA, GEORGE CUKOR, HOWARD HAWKS, ALFRED HITCHCOCK, VINCENTE MINNELLI, KING VIDOR, RAOUL WALSH AND WILLIAM A. WELLMAN. New York: Atheneum, 1975. 308 p.

Edited versions of television interviews for the series, "The Men Who Made the Movies," which premiered 4 November 1973 on WNET/13 in New York.

2113 _____. THE STARS. New York: Dial Press, 1962. 287 p. Index.

An admittedly impressionistic and fragmentary history of stars through brief sketches and photographs.

2114 Schumach, Murray. THE FACE ON THE CUTTING ROOM FLOOR: THE STORY OF MOVIE AND TELEVISION CENSORSHIP. New York: William Morrow and Co., 1964. 305 p. Illus., index.

A broad discussion of censorship in American movies through anecdotes and vignettes, with appendixes of samples of foreign censorship and the Motion Picture Production Code.

2115 Schuster, Mel, comp. MOTION PICTURE DIRECTORS: A BIBLIOGRAPHY OF MAGAZINE AND PERIODICAL ARTICLES, 1900-1972. Metuchen, N.J.: Scarecrow Press, 1973. 418 p.

Index to articles on directors, independent filmmakers, and animators from 340 magazines. Covers about twenty-three hundred names.

2116 _____. MOTION PICTURE PERFORMERS: A BIBLIOGRAPHY MAGAZINE AND PERIODICAL ARTICLES, 1900-1969. Metuchen, N.J.: Scarecrow Press, 1971. 702 p. Supplement No. 1, 1970-74, 1976. 783 p.

Lists magazine citations for performers.

2117 Sennett, Ted. LUNATICS AND LOVERS: A TRIBUTE TO THE GIDDY AND GLITTERING ERA OF THE SCREEN'S "SCREWBALL" AND ROMANTIC COMEDIES. New Rochelle, N.Y.: Arlington House, 1973. 368 p.

> A tribute to some two hundred films and one hundred performers.

2118 Shadoian, Jack. DREAMS AND DEAD ENDS: THE AMERICAN GANGSTER/CRIME FILM. Cambridge: MIT Press, 1977. 366 p. Notes, bibliog., index.

> The genre is examined through the discussion of eighteen films representative of its history and the cultural development of its imagery. Like dreams, genres are cultural metaphors and psychic mirrors.

2119 Sherman, Eric. DIRECTING THE FILM: FILM DIRECTORS ON THEIR ART. American Film Institute Series. Boston: Little, Brown, 1976. 352 p. Index.

> Based on interviews with some eighty-six filmmakers, the volume attempts to cover opinions on all aspects of directors' involvement in film.

2120 Silver, Alain. THE SAMURAI FILM. South Brunswick, N.J.: A.S. Barnes, 1977. 242 p. Glossary, bibliog., index.

> A history of the genre that examines the heritage films of individual directors and themes.

2121 Silver, Alain, and Ward, Elizabeth, eds. FILM NOIR: AN ENCYCLOPEDIC REFERENCE TO THE AMERICAN STYLE. Woodstock, N.Y.: Overlook Press, 1979. 393 p. Illus., credits, filmography, bibliog., index.

> Credits, stills, and synopses for noir films from 1927 to 1976, with appendixes arranging films according to chronology and personnel, and a brief discussion of the qualities of the style.

2122 Sitney, P. Adams, ed. THE AVANT-GARDE FILM: A READER OF THEORY AND CRITICISM. Anthology Film Archives Series, no. 3. New York: New York University Press, 1978. 295 p. Index.

> Thirty-three essays by filmmakers on interpretation and meaning.

2123 Sklar, Robert. MOVIE-MADE AMERICA: A SOCIAL HISTORY OF AMERICAN MOVIES. New York: Random House, 1975. 340 p. Notes, index.

> A broad cultural history of American film from the beginnings

through post-World War II that draws on the technology of the
medium, its audience, business organization, theaters, industry
leaders, government policies, and censors. The volume treats
the emergence of movie culture, the mass cultural context,
contributions of movies to mass culture, and the decline of
movies as an influential form.

2124 Smith, Julian. LOOKING AWAY: HOLLYWOOD AND VIETNAM.
New York: Charles Scribner's Sons, 1975. 236 p. Illus., bibliog.,
index.

Essays on films during the Korean War and the Vietnam War,
and consideration of the relationship between the film industry and the years of recent wars. Appendixes include an
aborted scenario by a South Vietnamese, a list of films re-
ceiving Department of Defense support from 1950 to 1968,
extracts from Department of Defense instructions on film
policies.

2125 Smith, Paul, ed. THE HISTORIAN AND FILM. London: Cambridge
University Press, 1976. 208 p. Bibliog., index.

Essays on resources, preservation, films as evidence, news-
reels, filmmaking, classroom practices, and history on the
public screen.

2126 Sobchack, Thomas. "Genre Film: A Classical Experience." LITERA-
TURE/FILM QUARTERLY 3 (Summer 1975): 196–204.

An essay relating the iconography and general conservatism
of structure of the genre film to classical form that reinforces
group solidarity. Contemporary filmmakers who tamper with
genres by changing them induce "in the audience a kind of
irrational radicalism, as opposed to a reasonable conformism."

2127 Solomon, Stanley J. BEYOND FORMULA: AMERICAN FILM GENRES.
New York: Harcourt, 1976. 310 p. Bibliog., index.

Exploration of the Western, the musical, horror and science
fiction, crime films, detective films, and war films through
the discussion of major genre films.

2128 Spears, Jack. THE CIVIL WAR ON THE SCREEN, AND OTHER ESSAYS.
South Brunswick, N.J.: A.S. Barnes, 1977. 240 p. Illus., filmography, bibliog., index.

A history of films in which the Civil War plays a major part,
with chapters on Alla Nazimova, Edwin S. Porter, and Louis
Wolheim.

2129 _____. HOLLYWOOD: THE GOLDEN ERA. South Brunswick, N.J.: A.S. Barnes, 1971. 440 p.

Essays on World War I movies, early animation, baseball movies, the movie doctor and the movie Indian; further essays on film personalities and collaborations.

2130 Spoto, Donald. COMERADO: HOLLYWOOD AND THE AMERICAN MAN. New York: New American Library, 1978. 231 p. Illus., index.

A discussion of such character types as "ordinary, charming, funny, sad, lawless, and strong," with some of their history in films.

2131 Springer, John Shipman. ALL TALKING! ALL SINGING! ALL DANCING!: A PICTORIAL HISTORY OF THE MOVIE MUSICAL. New York: Citadel Press, 1973. 256 p. Illus., song list, index.

Brief text with stills featuring performers.

2132 Stedman, Raymond William. THE SERIALS: SUSPENSE AND DRAMA BY INSTALLMENT. 2d. rev. ed. Norman: University of Oklahoma Press, 1978. 574 p. Bibliog., index, photos.

The best available discussion of fiction serials in American film, radio, television, and comics, with appendixes listing radio and television serials.

2133 Steen, Mike. HOLLYWOOD SPEAKS! AN ORAL HISTORY. New York: G.P. Putnam's Sons, 1974. 379 p.

A series of interviews with persons representative of credit categories. Interviewees include Henry Fonda, Rosalind Russell, Agnes Moorehead, David Cannon, Stewart Stern, William A. Wellman, Pandro S. Berman, James Pratt, Hank Moonjean, Randell Henderson, James Wong Howe, Preston Ames, Arthur Krams, Edith Head, Perc Westmore, Nellie Manley, Arnold Gillespie, Busby Berkeley, Fred Y. Smith, Bernard Freericks, John Green, Catalina Lawrence, Ruth Burch, Hal Roach, Sr., and Albert McCleery.

2134 Steinbrunner, Chris, and Goldblatt, Bert. CINEMA OF THE FANTASTIC. New York: Saturday Review Press, 1972. 282 p.

Discussions of a potpourri of science fiction and fantasy films from A TRIP TO THE MOON to FORBIDDEN PLANET.

2135 Stewart, John. FILMARAMA. Vol. 1, THE FORMIDABLE YEARS, 1893-1919. Metuchen, N.J.: Scarecrow Press, 1975. 394 p. Index, casting key.

Films listed for personalities involved.

2136 _____. FILMARAMA. Vol. 2, THE FLAMING YEARS, 1920-1929. Metuchen, N.J.: Scarecrow Press, 1977. 738 p. Casting key.

An extensive list of films arranged according to the names of the persons involved in the performance or production of them. Brief biographical sketches of Academy Award winners.

2137 Suid, Lawrence H. GUTS AND GLORY: GREAT AMERICAN WAR MOVIES. Reading, Mass.: Addison-Wesley Publishing Co., 1978. 357 p. Filmlist, notes, index.

Perceptive study of the military image in some seventy-five war movies, with chapters on films of the wars, changing images, themes, and military participation in filmmaking.

2138 Taylor, John Russell, and Jackson, Arthur. THE HOLLYWOOD MUSI-CAL. New York: McGraw-Hill, 1971. 279 p. Illus., filmographies, indexes to names, songs, titles.

An account of the films which discusses, briefly, history, composers, performers, and production of films from 1927 through the late 1960s.

2139 Thomas, Bob. WALT DISNEY: AN AMERICAN ORIGINAL. New York: Simon and Schuster, 1976. 312 p. Illus., filmography, tele-vision list, index.

Credits and plot summaries for the major Disney films.

2140 _____, ed. DIRECTORS IN ACTION. Indianapolis: Bobbs-Merrill, 1973. 283 p.

Articles collected from ACTION (Directors Guild publication) include interviews, appreciations, and surveys of the work of new directors. Recipients of the Directors Guild of America Award and D.W. Griffith Award are listed.

2141 Thomson, David. AMERICA IN THE DARK: HOLLYWOOD AND THE GIFT OF UNREALITY. New York: William Morrow and Co., 1977. 288 p.

See especially the chapter on "Man and the Mean Street" for detective films; "Woman's Realm and Man's Castle" for images of women; and the chapter on CITIZEN KANE.

2142 Toeplitz, Jerzy. HOLLYWOOD AND AFTER: THE CHANGING FACE OF THE AMERICAN CINEMA. Translation from the Polish by Boleslaw Sulik. London: George Allen and Unwin, 1974. 280 p. Notes and indexes.

A series of brief impressions of the contemporary film scene, divided into sections on recent changes, big budget movies, personnel changes, political emphases, violence and sex, the underground cinema, the impact of television, and new activities.

2143   Trent, Paul. THE IMAGE MAKERS: SIXTY YEARS OF HOLLYWOOD GLAMOUR. New York: McGraw-Hill, 1972. 327 p. Illus.

Survey of the stars.

2144   Trevelyan, John. WHAT THE CENSOR SAW. London: Michael Joseph, 1973. 275 p. Illus., bibliog., index.

A member of the British Board of Film Censors discusses the development of the board as a social institution, and comments on the activities of other similar bodies. Appendixes and various codes.

2145   Truitt, Evelyn Mack. WHO WAS WHO ON SCREEN: 1920-1971. 2d. ed. New York: R.R. Bowker, 1977. 505 p. Bibliog.

Lists dates and places of birth and death (often lists cause) for about nine thousand performers active from 1905 to 1975, together with chronological lists of their films. Includes celebrity and animal performances.

2146   Tudor, Andrew. "Genre: Theory and Mispractice in Film Criticism." SCREEN 11 (November-December 1970): 33-43.

Using the Western as a point of departure, Tudor emphasizes the difficulty of identifying genre films without using a priori criteria, and argues for the comparative use of the notion.

2147   _____. THEORIES OF FILM. New York: Viking Press, 1974. 168 p. Bibliog.

The author's interpretation of Eisenstein, Grierson, Bazin, Kracauer, auteur, and genre.

2148   Tuska, Jon. CLOSE-UP: THE HOLLYWOOD DIRECTOR. Metuchen, N.J.: Scarecrow Press, 1978. 444 p. Illus., filmographies, index.

Career studies of Billy Wilder, Frank Capra, William Wellman, William Wyler, John Huston, Alfred Hitchcock, Douglas Sirk, Henry King, and Spencer Gordon Bennet.

2149   _____. THE DETECTIVE IN HOLLYWOOD. Garden City, N.Y.: Doubleday, 1978. 410 p. Illus., index.

Beginning with the Sherlock Holmes films, Tuska examines Philo Vance films, hard-boiled fiction and films, marriage teams, series detectives, film noir, Hammett and Chandler, and the films that do not fit into any particular categories. Contains interview material not available elsewhere.

2150 _____. THE FILMING OF THE WEST. Garden City, N.Y.: Doubleday, 1976. 618 p. Illus., index.

An extensive historical account of Westerns from the beginnings through the early 70s, featuring one hundred films, their plots, and the lives of the personalities who were instrumental in making them.

2151 Tuska, Jon; Piekarski, Vicki; and Thiede, Karl, eds. CLOSE UP: THE CONTRACT DIRECTOR. Metuchen, N.J.: Scarecrow Press, 1976. 457 p. Filmographies, index.

Career studies of directors, with filmographies and some interview material included. The directors are Walter Lang, H. Bruce Humberstone, William Dieterle, Joseph Kane, William Witney, Lesley Selander, Yakima Canutt, Lewis Milestone, Edward Dmytryk, and Howard Hawks.

2152 Twomey, Alfred E., and McClure, Arthur F. THE VERSATILES: A STUDY OF SUPPORTING CHARACTER ACTORS AND ACTRESSES IN THE AMERICAN MOTION PICTURE, 1930-1955. South Brunswick, N.J.: A.S. Barnes and Co., 1969. 304 p. Illus., filmographies.

A broad selection of supporting actors and actresses, identified in still with birth date, birth location when known, and brief biographical sketches for better-known performers.

2153 Tyler, Parker. SCREENING THE SEXES: HOMOSEXUALITY IN THE MOVIES. New York: Holt, Rinehard and Winston, 1972. 367 p. Illus.

A sympathetic treatment of homosexual themes in film.

2154 _____. SEX PSYCHE ETCETERA IN THE FILM. New York: Horizon Press, 1969. 239 p. Index.

A perceptive psychological study of themes and conventions in film, including chapters on sex goddesses, male potency, symbols, costume romances, mass film criticism, visual education, individual films, and directors.

2155 Vale, Eugene. THE TECHNIQUE OF SCREENPLAY WRITING: AN ANALYSIS OF THE DRAMATIC STRUCTURE OF MOTION PICTURES. Rev. ed. New York: Grosset and Dunlap, Universal Library, 1973. 306 p. Index.

Straightforward discussion of writing and plotting in three
parts: form, dramatic construction, and story. First published in 1944.

2156   Vallance, Tom. THE AMERICAN MUSICAL. South Brunswick, N.J.:
A.S. Barnes, 1970. 240 p. Illus., index.

Filmographies and career sketches of some five hundred personalities involved with musicals.

2157   Vizzard, Jack. SEE NO EVIL: LIFE INSIDE A HOLLYWOOD CENSOR.
New York: Simon and Schuster, 1970. 381 p.

Ancecdotal confessions.

2158   Wagner, Geoffrey. THE NOVEL AND THE CINEMA. Cranbury, N.J.:
Associated University Presses, 1975. 394 p. Illus., bibliog., index.

Examination of literary "imagistic techniques and strategies"
which contributed to the development of cinematic styles in
European and American films.

2159   Wagner, Walter. YOU MUST REMEMBER THIS. New York: G.P.
Putnam's Sons, 1975. 320 p.

Interviews with a broad range of people related to the film
industry. The themes range from Jimmy Fidler on Hollywood
gossip to writing the script for THE TEN COMMANDMENTS.

2160   Walker, Alexander. THE CELLULOID SACRIFICE: ASPECTS OF SEX
IN THE MOVIES. New York: Hawthorn Books, 1967. 241 p. Illus.,
index.

The emphasis is on the portrayal of women stars. Included
are Theda Bara, Clara Bow, Mary Pickford, Mae West,
Marlene Dietrich, Greta Garbo, Jean Harlow, Marilyn
Monroe, and Elizabeth Taylor. Chapters on British and
American censorship and male leads conclude the volume.

2161   _____. STARDOM: THE HOLLYWOOD PHENOMENON. New York:
Stein and Day, 1970. 392 p. Appendixes, bibliog., index.

An exploration of the relationship between acting and the
star image, with discussion in later chapters on the public
qualities of the image. Roughly a history, the volume is
divided into parts on: innocence, experience, dedication,
extravagance, servitude, endurance, and emancipation and
after.

2162   Weaver, John. TWENTY YEARS OF SILENTS, 1908-1928. Metuchen,
N.J.: Scarecrow Press, 1971. 514 p.

Screen credits and vital statistics for performers, directors, and producers, and studios and distributors.

2163 Wheaton, Christopher D., and Jewell, Richard B., comps. PRIMARY CINEMA RESOURCES: AN INDEX TO SCREENPLAYS, INTERVIEWS AND SPECIAL COLLECTIONS AT THE UNIVERSITY OF SOUTHERN CALIFORNIA. Boston: G.K. Hall, 1975. 312 p. Index.

Listings of cataloged holdings of screenplays, interviews, and taped materials; indexed by titles, screenwriters, and personalities; with descriptions of materials in special collections.

2164 Whitney, John S. "A Filmography of Film Noir." JOURNAL OF POPULAR FILM 5, nos. 3-4 (1976): 321-71. Index.

Brief definition and extensive filmography, with credits and brief synopses of the film noir.

2165 Willis, Donald C. HORROR AND SCIENCE FICTION FILMS: A CHECKLIST. Metuchen, N.J.: Scarecrow Press, 1972. 612 p. Bibliog.

Filmography with credits, running time, and themes for horror, science fiction, and some suspense films through 1970, with a section on shorts, animations, and puppet films for 1930-71.

2166 Winston, Douglas Garrett. THE SCREENPLAY AS LITERATURE. Rutherford, N.J.: Fairleigh Dickinson University Press, 1973. 240 p. Notes, bibliog., index.

An introduction to the relationships between film and literature, with discussions of film language, narrative, dramatic aspects, standard screenplays, the portrayal of reality, literary adaptation, dream imagery, stream of consciousness, the antihero, psychoanalysis, "plotless" plots, and the underground cinema.

2167 Woll, Allen L. THE LATIN IMAGE IN AMERICAN FILM. Los Angeles: UCLA Latin American Center Publications, 1977. 126 p. Notes, filmography, bibliog., index.

Historical study of stereotyping through the examination of selected films.

2168 Wollen, Peter. SIGNS AND MEANING IN THE CINEMA. London: Secker & Warburg; British Film Institute, 1969. Reprint. Bloomington: Indian University Press, 1972. 168 p. Illus., bibliog.

An early attempt to bring film semiotics into respectability among critics. Divided into three sections dealing with

Sergi Eisenstein's aesthetics, auteur theory through discussion of John Ford and Howard Hawks, and a semiology of film.

2169 Wong, Eugene Franklin. ON VISUAL MEDIA RACISM: ASIANS IN THE AMERICAN MOTION PICTURES. New York: Arno Press, 1978. 321 p. Charts, notes, film list.

The volume is a reproduction of the author's 1977 University of Denver dissertation; it contains a history of Asian characterizations in American films, together with interviews with Asian-American actors and actresses.

2170 Wood, Michael. AMERICA IN THE MOVIES: OR, "SANTA MARIA, IT HAD SLIPPED MY MIND!" New York: Basic Books, 1975. 206 p. Index.

Impressionistic study of the relationship between film and American culture from the thirties through the early fifties. The volume covers a number of themes and is useful for Wood's interpretation of American individualism.

2171 Wright, Will. SIXGUNS AND SOCIETY: A STRUCTURAL STUDY OF THE WESTERN. Berkeley and Los Angeles: University of California Press, 1976. 217 p. Bibliog., index.

A structural analysis of the Western film, focusing on classical, vengeance, transition, and professional plots, with discussions of myth, social values, and methodology.

2172 Yacowar, Maurice. "Aspects of the Familiar: A Defense of Minority Stereotyping in the Popular Film." LITERATURE/FILM QUARTERLY 2 (Spring 1974): 129-39.

A defense of the use of popular stereotypes of women, Jews, blacks, and Indians. Such types are used as part of the popular iconography and should be considered in terms of their metaphorical appropriateness, rather than as realistic representatives of minority groups. The filmmaker cannot be criticized for drawing on the pool of types in the popular imagination, but has a responsibility "to extend and to replenish the humanity from which he has drawn his metaphors, not to permit a human type to freeze formulaic."

2173 Zinman, David H. SATURDAY AFTERNOON AT THE BIJOU. New Rochelle, N.Y.: Arlington House, 1973. 511 p. Illus., bibliog., index.

Informal examination of thirty series film groups, with credited filmographies.

NAME INDEX

In addition to authors, editors, compilers, translators, and other contributors to works cited in the text, this index includes all persons covered as subjects. For fictional names, such as characters in books, films, and television programs, see the subject index. Alphabetization is letter by letter and references are to entry numbers.

A

Name Index

Name Index

Peterson, Richard A. 967
Peterson, Theodore 1571, 1665
Peterson, William J. 429
Phelan, John M. 1602-3
Phelan, Rev. John J. 683
Philips, David Graham 1362
Phillips, David R. 430
Phillips, Gene D. 2074
Phillips, Leona R. 2075
Phillips-Birt, Douglas 846
Picasso, Pablo 132
Pickford, Mary 2160
Pieper, Josef 1296, 1375
Pierce, Charles 2076
Piekarski, Vicki 2151
Pike, Magnus 75
Pilkington, William T. 1527
Pinckney, Susan Shubrick 1528
Pincus, Edward 1999
Piper, H.D. 472
Pitts, Michael R. 1069, 2064-68
Pitz, Henry 597, 1723
Pleasants, Henry 1070
Plimpton, George 151, 807
Plowden, David 289
Poague, Leland A. 2076
Poe, Edgar Allan 1406, 1413, 1422, 1456
Pogel, Nancy 15a
Pohl, Frederick 1457
Polanski, Abraham 2107
Pollay, Richard W. 1176
Pollock, Bruce 1071
Pons, Valdo 523
Poole, Gray Johnson 615
Porfirio, Robert G. 2077
Porter, Cole 978
Porter, Edwin S. 1971, 2128
Porter, William T. 1667
Post, Emily 1338
Potamkin, Harry A. 2078
Powdermaker, Hortense 2079
Power, Tyrone 2071
Powers, Ron 1815
Pratt, Fletcher 1477
Pratt, John L. 847-48
Prawer, S.S. 2080
Predal, Rene 2081

Preminger, Otto 2107-8
Presbrey, Frank 1177
Prestbo, John A. 1554
Preston, Ivan L. 1178
Price, Edward T. 524
Price, Steven D. 1072
Propp, Vladimer 1822
Przebienda, Edward 324
Psathas, George 290
Pudovkin, Vsevolod 2039
Purdy, Jim 2090
Pye, Michael 2082
Pyle, C.C. 299
Pyle, Howard 1736
Pynchon, Thomas 1364

Q

Quantrill, Malcolm 616
Quayle, Eric 1450
Quest, Aleck 648
Quimby, Ian M.G. 525
Quimby, Phineas P. 302
Quinlan, Sterling 1816
Quinn, Arthur Hobson 1238-39
Quirk, Lawrence 2083

R

Rabkin, Eric S. 1493, 1499
Rabkin, Gerald 1901
Rabson, Carolyn 1073
Rachel, Frank R. 1126
Radcliffe, Ann 1423, 1425
Radcliffe, Elsa J. 1426
Radway, Janice 15a
Rae, John B. 526-27
Rafkin, Alan 1797
Rahill, Frank 1240
Rainey, Buck 1837
Raitt, Bonnie 1065
Rajec, Elizabeth M. 1372
Ralbovsky, Martin 850-51
Ramond, Charles 1179
Rapoport, Amos 528, 617
Rapp, George 302
Rapport, Samuel 291
Rausch, G. Jay 1412

Name Index

Name Index

Wood, Ann D. 330
Wood, Edward 1468
Wood, James Playsted 1190
Wood, Michael 2170
Wood, Nancy 316
Wood, Natalie 149
Wood, Norton 920
Wood, Sam 1880
Woodard, Gloria 1444
Woodlief, Annette M. 15a
Woods, Ralph L. 68
Woodward, Helen 1666
Woodward, Stanley 921-22
Woolfolk, Joanna 331
Woolfolk, William 331
Worth, Sol 1890
Wrenn, Charles G. 655
Wright, Basil 1999
Wright, David E. 1302
Wright, George 648
Wright, John K. 69
Wright, John L. 1797
Wright, Lawrence 546
Wright, Richard 1364
Wright, Richardson 332
Wright, Will 2171
Wrigley, Phil 803
Wroth, Lawrence C. 1628
Wurm, Stephen A. 58
Wykes, Joyce M. 600
Wyckoff, Alexander 597
Wykoff, Gene 1835
Wyler, William 1979, 2148
Wyllie, Irvin 463
Wynn, Ed 1307
Wyrick, Waneen 765

Y

Yacowar, Maurice 2172
Yarwood, Doreen 601
Yates, Donald 1392
Yates, Norris Wilson 1311, 1667
Yellin, David G. 1836
Yiannakis, Andrew 925
Yokelson, Doris 336
Young, Agatha (Agnes) Brooks 602
Young, James H. 464-65
Young, Lester 1090
Young, Neil 400
Young, Vernon 1960, 2046
Young, William C. 1254
Young, William H., Jr. 1704
Yurick, Sol 1386

Z

Zahorski, Kenneth J. 1505
Zanuck, Darryl F. 466
Zehnder, Leonard E. 1312
Zeiger, Arthur 1344
Zeigler, Earle F. 926-27
Zelomek, A.W. 152
Zenderland, Leila 466
Zeri, Bruno 623
Ziegfeld, Florenz 132, 1028, 1250, 1610
Zinman, David H. 2173
Zinsser, William 153
Zola, Emile 1378
Zucker, Wolfgang M. 49
Zuilen, A.J. van 1668
Zweig, Paul 1389

SUBJECT INDEX

In addition to topics covered in the text, this index includes all books, radio and television programs, comic books, comic strips, movies, and fictional characters treated as subjects. Persons covered as subjects are indexed in the Name Index. Alphabetization is letter by letter and references are to entry numbers.

D